CLAUDE LÉVI-STRAUSS
and
the MAKING of
STRUCTURAL
ANTHROPOLOGY

Marcel Hénaff

Translated by Mary Baker

University of Minnesota Press
Minneapolis
London

The University of Minnesota Press gratefully acknowledges financial assistance provided by the French Ministry of Culture for the translation of this book.

Published by the University of Minnesota Press
111 Third Avenue South, Suite 290
Minneapolis, MN 55401-2520
http://www.upress.umn.edu

Printed in the United States of America on acid-free paper

The University of Minnesota is an equal-opportunity educator and employer.

Library of Congress Cataloging-in-Publication Data

Hénaff, Marcel.
    [Claude Lévi-Strauss. English]
    Claude Lévi-Strauss and the making of structural anthropology / Marcel Hénaff : translated by Mary Baker.
        p.   cm.
    French ed. originally published: Paris: Belfond, c1991.
    Includes bibliographical references and index.
    ISBN 0-8166-2760-6 (alk. paper). – ISBN 0-8166-2761-4 (pbk. : alk. paper)
    1. Lévi-Strauss, Claude–Philosophy.   2. Structural anthropology.
3. Kinship.   I. Title.
GN21.L4H4613   1998
306–dc21   97–41271

10 09 08 07 06 05 04 03 02 01 00 99 98   10 9 8 7 6 5 4 3 2 1

Acknowledgments

The University of Minnesota Press thanks the Centre National du Livre, the French National Center for Books, and its office in New York for support for the publication of this book.

We also express appreciation to the Committee of Research, University of California, San Diego, for the grant awarded for the translation of this work.

Finally, we are particularly grateful to Jean-Louis Morhange, who scrupulously and remarkably verified the English translation of this work.

Abbreviations

AM   Lévi-Strauss, Claude. *Anthropology and Myth*. Trans. Roy
        Willis. Oxford: Blackwell, 1987. Originally published as *Paroles
        données* (Paris: Plon, 1984).

CCLS   ———. *Conversations with Claude Lévi-Strauss*. Trans. Paula
        Wissing. Chicago: University of Chicago Press, 1991. Origi-
        nally published as *De près et de loin* (Paris: Éditions Odile
        Jacob, 1988).

ESK   ———. *The Elementary Structures of Kinship*. Ed. Rodney
        Needham. Trans. James Harle Bell, John Richard von Sturmer,
        and Rodney Needham. Boston: Beacon Press, 1969. Originally
        published as *Les Structures élementaires de la parenté* (Paris:
        Presses Universitaires de France, 1949); revised edition, La Haye:
        Mouton, 1967.

GC   Charbonnier, Georges. *Conversations with Claude Lévi-Strauss*.
        Ed. Georges Charbonnier. Trans. John and Doreen Weight-
        man. London: Jonathan Cape, 1969. Originally published as
        Entretiens avec Claude Lévi-Strauss (Paris: Plon, 1961).

HA   Lévi-Strauss, Claude. *From Honey to Ashes*. Vol. 2 of *Mytholo-
        giques*. Trans. John and Doreen Weightman. New York: Harper
        and Row, 1973. Originally published as *Du miel au cendres*
        (Paris: Plon, 1966).

IMM   ———. *Introduction to the Work of Marcel Mauss*. Trans. Felic-
        ity Baker. London: Routledge and Kegan Paul, 1987. Originally
        published in Marcel Mauss, *Sociologie et anthropologie* (Paris:
        Presses Universitaires de France, 1950).

JP   ———. *The Jealous Potter*. Trans. Bénédicte Chorier. Chicago:
        University of Chicago Press, 1988. Originally published as *La
        Potière jalouse* (Paris: Plon, 1985).

NM   ———. *The Naked Man*. Vol. 4 of *Mythologiques*. Trans. John
        and Doreen Weightman. New York: Harper and Row, 1981.
        Originally published as *L'Homme nu* (Paris: Plon, 1971).

OTM   ———. *The Origin of Table Manners.* Vol. 3 of *Mythologiques.* Trans. John and Doreen Weightman. New York: Harper and Row, 1978. Originally published as *L'Origine des manières de table* (Paris: Plon, 1968).

RB   Bellour, Raymond. *Le Livre des autres.* Paris: 10 x 18, 1978. [Quotations from this work have been translated by me. *Trans.*]

RC   Lévi-Strauss, Claude. *The Raw and the Cooked.* Vol. 1 of *Mythologiques.* Trans. John and Doreen Weightman. New York: Harper and Row, 1969. Originally published as *Le Cru et le cuit* (Paris: Plon, 1964).

SA 1   ———. *Structural Anthropology.* Vol. 1. Trans. Claire Jacobson and Brooke Grundfest Schoepf. New York: Basic Books, 1963. Originally published as *Anthropologie structurale* (Paris: Plon, 1958).

SA 2   ———. *Structural Anthropology.* Vol. 2. Trans. Monique Layton. New York: Basic Books, 1976. Originally published as *Anthropologie structurale deux* (Paris: Plon, 1961).

SM   ———. *The Savage Mind.* Trans. George Weidenfeld and Nicolson Ltd. Chicago: University of Chicago Press, 1966. Originally published as *La Pensée sauvage* (Paris: Plon, 1962).

T   ———. *Totemism.* Trans. R. Needham. Boston: Beacon Press, 1963. Originally published as *Le Totémisme aujourd'hui* (Paris: Presses Universitaires de France, 1962).

TT   ———. *Tristes tropiques.* Trans. John and Doreen Weightman. New York: Atheneum, 1975. Originally published as *Tristes tropiques* (Paris: Plon, 1955); 2d ed., 1973.

VA   ———. *The View from Afar.* Trans. Joachim Neugroschel and Phoebe Hoss. New York: Basic Books, 1985. Originally published as *Le Regard éloigné* (Paris: Plon, 1983).

WM   ———. *The Way of Masks.* Trans. Sylvia Modelski. Seattle: University of Washington Press, 1982. Originally published as *La Voie des masques* (Geneva, 1975); new ed., Paris: Plon, 1979.

Note: "/b" following the date of a work given in a textual reference indicates that bibliographic data for that work can be found in the section of the bibliography entitled "Publications by Claude Lévi-Strauss," under "Books." The abbreviation "/a" indicates the reader should consult the section devoted to Lévi-Strauss's articles. The designation "/ow" indicates the section entitled "Other Works Cited in the Text."

Introduction

Lévi-Strauss and Structuralism

Rethinking the Heritage

Social facts are neither things nor ideas; they are structures.
— Merleau-Ponty 1964, 116–17

Today an introduction to Lévi-Strauss's work can neither emphasize the same issues nor use the same style and tone as those that appeared in the 1960s and 1970s. At the time, in France at least, structuralism seemed a triumphant theory, carrying hope for a renewal not only of disciplines that were well established (phonology, linguistics) or in the process of becoming established (semiology) or reestablishing themselves (ethnology, mythology, narratology) but also of others, formed long before and in very different domains, that had been in need of fresh methods (this was the case for certain movements in psychoanalysis, Marxism, history, and literary theory in general).

Must we admit this hope has faded? Rather, we must accept that it has been fulfilled so completely that today it appears exhausted. The movement was not devoid of extravagance, yet it was also not barren. The page has been turned, but it has not been torn out. It remains very much a part of the book written by that period.

This work does not propose to settle the debates and quarrels surrounding the "structuralist movement" at the time of its success. The file on this alone is enormous, and not all its aspects are equally interesting. There was a structuralist ideology, and it gave rise to a great variety of considerations, theories, even ramblings. The term "structure" has been used in such far-fetched senses that it would be tedious, even for the history of ideas, to reexamine all the variations.

Now, it must be admitted that Lévi-Strauss's own work only appears in better light from the point of view of its own domain, *anthropology*. Whatever reservations one may have and whatever criticisms one may make of it, as of any scientific writing, Lévi-Strauss's work remains very much above everything that too hastily invoked its example. Above all it has remained barely touched by all sorts of criticisms arising out of ignorance of the precise domain in which it was meant to develop.

It must be kept in mind that interventions came from many quarters: philosophy, history, psychology, psychoanalysis, literary criticism, Marxism, and so on. Lévi-Strauss, considered in spite of himself to be the "pope" of structuralism, was called upon to explain his theory in relation to areas of knowledge that were not familiar to him, regarding methods in which he could no longer recognize his own, with respect to stances that had nothing to do with the technical nature of his research, and finally regarding intellectual fads that he very quickly realized could be extremely harmful to the rigor and serene evaluation of his work, in the public mind as in the scientific community.

This is probably the reason he most often chose to stay away from such intellectual agitation and to engage in dialogue and debates only with researchers, either in the same discipline or in neighboring disciplines (history, folklore, linguistics, narratology, but also biology, demography, and so on), who questioned him about or were studying precise issues and who raised pertinent objections.

There was perhaps one exception to this retreat: debate with philosophers. This is understandable since it was from philosophy — and through taking issue with it — that Lévi-Strauss entered anthropology. He did not refuse dialogue with his former colleagues, but due to his original intimacy with them, he seems to have held a grudge against them. Such may have been the case when he responded to the manifestly irrelevant objections of Jean-François Revel in *Pourquoi des philosophes?* (1957). This appeared again in his response to the *Cahiers pour l'analyse* (1966) group where he took refuge behind the purely instrumental nature of the concepts he wields to explain that he need not provide their critical genealogy. Finally, there was the debate with Sartre on the relation between anthropology and history, of which the most complete testimony can be found in the last chapter of *The Savage Mind*. Lévi-Strauss, as is obvious, is not at ease with philosophers, and this is probably the very simple reason he, unlike many of them, refuses to set up structuralism as a philosophy. In the "Finale" of *The Naked Man*, he explains his position with a certain vigor:

> [A]lthough, from time to time, I take the trouble to indicate briefly in passing the philosophical implications that seem to arise from my work, I attach no importance to this aspect of it. I am more concerned to deny in advance what philosophers might read into my statements. I do not set my philosophy in opposition to theirs, since I have no philosophy of my own worth bothering about. . . . I am averse to any proposed philosophical exploitation of my work, and I shall do no more than point out that, in my view, my findings can, at best, only lead to the abjuration of what is called philosophy at the present time. (*NM* 638)

Certainly, one could object that the rejection of philosophy is not sufficient warrant for the belief that one is free from an implicit, unavowed philosophy. However, such an objection applies to any discourse. What must be noted here is precisely Lévi-Strauss's refusal to present structuralism as an explicitly stated philosophical position, for this allows him to demand the right to be excused from having to take a position outside of his domain of competence. That a particular area of knowledge and its method should give rise to philosophical issues in no way implies that such knowledge and such method should be eligible to be considered a philosophy. Holding to this healthy principle probably would have prevented many misunderstandings.

It is thus comprehensible that Lévi-Strauss considered himself unconcerned with all the excitement surrounding structuralism. He even explicitly criticized certain abusive and approximate uses of the term, for example, a number of developments in literary theory during the 1960s and 1970s. What was presented then under the label "structuralism" was most often a textual theory exhibiting two basic errors:

- first, a confusion between the notions of *order* and *structure*, as if the fact that a text presents a certain organization could immediately make it an object of the structural method, which is not particularly interested in organisms but in constants: speaking about the "structure of a text," *from this point of view,* is thus an anatomical metaphor that has at the very most a descriptive value;

- next, a confusion between the *formal approach* (or formalist approach) and the structural approach, a confusion that amounted to believing that abstracting out the material conditions for the existence of a cultural datum (such as literature and its various genres) could guarantee access to its essence, when it is the relation between the various levels of material expression that permits the appearance of a structure (thus a myth can be read according to various semantic levels, referring to contexts that are social, astronomical, culinary, meteorological, botanical, and so on). In contrast to what has been clumsily stated too often, structure (as opposed to form) is not indifferent to content: it is an invariable relation that links different contents. Lévi-Strauss reminds us of this in these terms (in an article on V. Propp): "*Form* is defined by opposition to material other than itself. But *structure* has no distinct content; it is content itself, apprehended in a logical organization conceived as a property of the real" (*SA* 2:115).

These two confusions also deprived many analyses, which were intended to be structural, of their scientific guarantees, especially of the possibility of external control, in other words, of confrontation of the interpretation with data from different autonomous levels. Lévi-Strauss always remains extremely vigilant on this point. He explains, for example, that in the study of myths the details must be congruent, and their congruency is verifiable by comparing sociological data with those regarding technological and economic conditions: climate, botany, zoology, and so on. Thus are "brought together the factors of a double external critique, one which reintroduces in the human sciences a system equivalent to the means of experimentation in the natural sciences" (*SA* 2:275). In contrast:

> The fundamental vice of literary criticism with structuralist pretensions stems from its too often being limited to a play of mirrors, in which it becomes impossible to distinguish the object from its symbolic image in the subject's consciousness.... This criticism — visionary and spell-binding — is structural to the extent that it makes use of a combinative system to support its reconstructions. But in so doing, it obviously presents structural analysis with raw material rather than a finished contribution. (*SA* 2:275)

In sum, Lévi-Strauss concludes, such criticism is itself an element of the mythologies of our time, and its claim to analyze texts and put them into perspective fails.

These very severe reservations concerning the unfounded theoretical extensions of structuralism seem to have been overlooked by many who, severe themselves, nonetheless believe it necessary to include Lévi-Strauss among those they criticize. Yet, in fact, he preceded them; thus it must be assumed that they either misunderstood or failed to read his work.

As a method, structural analysis is not a panacea and requires precise, well-defined procedures: those who can claim to have taken such an approach are not legion. This is why Lévi-Strauss insists on strictly limiting the use of the term "structuralism" (which, moreover, he uses rarely) to a few specialized works, refusing to include some very well-known names in philosophy and the human sciences. Addressing the author of a study concerning him who thought this label should not be applied to him, Lévi-Strauss wrote: "Shall I admit to you that I find it strange that one claims to remove me from structuralism while leaving as the sole occupants of that domain Lacan, Foucault, and Althusser? To do so is to turn the world upside down. In France there are three authentic structuralists: Benveniste, Dumézil, and I, and those whom you cite do not belong in the same group except as the result of an aberration" (letter to C. Backès-Clément, in Backès-Clément 1970, 196). Of course, Lévi-Strauss could have added a certain number of other names from outside France such as Roman Jakobson and also Erwin Panofsky, whom he characterizes elsewhere as "a great structuralist thinker" (RB 410).

Structuralism was fashionable for a time. Fortunately, it is so no longer. Moreover, as a scientific method, it never should have been. A science should be judged by its results in its domain, not by its success in popular opinion (which generally fascinates imitators more than it does serious researchers). So much the better, especially if it means that we are no longer going to try to apply structuralism to any and every subject. However, it has become (almost) fashionable to belatedly set obstacles in its path. The science's models, presuppositions, and resources are denounced as if they were moral failings, whereas what is at issue is an inevitable aging of intellectual tools, which is the common lot of the scientific world. These delayed retaliations no longer interest or bother anyone, and they are no more intellectually fruitful than the misplaced enthusiasm and celebration of the good years.

There is now only one truly interesting kind of question concerning structuralism (whether it be that of Lévi-Strauss or that of those who have extended the hypotheses and methods in specific research): *Has it or has it not* permitted the emergence of a new approach in the human sciences? *Has it or has it not* ensured a scientific advance in particular domains of research?

The answer is unquestionably *it has*. This is the case in the field of anthropology and, more specifically, in the domains in which Lévi-Strauss's research left its mark: kinship, the logic of sensible qualities, and myths. Such success cannot be denied without admitting prejudicial ignorance. The answer is equally positive in domains related to linguistics and anthropology, such as narratology, history, and poetics; theory of ritual, of folklore, of symbolic systems, and so on. The structural method certainly is not the last word in these disciplines, but it is nonetheless a kind of *minimal given* of which one is often no longer even conscious since it would be so difficult to express the issues without the new requirements it has brought to the study of texts and cultural phenomena. An anthropologist who is not considered particularly closely linked to structuralism writes:

> Quite apart from the wealth of insights that it contains, Lévi-Strauss's work seems to me to have a pivotal role in relation to two of anthropology's most urgent preoccupations. He tries very explicitly to place his work in relation to the irreducible polarities that the axes of classical anthropological research involve, whilst also assigning the same (symbolic) status to the different modalities of social organisation. He thus provides himself with the means of building an intellectually rigorous theory, and the most constructive of his critics are doubtless indebted to him for it. (Augé 1980, 50)

We can entertain certain reservations regarding structuralism precisely because it is now part of the obvious givens of our knowledge. Certainly, we can go further without it, but only because we implicitly suppose that it has become a starting point. The structural approach can be considered a *moment* that is not only pertinent but indispensable in certain domains where the exposition of constants (which is what it is essentially) is a condition for the intelligibility of the subject (this is the case for kinship systems, narrative forms, ritual mechanisms, modes of exchange, and so on). This approach does not preclude others: much to the contrary, it can provide their arguments with valuable elements. Thus structuralism finds its place as one method among others. It is a method that, at a certain time, some dreamed they could elevate to a philosophy when in fact they were merely producing superficial extrapolations, simultaneously rendering the method itself suspect in the eyes of many. This method, within its limits and in its specificity, merits simply the attention and respect due to any good tool. Things should have remained there, and this is now the point to which they can be brought back.

Nonetheless, what about the very special relation cemented between structural anthropology and linguistics? Certainly, using supporting texts to show how the former borrowed models from the latter, it is possible to highlight certain insufficiencies or deformations, sometimes even inaccuracies. This is possible and has been done. However, it is just as possible to repeat the operation for a multitude of cases in the history of ideas, which is full of models being imported in this way. The history of such importations reveals how a nascent science discovers in another science sufficient homologies regarding its subjects to be able, by reproducing its methods, to count on redefining its own domain and arriving at new, convincing results. Many examples could be given as evidence of such success, yet this kind of approach is not always explicit: the orientation is set by the dominant paradigm of the time.

It is certain that linguistics played this role in the 1950s and 1960s, and that, in many cases, the importation of its models proved justified and effective — at least when the research was conducted with rigor and real homologies could be revealed. Lévi-Strauss's work unquestionably fulfills these requirements. Recourse to examples from linguistics first allowed him to establish a relevant representation of kinship systems and thus rule out diffusionist and evolutionist explanations that prevented perception of the real coherence of the terms of each system as well as their internal dynamics (such as that of reciprocity, which regulates exogamous alliances and operates in different ways in restricted and generalized exchange). Likewise, linguistics put Lévi-Strauss on the track of a new approach in the study of myths by allowing him to show (as G. Dumézil had already established in his analysis of Indo-European mythology) that what is important is not the figures or themes as such but the system of their differences, of their reciprocal relations. Perhaps this does not exhaust the analysis of myths, but it nonetheless provides its only healthy foundation. That recourse to linguistics made this advance possible is all that matters. Lévi-Strauss himself was well aware of

the limits of this recourse when he increasingly looked to music to provide a more complex, more appropriate model. Thus it is not particularly
enlightening to know whether the linguistics to which he refers remains
too close to Ferdinand de Saussure's teaching (in fact, his sources were
mainly Jakobson and E. Benveniste) or whether his examples too frequently come from phonology. What is important is the unquestionable,
innovative results this methodological inspiration allowed him to obtain.
This is how a scientific work should be judged: it should not be decreed
after the fact that the results were not reached canonically. Scientific advances and intellectual adventures of any scope do not occur without
risk, audacity, or bending rules. Thus what is important in the choice of a
model is not to know whether it is used in strict and narrow conformity,
for that would produce nothing new. A model is, generally, a support for
an intuition to which it allows a method to be given. This is what counts
rather than the model itself, which has performed its duty well when it
has allowed a new schema to be recognized before it is transformed, enriched, and itself turned into a model for other branches of knowledge
searching for their own formulations. This point should be obvious, but
pointing it out may aid our inquiry.

This said, Lévi-Strauss has always tried to proceed with rigor: in his
work, audacity is never gratuitous. When he is bold, he is careful to
develop his point according to the scientific criteria and methods of his
profession. This cannot be said of all those who (sometimes claiming to
be following in his footsteps) have attempted to take the same approach
in other domains. Naturally, things took a turn for the worse when the
avidity of the media took hold of the affair, and hasty use of terms and
recourse to vague analogies ended up creating rhetoric that focused no
longer on the precision of analyses but on the use of passwords allowing
members of a tribe to be recognized. Anthropologists, moreover, know
better than anyone: words are never used merely to designate things; they
are also used to mark and permit recognition of those who use them. It
would thus be useful to provide a brief summary of the meanings of the
notions employed.

Structural Analysis

If a little structuralism leads away from the concrete, a lot of
structuralism leads back to it.   —*SA* 2:116

Not everything is structured, and there is not necessarily structure
everywhere.   —in RB 405

Lévi-Strauss writes, "Progress in this [anthropology] and other directions
would undoubtedly have been more substantial if general agreement had

existed among social anthropologists on the definition of social structure, the goals which may be achieved by its study, and the methodological principles to be applied at the different stages of research" (*SA* 1:302). We would also be more advanced in the evaluation of Lévi-Strauss's work if we could define at least the following three points: (1) For which objects is structural analysis particularly profitable? In other words, what is its field of relevance? (2) To which conception of structure does Lévi-Strauss's anthropology refer, and what does this choice imply? (3) What are the theoretical dividends of structural analysis, compared with other possible methods, and what are its limits?

The Method's Field of Relevance

Structural analysis is a certain perspective on objects of knowledge, on certain objects only. This is what is implied by the remark: "Any society at all is therefore comparable to a universe in which only discrete masses are highly structured" (*IMM* 18). Such would be the case for the kinship data for which, for anthropologists, "the notion of structure has found its chief application" (*SA* 1:279). Lévi-Strauss continues, "[A]nthropologists have generally chosen to express their theoretical views also in that connection" (*SA* 1:279). Thus it can be supposed that other aspects of social reality are less receptive to the structural approach simply because they are also less structured. One could, regarding the notion of *structure,* assert exactly what Lévi-Strauss remarked about that of *function:* to say that there are structures in a society is a truism; to say that everything is structured is absurd (see *SA* 1:13). Again, this is the limitation of which Lévi-Strauss reminds us, in opposition to certain critics who

> assume that the structural method, when applied to anthropology, is aimed at acquiring an exhaustive knowledge of societies. This is patently absurd. We simply wish to derive constants which are found at various times and in various places from an empirical richness and diversity that will always transcend our efforts at observation and description. (*SA* 1:82–83)

This is also what must be said of the culture/language homology: "[T]he conclusion which seems to me the most likely is that some kind of correlation exists between certain things on certain levels, and our main task is to determine what these things are and what these levels are" (*SA* 1:79).

It is thus very wrong to think one can claim that the structural method can pick up any object and always find in it pertinent elements (oppositions, differences) between which one could reveal a structural relation. As this study will show repeatedly, a structure is conceivable only where there is a sufficient degree of internal motivation (as opposed to arbitrariness): "I am ready to admit that there are, in the set of human activities, levels which can be structured and others which cannot. I choose classes of phenomena, types of societies, where the method is profitable" (in RB 49). This clarification by Lévi-Strauss is entirely essential (and it is astonishing it has escaped the vigilant eye of many harsh critics who attack, in consequence, an imaginary structuralism). It clearly indicates the field of relevance and, at the same time, the limits of the structural approach.

Primitive societies lend themselves particularly well to such an approach simply because their forms of organization are precisely, and most importantly, not only stable but tend constitutively toward stability. (Sahlins notes, "Structuralism developed in the first place out of the encounter with a type of society, the so-called primitive, distinguished by a special capacity to absorb perturbations introduced by the event with a minimum of systematic deformation" [Sahlins 1976, 23].) Moreover, in these societies, activities are limited and integrated. In the first instance there is resistance to change; in the second there is limitation of complexity. This, as will be seen regarding kinship, allows mechanical models to take precedence over statistical models (the latter being, to the contrary, more appropriate for the analysis of our societies due to their demographic size and the speed of the transformations they undergo).

A good example of a type of highly structured social organization, at least from the point of view of the kinship system, is found in Australia, in the Kariera system of matrimonial classes as described by A. R. Radcliffe-Brown. There are four such classes: *banaka, burung, karimera,* and *palyeri.* Alliances take place between the first two and between the last two, which results in the following: a *banaka* man always marries a *burung* woman, and their children are *palyeri;* a *burung* man always marries a *banaka* woman, and their children are *karimera;* a *palyeri* man always marries a *karimera* woman, and their children are *banaka;* a *karimera* man always marries a *palyeri* woman, and their children are *burung.* This excludes unions between close relatives while maintaining the possibility of marriage between cross-cousins.

This is a special example, and it is also presented in an ideal manner in order to accentuate the model. As always in this sort of case, reality is more nuanced and permits rules to be bent and adapted. Nonetheless, kinship systems provide a field particularly favorable to structural analysis (as are, for analogous reasons, phonetic systems in linguistics). This is because of their closed, finite nature (the effective terms and possible relations are limited) and because of their function, which is to differentiate and order positions and statuses and to link groups through individuals. Yet the same could be said of "totemic" systems of classification (which will be discussed in chapter 6), which appear as finite sets made up through the interlacing of series of differences and oppositions. Finally there remains another object favorable to the structural approach:

mythical narratives, particularly, it must be added, those of people without writing. The reason for this is simple and has been pointed out
by D. Sperber, for example. In a society without writing, any narrative (even a narrative relating real events) is memorizable only if some
of its aspects are simplified and others enriched. According to what immanent criterion? Essentially, the criterion is that the product have as
regular a structure as possible, thus bringing into play oppositions, inversions, and homologies. Oral memory leads the narrative toward the most
economical, effective, formula: "[I]n short, it is transformed into a culturally exemplary, psychologically salient object which, once adopted by
a society, becomes — precisely — a myth" (Sperber 1975, 79).

Lévi-Strauss himself emphasized this selective, structuring nature of
the oral tradition of people without writing, where

> only the structured levels will remain stable, since they rest on com-
> mon foundations, whereas the probabilist levels will be subject to
> extreme variability resulting from the personalities of successive
> narrators. However, during the process of oral transmission, these
> probabilist levels will rub against each other and wear each other
> down, thus gradually separating off from the bulk of the text what
> might be called its crystalline parts. (*NM* 626–27)

This is the argumentation of which Lévi-Strauss reminds Propp, who limits himself to the structuring of functions when what must be seen is
that it is the whole of the tale's or myth's discourse that tends to be not
only structured but even hyper-structured: "They owe to this property
their immediate perception as folk-tales or myths (and not as historical
or romantic narratives)" (*SA* 2:142). This is also why a third level, a
metalanguage of a specific type in relation to ordinary or other uses of
discourse, is added to the lexical and syntactical levels.

From these considerations a certain number of important consequences can be deduced immediately. The first is that because the
structural method may be appropriate for certain objects and not for
others, its use cannot be generalized. Thus we know that in linguistics
it is very successful when applied in phonology but much less so in syntax and lexicology; that in narratology it is very fruitful for analysis of
tales, myths, and popular traditions in general, but can be applied only
to a certain level or to certain aspects of narrative in novels or history.
In short, it is inadvisable to use it on objects in which the probabilis-
tic factor dominates the crystalline structure and in which the diachronic
element is more dominant than the synchronic.

The second consequence is of a theoretical order: it is difficult to see,
given these limitations of the method's field, how anyone could have
claimed to set up a "structuralist philosophy." That could amount only to
formulating the hypothesis of universal, all-inclusive structuring, which

would be nothing but hyper-rationalism. This is what some inconsiderately attribute to Lévi-Strauss by overlooking the limits he explicitly assigned to the field of application of his method. That he confined himself to the study of information gathered from people without writing, in other words hyper-structured objects (such as kinship, totemic classifications, rituals, and myths), does not permit one to suppose he claimed to submit all other data to these models. Moreover, he spared no effort in clarifying this point, as this remark also shows: "I propose to assume, as a working hypothesis, that the field open to structural study includes four major families of occupants: mathematical entities, the natural languages, musical works and myths" (*NM* 647). (It might be surprising not to find kinship systems in this list, but they fulfill the criterion only regarding elementary structures.)

The Notion of Structure

When Lévi-Strauss began to use the term "structure," he faced a number of rather different traditions concerning its definition. He clearly dissociates himself from some, while claiming ties to others. Let us perform a rapid review of these traditions.

First there is the common use of the term that refers to two models: the first is architectural (and historically it is indeed "the first"), which establishes the constructivist idea of the interconnectedness of parts in a whole (hence the adoption of this term by anatomists); the second is biological and refers to the idea of an organic unity of elements. This double inspiration, augmented by the growing influence of *Gestalttheorie,* can be seen in the definition in André Lalande's *Vocabulaire:* "A structure is a whole formed of interconnected phenomena, such that each phenomenon depends on the others and can be what it is only in relation to the others" (Lalande 1983). This definition is not incorrect, but it is not specific. It could be appropriate for any form of organization and does not allow us to differentiate between what is empirically observable and what is reconstructed by reason. It defines very general, minimal conditions for the existence of a structure. There is, therefore, no reason to reject it, though its heuristic value is extremely limited.

In fact, when Lévi-Strauss was writing his work on kinship, he was dealing with two very precise conceptions of the notion of structure: one was already dominant in his discipline, that of "social structure," developed by English and American anthropologists; the other, which he had just discovered, came from linguistics (notably through Jakobson's teaching, which led him to read Saussure and N. S. Trubetzkoy). Between these two conceptions there was no link but the term itself. Lévi-Strauss's originality was in his establishment of this link or, rather, in his formulation of the issues in a manner that led to a complete rethinking of the anthropological concept of structure from the starting point of that provided by linguistics.

One of the first to make consistent, specific use of the notion of structure in anthropology was Radcliffe-Brown. He defined his position in a 1940 article, "On Social Structure" (1940). According to him, social structure must be understood as the set of social relations organized in a system. In 1952 he took up his theses again in his classic *Structure and Function in Primitive Society*, writing: "The components or units of social structure are *persons*, and a person is a human being considered not as an organism but as occupying position in a social structure" (Radcliffe-Brown 1952, 9–10); it is thus understandable that he could have asserted: "Social structures are just as real as are individual organisms" (Radcliffe-Brown 1940, 3).

This use of the term "structure" was rapidly brought into question by other anthropologists. Thus A. L. Kroeber noted: "[T]he term 'social structure'...is tending to replace 'social organization' without appearing to add either content or emphasis of meaning" (Kroeber 1943, 105). In which case he was not wrong to add in the second edition of his *Anthropology*, "'Structure' appears to be just a yielding to a word that has a perfectly good meaning but which suddenly becomes fashionably attractive.... [I]n fact everything that is not wholly amorphous has a structure" (Kroeber 1948, 325). Note that at the time this criticism appeared, Lévi-Strauss had not yet published *The Elementary Structures of Kinship*.

We must recognize that Radcliffe-Brown later refined his conception by speaking of "structural form" (encompassing systems such as kinship, religion, and political institutions) and even of "structural principle" (such as what founds groups of first cousins or lines). Nonetheless, "social structure" is for him "the set of actually existing relations at a given moment of time, which link together certain human beings" (Radcliffe-Brown 1940, 4). This is the conception to which some remain faithful. For example, S. Nadel (1957) remains true when he gives this definition: "[S]tructure is a property of empirical data — of objects, events or series of events — ...and the data are said to exhibit structure inasmuch as they exhibit a definable articulation, an ordered arrangement of parts" (Nadel 1957, 7). By defending what could be called an empiricism of structure, Nadel opposes Lévi-Strauss, specifically, whose positions are actually very different. What are they?

Lévi-Strauss asks what it means to resort to the notion of structure in the analysis of social facts. What in particular does it provide, compared with other approaches? If "social structure" is in fact nothing other than the totality of social relations distinguishable in a given society, then one could grasp the structure through empirical observation alone. If such were the case, the expression "social structure" would be simply a synonym for "social organization," as Kroeber points out. There would thus be no theoretical dividend. All one would then produce would be an inventory of relations, which certainly would provide a good description of the organization, but would not attain what makes it intelligible, which is not directly available to observation but can be reached only through conceptual work, as in any science. Lévi-Strauss formulates his position in these terms: "The term 'social structure' has nothing to do with empirical reality but with models which are built up after it" (*SA* 1:279). Such social structure must not be confused with social relations, which are only "the raw materials out of which the models making up the social structure are built, while social structure can, by no means, be reduced to the ensemble of the social relations to be described in a given society" (*SA* 1:279).

Before explaining below what Lévi-Strauss means by "model building," it is appropriate to consider here what his view owes to linguistics. Lévi-Strauss came into contact with linguistics through Jakobson's teaching and through his conversations with him (in New York, beginning in 1941). In fact, it was precisely Jakobson (with Trubetzkoy and S. Karcevsky) who began using the term "structure" in linguistics in 1928, a term that was consecrated in the manifesto of the Prague circle the following year. The group's debt to Saussure was explicitly emphasized in this manifesto. Among members of the circle, the notion of structure tended to take the place of the Saussurian notion of system, but, in fact, both notions remained pertinent. If one thinks of the structure *of* a language, then it is a question of the system as a synchronic whole; if one studies structures *in* a language, then the term designates groups of invariable relations between terms (as has been demonstrated by phonology); when it is proven that these relations recur, then one speaks of a law of structure.

This, rapidly sketched, is the notion of structure to which Lévi-Strauss refers: what interests him most is the second aspect, which permits him (presupposing the system is given) to speak of structure as of a model, a conception that had first been developed in mathematics.

What is a *mathematical structure?* One of the best-known answers, that of the Bourbaki group, is the following:

> The feature common to the various notions ranged under this generic heading is that they all apply to sets of elements the nature of which *is not specified;* in order to define a structure, one or more relations involving these elements may be taken.... [I]t may then be postulated that this or these relations fulfil certain conditions (to be enumerated) which are the *axioms* of the structure envisaged. To develop the axiomatic theory of a given structure is to deduce all the logical consequences of its axioms, *forbidding oneself any*

other hypothesis concerning the elements under consideration (and especially any hypothesis with regard to their particular 'nature'). (Bourbaki 1948, 40–41)[1]

Descombes, who cites this text (1980, 85), remarks that Michel Serres is probably the only philosopher whose analysis of structural facts has been in accordance with this definition. Serres writes: "An analysis of a given cultural content, be it God, a table or a washbasin, *is structural when* (and *is structural only when*) it identifies such content as a model" (Serres 1968, 32, cited in Descombes 1980, 85).[2]

The notion of model is utterly central to an exact understanding of Lévi-Strauss's structuralism. What was to make his position original was his correction of the English and American sociological and anthropological approaches using a method inspired by structural linguistics. The mathematical conception of the notion of model is the major aspect of this reformulation, the main goal of which is defined thus: "The object of social-structure studies is to understand social relations with the aid of models" (*SA* 1:289). This formula defines the essence of Lévi-Strauss's opposition to theoreticians who identify social structure with the sum of empirically observable social relations. He writes, "[S]ocial relations consist of the raw materials out of which the models making up the social structure are built" (*SA* 1:279). If the model is a theoretical artifact and if it reveals the structure, then this is because the latter is not apparent. While it is "real," structure is not given in that it cannot be the object of immediate experience.

Access to structure is thus gained through the mediation of *models*. The pertinence of these models is limited neither to a given society nor to the societal domain alone. Lévi-Strauss considers that they must be general enough to apply to very different data. This very well-known text provides his definition:

> The question then becomes that of ascertaining what kind of model deserves the name "structure." This is not an anthropological question but one which belongs to the methodology of science in general. Keeping this in mind, we can say that a structure consists of a model meeting with several requirements.
>
> First, the structure exhibits the characteristics of a system. It is made up of several elements, none of which can undergo a change without effecting changes in all the other elements.
>
> Second, for any given model there should be a possibility of ordering a series of transformations resulting in a group of models of the same type.
>
> Third, the above properties make it possible to predict how the model will react if one or more of its elements are submitted to certain modifications.

Finally, the model should be constituted so as to make immediately intelligible all the observed facts. (*SA* 1:279–80)

(Each of these propositions should be discussed. Some researchers have already done so, and we will content ourselves with referring to their comments; for example, see Sperber in *Le Structuralisme en anthropologie* [1973, 89ff.].)

Lévi-Strauss asks that observation of facts not be confused with the development of methods that allow such facts to be used to construct models. What is at issue is thus whether it is possible to separate the two approaches without harming them. Yet in fact it is a question of two different levels corresponding to two stages of research:

- for the observation of facts, the rule must be to describe exhaustively, without a priori considerations. This is the ethnologist's task (or, if one prefers, the ethnographic stage of the ethnological approach);

- for the construction of models, the criterion is the following: the best model is that which, while presenting the simplest formula, restricts itself to observed facts only and can account for all such facts.

This seems obvious. Yet precisely in the case of kinship data, Lévi-Strauss thinks he has provided such clarification and simplification where extreme complication and confusion reigned.

What is clear is that this conception of structure no longer has much to do with that of Radcliffe-Brown and Nadel. Lévi-Strauss unquestionably turned his back on the empiricism of his precursors. In fact, he asked anthropology to proceed just like any science of observation: to be very empirical and meticulous regarding data gathering and very conceptual regarding the theorization of the set of such data.

Dividends of the Method and Its Limits

We might wonder what structural analysis permits, in what way it is more successful than other forms of analysis. The answer could be that the validity of its results is due to the fact that, regarding observed data, it always favors the membership of the data in a system, the present state of that system (rather than its genealogy), and its internal coherence. We will briefly show what these requisites (which, so presented, can appear general) mean more specifically in two domains in which Lévi-Strauss developed his research: kinship and mythology.

Take the case of preferential marriage of cross-cousins (the cousins from a collateral of the sex opposite to that of the mother or the father) and the prohibition on parallel cousins (from a collateral of the

same sex as the father or mother). Both present the same biological proximity, so how can this difference in treatment be explained? Traditional
explanations presented these situations as remnants of vanished institutions and as independent features. Lévi-Strauss rejected such genealogical
research, just as he considered no light would be shed by diffusionist theories, for in both cases an attempt is made to describe a transmission, but
the reason for what is transmitted is not described. Yet this is what must
be discovered — all the more so since this phenomenon appears in civilizations very distant from one another. It is clear, Lévi-Strauss notes,
that, whatever the mode of filiation, cross-cousins belong to different
moieties and parallel cousins belong to the same. The former are thus exogamous groups while the latter are like brothers and sisters. It remains
to be understood why marriage between cross-cousins is preferential (or
even prescriptive). This can be done only if marriage is situated in the
obligation of reciprocity between exogamous groups. This is an obligation that is itself the key to the incest prohibition, the origin of which
is not moral, psychological, or biological, but simply the form of gift/
countergift obligation realized by an alliance (thus on this point too Lévi-
Strauss challenges genealogical and diffusionist explications). In short,
what we have is a complex of closely related issues where heterogeneous
institutions were thought to be seen. The cross-cousin/parallel-cousin system thus forms a structure (of which the relations are invariable whatever
the mode of filiation or area of civilization), and this structure is closely
linked to that of exogamous alliance, which is the key to the incest prohibition. That prohibition is itself related to the two other types of essential
elements of kinship, which are consanguinity and filiation. This allows
the basic structure of any kinship relation to be defined: "We reduce
the kinship structure to the simplest conceivable element, the atom of
kinship, if I may say so, when we have a group consisting of a husband, a woman, [and] a representative of the group which has given the
woman to the man" (*SA* 1:72). This last relation is called *avuncular* because it is generally the maternal uncle (thus the brother of the husband's
spouse) who is the giver. (From which follows a completely different set
of structures dealing with positive and negative *attitudes,* as we will see
in chapter 3.)

In short, by bringing out the internal logic of relations and by verifying
it at a number of different levels of the system and in a number of fields of
observation, structural analysis establishes the current comprehensibility
of a set of data. This is what also allows a history to be pieced together
and changes to be understood: we now know how to situate the problem.
Such is the case, in the field of kinship, in instances of demographic crisis,
contact with other groups, the appearance of dual organizations, and so
on. (This will be discussed in chapters 3 and 4.)

The same could be said for the study of myths: purely historical or philological work, attempting to order versions and to find the true or original one, does not see that myths have a relation of transformation (through symmetry, reversal, or redundancy) and that all variations are, as such, equally interesting (see chapter 7).

From this point of view, the structural approach provided tremendous explanatory advances, particularly in domains that seemed either confused due to the supposition of accumulated remnants of institutions, like kinship, or which were thought to be fluid in nature and unamenable to systematization, like symbolism, sensible qualities, aesthetic productions, and mythologies.

However, such success does not authorize "generalized structuralism." Lévi-Strauss, moreover, was careful to refrain from this. Here we come back to our earlier remarks on the limits on the method's field of relevance. The essential point that causes problems in the end is that Lévi-Strauss favors system in relation to practice or, in Saussurian terms, *langue* in relation to *parole*. This anteriority of the virtual whole in relation to local and individual performance leads him to formulate the theory of possibles that often reappears in his work and that is summarized in the following hypothesis:

> The customs of a community, taken as a whole, always have a particular style and are reducible to systems. I am of the opinion that the number of such systems is not unlimited and that — in their games, dreams or wild imaginings — human societies, like individuals, never create absolutely, but merely choose certain combinations from an ideal repertoire that it should be possible to define. (*TT* 177)

Now we see: rather than a "Kantianism without a transcendental subject," as Paul Ricoeur proposed, Lévi-Strauss's thought would be better defined as a Leibnizianism without divine understanding.

The Lévi-Strauss Case

While all these clarifications are probably initially indispensable to dispelling misunderstandings and preventing hasty judgments, this book will nonetheless not be a defense and illustration of the work of Lévi-Strauss. It is intended simply as an exposition, a critical exposition as is required of any good intellectual discussion. Yet the critical evaluation here will not attempt to do battle with the shadow cast by structuralism over extinct quarrels and theoretical extensions. In contrast, it will review precise objections developed by certain ethnologists (such as E. Leach and R. Needham) and by philosophers who have taken the trouble to read the work carefully before discussing it (Ricoeur's remarks on the issue of myths and interpretation in general are a good example of this, as are G. Granger's analyses of syntax/semantics relations regarding the *Mythologiques*).

Finally, let us turn back to a relatively common criticism concerning Lévi-Strauss's structuralism. Often it has been called abstract. This reproach is due largely to a misunderstanding, for abstraction is required by all science in that, on one hand, science must construct its object and, on the other hand, when a datum is observed, science searches for constants to allow generalizations to be made. Anthropology can and must undertake this task if it is not to confine itself to a succession of descriptions that, in the name of respect for the uniqueness of each culture, attempt to justify a slothful empiricism. The work of abstraction supposes that of formalization, which does not necessarily result in formalism. What is proper to a formalism is to reason about models or general terms to which one attempts to submit empirical data. Lévi-Strauss's approach, always inductive, does precisely the opposite. It patiently gathers ethnographic data and teases structures out of very precise details. Many examples of this can be found in *The Savage Mind* and the *Mythologiques*. Bringing out the internal intelligibility of what is observed is part of the attention directed toward it.

It is paradoxical that such patient, audacious, serious, innovative work could have given rise to so much rejection and misunderstanding. At least we can say that such negative reactions were in inverse proportion and degree to the enthusiastic response. Yet we must admit that nothing similar occurred in response to the work of Dumézil, Jakobson, Benveniste, or Panofsky (to limit ourselves to the structuralist movement).

Two elements probably made Lévi-Strauss's case a little special.

Let us call the first "the founder's syndrome." What does this mean? Lévi-Strauss, unlike his French, English, and American colleagues of the same generation, did not have the benefit of any theoretical or practical academic anthropological training. Except for a truly philosophical intellectual training that he vehemently rejected, he really was an autodidact in anthropology. This makes his precise knowledge of the traditions of his discipline, its concepts, methods, problems, documentation, references, and field techniques, which is obvious even in his first writing, even more impressive. At no point could one dare to accuse him of amateurism, so sure are his judgments and so precise is his knowledge of cases (though this does not exclude errors or insufficiencies that are the shared fate of all researchers). This is thus a relatively rare case of successful self-teaching. What could have been a serious stumbling block was transformed into two advantages: a great independence of mind and an openness to the exploration of new paths. It was no small thing to set out free of the influence of *direct* masters to be revered or contested. Having arrived in anthropology as a visitor, Lévi-Strauss quickly settled down as a prince.

We are thus faced with one of those classic cases of a founder of a discipline or style of thought who knew he was beginning an intellectual dynasty and who therefore found himself in an exceptional situation (it is known that for this reason Freud never thought it necessary to submit himself to training analysis). A founder cannot ignore the fact that he also carries a heritage, but he questions it, transforms it, and uses it to present a work that will in turn have its own heirs. Lévi-Strauss is unquestionably conscious of his originality, and often, in his writing, he indicates the tasks awaiting those who will continue his research. Those who have followed him have often done so with the fervor and admiration inspired by a powerful, original body of work. Yet such a situation probably appeared irritating to those who neither shared the same theoretical perspectives nor accepted the same methodological choices.

A second element may have played an analogous role: Lévi-Strauss's repeatedly expressed desire to have a literary or artistic success. He admits that *Tristes tropiques* was originally meant to be the title of a novel. It was almost in frustration (as he himself avows) that he resolved to write, under this title and in a few months, an account of his travels, which as we know had highly successful sales. The scientific world does not much appreciate such confusion of genres. Yet aside from these rather involuntary worldly effects, our author remained profoundly attached to the desire to have success with a work that would be an artistic creation. He says, in fact, regarding the four volumes of the *Mythologiques,* that he had attempted to produce, in homage to Wagner and perhaps in rivalry with him, an equally grandiose and memorable tetralogy. Such desires for self-fulfillment and for the accomplishment of a lasting work, which Lévi-Strauss never separated from his most arduous technical research, are what make his scientific writing powerful and seductive. They are also what sometimes, as in the *Mythologiques,* make him take the position of a mediator, not as the spokesperson of a tradition but as the instrument, or moment of epiphany, of a system of thought still locked in the limbo of the virtual.

A few remarks to end this presentation.

Any reader of Lévi-Strauss is necessarily struck by a certain *tone.* This tone is that of restraint, sobriety. Lévi-Strauss clearly likes neither fancy words nor flamboyant effects. This tone is probably responsible for a certain classical coloring in his style. Undoubtedly, this style is primarily in accordance with an ethics of knowledge: advance only that which has been duly verified and can be checked. His is precision of information, clarity of documentary sources, restraint in interpretation, and rejection of explanatory redundancy.

Ethics of knowledge thus but also ethics of writing: this very great clarity is nonetheless never dull or banal. Making oneself understood is a minimal requirement of a scientist. To succeed in this with the greatest possible economy of words and the highest possible degree of sentential elegance is an additional pleasure. However, we must also speak of ethics in a third sense, which is more hidden, more unusual: this soberness could be a sort of tribute paid in exchange for the extreme boldness of his hypotheses. Few anthropologists have taken so many risks. (Lévi-Strauss himself was later amazed, though without regrets, that he had dared to publish *The Elementary Structures of Kinship* and the *Mythologiques*.) Little work in this domain has given rise to such rich and passionate reactions. It is as if the restrained tone were in inverse degree to the risk taken. Of course this tone and style are no guarantee of the scientific worth of the analyses, but they necessarily strike the reader and produce a kind of distance that seeks out the critical mind even as it provides the impression of reliability. This is clearly a detail, but details of this kind also indicate the qualities of a deeply original body of learned work that always intends to favor rigor of demonstration over charm of presentation.

There is thus, in his work, an accord between method, style, and object.

Chapter 1

The Anthropologist, the West, and the Others

The West Seen from Outside

One does not become an ethnologist and one cannot claim rigor in this discipline without a clear, methodical inquiry into the very special relation ethnological discourse has with its object. Within this relation is the boundary separating the West from other civilizations. Therefore, evaluation of this difference does not follow only from an ethical requirement or a concern with openness: it is part of the ethnologist's scientific approach. Perhaps this should be phrased: the epistemological difference between the method and its object merges, for ethnology, with the cultural difference noticeable between the Occident and other civilizations, and this distance precisely marks the location of the ethical requirement.

The problem is thus very special: it is to determine, simultaneously, the claims of a branch of knowledge and the specificity of its domain (as with any branch of knowledge) and to recognize that this methodological approach is inseparable from a judgment (or an attitude) regarding the difference in position between an observer (the Western ethnologist) and the observed (such and such primitive or traditional society). For epistemological issues, this ethical implication probably carries a danger: that of a self-denunciation of ethnological science by those engaged in it, either through recognition of a circumstantial link between its appearance and the colonization movement or through radical denial of its legitimacy through the argument that it amounts to an attempt at intellectual domination that would put the finishing touches on the project of economic and political domination.

Lévi-Strauss approached this debate in a straightforward manner, yet he refused the dilemma that would leave ethnology with only a choice between blind faith in the discipline or its very disappearance. His approach has two complementary aspects: first a historical reflection on the status of ethnology and then, most importantly, a reflection on the specificity of the West in its relation to other civilizations.

A Technique of *Dépaysement*

Voyages are to the science of societies what chemical analysis is to mineral science, what the collection of plants is to botany, in more general terms, what the observation of facts is to all natural sciences.   —Le Play 1879, v

It would be tempting to think of ethnology as a recent science connected to the history of modernity.[1] More precisely, it could be linked to the point in the West's evolution marked by its planetary expansion and brutal intrusion into numerous civilizations with millenary traditions and by the transformation of the latter into objects of its studies and knowledge.

This view is not incorrect and remains an essential aspect of current reality. Yet it is only partially true: ethnological interest has a much longer history. It began as soon as the idea of the relative value of local traditions was accepted and a comparison of lifestyles, habits, institutions, forms of thought, and religious representations was put into practice. This approach was already at work in Herodotus's *History*. Even though the Greek lifestyle is eventually presented as superior in that work (the others are uniformly "barbarian"), there is nonetheless an effort made to find parallels and to perform evaluations, which indicates the beginning of self-relativization, a very novel attitude regarding other peoples and civilizations. This shows that it was thought that such comparison could be instructive, that there was something to be learned through contact with others, that wisdom could be gained through traveling and leaving one's own surroundings. This might seem obvious to us today, yet it was an innovative, fresh idea for those who, over twenty-five centuries ago, ventured far out of their countries.

Lévi-Strauss did not propose we return so far back in time. He asked ethnology to recognize its beginnings in the Renaissance at the very earliest, in other words with the rediscovery of antiquity by the "humanists" and with the introduction of classical languages into college teaching: "[W]hen the Jesuits made Greek and Latin the basis of intellectual training, was that not a first form of ethnology? They recognized that no civilization can define itself if it does not have at its disposal some other civilizations for comparison" (*SA* 2:272). This is how generations of schoolchildren have since learned to put their "own culture in perspective" (*SA* 2:272) and have been "initiated into an intellectual method which is the same as ethnography, and which I would willingly call the *technique of estrangement*" (*SA* 2:272; emphasis added). This formulation reappears frequently in Lévi-Strauss's writing. The first benefit of this technique is to see one's own culture from a distance, to see oneself from the point of view of others. V. Segalen understood this very well: in Tahiti and in China, he discovered just as much about the extreme particularity of Paris and Brittany. For the traveler "living in such far-away places, ... home suddenly becomes powerfully different. From this oscillating double play, an untiring, inexhaustible diversity... " (Segalen 1978, 49). It is interesting to see historians describe an analogous experience. For instance, F. Braudel writes, "[S]uch surprise, such unfamiliarity, such distancing — these great highways to knowledge — are no less necessary to an understanding of all that surrounds us.... With regard to the present, the past too is a way of distancing yourself" (Braudel 1980, 37). He adds that a Frenchman who spends a week in London might not understand England any better, but he will never again see France in the same manner (Braudel 1980, 37; see identical considerations in Ariès 1954).

Yet for Lévi-Strauss this technique of *dépaysement* is not simply the product of know-how or of the attitude of a given observer: it indicates an entirely different aptitude that develops in certain traditions and creates a decisive difference in the destiny of civilizations. Those that do not or cannot learn to think about themselves in function of others will be dominated or absorbed sooner or later. This is no cause for rejoicing: much to the contrary. Yet we must admit that there is a kind of nemesis in this logic that ensures that human groups that are ignorant of, or that want to ignore, the rest of the species thus lose the means necessary to their own survival within that species.

What is henceforth mainly meant by *ethnocentrism* is the failing by which the West judges other cultures in comparison with its own. This limitative definition refers to an obvious point: that of the present hegemony of the Occident. In this it is the first, principal party concerned. However, ethnocentrism is in fact an attitude common to all peoples, including those we know have suffered from our domination, those we call "primitive":

> [F]or huge portions of the human species, and during tens of millennia, the notion [of humanity] seems to have been totally lacking. Mankind stops at the frontiers of the tribe, of the linguistic group, and sometimes even of the village, to the extent that a great many of the peoples called primitive call themselves by a name which means "men," ... thus implying that the other tribes, groups and villages have no part in human virtues or even human nature. (*SA* 2:329)

One of the paradoxes of the West is that it was one of the first civilizations to define itself explicitly in relation to others and assert the concept of universal humanity, while being the most hegemonic civilization that has ever appeared in history. However, it must be pointed out that its power merges with the expansion of modernity (scientific, technical, political) and that this destiny would perhaps have been the lot of any civilization, whatever its intentions.

To Become an Ethnologist

The foundation of the ethnologist's discourse on the object studied is the most empirical, poetical, and sometimes trivial and painful experience: that of the "field" or, more concretely, of the society in which the scientist has spent months or years.

In a work on general orientation titled "The Place of Anthropology in the Social Sciences," which was written at the request of UNESCO, Lévi-Strauss strikingly defines the training of an anthropologist as an initiation, even a conversion, for which field experience is the "crucial stage" (SA 1:373). Scientific synthesis is possible only if, first, another synthesis has occurred in the very experience of the researcher: the point at which the data of a society are grasped in their totality. Even if the researcher's knowledge later remains inferior to it, this experience will still remain the source of the richest hypotheses.

Lévi-Strauss compares such field experience with the training analysis imposed on future psychoanalysts. Neither can know what they are talking about, what they mean to conceptualize, except if they have undergone the test in their own development. As has been pointed out, there is the question of whether parallels can be drawn between the two experiences without supposing that anthropologists should be "anthropologized," as psychoanalysts are psychoanalyzed. Lévi-Strauss could answer Why not? at least if that means that, while in the radical dépaysement of another culture, one has passed the test of otherness and verified one's capacity to accept that culture and to think it. As in any kind of knowledge, the researcher must be recognized by the scientific community, so that in a way, strangely, the procedure begins to resemble an initiation ceremony: "Only experienced members of the profession, whose work shows that they have themselves passed the test, can decide if and when a candidate for the anthropological profession has, as a result of field work, accomplished that *inner revolution* that will really make him into a *new man*" (SA 1:373; emphasis added). We have to admit such a strangely religious tone is extremely rare in Lévi-Strauss's writing. It is hard to imagine that, for a rationalist generally so vigilant and inflexible, it is not a deliberately intended effect, unless we are precisely in the middle of the "blind spot" of this vision, which would be an indirect way of saying that the ethnologist's occupation is decidedly unlike any other.

In fact, it is not. Lévi-Strauss explains himself in a text written during the same period (which was also the time of *Tristes tropiques*) titled "Diogène couché" (1955a/a). Ethnologists, even if they want to submit to the Durkheimian method, which is to "treat social facts as things," cannot avoid carrying in themselves, to the very heart of their knowledge, the dividing line that separates their culture from that of the societies studied. Not only must the home culture be treated as if it were not so and the others as if they were, but one must also return to one's own culture to eliminate any danger of illusion in the experience of this reversal. In both cases an inside-outside relation is maintained, which means always remaining in one culture yet always being in the other. This is not acrobatics or dialectical ruse: it is a crossing where the real travel in space and in the areas of investigation necessarily becomes an intellectual and spiritual voyage in knowledge:

> Here the voyage can be seen as a symbol. By traveling, the ethnographer — unlike a so-called explorer or tourist — plays with his position in the world, crosses its boundaries. He does not travel between the countries of the savages and those of the civilized: in whatever direction he travels, he *returns from among the dead.* By submitting himself to the test of social experiences irreducible to his own, his own traditions and beliefs, by performing an autopsy on his own society, he is truly *dead to his world,* and if he manages to return, after having reorganized the disjointed parts of his cultural tradition, he will still remain a *resurrected being.* (Lévi-Strauss 1955a/a, 30)

Or a ghost . . .

This makes it easier to understand in what way an apprentice ethnologist is (or was) asked, through field experience, to become a "new man." That the language here, as was noted, is religious, even explicitly Christian in its terminology, is obvious. That this formulation was accepted by the author is more than probable. Moreover, whatever the references of this lexicon, these formulations refer to very ancient forms of wisdom: they are found in all protocols on education. They teach us that no true knowledge can be acquired without an interior transformation (*periagôgè* [conversion], as the Pythagoreans and Platonists would say) of the person aspiring to knowledge. However, the test of *dépaysement,* the crossing of otherness, is not simply a condition of access to knowledge for the anthropologist. It is a questioning of the discipline itself, of its origin and its status. The anthropologist's task is never innocent, even if, compared to other research in other fields, it is more often intended and undertaken to defend the societies studied.

Within and without, near and far, engaged and critical, and so on — it seems that Lévi-Strauss does not want to evade any of the paradoxes of his profession or allow himself to be caught in flagrant naïveté. This sheds only more light on the fragility of the position of this discipline. It is closer than any other to the experienced frontier and the theoretical heart of the civilization where it was born and where it develops.

False Differences, True Identity

From Montaigne to contemporary anthropologists, through Las Casas, Rousseau, and Diderot, to list only a few famous names, many thinkers, writers, and scholars have protested against the conquest, the subjection and especially the destruction of primitive cultures by European conquerors. We must continue to have such just and necessary reactions. Nonetheless, even in much work in anthropology today, an undiscussed certainty animates these protests: that these cultures are fundamentally different from our own. Yet instead of scorning this difference, as did the conquerors and colonizers, the desire is now to increase esteem for it, defend it, save it.

What is interesting about Lévi-Strauss's approach is that it tells us something completely different. He is not content to assert: let them live as they are and as they want to be; respect their "choice...." He does say this, and the issue is clearly close to his heart, but primarily he asks us to reflect on this truth: between these people and us, between their culture and ours, there is precisely no *fundamental* difference, in spite of the cultural difference.

This is not simply a question of asserting that we are a single humanity and deducing the moral obligations that follow — which is no negligible enterprise. Lévi-Strauss's main message is something that most omit but that is just as essential. It is that it is the same *mind*, with the same logic, the same categories, the same requirements of order and rigor, in short the same capacities for understanding, that operates in the makeup of kinship systems, classification of natural species, organization of mythical narratives, and the most elaborate forms of our science. This is certainly not the level at which one should try to situate the difference, which had (and has) to do with the modalities of the relation to the natural world. This relation, in the case of primitive societies (in other words, generally, societies without writing), is dominated by a principle of balanced exchange while, in our societies, it is dominated by a principle of cumulative transformations supposing an indefinite increase in technical aids. Historically, these are two possible human responses to our situation in the natural world and in relation to other living species.

It is thus not sufficient to assert the universal identity of humanity, while proclaiming differing cultures, in order to found an ethic of respect for primitive societies. That would result precisely in a purely moral, or rather moralizing, position: tolerance, openness, the rights of man. This is important, but it is a little thin. Primitive peoples would be maintained in enigmatic, even mystifying, otherness. By framing the problem in terms of analysis of the categories of the human mind, Lévi-Strauss, without challenging the *present* urgency of a moral position, places himself on a rigorously anthropological level. In this way he unquestionably seems to reduce such otherness, but the immediate result is that we rediscover it in ourselves. The boundary disappears; certainly, however, we then see that the disappearance of primitive societies is also that of our humanity. In the shared heritage of our species's possibilities, a whole section comes untied and falls away. Not only do so-called primitive cultures disappear from history, one of humanity's — all humanity's — choices of essential modes of being is destroyed.

The Epistemology of Otherness

Thus we must ask: What is the origin of ethnological knowledge? What kind of knowledge does it make possible? What is its specific object? In order to answer these questions, we must first consider the fact of the very existence of this discipline: "It has sometimes been said that European society is the only one which has produced anthropologists, and that therein lies its greatness. Anthropologists may wish to deny it other forms of superiority, but they must respect this one, since without it they themselves would not exist" (*TT* 389).

There is something impossible in the position of ethnologists: through their work they are in the best position to appreciate and defend forms of civilization and ways of life entirely distant from those of the West (from which ethnologists generally come). Yet, at the same time, they understand better than anyone that their very activity (performing inventories, recording, classifying, and so on) is not separable from the immense task of rational explanation and technical transformation of the world that Western science has assigned itself. Ethnology is a daughter of this history, and yet ethnologists intend to defend the societies they study from the aggressions inflicted on them by the West. Today such aggressions do not generally have the direct nature of those of colonial times (massacres, expropriations, illnesses): they are more often involuntary, produced simply by disturbances caused by the introduction of new technologies or lifestyles incompatible with traditional forms of culture. Thus, ethnologists cannot be unaware that their presence itself, like their form of research, is, though in a more passive, subtle form, also an aggression. The learning in which their "object" (a given society) is wrapped belongs to the general process of mastery that the West continues to develop. Ethnologists go to study primitive people, but the latter never claim to go to study Westerners. The relation is totally unbalanced, or at least asymmetrical. This is precisely the point at which things become unclear. Ethnologists study in the name of science, but do those who are questioned and analyzed answer in the name of something? What type of relation is produced between these two groups?

The inequality of this relation shows that one of the first problems that arises here is that of *objectivity*. This is an essential problem for a discipline that claims to be scientific. Objectivity seems at once excessively granted and subject to caution. How so?

First it appears that objectivity proceeds from the fact that the observers (ethnologists in this case) are exterior to their objects, in other words to the societies they study: "Since we are no longer agents but spectators of the transformations which are taking place, we are all the better able to compare and evaluate their future and their past, since these remain subjects for aesthetic contemplation and intellectual reflection, instead of being brought home to us in the form of mental anxiety" (*TT* 384). This taking of distance is what ethnologists cannot do in their own society: whether they like it or not, in their own society they remain party to the process.

The desire for objectivity leads to recognizing, in other societies, very precise knowledge, elaborate technologies, which in many cases provide solutions superior to ours (for example, Inuit clothing and housing designs of which we have only recently been able to understand the physical and physiological principles). Yet it is precisely through performing this sort of reevaluation that we run the risk of eliminating the desired objectivity, for such reevaluation submits societies to criteria that are not their own and also judges them in accordance with goals that belong to us. In certain cases, this allows us to admire their success, but in most other cases it leads us to note our own superiority. By sincerely recognizing the merits of others, merits established in conformity with our norms, we implicitly give ourselves the right to judge them according to our values in many other domains (as is demonstrated by the misunderstandings and misinterpretations regarding the issue of anthropophagy).

Must we thus renounce all value judgments, all comparisons? Indeed, this follows, and also we "must accept the fact that each society has made a certain choice, within the range of existing human possibilities, and that the various choices cannot be compared with each other: they are all equally valid" (*TT* 385–86). However, this apparently neutral position proves to be purely eclectic and in turn gives rise to other difficulties: it implies that, regarding other societies, we accept everything without discrimination, including practices we would consider intolerable in our own. Thus the paradoxical attitude of the ethnologist: "critic at home and a conformist abroad" (*TT* 386).

We have to admit that this is a very difficult position to hold. Ethnocentrism can no more be avoided through a goodwill that assigns the same merits to others as to oneself, than through a refusal to compare that suspends all judgment. Finally, accepting the burden of the West's wrongdoing does not amount to assigning a certificate of sainthood to other civilizations. In the end, ethnologists can neither naïvely commit themselves nor slyly shirk their duty. Whether they like it or not, they cannot avoid judging. Therefore, the question is: How can such judgment be given a foundation acceptable *to all?* "All" means both to the society under study and to the ethnologist's original one. This is not impossible so long as one can provide another dimension and another goal for the work of *comparison.*

To compare would no longer be to place the West ("our society") in parallel with a given primitive society, an object of study (or even non-Western societies taken as a whole). In fact, it is a question of giving free reign to the structural method itself, which does not aim simply to establish local homologies but intends to bring out models relevant to all manifestations of the human mind (since this is, indeed, for Lévi-Strauss, how different cultures must be understood). Thus it is a question neither of positing an ideal universality (which, in the ethnological eye, rapidly proves to be nothing but the point of view of certain forms of Western thought) nor of looking for a sort of common denominator for radically different societies. The goal is, through an approach that is both theoretical and empirical, to reveal "the characteristics common to the majority of human societies" (*TT* 391) in order to "postulate a type, of which no society is a faithful realization" (*TT* 391), or

> to build a theoretical model of human society, which does not correspond to any observable reality.... But the model — this is Rousseau's solution — is eternal and universal. Other societies are perhaps no better than our own; even if we are inclined to believe they are, we have no method at our disposal for proving it. (*TT 392*)

By varying perspectives, the reflective work that springs from the meeting of several societies gives pragmatic access to a universality that is in no way ideal but that leads to a plausible determination of the way of life that could be most appropriate for the human species.

Above all, Lévi-Strauss understands that anthropology has to enter a new era: it can no longer simply receive and gather details about other civilizations, which are in many cases endangered. While to do so would still be relevant, it would no longer be sufficient because such studies, such data-gathering (which is often the only possible remaining form for saving the memory), are in reality also very precise experiences of humanity as such.

Portrait of the Ethnologist as Astronomer

Anthropology is...in a situation quite comparable to that of
astronomy.   —Lévi-Strauss 1958, 28

...the ethnologist's mission as astronomer of the human con-
stellations.   —*IMM* 66

More than once in his writing, Lévi-Strauss made a parallel between the
position of the anthropologist and that of the astronomer. Not that he
compares "exotic" civilizations to planets or even less their populations
to extraterrestrials....He was interested in proposing an *analogon* as
telling and also as relevant as possible for the position of the observer in
anthropology. Why astronomy? Because the type of knowledge it develops is very directly proportional to the limits, but also to the advantages,
that *distance* imposes.

Astronomy is obliged to construct the science of an object that necessarily remains extremely distant. This distance does not prevent the
development of very precise knowledge: to the contrary, it is an important factor. It acts as a filter; it forces us to retain only what is relevant
in this distancing. It allows properties to be brought out that would not
be perceptible close up. Distance is thus, in this case, not a limit but the
raison d'être of a specific science.

This is an analogy. After stating it, we must ask what it means more
precisely. First we must set aside the most obvious answers, simple reflections of very old prejudices. One would be to speak of distance in space
and thus to take Europe as the center of reference. The other would be to
consider distance in time, which is probably what is presupposed by the
usual concepts of the "primitive" and the "archaic." For other peoples, it
is indeed we who are very far away, exotic, even uncultured (all travelers
know this, or should know it...).

What is at issue then? Is distance due to the nature of the object or
to the position of the observer? Probably we must answer that it has
to do with both. The nature of the object? The point of this is not to
say that "primitive" societies have a different essence (no more so than
do heavenly bodies) but that today they are a privileged experience of
organization that allows us to isolate the essential aspects that are problems in all societies: "[T]hese societies offer man an image of his social
life — reduced on the one hand (because of their small population) and
balanced on the other (due both to their entropy from the absence of
social classes and a true, albeit illusory, repudiation of history by those
societies themselves)" (*SA* 2:63).

The position of the observer, in this case the ethnologist, is linked
to the following target in anthropology: "The ultimate goal is not to

know what the societies under study 'are' — each on its own account — but to discover how they differ from one another" (SA 2:63). This neither amounts to disqualifying prolonged, painstaking field study nor to denying the profound diversity of cultures. It amounts to understanding universality in a completely different way: not by classifying similarities but by accounting for the appearance of constants in different sets (which demands detailed knowledge of those sets, just as it is required by structural comparison). From then on what are obstacles to a greater proximity are transformed into instruments for a more general knowledge. Here we find Lévi-Strauss's constant affirmation that anthropology must be a science of necessary relations. Ethnographic monographs have no purpose except to lead to this perspective. To consider them independently is to eliminate their scientific interest.

From this point of view there is an essential difference for Lévi-Strauss between sociologists and ethnologists. Sociologists aim primarily to explain their own societies, and their learning remains marked by the mind of their societies. In the case of anthropologists, something very special occurs (thus the initiation language used by Lévi-Strauss to describe their training). Anthropologists are no longer in their societies; they are in the interstice, or in-between, of two, or even several, cultures. They cannot naïvely claim to abstract themselves from their own, but they give themselves the means, through methodical comparison, of considering it from afar, of thinking of it relative to others. They may even think of all cultures relative to all others, which is the very experience of the revelation of structures:

> While sociology seeks to advance the social science of the observer, anthropology seeks to advance that of what is observed — either by endeavoring to reproduce, in its description of strange and remote societies, the standpoint of the natives themselves, or by broadening its subject so as to cover the observer's society but at the same time trying to evolve a frame of reference based on ethnographical experience and independent both of the observer and of what he is observing. (SA 1:363)

Lévi-Strauss goes so far as to say that the ethnologist must succeed in this manner "to formulate a theory applicable not only to his own fellow countrymen and contemporaries, but to the most distant native population" (SA 1:363) and to "reason on the basis of concepts which are valid not merely for an honest and objective observer, but for all possible observers" (SA 1:364).

Such a formulation might seem very ambitious. It amounts to relativizing all cultures (starting with that of the observer) from the point of view of the only acceptable universality: that of the human mind, which has the same abilities in all places and at all times. Anthropology's task is

to attain these deep structures by varying perspectives. This is how anthropologists' own cultures can be made particular cases within a greater
set, exactly as Euclidean geometry has become a particular case within a
system of differently structured spaces. Such is its epistemological task,
which must go beyond simple self-criticism of cultural hegemony:

> We must then resist the appeal of a naive objectivism, but without
> failing to recognize that the very precariousness of our position as
> observers brings us unhoped-for guarantees of objectivity. It is inso-
> far as so-called primitive societies are far distant from our own that
> we can grasp in them those "acts of general functioning" of which
> Mauss spoke, and which stand a chance of being "more universal"
> and having "more reality." (*SA* 2:28)

Nonetheless, the portrait of the ethnologist as astronomer could be
deceiving if it were to lead one to believe that distance in thought means
absence of direct experience with particular cultures. The truth is to the
contrary. What must be said then is that ethnologists resemble strange
astronomers who first go to the planets they observe and describe. The
greatest distance (with the learning this makes possible) is born of the
greatest proximity. Was the austere scholar first a savage by adoption?
This is poorly worded (but someone like A. Michaux would say it without hesitation, so great is his traveler's irony). Ethnologists remain dual
beings, observers who must become as distant as what they observe.
"They try to behave as if they came from a faraway planet and as if
all that is human were foreign to them" (conversation cited in Backès-
Clément 1970, 206), and so nothing human seems to them to be spared
their attempt to understand it.

The Nature of the West

Western civilization has proved to be more cumulative than the
others.   —*SA* 2:350

Ethnologists can ignore neither the very peculiar position of their discipline nor the cultural division crossing it and defining its originality and
requirements. At the same time, they must understand the essential reasons for this division. In other terms, they must understand why the West
has taken a technological lead that ensures its historically unprecedented
hegemony. What process, what choices, led to the Western tradition's
adoption of its particular relation to the natural world? What about
the process and choices, from this point of view, in so-called primitive
societies?

The answer to these questions first supposes recourse to descriptive
categories able to account for this difference in a purely objective man-

ner. Yet it is impossible, in this affair, to remain faithful to one point and to renounce all value judgments. Moreover, we must wonder if this difference does not refer back to a violent situation, to a destructive process for which the West is responsible.

In order to mark the difference between Western civilization and the others, in particular primitive societies, what is generally emphasized is the capacity of the former to accumulate knowledge, discoveries, and techniques. This is precisely where so-called primitive societies would be lacking and what would also explain their imperviousness to development. We can thus wonder from what angle we should consider comparison of these societies with those that, like ours, belong to industrial civilization. Is it possible, without running into paradox, to do without the idea of *progress?* If not, how can we avoid situating societies that have little material development and societies with very advanced technology on a line of development? In short, even if well-intentioned anthropologists aim not only to restore cultural dignity but to bring out the original techniques and knowledge of the societies they study, do they not risk achieving nothing greater than an admirable but vain attempt at compensation?

The discrepancy is unquestionable, and to claim to restore esteem to primitive societies by denying the idea of progress is an approach both simplistic and false. The reason for this is, explains Lévi-Strauss, that all societies, including those that we now call primitive, have experienced considerable technological transformations. In short, the notion of progress is applicable to them just as to any other society (for example, the achievements, made over several thousand years, in pre-Columbian America). This means that these societies have necessarily changed over time and that, like all others, they are in this respect "in history" or rather in a history (unless one naïvely considers our own as the exclusive point of reference).

There is thus no point in opposing progress (that of the Western world) to an illusory nonprogress (that of populations supposed to have remained in a mode of existence as close as possible to nature). What must be explained is rather the plurality and occasional divergence of a number of lines of progress. In short, two main prejudices must be challenged: (1) the evolutionist prejudice that assigns a single, favored line to different movements of transformation by making them converge toward the civilization in which scientific and technical achievements appear greatest; and (2) the continuist prejudice that imagines permanent progress shielded from all phenomena of rupture or regression.

To the first presupposition, Lévi-Strauss opposes the reality of a plurality of evolutions and transformations. Thus divisions into ages, intended to order prehistoric facts (later, middle, early Paleolithic), do not correspond to any global development on the planet, for depending on the region and the continent, these different levels coexisted; some areas knew techniques of which others were ignorant; and the mastery of certain techniques was lost in later times. In short, "none of this aims at denying the reality of a progress of mankind, but it invites us to consider it with greater care. The development of prehistoric and archaeological knowledge tends to *spread out in space* those forms of civilizations which we imagined as *spread out in time*" (*SA* 2:337).

Lévi-Strauss proposes the continuist prejudice be eliminated through recourse to a statistical model that leaves great room for chance locally, even if the result of the whole can be predictable. As in a game, the transformations result from a series of moves: some winning, some losing. The correct metaphor would be that of the knight in a game of chess, which moves in various combinations, but never in the same direction. The same holds for history and the progress that appears in it. "It is only from time to time that history is cumulative — in other words that the numbers can be added up to form a favorable combination" (*SA* 2:338).

Such favorable combinations have appeared in different places on the planet. Pre-Columbian America experienced particularly rich ones in terms of inventions and innovations. Yet assessment of the twentieth century reveals that Western civilization holds the greatest number of winning cards. Nothing in it has made it naturally more apt to make technical inventions than the others. It has proven itself simply "more cumulative." It is thus this capacity (which is not in itself of a superior nature) that must be understood.

Homeostasis and Entropy

The clearest, most interesting answer Lévi-Strauss has given to this question is that which appears in *Conversations with Claude Lévi-Strauss* (GC) in which he is interviewed by Georges Charbonnier. There Lévi-Strauss proposes to consider primitive societies as societies in which regulations aim above all to maintain a maximum of balance and unity. This goal implies the need to eliminate any risk that an individual or a group within the society would be excluded, thus the need to prevent internal divisions from appearing. This explains the procedures and rites of unanimity preceding important decisions and, more generally, the various regulations made to prevent any political or economic power from becoming autonomous in a separate sphere. Such a society tends toward maximum internal equilibrium, in other words toward homeostasis. It can be said to have minimal entropy. Its model could be that of a machine that requires only a little initial power (as in the case of a spring-loaded clock) to keep it working.

Western societies, to the contrary, can be referred to a steam-engine model, in that they produce a very large amount of work by consuming an equally large amount of energy (thus the expression "hot societies" in this case, in contrast to others that are called "cold"). Here the motor is made up of the tension between the dominant and the dominated, decision makers and producers. There is an accumulation of knowledge, techniques, and goods, but at the cost of very high social entropy (inequalities, disorder, conflict). We might say that the initial conditions supposed by this sort of society are the appearance of writing, development of sedentary agriculture, urban organization and concentration of population, formation of a separate sphere of power, and, finally, orientation of human work toward the production of a surplus to be accumulated and negotiated. Such societies are necessarily caught up in change without foreseeable limits and can find equilibrium only in movement, in other words in ever-increasing technological development. Their present planetary hegemony follows from this logic.

Clearly the ups and downs of this domination, of which the colonization movement beginning in the sixteenth century is the most obvious — but not the only — example, cannot be ignored by anthropologists. Better than anyone else immersed in the Western world, they know that the traditional forms of the other civilizations are fated to dissolution and even to disappearance. Better than anyone they know (or should know) that their enterprise still belongs, in its very presuppositions, to the West's project of mastery. Yet if they do not abandon their work it is simply because no one else, in the generalized drowning of traditional cultures provoked by the expansion of modernity, is able to transform a memory being extinguished into knowledge and to transmit to tomorrow's humanity testimony of forms of thought and life that cannot be ignored without denying humankind's very being, since these forms were, for thousands of years, its essential reality.

In Lévi-Strauss's eyes, this is indeed, in spite of everything, the urgent task and responsibility of anthropologists. They are neither simple data-gatherers nor saviors. Their task remains ordered in accordance with knowledge, which very well may be burdened still with the prejudices of its culture. Yet the effort to gather and understand the cultures of others, just when they are most endangered, is to be neither scorned nor considered useless. It will be even better respected if anthropologists themselves remain critical of the reasons that have given rise to the approach and do not forget the conditions in which their learning was born.

Chapter 2

The Movement of Reciprocity

Lévi-Strauss's first major work, which established (not without a little controversy) his intellectual authority in the anthropological domain, was *The Elementary Structures of Kinship*. It could be claimed that this study, which was devoted to the regulating principles and empirical manifestations of various kinship systems, should be read essentially as the theoretical development, in the domain of kinship, of Marcel Mauss's theses in *The Gift*. Yet it should also be said that Mauss's theory of the gift can be wholly understood only if we consider the degree to which the play of gift/countergift takes place primarily in the framework of kinship relations, in other words in matrimonial alliances. This relation of reciprocity holds the key to the enigma of the incest prohibition. It explains the system of exogamy but more importantly sheds light in a remarkable way on certain more specific aspects of alliance, such as that of marriage — whether it be preferential or prescriptive — of cross-cousins and that of the very widespread existence of dual organizations in areas of culture not known to be related. It also elucidates the role of the maternal uncle in certain systems and that of the goods involved in an alliance.

Generally, reciprocity requires that the groups mutually recognize each other, and this mutual recognition appears to be proper to human societies. Yet, contrary to what a superficial reading might lead one to believe, reciprocity cannot be reduced to a simple relation of exchange. It might be said that it is fundamentally the manifestation of a *constitutive mutuality,* in which hostile relations (war, raiding, abduction) form the negative extreme, while exchange relations (gifts, alliances, commerce) form the positive extreme. This fundamental relation of reciprocity has nothing to do with an exchangist explanation of society, with an interactionist theory, or for that matter with a static conception of structures (hence the small degree of relevance of certain criticisms made in this vein). The only issue is rather: Does the observation of the facts of reciprocity (the obligation to give and receive) allow one to establish their universal nature? This is the kind of question asked by certain English and American anthropologists (such as Needham), and it requires more serious consideration.

A Question of Principle

First let us note the title of chapter 5: "The Principle of Reciprocity." Where one might have expected the word "phenomenon" or "fact," Lévi-Strauss does not shrink from proposing "principle." This might be surprising, yet his audacity has to be appreciated. It is clear that for Lévi-Strauss the practice of exchange between groups attains a point that goes beyond simple facts and forces us to consider it as a general or even universal form of social behavior. Lévi-Strauss's view here is directly related to the way in which the issue of the incest prohibition is resolved. In particular, it brings out the importance of the *third party who offers the gift,* of which the maternal uncle is the prime example, even if he is not the only one and is not always present.

Given this information, and before seeing in more detail what Lévi-Strauss means by the phrase "principle of reciprocity," it may be useful, or even indispensable, to reflect on the status of such notions in anthropology. Thus in a work published in 1969, Meyer Fortes (one of the most well-known contemporary British anthropologists, who held the prestigious Cambridge chair) stated what he called the "axiom of amity," which can be summarized by this assertion: "Where kinship is demonstrable or assumed, . . . there amity must prevail" (Fortes 1969, 234). This "prescriptive altruism" can extend quite far: "Its roots are in the familial domain and it embraces the bilateral kinship linkages of this domain. Kin by complementary filiation are also embraced within the orbit of kinship amity" (Fortes 1969, 234).

Commenting on this work, Needham (in *Rethinking Kinship and Marriage* [1971]) delivers an acerbic criticism (Needham 1971, xcvi ff.) of this supposed axiom, noting first that it simply contains one of Radcliffe-Brown's ideas concerning the extension of a feeling of goodwill from within the elementary family, which allows no specific attitude to be determined. "In the end, it seems to me, both the axiom and its converse are empty tautologies, expressing no more than a particular presupposition of what 'kinship' really is" (Needham 1971, xcvii). Needham continues with this irrevocable judgment: "Now I do not wish to sound at all derisive in drawing out this flat conclusion, but only to exemplify with a recent and prominent case the kind of theoretical failure to which a grandiose conception of anthropological inquiry tends to lead" (Needham 1971, xcvii).

One might wonder whether the statement of the *principle of reciprocity* does not risk being cut down by this sort of criticism. Yet, in the work mentioned, neither Needham nor the other contributors question (or discuss for that matter) this principle. Nonetheless, it is easy to imagine how the claim to state a principle in anthropology would appear suspicious to them. Either that, or they considered such a principle to remain epistemologically wholly undetermined: neither falsifiable nor verifiable. Thus not very interesting.

There still remains one hypothesis: gift/countergift relations are perfectly well known and proven. Ever since Mauss's famous analyses, no one has dreamed of questioning their reality. Anthropological material on this subject is vast. The data are specific, and their interpretation is the object of no notable dissent. From this point of view, Lévi-Strauss chose very solid ground. His originality was to show that the exchange of goods, women, and words forms one and the same procedure (not only on the level of signs but on the level of values, which is symbolic), and moreover it was to postulate that this play of exchange is coextensive with the very fact of alliance and that which prescribes its necessity: the incest prohibition. From this follows the possibility of establishing reciprocity as a principle. In order to grasp this, we must return to the "spirit of the gift" in Mauss's analyses.

Mauss and the "Total Social Fact"

It is difficult for some to understand the importance Lévi-Strauss assigns the notion of reciprocity; some go to the point of judging the notion obscure or considering it inoperative; this difficulty arises because they do not realize the degree to which the weight of the heritage from Emile Durkheim and especially from Mauss is noticeable in the exposition of this "principle." The influence of Durkheim can be seen in the way that, on this issue in particular, the spotlight is placed on the fact that the social precedes and explains the individual. What does this mean? It means precisely that the action of giving and the modalities of the responses cannot be explained by a psychological disposition or by an initiative by members of the group. They are, to the contrary, the manifestations of a necessity that comes from the group itself and that is constitutive of its collective being.

As for Mauss, direct reference is made to his work *The Gift*. From this text, considered as having exemplary, even fundamental, value, Lévi-Strauss extracts the three essential conclusions for anthropology:

- "that exchange in primitive societies consists not so much in economic transactions as in reciprocal gifts";

- "that these reciprocal gifts have a far more important function in those societies than in our own";

- "that this primitive form of exchange is not merely nor essentially of an economic nature but is what he [Mauss] aptly calls 'a total social fact,' that is, an event which has a significance that is at once social and religious, magic and economic, utilitarian and sentimental, jural and moral" (*ESK* 52). "It is a question of a universal mode of culture, although not everywhere equally developed" (*ESK* 53).

In the various societies that were the subjects of Mauss's and Lévi-Strauss's studies, it appeared that this form of reciprocal gift-giving occurs generally during specific celebrations (marriages, funerals, war-alliances, religious celebrations); that reciprocity on such occasions takes on an obligatory nature; that this exchange is marked, in certain cases, by *one-upmanship;* and that it is meant to ensure an increase in *prestige.* It can thus take extreme forms, extending even to the destruction of the goods displayed ("[G]reater prestige results from the destruction of wealth than from its distribution" [*ESK* 55]). This extreme form is what Mauss proposes be called "potlatch," which is the term used by the Indian tribes of the Northwest Coast of North America.

This increase in prestige is probably the determining factor in such challenge-like exchange. Such transactions are not only not economic in nature; they could even be called antieconomic. They permit no profit; they target no utilitarian consumption. The advantage gained remains immaterial: its object is pure status. Here, thus, wealth has no accumulative end. It exists only to be expended or distributed. It is not in itself a source of prestige; instead it provides prestige because it is given or sacrificed.

From this we can conclude first that there are two very different types of exchange:

• that which can be called ordinary and which is limited to utilitarian goods: it has an economic nature and is generally very limited in societies that tend to subsist as autonomously as possible (yet even then such exchanges cannot avoid the symbolic weight of reciprocity);

• that which has as its object precious objects (such as the copper engravings, woven blankets, and ceremonial clothing exchanged during the potlatches of the Northwest Coast Amerindians). Such objects given or sacrificed during ceremonies *are symbolically enriched by the exchange itself* (which is what Lévi-Strauss calls the "synthetic nature of the gift"). This is indeed remarkable and requires clarification through anthropological analysis, especially since the exchange of women — let us read "matrimonial alliance" — is at the heart of this procedure.

Reciprocity as Such

What actually occurs in this exchange, what constantly makes it a requirement, remains utterly incomprehensible from the point of view of economic rationality. The increase in prestige ensured in the case of potlatch is only an extreme form of this exchange. Often the reason the exchange takes place can be found only in itself. There is a multitude of examples in which the objects exchanged are identical, which clearly means that the object of those exchanges is not to acquire a good or make a profit. ("In fact, the exchange does not bring a tangible result such as is the case in commercial transactions in our own society" [*ESK* 54].) Its "dividend" here (one might as well say its "meaning") is absorbed into the very fact of exchanging, in other words into the manifestation of reciprocity as such. This may appear strange.

At this point we can understand what Lévi-Strauss means by "principle" when he speaks of reciprocity, for what must be understood is why "there is much more in the exchange itself than in the things exchanged" (*ESK* 59). What occurs is not simply a manifestation of goodwill or generosity but *the recognition of the other as such*. So be it, but why is this recognition important? Is it a requirement that is peculiar to primitive and traditional societies, or is it still visible in our own? In order to make himself understood, Lévi-Strauss proposes the story of a dining experience:

> We have very often observed the ceremonial aspect of the meal in the lower-priced restaurants in the south of France, especially in those regions where wine is the principal industry and is surrounded by a sort of mystical respect which makes it "rich food" *par excellence*. In the small restaurants where wine is included in the price of the meal, each customer finds in front of his plate a modest bottle of wine, more often than not very bad. This bottle is similar to his neighbor's bottle, as are the portions of meat and vegetables which a waitress passes around. Nevertheless, a remarkable difference in attitude towards the wine and the food is immediately manifested. Food serves the body's needs and the wine its taste for luxury, the first serving to nourish, the second to honor. Each person at the table eats, so to speak, for himself, and the noting of a trifling slight in the way he has been served arouses bitterness toward the more favored, and a jealous complaint to the proprietor. But it is entirely different with the wine. If a bottle should be insufficiently filled, its owner will good-humoredly appeal to his neighbor's judgment. And the proprietor will face, not the demand of an individual victim, but a group complaint. In other words, wine is a social commodity, while the *plat du jour* is a personal commodity. The little bottle may contain exactly one glassful, yet the contents will be poured out, not into the owner's glass, but into his neighbor's. And his neighbor will immediately make a corresponding gesture of reciprocity. (*ESK* 58)

"What has happened?" asks Lévi-Strauss. Apparently nothing but an incomprehensible action of reciprocal substitution of a serving of wine. In reality what takes place is an action of considerable meaning. Two strangers who know nothing about each other, but are brought together during a meal, face each other in a situation in which there is a good deal of promiscuity. They have the choice of establishing contact or ignoring each other. If they choose the latter they have to accept the tension and embarrassment such refusal entails:

> This is the fleeting but difficult situation resolved by the exchanging of wine. It is an assertion of good grace which does away with the mutual uncertainty. It substitutes a social relationship for spatial juxtaposition. But it is also more than that. The partner who was entitled to maintain his reserve is persuaded to give it up. Wine offered calls for wine returned, cordiality requires cordiality. ... Further, the acceptance of this offer sanctions another offer, for conversation. (*ESK* 59)

This little story and its analysis are admirable in that from a limited segment of "fresh traces of very primitive psycho-social experiences" (*ESK* 60), we are led to see the general principle of reciprocity. For, in this case as in many other cases, it is a question of going from indifference to dialogue, not because of morals or social constraints but because in this reciprocity the social fact asserts itself as the properly human, or cultural, level. In the example we have just read, the exchange has, materially, no meaning and could even seem absurd, yet the gesture has, symbolically, considerable significance. It is simply the declaration that the relation precedes (logically, not ontologically) the individuals, that this anteriority binds them while fulfilling them: sociality is given with this symbolic recognition, and from then on everyone is included in it. Yet such sociality exists only in the unceasing performance of the gestures and rituals that manifest its structure. These remarks could nonetheless run the risk of seeming too general if it were not shown how this performance is effected on special occasions and regarding specific goods. Certain goods (depending on the culture and circumstances) appear to have in themselves a social nature. They are virtually designated as belonging wholly to sharing and exchange. This is the case with any food that does not primarily serve to satisfy the requirements of physiological needs and that has a luxurious quality demanding it be consumed in company, most often festive. Examples are still very numerous in the West today: "A bottle of vintage wine, a rare liqueur, a fois gras, pricks the owner's conscience with the claim of someone else. These are some of the delicacies which one would not buy and consume alone without a vague feeling of guilt" (*ESK* 57).

This example, which is close to us, allows us to recognize the same logic in very different civilizations, such as ceremonial Polynesian meetings that require that each group avoid consuming the food it has brought, but rather eat that brought by the others. There is shame for a group if one of its members takes from his or her "own basket" (*ESK* 58) and still greater shame — to which contempt and anger may be added — for anyone who secretly eats a ceremonial dish.

What is the nature of this rejection? It is, according to Lévi-Strauss, of exactly the same nature as the incest prohibition: "It seems that the group confusedly sees a sort of *social interest* in the individual accomplishment of an act which normally requires collective participation" (*ESK* 58; emphasis added). One might think that here this is simply an interesting analogy. Not at all, for there is much more to it. This example allows us to grasp the whole dimension of the incest prohibition. Its role is certainly fundamental and unavoidable in the institution of the human world as such, in other words inasmuch as it is distinguished from the purely natural universe, but this role integrates itself into the permanent, underlying, more general movement of reciprocity. At a certain level it is the condition for it: at another it is nothing but the expression of it. What is expressed is the necessary recognition of the otherness (of the neighbor or of the other group) that ensures that in each situation there is humanity. In order to understand this we must go back to the problem of the incest prohibition and what explains its universality.

The Incest Prohibition and Exogamous Alliance

There is thus an essential relation between the issue of the incest prohibition and the phenomenon of reciprocity. Lévi-Strauss establishes the necessary nature of this relation as he provides a clear, conclusive explanation of what was considered to be an enigma. It was thought of as an enigma because this prohibition is both universal (like a law of nature) and a social rule (thus belonging to culture).

In chapter 2 of *The Elementary Structures of Kinship*, Lévi-Strauss evaluates the various theories that have been developed to explain the incest prohibition, and he exposes their contradictions. In summary, we can say that biological explanations may be universalized (because they are based on nature) but are false; while historical and cultural explanations may be true (since they deal with observable facts) but cannot be universalized.

The biological argument, according to which incest would be perceived spontaneously by the group as a behavior that carries the risk of degeneracy, comes up against the results of scientific observation. We know that endogamous reproduction in animal and plant species is precisely what ensures the stability of a line or type — the instability linked to the appearance of recessive traits appears only at the beginning of a process of selection. Lévi-Strauss refers to various works, such as those of E. M. East, which permit the conclusion that the dangers of endogamy would not have appeared if humanity had been endogamous from the beginning. It is thus unlikely that a sort of obscure collective knowledge of a biological danger would have led to the prohibition, when we know that such a danger is most probably one of the prohibition's effects. Above all, this theory does not touch the paradox that close blood-relatives are not prohibited while biologically very distant partners are. If instinct is at work here, it is seriously out of tune.

The other, psychocultural, explanation invokes an instinctive horror of incest that would be due to the absence of sexual stimulation on the part of sexual partners exposed to too great a proximity. It is remarkable (even amusing) to note that this same proximity is what psychoanalysis invokes to draw the opposite conclusion. Ethnographic data and mythical narratives show that the truth is rather on the side of attraction ("The desire for a wife begins with the sister," says an Azande proverb quoted in *ESK* 17), but probably not for the reasons cited by Freud. Whatever the case, a simple argument can be used against the partisans of natural repulsion: Why forbid what no one wants or dreams of doing? That would be a sociological absurdity. To the contrary, what should be remembered is this obvious methodological principle: "Society expressly forbids only that which society brings about" (*ESK* 18).

What remain, thus, are those explanations that assign the prohibition a social origin but always make it the remains of ancient, otherwise vanished practices that led to exogamy, such as the kidnapping of women in warrior tribes (this is the position of John McLennan and Herbert Spencer). The prohibition thus remains only as a distant sign of this cause. This amounts to saying that it has no present reason to exist. The same criticism can be made of Durkheim, who also resorts to a genealogical explanation: the origin of exogamy would be in religious prohibitions concerning menstrual bleeding, itself linked to the blood of the clan and thus to the totem. Thus for Durkheim too, "the prohibition of incest is a remnant of exogamy" (*ESK* 21). The ethnographic data he uses are, though perhaps not well interpreted, much better documented than those used by McLennan and Spencer. However, in both cases: (1) the data used are particular and impossible to generalize; and (2) between the different points in the proposed genealogy, no necessary connection is shown.

Two requirements are thus placed on the anthropologist: the explanation of what is a social rule must be discovered in the society itself, and a universal reason for a universally followed rule must be provided. In other words, unlike most other anthropologists of his generation, who preferred to abandon this problem as unsolvable, Lévi-Strauss considers that it is not only possible but necessary to reopen the debate, but only on the condition that the statement of the problem be revised, for the issue no longer regards the genealogy of an institution: it concerns understanding its logical coherency. This coherency may then take different forms depending on combinatory possibilities and not on unverified, unverifiable events.

The prohibition is a social rule, but is its origin social? For if it is, how can its universality be explained? To be able to answer these two questions would be to solve the problem. We know that in all complex living species, including our own, biological reproduction supposes the union of two partners of opposite sex. Nature demands nothing else. It leaves the choice of partner undetermined. Between this necessity and this indeterminacy slips the social rule, which states which partners are possible or permitted and, to the contrary, which are forbidden. Thus the rule rests on a fact of nature (the necessary union), and it gives that fact a cultural value (permitted or prohibited union). What was a necessity becomes a choice: the union is transformed into an alliance. In this sense the incest prohibition is indeed the kingpin connecting two worlds, or rather it is the passage from one order to the other. Through this we see that the cultural universality of the rule is grafted directly onto the natural universality of the union.

Establishing this articulation is not, however, sufficient to explain why the human species, unlike other species, considers it necessary to specify the partner, and we also do not yet know what modalities govern this choice. The existence of the prohibition at least shows that the decision on the union is withdrawn from blood relatives to be given to the social group. In other words, society as an institution asserts itself here:

> The prime rôle of culture is to ensure the group's existence as a group, and consequently, in this domain as in all others, to replace chance by organization. The prohibition of incest is a certain form, and even highly varied forms, of intervention. But it is intervention over and above anything else; even more exactly, it is *the* intervention. (*ESK* 32)

This priority of the social group over the consanguineous group (which could be translated as that of the society over the family) demonstrates the positive nature of the prohibition: it is in no way a moral prescription or inspired by an obscure capacity for biological prevention. It simply and essentially means that for every woman given up by her relations, another one will be made available by another group of relations. This reciprocal recognition is precisely what takes us from the natural necessity of the union to the instituted rule of alliance. In short, it is why there is society and not simply a biological group. It also entails that paternity or fraternity do not entitle one to claim a spouse. At the same time the prohibition places the young woman in an external position in relation to her group of blood-relations. She is virtually freed from her dependency in this respect (she is necessarily destined to go into the other group), and simultaneously she is virtually nonexclusively available to all those seeking spouses in the other group. "[T]he logical end of the incest prohibition is 'to freeze' women within the family, so that their distribution, or the competition for them, is within the group and under group and not private control" (*ESK* 45).

The incest prohibition has thus one and only one goal: to make the consanguineous group exogamous, to deliver it from its natural confinement in order to establish and maintain the social group as such, to give the latter authority over the former. Only by this constraint on exchange, which is reciprocal recognition through the interdependence created by the movement of the received and the returned, does a properly social link take up and transform the natural relation. This movement and obligation prevent the social group from breaking up "into a multitude of families, forming so many closed systems or sealed monads which no pre-established harmony could prevent from proliferating or from coming into conflict" (*ESK* 479). This allows the following conclusion to be drawn:

> Like exogamy, which is its widened social application, the prohibition of incest is a rule of reciprocity. The woman whom one does not take, and whom one may not take, is, for that very reason, offered up. To whom is she offered? Sometimes to a group defined by institutions, and sometimes to an indeterminate and ever-open collectivity limited only by the exclusion of near relatives, such as in our own society. (*ESK* 51)

The incest prohibition is not foremost a prohibition on sexuality but has to do with matrimonial alliance. "Incest is socially absurd before it is morally culpable" (*ESK* 485). It is neither considered nor even desired simply because everyone sees it as a considerable social disadvantage. Inversely, in certain populations, occasional incestuous relations are sometimes ignored so long as there are no regrettable social consequences (pregnancy or refusal to be separated, for example), in other words, as long as the possibilities of alliance are not endangered. In modern societies, where the social link is no longer either essentially engendered by marriage or carried by kinship relations, the positive function of the prohibition as a rule of reciprocity is no longer perceived. This explains the temptation to account for its origin from the individual structure of desire (as Freud attempted to do) or to legitimize its necessity through a purely moral or biological argument.

What Lévi-Strauss, in any case, establishes in a lucid and utterly convincing manner is that the incest prohibition springs from the obligation to give and that, in contrast, "incest, in the broadest sense of the word, consists in obtaining by oneself, and for oneself, instead of by another, and for another" (*ESK* 489). The prohibition does not follow from an article of sexual morality. It is a question of receiving from another, more precisely, from another group, that which nature would allow one to give to oneself. The prohibition is the very seed of the sovereignty of the social group, as a culturally determined order, over the consanguineous group, as a natural fact.

It might seem surprising that certain anthropologists, who are nonetheless brilliant and subtle, remain closed to this argument. This is the case of Needham. In the collective work mentioned above (*Rethinking Kinship and Marriage* [1971]), even the word "reciprocity" does not appear in the index, which is very detailed. Needham himself devotes a few very critical pages (24–29) to the issue of the incest prohibition. Regarding Lévi-Strauss, he mentions only the formula: "The incest prohibition is...culture itself" (*ESK* 12) and the sentence asserting its universality. Needham reasons that this prohibition seems important in certain cultures, less so in others. It is thus not a homogenous class of social facts. The issue is, in his view, that "the difficulties arise from the invalid constitution of a class and, especially clearly, the unbounded exercise of the craving for generality....A structural theory is unlikely to serve, since there are no systematic resemblances among all known sets of prohibitions" (Needham 1971, 28).

These remarks would be pertinent if one could isolate the prohibition from the facts about exogamy and if one considered the logic of reciprocity dismissed. This, however, amounts to refusing to call the prohibition a "total social fact." This is indeed what Needham does throughout his argumentation, which ends in the following remark: "All that is common to incest prohibitions is the feature of prohibition itself" (Needham 1971, 28). This is short and insufficient. Where lies the problem according to Needham? It is summarized in the following critical requirement:

> Each set of cultural prohibitions forms a coherent but variable assemblage of rules; the contextual explication of these rules demands a recourse to history, language, moral concepts, and many other contingent particulars. The various sets of prohibitions thus do not compose a concrete class such as might be open to a unitary explanation; the functional or semantic explication of the rules of one society may not apply at all to those of another. (Needham 1971, 28)

It is clear that Lévi-Strauss could subscribe without hesitation to this proposition applying to prohibitions in general since he formulates it many times regarding many other issues (analysis of myths, and so on). Yet he would continue to maintain that the incest prohibition, whatever form it might take in a given culture, has a unique nature due to two elements that remain the same: (1) it is a universal prohibition; and (2) it is defined by a rule of reciprocity. These are not "generalizations": these are conclusions to which ethnographic study has led.

The objections raised by Needham lose some of their relevance when one ceases to think of the incest prohibition as an isolated phenomenon. Yet how can it be considered a "total social phenomenon" if it is separated from the practices it is meant to make necessary: those of reciprocity? This would suppose that the logic of reciprocity were itself understood and accepted (which it does not seem to be in the case of Needham). There are perfectly good grounds to demand that the various expressions of the prohibition belong to a homogenous class of facts, but one must not begin by unduly limiting the definition of that class. The incest prohibition is only the principal form (because without it the others would not endure) of a set of relations and institutions that cover all of social life. It is as important to understand that incest is a rupture of reciprocity as it is to see that the refusal to share what is considered a nonprivative good constitutes "social incest." If incest is a refusal of reciprocity, then inversely any refusal of reciprocity takes on an incestuous nature. Thus there is an expansion and dissemination of the connotations linked to the opposition of the incest/reciprocity terms. However, this is not alone in being a possible object of symbolic treatment. In many myths, where what is at issue is the formulation of a balanced life, of a "good distance," incest can mean an excess of proximity, as animality can mean an excess of distance (but here the subject and attribute can change places, and this would be, to the contrary, excessive nearness that would signal the incestuous situation, and so on).

By following this path, very clearly indicated by Lévi-Strauss moreover, certain researchers have been able to demonstrate the wealth of analogical reasoning related to the practice of this prohibition, which is all the more pregnant since it founds social life. F. Héritier, for example, in an essay titled "The Symbolics of Incest and Its Prohibition" (in Izard and Smith 1982), shows in a remarkable way that the problem of the incest prohibition is never limited to sexual relations alone but reverberates in all representations of the individual, the world, the social organization, and the relations between these three aspects. In the African examples analyzed in her study, incest appears as a cumulation of identicalness and thus as a danger for the equilibrium of opposites (hot-cold, dry-wet, and so on) on which the equilibrium of the physical and social universe depends. Incest is the form par excellence of the abuse of identicalness just as, reciprocally, any excess of identicalness is stated in the terminology of incest. In short, a "total social fact" is a fact that is much more than social: it is also cosmic, religious, logical, aesthetic, moral, and so on. This is, moreover, what we will learn from the analysis of myths.

Marriage as Exchange of Women

Exchange, as a total phenomenon, is from the first a total exchange, comprising food, manufactured objects, and that most precious category of goods, women. Doubtless we are a long way from the strangers in the restaurant, and perhaps it will seem startling to suggest that the reluctance of the southern French peasant to drink from his own flask of wine provides the model by which the prohibition of incest might be explained. Clearly the prohibition does not result from this reluctance. Nevertheless, we believe that both are phenomena of the same type, that they are elements of the same cultural complex, or more exactly the basic complex of culture.

—*ESK* 60–61

These remarks are important because they allow us to widen the perspective on the institution of marriage and at the same time to understand the incest prohibition starting with the total system of the culture in which it is certainly the cornerstone (since it is a condition for its existence), but of which it is also only one element among others. It is "not only that the system of prestations *includes* marriage, but also that it *keeps it going*" (*ESK* 66–67), for the prohibition makes exogamy possible and necessary. It forces each group to give women to other groups (in each case in accordance with very specific conditions and rules). However, what is important to note is that this action of giving is inseparable from a set of other prestations that make it a syncretic manifestation of reciprocity. In this case again we are dealing with what Mauss calls a "total social fact."

It is thus understandable how any infraction of the logic of reciprocity (solitary consumption of food, for example) takes on an *incestuous* character and, symmetrically and inversely, why matrimonial alliance brings with it all of reciprocity's forms. "It would then be false to say that one exchanges or gives gifts at the same time that one exchanges or gives women. For the woman herself is nothing other than one of these gifts, the supreme gift among those that can only be obtained in the form of reciprocal gifts" (*ESK* 65).

Reciprocity defines a very special domain: that of *goods or persons that cannot be obtained privately*. Even though they may permit private use or relationships, they remain, in their essence, that by which or by whom the community is instituted. From this point of view reciprocity is indeed a principle: it cannot be derived from the institution of the society. Rather, it creates the possibility of the society. The various modes of exchange are possible only because of this. The initial, founding relation is that of the reciprocal gift: it is essentially agonistic, an act of recognition of the group as such, a way out of the natural circle of consanguinity, a manifestation of the symbolic order of alliance. This is indeed also why it continues to exist in our modernity, even though many other types of activity have relegated its expression to forms that seem marginal to us. The present hegemony of contractual modes of exchange (such as commerce) makes its perception difficult but in no way diminishes its reality.

Some have confessed to being upset or even shocked by the expression "exchange of women," thus reproaching Lévi-Strauss's theory for endorsing the reduction of women to goods to be used by men (see *SA* 1:61). Some anthropologists have even considered these formulations unacceptable from an ethical point of view. M. Sahlins notes, "an interesting number of British and American ethnologists recoiled at once from the idea, refusing for their part to 'treat women as commodities.' Without wanting to decide the issue, at least not in these terms, I do wonder whether the Anglo-American distrust was ethnocentric" (Sahlins 1972, 181). What they have not understood, explains Sahlins, is the very nature of alliance, its nature as a total prestation. Here ethnocentrism consists in projecting the separation existing in our society between the world of business and that of individual relations onto primitive societies, thus supposing "an eternal separation of the economic, having to do with getting and spending, and besides always a little off-color, from the social sphere of moral relationships" (Sahlins 1972, 181).

Lévi-Strauss was a little surprised by this sort of confusion, and he later explained his position, though *The Elementary Structures of Kinship* was already sufficiently explicit. Before discussing his argument in depth, we must note that the anthropologist's task is in any case not to propose an ethical critique of the facts but to establish their objectivity and explain the reasons behind them. The facts are the following: "[I]t is men who exchange women, and not vice versa" (*ESK* 115). In other words, in matrimonial alliances, the other group does not demand a man, but indeed a woman. If such is the case (and here we are coming to the reasons), it is because women are recognized as belonging to the sex by which the biological continuity of the group passes. It is in this sense, and this sense only, that women can be said to be "the most precious good." This esteem and the rites of exchange that follow from it can be seen in all primitive and traditional societies (and can still be identified in a latent state in modern societies). In itself this does not imply a diminution of the status of women, but that such a diminution effectively occurs in most societies requires that other elements be taken into account, elements that Lévi-Strauss does not attempt to define since to do so would be to leave the framework of his analysis. He himself indicates that he confines himself to the structures of communication and leaves aside those of subordination.

Let us thus take a closer look at his discussion of the function of women in the process of reciprocity. As we saw regarding the explanation of the incest prohibition, nature prescribes the union of partners but

leaves the choice of partner undetermined. This is the point at which social intervention comes in: the partner must be chosen from the other
group, and the partner from, or who should join, the other group can
be only a woman. A passage made obligatory by biological reproduction
(which is a natural constraint) becomes thus also a special support and
sign of reciprocity (which is an invention of culture). Thus it is always a
woman, necessarily, who is received or given up by a group. This makes
it understandable that the exchange would be indexed, at least formally
from the point of view of men, since every woman is first a daughter
given by a father or a sister given by a brother, in other words by a member of the same group but of opposite sex and who would be able, in
principle, to have procreative relations with her. All daughters and sisters
are thus initially possible wives. All fathers and brothers are thus initially wife-givers. The incest prohibition has no other meaning. Women
as signs and instruments of alliance — the act of reciprocity that manifests the social as such and its preeminence — are necessarily linked to
all other acts of exchange, to all forms of gift/countergift, to all goods
considered precious, unobtainable privately.

"[M]atrimonial exchange is only a particular case of those forms of
multiple exchange embracing material goods, rights and persons" (*ESK*
113). The prohibition on the daughter or sister is not, in itself, related to
the fact that she is a member of the group, for her degree of proximity
is neither more nor less great than that of sons and brothers. It is due
to a possibility indicated by nature, immediately assumed in principle by
culture: that of manifesting reciprocity. Thus, in the relations between
the exogamous moieties of some aborigines of southern Australia, all
exchanges are concentrated around the figure of the woman:

> The sole reason is that she is *same* whereas she must (and can) be-
> come *other*. Once she becomes *other* (by her allocation to men of
> the opposite moiety), she therefore becomes liable to play the same
> rôle, *vis-à-vis* the men of her own moiety, as she originally played
> to the men of the opposite moiety. In feasts, the same presents can
> be exchanged; in the custom of *kopara*, the same women that were
> originally offered can be exchanged in return. All that is necessary
> on either side is the *sign of otherness,* which is the outcome of a
> certain position in a structure and not of any innate characteristic.
> (*ESK* 114)

Obviously we can imagine the extreme ambivalence that can mark this
"position in the structure" since it defines a woman as the beneficiary
of an essential, unavoidable function, but with a power that is, for her,
passive. In contrast, while she is a sign and a value in an exchange, she
nonetheless remains herself a producer of signs and values. All that is
required is that this position in the structure be modified (as in the caste

system, as we will see later) for roles to change, and with them, attitudes. From this it is not difficult to understand the inevitable transformations wrought by modern society.

Marriage of Cross-Cousins

This presentation of the "principle of reciprocity" would already be of certain value insofar as it allows us to account for the specific nature of exchanges between groups, for the supraeconomic nature of these exchanges, and finally for the nature of alliance as a "total social fact." However, this would merely add to Mauss's analyses by confirming and completing them. This presentation of the principle is only the methodological introduction to its various applications, first among which is the enigma posed by the marriage of cross-cousins and, at the same time, that of the prohibition of marriage between parallel cousins.

Let us briefly go over, for readers unfamiliar with anthropological terminology, the difference between these two forms of kinship:

- cousins from the marriages of siblings of the opposite sex are called "cross." In other words, cross-cousins are cousins from the marriage of the mother's brother or of that of the father's sister, in short the children of the maternal uncle and of the paternal aunt;

- cousins from the marriages of siblings of the same sex are called "parallel." In other words, parallel cousins are cousins from the marriage of the mother's sister or of the father's brother, in short the children of the maternal aunt and the paternal uncle (see figure 1).

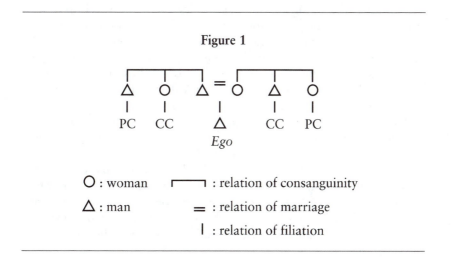

Figure 1

O : woman   ⌐⌐ : relation of consanguinity

Δ : man   = : relation of marriage

| : relation of filiation

Why is it that in the case of cross-cousins, marriage is not only possible but often even preferential or obligatory, and why is it that in the case of parallel cousins it is strictly prohibited? This enigma only seems greater when we consider that, from the biological point of view, the degree of proximity is the same in both cases:

> It is precisely because cross-cousin marriage disregards the biological factor that it should be able to establish that the origin of the incest prohibition is purely social, and furthermore to reveal what its real nature is. It is not enough to repeat that the prohibition of incest is not based on biological grounds. What then is its basis? This is the real question, and while it remains unanswered the problem cannot be said to have been resolved. For the most part, an answer to this is very difficult to give because the prohibited degrees of kinship, taken as a whole, are biologically closer than the permitted degrees. Consequently, there is always a doubt as to whether it is the biological degree, or the social degree, which is the basis of the institution. The difficulty is completely eliminated only in the case of cross-cousin marriage, for if we can understand why degrees of kinship which are equivalent from a biological point of view are nevertheless considered completely dissimilar from the social point of view, we can claim to have discovered the principle, not only of cross-cousin marriage, but of the incest prohibition itself. (ESK 122)

We probably must emphasize what is at stake here. Actually, it is significant for Lévi-Strauss's theoretical undertaking, for to provide a satisfactory answer to the problem posed by the marriage of cross-cousins is also to verify the pertinence of the principle of reciprocity. It is to confirm the hypothesis of the purely social origin of the incest prohibition, and it is also, on the methodological level, to demonstrate the mode of existence of a structure and show the rigor of its operation. This is why we can consider the issue of the marriage of cross-cousins to be a crucial element in Lévi-Strauss's exposition. (He himself underlines its "exceptional importance" [ESK 121].)

However, before coming to this solution, we must take stock of the difficulties. They were due mainly to the methodological presuppositions of anthropologists, for the marriage of cross-cousins implies two levels: that of the aspect of supposing a level of matrimonial *classes* (men and women seem to be distributed exactly according to a dual organization, in other words, into exogamous moieties) and that of the aspect of assuming another level, which is that of preferential *relations* between individuals (each man and each woman has the possibility of finding a cross-cousin spouse).

In the first case it is a question of knowing if the logic of dual organizations explains the marriage of cross-cousins or if it is independent of, or even logically prior to, such marriage. In the second case the issue is why there is a prohibition on parallel cousins while for cross-cousins, who are just as close biologically, there is not only the possibility of union but preferential, or even imposed, union.

On the first point Lévi-Strauss notes the methodological failures of the first generation of anthropologists (Lewis Morgan, Edward Tylor, William Perry), who considered the marriage of cross-cousins to be a somewhat irrational remnant from an institution that has vanished and that could be a mode of a dual organization. This explanation is frankly historicist. Above all it leaves whole the enigma of the difference in status between cross-cousins and parallel cousins. What is the source of this failure?

> What should have been done, on the contrary, was to treat cross-cousin marriage, rules of exogamy, and dual organization *as so many examples of one basic structure....* It was especially necessary to see that, of the three types of institutions, cross-cousin marriage is the most significant, making the analysis of this form of marriage the veritable *experimentum crucis* in the study of marriage prohibitions. (*ESK* 123)

This experiment is crucial indeed because this form is documented independently in a great number of very different societies. This, while not showing a universality comparable to that of the incest prohibition, provides it with a degree of universality sufficient for it to be legitimate to think that what produces it is independent of purely local experiences and traditions.

What is this "fundamental structure," and why does the case of cross-cousins illustrate its efficiency better than others? This is the question Lévi-Strauss intends to answer. In order to arrive at the solution, a certain number of facts must be established:

- The first is that the difference in status between cross-cousins and parallel cousins leads us to suppose that at the level of the parents' generation, the relation brother-sister and sister-brother is radically different from the relation brother-brother and sister-sister. The system of appellations confirms this division by, in most cases, assimilating under the same term the father's brother and the mother's sister (an assimilation that sometimes even extends to the grandparents' generation).

- This division then reveals the difference in status (relayed by the differences in attitudes) between the direct and the collateral lines.

To put it differently, the radical difference in status between cross-cousins and parallel cousins must be read in the different status of their parents: on one side, Ego's maternal uncle and aunt; on the other side, Ego's paternal uncle and aunt.

Moreover, there is no point in explaining the marriage of cross-cousins as the positive side of the prohibition weighing on the union of parallel cousins. Affinity in one case cannot be explained as a response to exclusion in the other. What is required is a common reason that would simultaneously explain both choices. This reason exists, and Lévi-Strauss must be awarded the credit for having been the first to formulate it clearly and coherently.

What does he tell us? He tells us that marriage between cross-cousins is simply an example of "marriage by exchange," in other words of the rigorous practice, in alliance, of the principle of reciprocity. Concretely this means that for a woman given up by a group, there must be another restored *by the receiving group and by no other*. If we take as an example two patrilineal, patrilocal groups, A and B (which is the simplest example, for many other situations are possible), it appears that every related woman is a woman lost to the group and that every woman married is a woman gained. Thus for every woman who comes from B to A, the male children of A are in debt to the men of B, and the latter are creditors of those of A.

Allow us to put this differently. Let there be two patrilineal groups A and B. An *a* man (Ego) marries a *b* woman, and their children will be *a*, as will be the children of the man's brother; in other words, the children will be parallel cousins. However, the sister of the man is *a* and marries a *b* man, so having *b* children, who are cross-cousins of the *a* man's children. Since they are *a* and *b*, the cross-cousins belong to different clans (or to any other form of group). Since they are only *a* or only *b*, the parallel cousins belong to the same group. The relations between cross-cousins can thus be exogamous, and most primitive societies have considered it logical that they be so necessarily. Marriage between parallel cousins would mean pure endogamy (an *a* man would marry an *a* woman), which is the same thing as marrying one's sister who is also *a*. The natural consanguineous group would not receive its laws from the social group. By obliging *a* to marry *b*, and *b* to marry *a*, the incest prohibition manifests both the sovereignty of the group and the relation of reciprocity. Marriage between cross-cousins ensures reciprocity in each generation: *a* received a *b* woman, but a *b* man will marry his *a* daughter, and their *b* daughter will marry an *a* man. (This is the simplest, most typical case, as we will see in the next chapter, of what Lévi-Strauss calls *restricted exchange* in opposition to more complex forms of *generalized exchange*.) The above description can be seen synoptically in figure 2 (*ESK* 131).

Figure 2

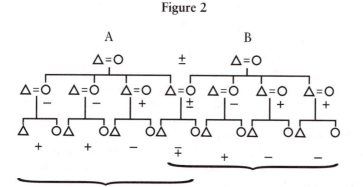

△ man   ○ woman   △=○ husband and wife   △ ○ brother and sister
Cousins in the (+ −) relation are cross;
those in the (+ +) or (− −) relation are parallel

Because James Frazer did not see that marriage between cross-cousins (in which he had nonetheless recognized a typical case of marriage by exchange) was regulated by the requirements of reciprocity, he also did not see that the prohibition on marriage between parallel cousins (which he treats as a totally separate problem) was its immediate and necessary consequence. By bringing out this connection, Lévi-Strauss offers the first coherent, clear, irreproachable solution to this old anthropological enigma. He formulates his conclusion in these terms:

> Thus, the notion of reciprocity allows the dichotomy of cousins to be immediately deduced. In other words, two male cousins who are both in the credit position towards their father's group (and in the debit position with regard to their mother's group) cannot exchange their sisters any more than could two male cousins in a credit position with regard to their mother's group (and debit position with regard to the father's group). This intimate arrangement would leave somewhere outside not only groups which did not make restitution, but also groups which did not receive anything, and marriage in both would be a unilateral transfer. In the final analysis, therefore, cross-cousin marriage simply expresses the fact that marriage must always be a giving and a receiving, but that one can receive only from him who is obliged to give, and that the giving must be to him who has a right to receive, for the mutual gift between debtors tends to be privilege, whereas the mutual gift between creditors leads inevitably to extinction. (*ESK* 131)

The marriage of cross-cousins is thus the simplest, most obvious way to establish a relation of alliance, in other words, of reciprocity, between two consanguineous groups. It is thus not surprising that this type of marriage appears in different places all over the map of traditional populations. It is the most obvious solution to a single problem, and there is nothing surprising in the fact that it is formulated in the same way everywhere if we accept that the mental equipment is also the same in all people. (It is thus perfectly pointless to resort to diffusionist hypotheses to explain the extension of the phenomenon.) Better yet, this explanation also allows us to understand another particularity within this type of marriage: marriage between matrilineal cross-cousins is more frequent and more positive than that between patrilineal cross-cousins. In other words, it is more preferable for Ego to marry the daughter of his mother's brother than the daughter of his father's sister. This hierarchy of value within the "cross-cousin" type itself has seemed equally mysterious to anthropologists. Now, if one takes into account how the movement of reciprocity is organized in both cases, one sees, notes Lévi-Strauss, that it remains open and dynamic in the case of matrilineal cousins, but that it tends to close and extinguish in the other (*ESK* 443) (see figure 3).

Figure 3

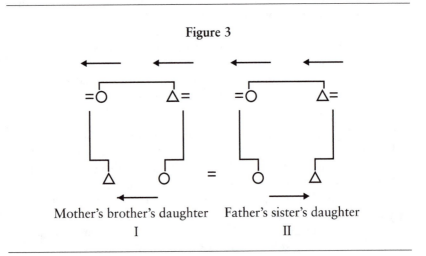

Mother's brother's daughter   Father's sister's daughter
              I   II

In the case of matrilineal cross-cousins, there are asymmetrical pairs at all levels (in other words, one is always in a cross-situation), while in the case of patrilineal cross-cousins, there is a mixture of symmetrical and asymmetrical pairs. This would not be important if it were not also that this formal difference corresponds to a difference in the movement of reciprocity. In the first case, the movement is always oriented in the same direction and remains open. Here we are already in the system of generalized exchange. In the second case, the movement comes back on itself and closes. Here we remain in the framework of restricted exchange. The compensation in reciprocity occurs more rapidly but also wears out more quickly, since the cycles are very short and, above all, are limited thus to two groups and cannot extend to the whole of the society. The social ties are more fragile since what is lacking, unlike in the other case, is the ability to imagine long-term reciprocity. This lack of confidence is seen clearly in populations in which marriage with a patrilineal female cross-cousin appears: there it is qualified by terms that are not very flattering and that denounce withdrawing into oneself, going against the grain. They even go so far as to see in this sort of marriage a lack of reciprocity that makes it close to incest. "To speak in mathematical terms, incest is the 'limit' of reciprocity, i.e. the point at which it cancels itself out. And what incest is to reciprocity in general, such is the lowest form of reciprocity (patrilineal marriage) in relation to the highest form (matrilineal marriage)" (*ESK* 454).

What does this mean? At least the following: not only that the movement of reciprocity allows us to understand the marriage of cross-cousins but that this reciprocity itself has degrees, depending on whether it is limited to a closed set or whether it ensures a wider circulation and thus greater integration of the social group. Thus we can see how *The Gift* opened the way to the revelation of a logic that governs, through the organization of alliance, all kinship relations and that, thanks to the principle of reciprocity, allows the comprehension that the prohibition on marriage between parallel cousins and the preferential marriage of cross-cousins, along with the particular approbation of matrilineal cross-cousins, constitute a single problem. It is undoubtedly to Lévi-Strauss's credit that he was able to perceive this relation and draw out, with exemplary rigor and clarity, its consequences on a certain number of phenomena considered until then to be unamenable to coherent explanation.

Dual Organizations

There is another type of problem with which anthropology has been confronted regularly ever since its conception and that has resulted in explanations as numerous as they are divergent. It is that of *dual organizations*. Here again Lévi-Strauss thinks that the solution is to be found in the logic of reciprocity. Here again his demonstration is of great clarity.

What is a dual organization?

This term defines a system in which the members of the community, whether it be a tribe or a village, are divided into two parts which maintain complex relationships varying from open hostility to very close intimacy, and with which various forms of rivalry and co-operation are usually associated. (*ESK* 69)

How should we understand the fact that there is a division into moieties superimposed on the apparently simpler, more logical clan division, and that the division into moieties seems most often to complicate it, for no reason, by introducing new levels of exogamy? Faced with what appears to be a phenomenon with little rationality, many anthropologists have advanced the hypothesis that such dual organizations are the remains of the union of two heterogenous groups or populations, and, in support of this thesis, there are many cases in which such unions have been observed. This, however, does not alter the problem in other cases and, above all, does not help us to understand the logic proper to such organizations: the attitudes and rituals of sharing and rivalry. Clearly the phenomenon of reciprocity is predominant here. The historicist point of view thus found its argument here: reciprocity is proper to dual organizations that are themselves the results of the fusion of two different populations. This would permit the genealogy of exogamy, of the facts of exchange, of rivalry behavior, and so on, to be established. In short, reciprocity would appear where the meeting of two groups requires good manners, compromises, and gestures of exchange.

Yet the existence of dual organizations can be seen in many cases in which such events have not taken place. On this point again, Lévi-Strauss, while not failing to recognize the historical fact of the union of two populations that could have provided a natural stimulus for the division into moieties, attempts to show that the constraint is internal, that its nature is structural. What he again finds operating here is precisely the principle of *reciprocity*. "[T]he dual system does not give rise to reciprocity, but merely gives it form" (*ESK* 70). Such reciprocity finds one of its oldest expressions in the dual organization. It seems in fact to be "a functional character peculiar to archaic cultures" (*ESK* 70). It will allow us to understand the notion of a *matrimonial class*. However if, as Tylor and Frazer presupposed, one sees the source of kinship classificatory systems in dual organizations, then that amounts to considering such systems as a primary phenomenon and situating that of reciprocity among its consequences. Lévi-Strauss postulates the inverse order.

The main question that ethnologists then must answer is how the dual system superimposes itself on, or connects to, the clan system. One can very well exist without the other, but when both are found at once, what are the rules of alliance, in other words, of exogamy? Clan exogamy, insofar as it limits itself to forbidding marriage within one's own clan, provides a negative rule, at most. It leaves the choice otherwise undetermined (this means undetermined within the set of other clans). The existence of a division into moieties can then modify this situation: the other moiety is that with which marriages *must* take place. This well-known difference allows a definition to be proposed: "The term *clan* will be reserved for unilineal groupings which, in that they are exogamous, permit a purely negative definition, and the term *class,* or more exactly, *marriage class,* to those groupings which permit a positive determination of the modalities of exchange" (*ESK* 73). In concrete situations things are not so simple, and Lévi-Strauss gives obvious examples of this (such as the case of the Bororo, where to clan exogamy is added divisions into upper, middle, and lower; and also the case of Australian matrimonial classes that are independent of clans).

This distinction between *clan* and *class* is of capital importance, insofar as it prevents confusion of levels, when a society finds itself reduced to two clans: the negative exogamous injunction becomes positive (which means it identifies not only the partner who is forbidden but the one who is prescribed). The clan thus comes to have the same function as a dual organization. This does not mean that it would be the origin of such organization. In a general way the dual system is not so much an institution as a "principle of organization" (*ESK* 75). It is only one of the "formulations of the principle of reciprocity" (*ESK* 75). This can concern religious and political activities, sports competitions, just as it can, but does not necessarily, extend to the system of marriage.

Now all the classical difficulties with this issue can be eliminated, or at least the underlying reasons for them have been clearly identified. What were considered unconnected facts for which a causal hierarchy was to be discovered (for example: fusion of two groups, demographic reduction to two clans, and so on) were in fact different manifestations of the same fundamental requirement, which has to do with the logic of reciprocity. This logic follows a path identical to that which Lévi-Strauss was later to call (beginning in *The Savage Mind) bricolage:*[1] this logic uses anything available to achieve its goal; it manifests itself using whatever media are appropriate. The heterogenous nature of dual facts is then no longer a problem. What is important thus is to not

confuse the principle of reciprocity, which is always at work and always oriented in the same direction, with the often brittle and almost always incomplete institutional structures continually used by it to realize the same ends. The contrast, the apparent contradiction we might almost say, between the functional permanence of systems of reciprocity, and the contingency of the institutional matter placed at their disposal by history, and moreover ceaselessly reshaped by it, is supplementary proof of the instrumentality of these systems. Whatever the changes, the same force is always at work, and it is always to the same effect that it organizes the elements offered or abandoned to it. (*ESK* 76)

Each time he has a chance to come back to this problem, Lévi-Strauss insists on the value of the dual organization as a *method,* on its ability to treat different contents according to a single principle, that of reciprocity. This it does either by taking over existing data, by orienting accidental modifications toward itself, or by giving rise to new practices likely to produce bonds or to create rivalry (simulated or not).

Thus dual organization can be explained by a reciprocity relation between two moieties. The most obvious, general case of such a relation is precisely that of marriage between cross-cousins, for whatever the mode of filiation (patrilineal or matrilineal), the children of the mother's brother and of the father's sister are placed in a moiety different from that of the subject. They are thus the first collaterals with whom marriage is possible. This is most often confirmed by the appellations they are given ("husbands" and "wives," whereas parallel cousins are called "brothers" and "sisters"). Cross-cousins therefore seem to present themselves as an exemplary case of exogamous moieties. At this point, the question anthropologists asked was: Does the anteriority of dual organizations explain the marriage of cross-cousins, or should such marriage be considered independently? In one case, we are led to diffusionist and evolutionist hypotheses for which there are no rigorously verifiable data. In the other case, we must admit that primitive thought resolved an extremely complex problem with extraordinary logic and coherency, a possibility that seemed unlikely to many observers. The problem was thus not in the object but in the prejudices concerning that object.

The problem (as we saw above) is that of the organization of cycles of reciprocity. From this point of view, the marriage of cross-cousins provides an astonishingly perfect solution. Here we must speak of a "regulating principle" and say of this one that it "can have a rational value without being rationally conceived" (*ESK* 101). Must we now adopt the view opposite to that of the evolutionists and propose to derive the dual organization from the marriage of cross-cousins? What must be said instead is that in both cases there is an original system of reciprocity driven by its own logic. In the case of dual organizations, *an entire class of individuals* is designated for exogamous exchange. It is thus a "global system, engaging the group in its totality" (*ESK* 102). In the other case, it is a question of *a relationship between individuals:* the problem is resolved case by case (and often with a certain degree of flexibility depending on the individuals available).

In dual organizations, the *class* of possible spouses is well-defined, while the *relations* between individuals remain undetermined. We find the inverse situation with the marriage of cross-cousins, which defines the possible (or even prescribed) spouse in a very individualized way, with the risk (as in very restricted groups) that no individual will correspond to the designated position. The two formulations should not, thus, be situated on a chronological line that would place one before the other. In fact, "the two institutions are in contrast, one being crystallized, the other flexible" (*ESK* 103). They are two functional responses to the same requirement of reciprocity. This explains why cross-cousin marriage appears where dual organizations are lacking (as is the case in certain regions of Melanesia).

After the enigma of the marriage of cross-cousins, we find that of the disparate appearance of dual organizations resolved. Credit must be given to Lévi-Strauss's method for this undoubtedly impressive result. Yet Lévi-Strauss does not stop on such a fruitful path. He pushes the hypothesis further, regarding the various forms of dual organization, by supposing that to "understand their common basis, inquiry must be directed to certain fundamental structures of the human mind, rather than to some privileged region of the world or to a certain period in the history of civilization" (*ESK* 75). This hypothesis is perfectly coherent with the statement of a *principle* (that of reciprocity), but this will be the subject of another chapter in the present study.

Remark on the Caste System and Reciprocity

The rules of reciprocity transform in a wholly remarkable way when we turn to a system founded on professional specialization and thus on complementarity of services. At once the exchange of women and the distribution of prestations are completely upset. In the caste system, differentiation is ensured thanks to professional specialization; thus it is at this level that contrasts and oppositions appear. This is also the level at which, in consequence, reciprocity can operate: it no longer has a reason to be accomplished through exogamous exchange. Thus "true reciprocity being otherwise secured, endogamy is made available" (*SM* 126).

Between clan exogamy and caste endogamy, we see clearly how the function of marriage and thus the role of women are transformed. In the first case, a natural difference (woman-man) is translated into a cultural difference: the system of possible and impossible alliances, the degrees of prohibition or permission, and the many relations that develop from this (the position of individuals in the system, relations between the groups, and so on) make possible a very complex coding of social life. Kinship relations become the point of reference of social activities. They are thus first among cultural codes, and their imperative nature explains their importance.

In the caste system, cultural identity is manifested by one's trade or profession. There is the possibility of marriage within the same caste, a possibility that becomes a prescription. It is no longer the exchange of women that guarantees the specificity of the cultural organization; thus it is not surprising that there is a simultaneous renaturalization of women.

Against the Economist Illusion: The Cases of
Marriage by Exchange and Marriage by Purchase

[T]his exchange [which occurs when groups periodically settle grievances] is not a business transaction — not a mere bartering — but a means of expressing and cementing friendship.
— Elkin 1931, 197–98

It is our western societies who have recently made man an "economic animal."
— Mauss 1990, 76

In Lévi-Strauss's work, the notion of exchange has a very precise status. Exchange is the exercise of reciprocity. This formulation might seem obvious or even redundant. A simple example will prove it is not. It is the case of what is usually called "marriage by exchange." This formulation means that one group cannot obtain a spouse for one of its members except if it also offers one to the providing group. Without this, the marriage cannot take place. No present, amount of money, or gain in status can be considered equal to the gift of a woman. The only equivalent is the offer of another woman. This strict reciprocity is what is known as exchange:

> Exchange is not a complex edifice built on the obligations of giving, receiving and returning, with the help of some emotional-mystical cement. It is a synthesis immediately given to, and given by, symbolic thought, which in exchange as in any other form of communication, surmounts the contradiction inherent in it; that is the contradiction of perceiving things as elements of dialogue, in respect of self and others simultaneously, and destined by nature to pass from the one to the other. The fact that those things may be *the one's* or *the other's* represents a situation which is derivative from the initial relational aspect. (*IMM* 58–59)

Reciprocity is thus a principle. It is a *universal* given of human societies (since outside of alliance there is only animal society). Nothing could be more incorrect or misleading than to view this reciprocity as an economic fact. It is probably very difficult for minds formed in an industrial, mercantile civilization, which has made economics its main activity, to refrain from giving an economic meaning to exchange relations found in other types of society, relations such as that of marriage, which, in most traditional societies, results in an intense circulation of goods. Our temptation is then, given our experience, which is dominated by commercial exchange and profitable production, to perform a recursive reading of social behavior that we believe to be identical to our own.

On this point, Lévi-Strauss notes that more than one anthropologist has been caught out. This is especially clear with respect to the system of marriage by exchange. Frazer, for example, who was perfectly able to uncover the link between this type of marriage and that of cross-cousins, fell under the *economist illusion* when he tried to provide the *reason* for this link. According to him, this is a trade ("a simple case of barter" [Frazer 1919, 2:220; cited in *ESK* 138]), which allows poor trading partners to participate at lower cost. Frazer's conviction is clear: "For under the surface alike of savagery and of civilization the economic forces are as constant and uniform in their operations as the forces of nature, of which indeed they are merely a peculiarly complex manifestation" (Frazer 1919, 2:220; quoted in *ESK* 138).

Under this hypothesis (which concords, for reasons that are less surprising than one might think, with Marxist anthropology), we must say that purchase is fundamental because economic logic is in some way inherent in it. This is why for Frazer there is, *from this point of view,* no real difference between the case of cross-cousins and that of parallel cousins. Therefore, the observable difference can come, according to him, only from some obscure historical leftover. What Frazer does not see is that this difference is due to two very different systems of relations. In the case of cross-cousins, we are in the cycle of reciprocity that renders exchange (a woman given for a woman previously received) the only possible form of relation. By considering the question from an economic angle, one prevents oneself from understanding this logic and thus from accounting for the essential difference that appears between forms of alliance (permitted, prescribed, or prohibited). An exchange is thus not a substitute for a purchase for people who are excessively economically limited and lacking in other forms of payment: "[F]ar from exchange being a form of purchase, purchase must be seen as a form of exchange" (*ESK* 138). This anteriority appears even more clearly when the exchange seems to provide, from the economic point of view, only a zero-sum result, in other words when the goods transferred are of identical nature or value. The actions of giving and receiving seem then to neutralize each other (we have already seen an example of this apparent redundancy in the exchange of carafes of wine in a restaurant). These cases are very frequent in ethnographic observation and are far from having to be judged as economically aberrant (which tends to be the opinion of Frazer and many others). What must be seen is that they are situated in an entirely different logic and express the essence of exchange as such: "The exchange relationship comes before the things exchanged and is independent of them" (*ESK* 139). Thus the transfer is not neutral; the game is not zero-sum. The goods in circulation gain value from the very fact that they have been exchanged, from having been that through which reciprocity was manifested, because they are the testimony, the symbolic guarantees, of reciprocity.

This same logic can be found in a procedure that could seem to contradict it and that has been called "marriage by purchase." The Katchin of Burma have a remarkable example of this in which a "bride-price" seems to exist. The prestations required are not only considerable; they are extremely complicated because they specify a great number of the members of the bride's family: price of the brother or the cousin, price of the uncle, price of the aunt, price of the mother, price of the slave, and so on. Moreover, this is but a preliminary to the "grand payment" to the father. Each "price" can also be subdivided into different payments assigned to various actions or procedures. Thus the price of the aunt (who must present her niece to the latter's future husband) can, for the single "small payment," include up to twelve fees (for making the trip, for entering the house, for climbing the ladder, for sitting down, for discussing, and so on).

Here we have a system that belongs not to closed exchange (A gives to B, who gives back to A) but to generalized exchange (of which we will speak in the next chapter) and that requires A to give to B, who gives to C, who gives to D, who gives to A. It is thus a long, indirect cycle since one does not receive a spouse from the group to which one has given a spouse. The system is balanced because the cycle, in the end, closes itself and all give and receive spouses. We see thus the role of the goods exchanged: they are at once guarantees and operators of the alliance, a sort of mobile collective treasure, the movement of which is inverse to that of the movement of spouses (see figure 4).

Figure 4

wives	$\longrightarrow$	$\longrightarrow$	$\longrightarrow$	$\longrightarrow$	
	A	B	C	D	A...
goods	$\longleftarrow$	$\longleftarrow$	$\longleftarrow$	$\longleftarrow$	

These goods are not the price in the sense of a direct equivalence. They are only the symbolic mediators and pledges of permanent global reciprocity. Yet in reality it is always *wives that are exchanged for wives and not for goods* (as Lévi-Strauss reminds Leach, who had misunderstood this argument [see *ESK* 238]). The goods received today from one group are the pledges for the wife that one's own group will receive tomorrow from another group. From this we can see that it is the whole group, at all levels of kinship and in all the procedures necessary for the exchange, that is engaged in the matrimonial alliance. Not only is the payment total in that it involves all aspects of the exchange procedure; it is also total in that what goes for alliance goes for "vengeance": the debt incurred for an insult or transgression (crime, adultery, and so on) follows the same path as that of exogamy, according to the schema A ---> B ---> C ---> D ---> A. This clearly shows that reciprocity must be understood in its agonistic implications as much as in the practices of mutual giving. The mediation of goods in alliance, far from making them equivalent to women, ensures to the contrary that alliance invades all of social life and that reciprocity regulates its movement. A work by M. Leenhardt regarding Kanaka alliances describes this well:

> They exchanged their sisters, and had it been a bargain they would have called it quits. But this exchange is not a bargain, it is an arrangement for the future, a social contract: the child that each has by the woman received goes back to take the place that this woman has left among her mother's people; from generation to generation new gaps are filled alternately in the same way. (Leenhardt 1930, 71; cited in *ESK* 435)

We probably have a better understanding of it now, for in relations between groups, reciprocity plays the most important role: reciprocity is primary. Its genesis is not to be explained by the attitudes of individuals because it is what makes possible the explanation of these attitudes. The theoretical task is to bring out its irreducible nature. From this point of view there is a limit to "genealogical" research. Reciprocity (like the symbolic order of which it is one of the privileged manifestations) is the mode of being of humans as such or, if one prefers, of social existence as the ordering of culture. Reciprocity means that the natural organization, or consanguineous family, by which the biological continuity of the group passes, cannot close upon itself without preventing the very possibility of the group as human society, as an institution. Reciprocity resolves this contradiction: *it allows one to remain alone while receiving from others that which one most desires for oneself.* Women are this "sign of otherness," this mediation between oneself and others. Thus the value of reciprocity, attached to what is rare and not a magical principle — such as the Maori *hau* cited by Mauss — is what explains the requirement that certain goods circulate (here we can refer to the excellent commentary by Sahlins, in "The Spirit of the Gift," chapter 5 of *Stone Age Economics* [1972]).

The incest prohibition shows that humans recognize themselves by distinguishing themselves from other species that establish no difference between blood-relations. To desire this distinction is to forbid oneself union with the nearest woman, daughter or sister, and it is thus to leave her available to another group. This is possible only *on the condition that the other necessarily imposes the same constraint on himself.* The obligation to give and receive, the play of gift/countergift, is not something that emerges in society but indeed what institutes society. This unconditional requirement is what is constantly affirmed and confirmed in the principle of reciprocity and in the practices that follow from it. Reciprocity is not something added on to a social reality that would be the synthesis of individual positions (in accordance with the Enlightenment schema that proceeded by transferring onto the origins, as a fact of nature, the nascent isolation of the modern individual). It is what institutes and indicates the sociality proper to humankind, what we call "culture." The reciprocity of which Lévi-Strauss speaks does not originate in an admirable attitude of generosity. It is not engendered by a psychological or moral feeling: such a feeling follows from it as an effect, and this effect, in turn, reinforces its logical necessity by giving it the value of a highly estimable, and effectively esteemed, behavior. This is a Durkheimian position of incontestable pertinence (one that is not always fully understood by the methodological individualism of the Anglo-American tradition).

These analyses allow us to respond to two types of objection.

The first concerns the criticism of "general principles" made by Needham. It is clear that his denunciation of Fortes's "axiom of amity" and of Radcliffe-Brown's a priori benevolence cannot be applied to Lévi-Strauss's "principle of reciprocity." What Lévi-Strauss has brought out, from a constant, universal datum — the incest prohibition and its corollary, exogamy — is the no-less-constant, universal rule that governs the way it operates: that of reciprocal exchange. This is not a feeling of benevolence but an immediate fact of human societies, a regulating principle the logical implications of which explain, in all their aspects, forms of marriage and thus of kinship, as we will see better in the next chapter.

The second objection concerns the accusation of exchangism directed at Lévi-Strauss's theory. This criticism comes essentially from the Marxist sphere of influence and is due to a misunderstanding. In reciprocity there is no exchange in the precisely economic sense that this term has acquired in our societies. What is first a necessary affirmation of human order — as a social organization — cannot be seen in a recurring manner in terms of contractual relations and profitable exchange. As such an affirmation, the reciprocity at issue here has nothing to do with commercial relations. It is precisely when one attempts to understand it using a mercantile schema that it becomes absurd, in other words, economically irrational. Lévi-Strauss says nothing else. Thus when his critics complain he has developed an exchangist ideology, this means, in their minds, a market ideology, which shows they have understood reciprocity as profitable exchange. Yet reciprocity is the exact negation of this: the exchange is worth more than the things exchanged. Such criticism is thus itself victim of the presuppositions it denounces.

This said, even if reciprocity has in itself no economic meaning, and even if production and exchange of useful goods are limited, this does not mean that the forms of material existence of the societies considered are unimportant. It means that their role is not determinant in the institutions that ensure their organization. This is also probably why the fundamental symbolic structure presents itself to be read in such societies in a virtually direct manner, when it seems to exist only in a residual or buried state in modern societies. In modern societies such a structure can no longer be what organizes the whole social order, for the social order no longer depends on kinship relations, but on technical (economic, administrative) regulations. This is so unless we must admit that such a structure is much more present than we think, not only in interindividual relations but also in relations between groups and institutions. To show this could be the task of an anthropology of modern societies.

Chapter 3

Structures of Kinship

Of all social facts, those concerning kinship and marriage display to the highest degree the aspects of permanency, systematism and continuity even in change, which open the way to scientific analysis.[1]

Analysis of reciprocity has led us to the heart of the problems regarding kinship. Now we must focus on them by presenting the results of *The Elementary Structures of Kinship,* and also other shorter studies that Lévi-Strauss published later.

However, first we have to ask why this domain was chosen in the study of savage societies. Why not rites or forms of material production, or power relations, and so on? Lévi-Strauss's answer is simple: only kinship data present an internal logic comparable to the system of language. In short, only such data are susceptible to purely synchronic analysis. We know that it was by rejecting the philological, historical approach that Saussure claimed to elevate linguistics to the rank of rigorous science. Likewise, it is by performing a similar methodological recentering regarding kinship data that Lévi-Strauss intended to open, for ethnology, a new era of properly scientific research. Certainly he did not claim that research predating his own lacked rigor or method. Data collection, efforts at classification, and even attempts at global interpretation lacked neither aspect. The difficulty lay in the fact that none of this work allowed a global theory to be constructed. Between various problems posed by kinship systems (as we have seen, that of the different treatment of cross-cousins and parallel cousins, that of the existence or nonexistence of matrimonial classes, that of the presence of bilineal and unilineal systems of relation, and so on), relations were indeed suspected, but there was no way to articulate them clearly, coherently, and unquestionably.

By reexamining the roots of the kinship problem beginning with the issue of the incest prohibition and the "principle of reciprocity," Lévi-Strauss could present a body of hypotheses that both remarkably simplified and shed new light on a large number of phenomena that, until then, had remained entirely disparate and obscure:

It has been shown that the complete set of marriage regulations operating in human societies, and usually classified under different headings, such as incest prohibitions, preferential forms of marriage, and the like, can be interpreted as being so many different ways of insuring the circulation of women within the social group or of substituting the mechanism of a sociologically determined affinity for that of biologically determined consanguinity. (*SA 1:60*)

Problems and Controversies

Since the publication of *The Elementary Structures of Kinship*, it has seemed difficult for anthropologists to approach this field of investigation without situating themselves, in one way or another, in relation to Lévi-Strauss's work. His theses and demonstrations are extended, or completed and confirmed, or, to the contrary, disproved or even rejected: in every case they must be taken into account.

It is well known that Anglo-American (and especially British) anthropologists have proved to be the most reticent regarding a book with a stated ambition that has most often appeared to them to lack not empirical foundation (the documentation of the work is considerable) but deep analysis of certain systems. It is thus remarkable to note that it is one of the leaders of this critical current, R. Needham, who, with a few collaborators, undertook the English translation of Lévi-Strauss's thesis. The same anthropologist also led a significant colloquium (at Bristol University in 1970) focusing on kinship issues. The work that came out of this colloquium (Needham 1971), while not an anti–Lévi-Strauss war tract, is not far from resembling one. To be sure, Needham declares he does not claim to challenge "the sheer intellectual excitement that Lévi-Strauss's classical monograph has to offer, or the theoretical stimulation that can be had from it by anyone who seriously tries to master its argument" (Needham 1971, xcii). However, after these introductory compliments come his reservations: "[I]t suffers from serious lacks as regards sources..., it contains numerous ethnographical errors and misinterpretations of the facts" (Needham 1971, xci).

In fact, as early as his 1947 preface, Lévi-Strauss himself envisaged the possibility that some points would be lacking when he wrote: "[N]o claim is made the work is free from errors of fact and interpretation" (*ESK* xxiv). The great number of documents discussed and the variety of fields covered did make such inadequacies plausible. The author thus requested the indulgence of specialists in the various domains involved, and above all that there be an exchange that would allow errors to be rectified and the proposed hypotheses to be analyzed. In the second preface (1967), he renews his declaration of the weaknesses of the work ("On reading it today, the documentation seems tedious and the expression old-fashioned" [*ESK* xxvii]), but he immediately adds: "Nevertheless I reject not one part of the theoretical inspiration or of the method, nor any of the principles of interpretation" (*ESK* xxvii). He then remarks that, amusingly, criticisms have most often been centered on typographical errors, or due to a foreign reader's lack of knowledge of the French language (the English translation appeared only in 1971), and he adds: "I have also been taken to task for ethnographic errors when the evidence itself comes from reputable observers whom I quoted without using inverted commas because the source reference was given a little later" (*ESK* xxviii). Lévi-Strauss most often responds to such criticisms by pointing out an appropriate passage in his work that shows that, in most cases, the misunderstanding was purely material or that he had already foreseen the objection or that one of his analyses was simply unknown to his critic, thus causing the point of the criticism to disappear.

However, the disagreements with certain anthropologists (such as Needham and Leach) seem more serious when we consider that these researchers are excellent readers who sometimes challenge, or simply set aside, the very foundations of Lévi-Strauss's approach. Thus Needham clearly questions Lévi-Strauss's explanation of the incest prohibition (see the preceding chapter) or at least attaches little importance to the principle and consequences of this explanation (that it is primarily a question of reciprocity and that it is the exchange of women, thus alliance, that regulates its necessity).

Needham goes even further by questioning the very notion of *kinship*. It is true that it is a term susceptible to very wide, even undetermined, use since it can cover very different data: matrimonial alliances, transmissible rights, relations between consanguineous relatives, genealogical statuses, rules of residence, rules of filiation, and so on. Needham writes:

> I am not denying, therefore, that the word 'kinship' is useful; and still less should I wish to try to reform our professional vocabulary by narrowing the definition of the word, or, on the other hand, by urging that it be abandoned altogether. What I am saying is that it does not denote a discriminate class of phenomena or a distinct type of theory. . . . [A]nthropologists do often get into trouble, of a time wasting and discouraging sort, when they argue about what kinship really is or when they try to propound some general theory based on the presumption that kinship has a distinct and concrete identity.

To put it very bluntly, then, there is no such thing as kinship and it follows that there can be no such thing as kinship theory. (Needham 1971, 5)

One of the participants in the colloquium, M. Southwold, makes this criticism more radical: "In a loose sense, I should agree that the term 'kinship' is 'meaningless': and if we were all agreed about that enough to avoid ever using it, I should have accomplished half my purpose" (Southwold 1971, 40). It is a question, again according to this author, of agreeing on the definitions, and first on what a definition is. He then shows how poorly our terminology accounts for what are called kinship relations in other societies: "No account is taken of the fact that, although the term thus equated with, say, 'father,' is indeed applied to a person's father, it is much more often applied to persons who are *not* his father" (Southwold 1971, 39). Every ethnologist knows — or should know — that. There can be only approval for the greatest critical vigilance on this point. It is certain that kinship systems are extremely diverse and that the values attached to appellations differ, not only in relation to the ethnologist's culture but generally in all cultures taken relative to each other. This said, it is relatively sterile to deduce from this that the very term "kinship" should be excluded.

Here an excess of nominalism must be fought with a minimum of conventionalism: it must be understood that the value of terms is relative. Thus, whatever the society, there are always three components: consanguinity, filiation, alliance. Let us call "kinship" the relations generated by these three universal types of relation. Moreover, it is not because the forms of kinship are, in our society, less rich and less complex than in other societies that the term itself should pose a problem.

In contrast, what must be clear in the mind of the ethnologist is that, in the societies under study, the relations called kinship most often cover, or profoundly affect, all social relations (regarding a third party, one is generally either allied, consanguine, ascendant, or descendant, with all the nuances and degrees of the system). For us, for whom kinship relations cede to professional, administrative, political, or associative relations, or simply to the gender difference (man/woman), it is clear that the value of the term loses in social content what it gains in psychological meaning in the restricted circle of the biological family. Understanding this distance (and at the same time the profound differences in kinship statuses) requires a little sociology and at least as much history. This is what is apparently lacking in the exclusively logical argument of Southwold and, to a lesser degree, in that of Needham.

However, in order to grasp these recent discussions, we must reexamine Lévi-Strauss's early approach and evaluate its foundation.

Kinship and Language

Sociology would certainly be further advanced had it proceeded
everywhere in imitation of the linguists.   — Mauss 1972c, 20

[A]nalogies, properly used, are important aids to scientific thinking.
                                              — Radcliffe-Brown 1952, 195

The way kinship data were analyzed required extensive renovation. For
Lévi-Strauss this primarily meant replacing the theoretical model for analyzing the subject. Lévi-Strauss chose to borrow a model from linguistics.
This choice was not arbitrary, at least in his eyes. He writes, "The kinship system *is* a language" (*SA* 1:47; emphasis added). In another work
he proposes, more prudently, to treat "marriage regulations and kinship
systems *as a kind of language*" (*SA* 1:61; emphasis added). Our first task
is to see what led Lévi-Strauss to this identification: this will allow us
to evaluate the results of his hypothesis. Then we will ask whether his
method is valid and if it stands up to critical examination.

In 1951 Lévi-Strauss wrote, "Among all social phenomena, language
alone has thus far been studied in a manner which permits it to serve as
the object of truly scientific analysis" (*SA* 1:58). Based on this, he intends
to propose that anthropology look for models in linguistics. However,
such a choice is legitimate only if there initially appears to be enough
analogies between the objects of these two disciplines for a transfer of
method to be conceivable. It is all the more necessary to examine Lévi-
Strauss's arguments on this point carefully since it is one of the areas on
which his critics have concentrated.

Thus the issue is not simply to know what is shared by language and
society (for that they share elements is a long-standing certainty) but to
determine the angle from which social phenomena and facts of language
can be treated in the same way. Or rather, it is a question of knowing
whether the former can be assimilated to the latter, since it is indeed anthropology that is asking for a lesson from linguistics. Now, to eliminate
the distance between these two notions, it suffices to bring them back
to their common ground: culture. In effect, on one hand, culture defines
itself through language, and, on the other hand, the totality of culture's
manifestations is the very object of anthropology.

However, first we must understand the intrinsic link between language
and culture. Language is at once culture's condition, its result, and one of
its elements among others. It is the condition for culture because it is first
that which mediates the rupture with the natural order. It is the ordering of the world. Logical construction is achieved in it and by it, through
oppositions and correlations. Language is thus the matrix of meanings
carried by culture, and it is indeed through the formation of his or her

language that each individual, from childhood, acquires knowledge of the society that is home and into which he or she is integrated. "Language, from this point of view, may appear as laying a kind of foundation for the more complex structures which correspond to the different aspects of culture" (*SA* 1:69). Next language results from culture in that it reflects its material modalities (climate, subsistence techniques, and so on), traditions, and institutions. Finally, language is but a part of culture if we put it on the same level as all the other elements such as tools, customs, forms of organization, and so on.

The language/culture link thus seems intrinsic. We can therefore suppose that between the two domains there is the likelihood of encountering not only analogies but structural identities. From this initial point of view it is already legitimate to ask linguistics to perhaps provide models for anthropology without the distance between the two fields appearing excessive, in other words, without the homologies that are identified seeming arbitrary. Above all we must add that, for Lévi-Strauss, language and culture essentially belong to the *symbolic field* and that it is under the hypothesis of this formal unity that their structures respond to each other and link together. Already, this could be sufficient to provide a foundation for the importation of linguistic models into anthropology. However, Lévi-Strauss means to reinforce the connection between the two fields by resorting to an even "wider" concept because such a concept would allow greater generalization and thus more open use by the human sciences. This concept is *communication.*

Clearly with such a concept there is a change in level. Linguistics itself is then no more than a chapter in cybernetics (a term popularized by N. Wiener in a book, *Cybernetics* [1948], which had profound echoes in most research in the human sciences). This theory entails a complete reconsideration of culture and social institutions. For Lévi-Strauss it allows the elegant, almost miraculous, unification of the three levels of activity that are involved in the "total social fact" of *alliance,* "since the rules of kinship and marriage serve to insure the circulation of women between groups, just as economic rules serve to insure the circulation of goods and services, and linguistic rules the circulation of messages" (*SA* 1:83).

Perhaps this is so, but we may wonder if it is legitimate to use the same terms to describe very different phenomena. One runs the risk of playing on words regarding the term "communication," which in the case of the exchange of women is identified with "circulation." Some criticisms have emphasized the inappropriate nature of this formulation. Thus Sperber (1985b, 68ff.) notes that: (1) even if one admits that the circulation of women is the central aspect of kinship relations, one cannot underestimate the other aspects that do not follow directly from such circulation, such as the transmission of rights, property, knowledge, attitudes, and so on (however, Lévi-Strauss would note here that precisely these exchanges are inseparable from the total exchange of alliance); and (2) language is not specifically defined by the circulation of words except on the level of *speech* (*parole* in Saussurian terms) or *performance* (in Chomskian terms); thus one cannot suppose it on the level of *langue* (or *competence*), which is rather its condition of possibility. The essential difference between language and kinship would then be this:

> A language is a *code* which determines which messages are available for (among other possible uses) circulation in the social network to which the interlocutors belong. By contrast, a marriage system is a *network,* whose structure determines which channels between social groups are open to the "circulation of women." Women are made available not by any kind of a code, but through biological reproduction. (Sperber 1985b, 68)

The joke at the end, meant as a healthy call to reality, should not however allow us to forget that in human societies biological reproduction is always culturally marked, always given symbolic value. This is indeed the level at which it is considered by Lévi-Strauss. It would thus be appropriate to say that network structures are coupled with code structures.

Furthermore, it must be noted that regarding the analogy between kinship and language, on one hand, and the use of the concept of communication, on the other hand, Lévi-Strauss does not proceed without taking precautions. This has not, in general, been taken sufficiently into account. First he constantly emphasizes the fact that it is a question of an *analogy.* "A too literal adherence to linguistic method actually betrays its very essence" (*SA* 1:36). Lévi-Strauss was thus right to correct himself: kinship is not a language, it is *like* a language. There is similarity in form, but certainly not in function.

For him there is also no question of identifying language and culture (in order to facilitate the treatment of the homologies between kinship and language). Precisely, Lévi-Strauss reminds his critics that on this issue he explicitly proposed to exclude two hypotheses: "[B]etween culture and language there cannot be *no* relations at all, and there cannot be 100 per cent correlation either" (*SA* 1:79). Such a hypothesis would, he adds, be coupled with a logical error since one would have to postulate that the whole is equivalent to a part. This is precisely what Lévi-Strauss criticizes in the American metalinguistics of the 1950s, which attempted to find term-to-term equivalencies between "highly elaborate linguistic data" and purely empirical "ethnographical observations": "Thus they compare objects of dissimilar nature and run the risk of achieving nothing but truisms or weak hypotheses" (*SA* 1:85). Even today, many criticisms of Lévi-Strauss seem to ignore these methodological reservations and accuse him of the very thing he censures and tries to avoid. There are two possibilities: either these criticisms follow from superficial reading, or Lévi-Strauss does the opposite of what he says. We will find the former interpretation to be correct.

Likewise, regarding the use of the concept of communication and the possibility of bringing it into play in the three levels of alliance (women, goods, and messages), Lévi-Strauss makes the following point:

> These three forms of communication are also forms of exchange which are obviously interrelated (because marriage relations are as-sociated with economic prestations and language comes into play at all levels). It is therefore legitimate to seek homologies between them and define the formal characteristics of each type consid-ered independently and so the transformations which make the transition possible from one to another. (*SA* 1:83)

Note the methodological precautions: "homologies," "formal character-istics," "transformations." It is thus not a question of identifying fields, of confusing objects, or of establishing an equivalency of content. Yet we must go further. What type of linguistic discipline could be capable of providing a model for anthropology?

This was, until now, the general, preliminary problem of the use of linguistic models in the analysis of social data. More simply, it was the problem of the possible homology between language and culture. These issues open up a theoretical field and inspire significant epistemological debates, but they do not yet provide a tool. Everything depends in fact on which linguistics one intends to use as inspiration. Concerning historical or philological linguistics, there already were collaborations with sociol-ogy (relations between terms and customs, remnants in the vocabulary of lost relations, and so on). This provides complementary information and sheds light on behavior, but it is not a methodological revolution.

Lévi-Strauss asks one of the branches of linguistics to provide this tool. This branch, *phonology*, is the one that, at the time, had made the most impressive progress and had been able to turn itself into a truly scien-tific discipline. In this domain, Lévi-Strauss recognizes his special debt to Trubetzkoy and salutes his article-program of 1933 in which are de-fined the "four basic operations" of the new phonology: they were to become, word for word, Lévi-Strauss's research program for anthropol-ogy. For Trubetzkoy, they could be summarized by the following four points: (1) phonology passes from the study of conscious linguistic phe-nomena to that of their unconscious infrastructure; (2) in phonology, terms have no interest as independent entities; only the relations between the terms count; (3) phonology introduces the notion of system; and (4) phonology aims to discover general laws, to be found by induction or deduction (which, says Trubetzkoy, "give them absolute character" (Trubetzkoy 1933; quoted in *SA* 1:33).

Lévi-Strauss makes this promising observation: "[F]or the first time, a social science is able to formulate necessary relationships" (*SA* 1:33). This is another way of saying that for the first time a social science had attained the same level of objectivity as the natural and physical sciences. Thus in the social domain there are facts that possess the same universality as that which is postulated in the natural order. To accept this is not only to envisage reorienting future sociological and anthropological research; it is to recognize a veritable methodological revolution. "But when an event of this importance takes place in one of the sciences of man, it is not only permissible for, but required of, representatives of related disciplines immediately to examine its consequences and its possible application to phenomena of another order" (*SA* 1:33–34). Indeed, in the envisaged collaboration between linguists and sociologists (and anthropologists) it is no longer a question of exchanging information or completing analyses; it is a question of knowing whether the subject studied by the latter can be treated in the same way as phonologists treat the sounds in a language. For Lévi-Strauss, the answer is in the affirmative, at least in one specific domain of anthropology, *kinship* relations:

> Like phonemes, kinship terms are elements of meaning; like phonemes, they acquire meaning only if they are integrated into systems. "Kinship systems," like "phonemic systems," are built by the mind on the level of unconscious thought. Finally,...in the case of kinship as well as linguistics, the observable phenomena result from the action of laws which are general but implicit. (*SA* 1:34)

This assimilation of kinship terms to phonemes might seem curious and even suspect. In fact it was immediately questioned by a number of critics. Thus, on this point too, we must take careful note of the methodological precautions Lévi-Strauss imposes on himself before beginning any investigation:

> The problem can therefore be formulated as follows: Although they belong to *another order of reality,* kinship phenomena are *of the same type* as linguistic phenomena. Can the anthropologist, using a method analogous *in form* (if not in content) to the method used in structural linguistics, achieve the same kind of progress in his own science as that which has taken place in linguistics? (*SA* 1:34)

Once these precautions are taken, there is in principle nothing to prevent this approach from being followed. All that is necessary and sufficient is that kinship phenomena lend themselves to such modeling. Lévi-Strauss's task is thus to convince us of the formal identity of kinship terms and phonemes. This means that they can be studied as synchronic wholes and that they are first determined by internal constraints. The requirements of the model can go no further without taking risks, for the two domains do not have the same functions at all. Here again hasty identifications must be avoided: "The superficial analogy between phonemic systems and kinship systems is so strong that it immediately sets us on the wrong track. It is incorrect to equate kinship terms and linguistic phonemes from the viewpoint of their formal treatment" (SA 1:35). This restriction may seem surprising and in contradiction with the propositions, made only two pages earlier, that kinship phenomena be treated like the phonemes of language. This aids us to better understand what Lévi-Strauss means when he speaks of models. A model determines a method. It does not imply the identification of the objects of the field of application with those of the original field. Phonology, after all, has provided Lévi-Strauss with only an efficient heuristic analogy. He himself says this, and he stands by it: reminding ourselves of it may prove useful.

Structures: Elementary and Complex

What allows Lévi-Strauss to fill out his study program and to verify the validity of his hypotheses is the choice he announces at the beginning to restrict himself to "elementary kinship structures." What does this mean? What distinction should be made between elementary structures and complex structures?

The definition of this is provided in the first lines of his 1947 preface:

Elementary structures of kinship are those systems in which the nomenclature permits the immediate determination of the circle of kin and that of affines, that is, those systems which prescribe marriage with a certain type of relative or, alternatively, those which, while defining all members of the society as relatives, divide them into two categories, viz., possible spouses and prohibited spouses.

The term "complex structures" is reserved for systems which limit themselves to defining the circle of relatives and leave the determination of the spouse to other mechanisms, economic or psychological. (ESK xxiii)

It might be tempting to see in these definitions the affirmation of the difference between societies called primitive and those considered modern. This would be to ignore that the latter formula exists in the former societies. The classical example is that of the "Crow-Omaha" kinship system. The fundamental principle of this system (named for the North American Indian tribes regarding which it was first defined) can be summarized by this: all clans not expressly forbidden are permitted. If we replace the term "clan" by "individual," it becomes immediately apparent how such a formulation could be close to that of modern societies (in other words, mainly Western societies or societies that are very Westernized), where all partners not belonging to the circle of the biological family are considered permissible.

In fact, the Crow-Omaha system is an intermediary case (it is considered a semicomplex system), but before coming back to this, we must ask whether the definition Lévi-Strauss gives of elementary structures properly covers all of the systems to which he proposes to apply his hypotheses. This is, in any case, the question asked by Needham (1962), who considers that these hypotheses are verifiable only for *prescriptive* systems and thus are not valid for the more flexible category of *preferential* marriages. If this were the case, it would mean that *The Elementary Structures of Kinship* and its hypotheses would concern only a very restricted category of marriages. This would prohibit the generalization of the hypotheses of the work to the whole of elementary kinship structures.

Lévi-Strauss responds to these objections in two places: "The Future of Kinship Studies" (1965) and "Preface to the Second Edition" of *The Elementary Structures of Kinship* (which largely restates the 1965 article). Essentially, his reply can be stated as follows. Needham and those who concur with him have conflated the opposition between "prescriptive marriage" and "preferential marriage" with the opposition between "elementary structures" and "complex structures." Instead, these two types of marriage are two aspects belonging to elementary structures. Obligation and preference are not alternatives, but two extremes between which solutions can be found that are closer to one or to the other. Thus when obligation is strictly respected, we are close to the theoretical model, and when it is practiced with accommodations, we are heading toward the preferential formula. Moreover, this is indeed how the indigenous people perceive it, as has been shown in numerous studies. "Rather let us own that the notions of prescriptive and preferential marriage are relative: a preferential system is prescriptive when envisaged at the model level; a prescriptive system must be preferential when envisaged on the level of reality" (*ESK* xxxiii). Practically, this would allow us to turn around the argument of those who radically oppose the two forms and to assert: "Accordingly, if the system can be called prescriptive it is in so far as it is preferential first. If it is not also preferential its prescriptive aspect vanishes" (*ESK* xxxiii).

This clarification also allows us to better define the field of *elementary structures,* which are both prescriptive and preferential. What sets them apart in relation to complex structures is first the fact that alliance is not conceivable except between partners between which there is a defined kinship relation. In other words, preference is not subjective: the system presides over the choice. "In other words, the imperative or desirable relationship is a function of the social structure" (*ESK* xxxiv), which appears in the procedure by which partners are selected. This is not the case for complex structures, where the margin of individual choice is virtually unlimited, even if the subjective criteria prove to be socially determined not at the level of structure but at the level of representations (although it is possible to show the existence of isolated populations functioning like endogamic wholes).

Nonetheless, the fact that complex structures are the most wide-spread formula in modern societies should not lead to the conclusion that they are necessarily the fruit of an evolution toward modernity. This is no more valid (as we will see later) than the notion that the conjugal, monogamous family is specifically modern (this kind of family is proven to exist in all sorts of societies with varying degrees of technological and economic development). In short, noting that complex structures are particularly well adapted to modern societies does not allow us to place them on a time line where their position would be more recent and where, by the same stroke, the others would be made to look archaic. At most we can note that modern societies are especially suited to a form of kinship that existed previously and to which they have given greater importance and a particular orientation:

> We understand better that the line separating societies traditionally called primitive from those called civilized does not in any way coincide with that between elementary structures of kinship and complex structures. Among the so-called "primitive" societies heterogenous types exist.... A large number of societies in fact relate to complex structures of kinship. (*AM* 128)

From the methodological point of view, a simple difference appears between elementary structures and complex structures: the former refer to mechanical models (the terms related in the model are on the same scale as the elements observed); the latter correspond to statistical models (the relations correspond to probabilities and express averages). In the first case, the system designates the type of partner possible in a prescriptive manner (whether it is a question of classes, as in dual organizations, or of relations, as in the case of cross-cousins); in the second case, the system designates as possible everyone who is not forbidden. We can see how the second formula is particularly suitable for societies called historical since what, among other things, makes them so is precisely the margin of individual choice permitted by institutions and the fact that cycles of reciprocity no longer close: they are diluted and lose their thread in the indeterminacy and "internationality" of alliances. In elementary kinship structures, diachrony remains internal in that the event (the alliance) is determined by the structure, while in complex structures it is the sum of events that brings out the structure statistically; diachrony then becomes the essential support and common element of a structural dispersal. Beyond a certain threshold (which many other aspects combine to cross) this diachrony imposes itself as "history."

Restricted and Generalized Exchange

The entire discussion of *The Elementary Structures of Kinship* aims to establish the pertinence of the "principle of reciprocity," in other words, to establish its heuristic value in making sense of the variety of types of alliance and thus the kinship systems that follow from them. The general principle, as we have seen, amounts to this: for every woman given up by a group, there must be a woman received in return. However, this formulation is susceptible to two fundamental applications: either this form of gift/countergift is *direct* (*A* gives to *B*, who gives back to *A*), or else it is *indirect* (*A* gives to *B*, who gives to *C*, and so on, who gives back to *A*). We will see that this schema, which appears simple, covers situations of extreme complexity but allows the introduction of order and coherence. It is, in any case, to Lévi-Strauss's credit to have identified the existence of these two types of system and to have seen their fundamental difference. Better yet, he was able to show that, in certain cases, there are mixed systems and that mechanisms that had until then seemed aberrant to anthropologists were in reality perfectly well constructed when considered from this dual point of view.

How is *restricted exchange* defined?

"The term 'restricted exchange' includes any system which effectively or functionally divides the group into a certain number of pairs of exchange-units, so that, for any one pair X-Y there is a reciprocal exchange relationship" (*ESK* 146). What is vital in this definition is the notion of "pairs." The relation of matrimonial reciprocity takes the following form: if a man *X* weds a woman *Y*, a man *Y* must be able to wed a woman *X*. The most common division of a group into exogamous moieties is that based on either patrilineal or matrilineal filiation, but if these forms are superimposed there is a double dichotomy and thus a system with four sections instead of two moieties.

What about *generalized exchange*?

Lévi-Strauss's formulation of this is simple and clear: "Generalized exchange establishes a system of operations conducted 'on credit.' *A* surrenders a daughter or sister to *B*, who surrenders one to *C*, who, in turn, will surrender one to *A*" (*ESK* 265). Of course, the study of specific societies shows that things are not so simple and that a great number of parameters can complicate the schema. However, Lévi-Strauss's schema is essentially verified, and now we must state the conditions.

First we note that the group that receives and the one that gives are not in a direct relation of reciprocity (in other words, one does not receive from the group to which one has given). There is thus an element of trust that intervenes and that supposes that the cycle will close in the end. Generalized exchange both postulates and gives rise to stronger social ties and greater solidarity between the partners than restricted exchange. The risk taken is the measure of the certainty engendered by the group and by the strength of the tradition linked to the rules followed. "The belief is the basis of trust, and confidence opens credit. In the final analysis, the whole system exists only because the group adopting it is prepared, in the broadest meaning of the term, to *speculate*" (*ESK* 265).

Here another consideration comes into play, that of demographic size. As appropriate and sufficient as restricted exchange is for small societies, it is just as inappropriate for societies with a denser, larger population. For the speculative act mentioned above must be understood as having its usual meaning, but also in its wider sense: "[T]he speculation brings a profit, in the sense that with generalized exchange the group can live as richly and as complexly as its size, structure and density allow" (*ESK* 265). While restricted exchange resolves the problem of increases in the group's size by adding subsections (as can be seen in many societies in Australia), generalized exchange allows new members to be integrated without the modification of the composition of the group. It substitutes an organic formula (a "regulating principle" [*ESK* 441]) for a mechanical formula.

The two forms of exchange, moreover, do not suppose the same relation to time and space. In the first case there is a dichotomy between the spatial organization (local groups) and the temporal organization (generations and age groups). What links them, in groups that are always limited, are rules of filiation. "These rules, however, only succeed in restoring unity by, as it were, spreading it out in time, in other words at the price of a *loss*, i.e., the loss of time" (*ESK* 265).

Generalized exchange, to the contrary, has no such constraints. It permits a synchronic multiplicity of combinations. It even calls on them to compensate the initial risk through the accumulation of guarantees and security. *Polygamy* thus appears as one of these solutions because it increases the circle of allies, a solution made even more tempting when the credit concerns the entire line, no longer simply a specific degree of kinship. Thus the appearance of the seeds of feudalism wherever this form of exchange is dominant (the Katchin of Burma provide a particularly good example of this, which Lévi-Strauss analyzes in detail). This logic leads generalized exchange to a sort of internal contradiction because it "presupposes equality, and is a source of inequality" (*ESK* 266). The "speculation" it creates (monopolization of spouses, increase in guarantees) engenders differences in situation and thus in status: noble lines and common lines. Thus there necessarily will be marriages between partners with different statuses, or *anisogamy*. Progressively factors creating tension dominate the integrative factors, and the system slides into ruin: "[G]eneralized exchange can in fact facilitate the integration of groups of different ethnic origins, as well as lead to the development of differences within an ethnically homogenous society" (*ESK* 417).

Filiation and Lineal Asymmetry

The conception of alliance made possible through comprehension of the rules of reciprocity is also what allows Lévi-Strauss to clarify certain classical difficulties inherent in the asymmetry that can be noted between matrilineal and patrilineal systems.

First, there is no support for the theory that these two formulas could be situated on a time line, one as an older and the other as a more recent system:

> It is possible, and even probable, that sociologists who defend the theory that all human societies have passed from a matrilineal stage to a patrilineal stage have been victims of an optical illusion, and that, in fact, any human group might, in the course of centuries, develop alternately matrilineal or patrilineal characteristics, without the most fundamental elements of its structure being profoundly affected by it. (*ESK* 409)

In any case, one of the striking features of the modern family (let us mean by this the present type of Western family) is the predominance of bilineal filiation: paternal and maternal (regarding rights, inheritance, and so on, with a paternal advantage for the transmission of the name). In contrast, in societies we call primitive, what appears most constantly is recognition of kinship according to only one of these lines. However, this apparently obvious statement is not as strong as was imagined, for it is rare that a unilineal society does not set up procedures for the recognition of rights regarding the other line or that such a society does not at least compensate for the absence of such procedures by very real, if not institutional, attitudes and customs.

However, as Lévi-Strauss notes, new studies tend to show that cognatic systems (systems based on equal recognition of both lines) are much more frequent than previously thought. (They account for nearly a third of cases, but these cases tend to be outside the framework of elementary structures.) The difference between patrilineal and matrilineal systems is not, except from a formal point of view, that of two equivalent lines: "To be unmindful of this would be to overlook the basic fact that it is men who exchange women, and not vice versa" (*ESK* 115). Matrilineal systems are generally accompanied by patrilocal residence: the mother is thus on foreign ground with her children. This however does not necessarily mean she has an inferior position, for she is the vehicle through which her group (the spouse-giver in relation to the group in which she lives) marks its presence and power. "Matrilineal descent is the authority of the woman's father or brother extended to the brother-in-law's village" (*ESK* 116). Cases of matrilocal residence, when the husband is exiled to his brother-in-law's home, are rather rare. Nonetheless, does the wife have any specific powers in such cases? To think so would be to forget that authority over her husband is devolved to her father or brothers, rather than to her.

Appellation and Attitude

Can the study of kinship systems be restricted to the inventory of kinship terms and the analysis of logical relations that are established between the individuals and groups designated by such terms? Such a limitation ignores other facts that strike all observers: the regularity of certain attitudes within a given system. These can be, for example, the nephew's attitude of respect toward his maternal uncle; relations of suspicion between spouses; an extreme closeness, or else a systematic distance, between brothers and sisters; or finally a taboo concerning one's in-laws. How should such data be interpreted? Is there a law that could explain their recurrence? In short we are in the presence of a system no less important than that which is represented by the terminology. We must thus suppose that systems of kinship taken as a whole include two very different levels of reality: (1) the system of *appellations* made up of the kinship vocabulary; and (2) the system of *attitudes* that is the set of behaviors of individuals (or classes of individuals) in their kinship relations.

These two levels each raise a specific difficulty, and the difficulties they raise are inversely symmetrical. In the first case, we can construct the system relatively easily, but we cannot determine its function. In the second case, the function is obvious (that of ensuring the cohesion and equilibrium of the group), but the system remains undetermined. We must thus say that the kinship system is dual and that it can be grasped at the intersection of its two subsets. The problem of the relation between the two is that certain attitudes are strictly determined by appellations and others, contrary to what Radcliffe-Brown thought, are not. There is no way to prove that it is possible to deduce the attitudes from knowledge of the terms (the formal treatment of the latter remains thus purely sterile). However, this difficulty renders the problem even more interesting: these attitudes can be conceived as "secondary elaborations, which serve to resolve the contradictions and overcome the deficiencies inherent in the terminological system.... The system of attitudes constitutes rather a dynamic integration of the system of terminology" (*SA* 1:38–39).

The most classic example is provided by the special, complex relationship that exists between the maternal uncle and his nephew, in short what has been called the *avuncular relationship*. In order to explain this phenomenon, traditional anthropology had suggested all sorts of hypotheses about vanished institutions of which this relation would be the relic. Yet there was a definite sense that the facts observed were not arbitrary or nonsensical since everywhere such relations could be observed, it was clear that certain traits were favored and others excluded. Thus it was possible to observe either that there was a relation of authority of the uncle over the nephew (the latter behaved deferentially or submissively) or that the nephew had a relation of familiarity to, or even superiority over, his uncle. In each case, a specific attitude toward the father seemed to follow: trusting in the former case, distant in the latter. How could such recurring pairs of attitudes be explained? Radcliffe-Brown acted as a precursor when he showed, using a South African example, that the former schema belonged to matrilineal filiation while the latter belonged to patrilineal filiation. It was unquestionable progress in research to have understood that the problem was related to the mode of filiation and that it thus belonged not to random events in a confused evolution but to a logic internal to kinship systems. Above all it was essential to have pointed out that the relation to the uncle and that to the father formed an antithetical pair. Yet was Radcliffe-Brown's explanation generalizable? In other words, was the mode of filiation the place to look for the reason behind the positive or negative nature of the avuncular relationship? Certainly not, according to Lévi-Strauss, for to do so would be to forget that the avuncular relationship is absent in several matrilineal and patrilineal societies and above all that even in societies with this relationship, there can be situations that are the inverse of Radcliffe-Brown's schemas. Thus, according to B. Malinowski's observations, among the indigenous people of the Trobriand Islands, who have a matrilineal social organization, it can be noted that the relations between the maternal uncle and the nephew are antagonistic and that those between father and son are the ones that are familiar and trusting. Moreover, there is in this case a rigorous prohibition on brother/sister relations and a very tender relation between husband and wife. There is thus a new problem: Are these two pairs of relations related to the preceding ones?

Lévi-Strauss pursues the inquiry and finds that the Siuai of Bougainville, who are also matrilineal, have relations comparable to those of the Trobriand Islanders between uncle and nephew and thus between father and son, but opposite relations regarding spouses (hostility) and brothers and sisters (reciprocal confidence). This last set of attitudes is the same as that of the indigenous people of Lake Kutubu in New Guinea, who are patrilineal, but it is inverted in the case of the Tonga of Polynesia, who are also patrilineal. As for the Cherkesse of Caucasia, who are patrilineal, the situation is the following: the maternal uncle helps and protects his nephew, while hostility appears between father and son, and there is extreme tenderness and confidence between brother and sister, but an official distance between spouses. This is exactly the inverse situation of that of the Trobriand Islanders. All these examples can be represented by figure 5 (see *SA* 1:45).

Figure 5

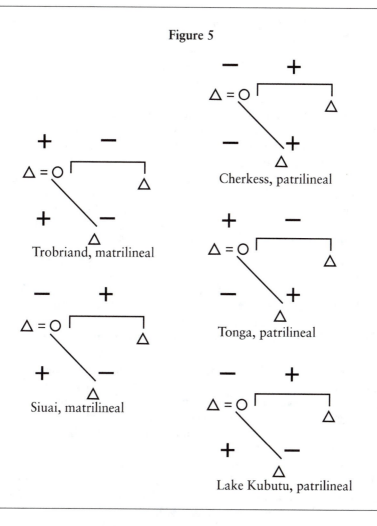

Trobriand, matrilineal

Siuai, matrilineal

Cherkess, patrilineal

Tonga, patrilineal

Lake Kubutu, patrilineal

We immediately see that the mode of filiation (patrilineal or matrilineal), while essential in each case, is not a pertinent explanatory principle since it does not lead to stable relations. Lévi-Strauss asks what we can conclude from this. First, concerning the *terms,* the avuncular relation is not limited to two terms; it includes four: a brother (the uncle), a sister (the wife given), a brother-in-law (the husband), and a nephew. Next, concerning the *relations,* the set of reported facts allows us to suppose a global system that includes four organically linked types: brother/sister, husband/wife, father/son, maternal uncle/sister's son. The examples studied, explains Lévi-Strauss, can be considered as the application of a law that he proposes to formulate as follows: "*In both groups, the relation*

*between maternal uncle and nephew is to the relation between brother
and sister as the relation between father and son is to that between
husband and wife. Thus if we know one pair of relations, it is always
possible to infer the other"* (SA 1:42; emphasis added).

The formulation of this law provoked a very rich, vigorous anthropological debate, but before coming back to it we shall propose a number of
general remarks. The first, methodological in nature, is that here we are
in the presence of a good example of structuralist comparison since the
approach consists in bringing out the shared traits in groups of relations
of the same type, but taken from societies very distant from one another
and without any probable relations, present or past. This is indeed the
kind of phenomenon that led Lévi-Strauss to resort to the concept of the
human mind as the common armature of such logical systems. Whatever
events and changes might lead to given systems, there is nonetheless an
immanent relation between these systems, defined by a structural identity.

The second remark is that an internal logic of implication and exclusion regulates the relations between the pairs of terms and allows us to
deduce the combinations that are possible and those that are not. We are
thus dealing with necessary relations, which should confer upon kinship
analysis, on this point at least, the status of an objective science.

However, and this is the third remark, we must not lose sight of the
fact that we are dealing with a model. The signs + and − mark, above all,
tendencies: familiarity, friendship, confidence, on the one hand; hostility, antagonism, simple reserve, on the other hand. Their value is mainly
differential, not absolute. "This is an oversimplification but we can ten-
tatively make use of it" (SA 1:44). Lévi-Strauss himself seems thus to
indicate that his schemas should be understood flexibly, like the law that
explains them.

This leads us directly to the debate that developed regarding this "law
of the atom of kinship." This law has sparked the interest of British anthropologists in particular. Fortes (1969) challenges Lévi-Strauss's formal
approach and attributes only Radcliffe-Brown with the discovery of a
"logic of emotions" in kinship relations, but Needham takes up the debate in a significant work (1962) and gives Lévi-Strauss the credit for
a formulation that he considers was inspired by Durkheim and Mauss.
However, studies undertaken by other researchers, such as C. M. Turnbull, J. D. McKnight, and P. Rigby, lead Needham to conclude prudently
that Lévi-Strauss's formulation, while accurate and fruitful, is not verified in all cases: "[A]nybody who had tested it at all knew that it was
not universal. The really interesting thing was that in a significant number of cases it seemed to work" (Needham 1971, xlix). This is probably
a sufficient degree of induction for the human sciences. Certainly Lévi-
Strauss dreamed of stronger objectivity for them, comparable to that of
the natural sciences, and yet he himself, regarding a debate of the same

type, proposed that *statistical correlation* not be confused with *logical connection* (*SA* 1:322n.105).

This said, another problem remains. As we recall, Lévi-Strauss shows that the mode of filiation is not explanatory. He limits himself to noting the invariability of the correlations between two pairs of coupled terms. He does not give a reason for these attitudes. Needham himself, responding to Fortes, asserts that there is nothing to explain and that, following Wittgenstein's recommendation, the difficulty is resolved by an appropriate description (Needham 1971, lv).

It is thus surprising that here Lévi-Strauss does not explicitly refer to the principle of reciprocity that, in many similar cases, allowed him to elucidate the reasons for an attitude precisely like that existing between a nephew and his maternal uncle. The former's deference to the latter is regularly motivated, when the wife is a matrilineal cross-cousin, by the fact that the uncle then appears as the wife-giver to the nephew, but in cases when the uncle can claim the daughter of his sister, the nephew finds himself in the giver's position since, through union with his niece, the uncle becomes (or can become) the brother-in-law of his nephew: here the attitudes are inverted.

Without now entering into consideration of the multitude of possible combinations related to modes of filiation, there remains one fact on which observers generally agree (and which shows the pertinence of the very Maussian hypothesis of reciprocity, which some would like to ignore): the prestige, rank, superiority, and thus the attitude of authority always falls to spouse-givers; the dependence and attitude of submission or deference always fall to the receivers. Should not the question asked about each attitude be: Who gives? Who receives? or, at least, Who belongs to the creditor group and who to the debtor group? (There are, however, situations in which the takers have the upper hand, but this is when we tend to leave the framework of elementary structures, as is shown by the evolution of alliances in medieval Europe.)

Moreover, the avuncular relationship is not necessarily what comes into play in all forms of attitudes of the various kinship systems. It is not directly relevant to explaining, for example, the relations between individuals belonging to alternate generations or other more specific situations. The avuncular relationship is exemplary in that the uncle's privileged position is that of being a spouse-giver, of giving his sister to the other group, in short, of being the one through whom passes, and on whom depends, the movement of reciprocity. This, in the very mediated formula of generalized exchange, supposes, as we have seen, long-term confidence that everyone will respect the rules and give as much as was received. Each individual is thus, at a certain time, the pivotal point of the circulation: the weaver between whose hands passes the shuttle carrying the thread of the social bond. The maternal uncle is the exemplary case of this, but any other giver assumes the same function, which is simultaneously logical, symbolic, and social.

We are provided with a good example in the first of the two concluding chapters of *The Elementary Structures of Kinship* (chapter 28). Here there is a general explanation of the prohibition on parents-in-law. The example in question concerns the Tonga (a Southern Bantu population), among whom a very special, extremely respectful relationship can be observed between the husband and the wife of his wife's brother. The wife of his brother-in-law thus receives a ceremonial title: "great *mukōnwana.*"

Certain anthropologists have advanced the thesis that this sister-in-law was considered to be a mother-in-law apparent because of a right over the daughter of the woman's brother. However, the origin of this right must be explained, as must be the reason it engenders an attitude considered extreme. Lévi-Strauss, faithful to his method, looks for the solution in the rules and symbolism of reciprocity. Among the Tonga, marriage is accompanied by the giving, by the husband's family to the wife's family, of a set of presents called *lobola,* the main component of which is a herd of cattle (see figure 6).

Figure 6

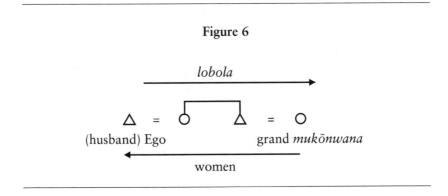

This *lobola* is not properly speaking a payment because at no point is the woman acquired appropriable by the group that receives her. To the contrary, her own group continues to protect her and to watch over her rights. The *lobola* received by the woman's family cannot be consumed or be the object of any business transaction. It has one purpose and one purpose only: to allow the brother of the wife to acquire a spouse in turn. "She has been bought with the[2] husband's cattle. In our opinion, one need look no further for the reasons for the special attitude of the husband towards his 'great mukōnwana.' Any contact or intimacy between them would have been socially dangerous" (*ESK* 468). The husband (Ego), through the intermediary of the *lobola* given to his wife's family, allows the latter's brother to marry. The spouse of the brother-in-law is thus equivalent to a sister of Ego. For him the entire process is as if, from the beginning, he had obtained his own spouse in exchange for the great *mukōnwana*. She is thus symbolically of his blood, of his clan; she "is his cattle" (thus the Tonga taboos on livestock and its products — milk, meat — as is the case with other pastoral peoples). The respect he has for her is in proportion to the rights he has over her (she is the symbol and token of the *lobola*) and to the impossibility of exercising them since she is like his sister: relations between them would thus be incestuous. Here we have a typical case of generalized exchange and mediation of this exchange by goods as symbolic substitutes for the wife (here again we see the problem of marriage said to be "by purchase": we can see how this model is erroneous since it is not a question of purchase but of symbolic equivalence).

Can we say that the schema concerning attitudes, brought out above, is no longer relevant here? This would be to overlook the fact that, in the present case, the husband finds himself, in relation to the wife of his wife's brother, in a position equivalent to that of the uncle in other systems, while his brother-in-law is in that of the nephew. The attitudes confirm this. We thus rediscover our schema after a substitution of terms, and we see once more that, whatever the mode of filiation, the solution can be found by looking at modes of alliance, in other words at the forms of organization of the system of reciprocity, of the social play of givers and takers.

The Giving Third Party:
Alliance and the Atom of Kinship

All the novelty of Lévi-Strauss's explanation of kinship systems rests thus on the phenomenon of alliance, which means that in all human societies the biological link immediately becomes a social tie, a tie defined and controlled by the group. The union of two individuals is always mediated by a third party (let us call this person the "giving third party") representing the group that gives a wife to the receiving group. This is, as we saw earlier, the positive meaning of the incest prohibition. All the rest follows from this necessity.

In spite of the esteem Lévi-Strauss very often expresses for the English and American ethnologists of the preceding generation (first among which we must name Radcliffe-Brown), he is consistently severe in his criticism on one point, that concerning their essentially biological conception of the family, namely, the model made up of the father, the mother, and their children. It is probably not pure chance that this biological model also coincides with the "nuclear family" as conceived of by modern Western society. "The unit of structure from which a kinship is built up is the group which I call an 'elementary family,' consisting of a man and his wife and their children" (Radcliffe-Brown 1941, 2; quoted in *SA* 1:50). This is the basic group Radcliffe-Brown adopts to construct the system of kinship relations, yet this atom of kinship, explains Lévi-Strauss, is not relevant. The entire demonstration in *The Elementary Structures of Kinship* tends precisely to show that there cannot be an elementary kinship unit without the inclusion of at least three types of relations: (1) relations of filiation; (2) relations of consanguinity; and (3) relations of alliance. What is important here is precisely the *relation of alliance* because it means that the wife is always received from another group, or more precisely from one of her relations, who is very often and exemplarily her brother, in other words, the maternal uncle (in relation to Ego).

Why include the uncle (or any other wife-giver) in the schema of the family or, if one prefers, among the basic elements of all kinship systems? Because the determining fact in the institution of the family, or rather in the phenomenon of kinship, is the *relation of reciprocity.* It is the fact that marriage means first the alliance of two groups and that this alliance enters into a complex process of prestations and counterprestations in accordance with a cycle that can extend over several generations. At the base of this cycle, of which alliance is the essential point as a "total social fact," there is, on the part of the group that gives the wife, a gesture of renunciation by the father for his daughter or by the brother for his sister, through which appears the universality of the incest prohibition. Any kinship structure that did not integrate this necessary aspect of alliance would be lacking precisely what is essential to the kinship relation. Thus Lévi-Strauss's conclusion:

> We reduce the kinship structure to the simplest conceivable element, the atom of kinship, if I may say so, when we have a group consisting of a husband, a woman, a representative of the group which has given the woman to the man — since incest prohibitions make it impossible in all societies for the unit of kinship to consist of one family, it must always link two families, two consanguineous groups. (*SA* 1:72)

Here again we see the existence of a system, the preeminence (not the preexistence) of relations over terms, and, concretely, of the rule of the group over the choice of individuals. In the present case this means that alliance cannot be created from individuals (husband, wife); rather, from the start, we must consider the existence of reciprocity as constitutive and in consequence the position of the giver as primary. "Thus we do not need to explain how the maternal uncle emerged in the kinship structure: He does not emerge — he is present initially. Indeed, the presence of the maternal uncle is a necessary precondition for the structure to exist"

(*SA* 1:46). (Note that in his *Introduction to the Work of Marcel Mauss*, Lévi-Strauss uses the same type of formulation regarding symbolic systems, but it is because here, according to him, we truly attain the central point of the system.)

At this point an objection arises (which could be an objection generalizable to the structuralist approach). It can be formulated as follows: kinship does not exist for itself, but in view of the renewal and maintenance of the group. It thus has a dynamic aspect, a goal, that would require that limitations be placed on the structural point of view, which is then seen as static. Is this a good objection? In fact, notes Lévi-Strauss, this dynamic is already included in the way reciprocity and the system of alliance are conceived since what constantly reactivates reciprocity is the initial disequilibrium between the group that gives and the group that receives. This disequilibrium must be corrected endlessly, generation after generation. Thus we can see how the diachronic establishes itself as a condition on the synchronic mechanism. This also reveals that the goal, in this case, cannot be reduced to the biological aspect (assurance of the reproduction of the group) but affirms itself as a properly cultural fact: that of reciprocity, which is symbolic in nature.

On a point such as this, Lévi-Strauss's approach asserts itself in all its originality. Here we again find his criticism of the purely biological conception of the family noted above regarding Anglo-American anthropology. This biological aspect, says Lévi-Strauss, exists, and its existence is necessary. However, to present this necessity as a primary (or ultimate) sociological truth is not only erroneous but dangerous, because it is to forbid understanding of the specificity of kinship data: "But what confers upon kinship its socio-cultural character is not what it retains from nature, but, rather, the essential way in which it diverges from nature.... [I]n human society, kinship is allowed to establish and perpetuate itself only through specific forms of marriage" (*SA* 1:50–51).

Considered in itself, the so-called biological family means nothing. In other words, it does not allow us to understand even the slightest social fact. It is an empty term. This term gains meaning only in its relation to other terms, in short, in the system of alliance, in the general system of relations. It is indeed through the system that it is possible to conceive the terms, and this is why recourse to a model, such as the one offered by linguistics, which operates according to such a requirement, proves to be valid for Lévi-Strauss.

The Family from the Anthropological Perspective

Anthropological analyses of kinship data in primitive societies can significantly clarify problems of kinship in Western societies. The differences are not of nature but of degree. Lévi-Strauss notes, in a general study entitled "The Family" (*VA* 39–62), that the archaist and historicist prejudices in the West could be summed up in this implicit syllogism: since our history, we believe, is that of the most complex, refined evolution, very ancient, primitive forms of the family are necessarily opposite to our present, conjugal, monogamous forms, which are supposed to be the fruit of a long evolution. This explains the advancement of the entirely fantastic hypothesis of an "original" predominance of "group marriages" and of "undifferentiated families" (such hypotheses can be found in the work of authors as respectable as Frazer). It is thus important to put things in perspective and to situate the facts about our tradition in relation to those of other societies.

First it must be emphasized that the West has no monopoly on the conjugal, monogamous family, even though these characteristics are claimed by the Christian tradition as values to which it attaches the greatest importance. The monogamous family exists in all sorts of societies. It is not a special indicator of "evolved civilization" since it is very frequently found in populations with a very limited level of technology (absence of weaving and pottery). Thus it does not succeed polygamy as what is modern succeeds the archaic. Recourse to one or the other formula is most often due to social regulations that have nothing to do with religious or moral criteria. Nothing here allows these forms to be situated on a time line of historical evolution.

Another very widespread prejudice is that societies called primitive exercise very strong constraints over the sexuality of young people to the point of limiting its expression to the matrimonial institution. Such a generalization is without foundation. Observation of the facts (which vary with almost every society) indicates instead a rather large tolerance of premarital sexuality, extending in some cases to institutional promiscuity (as with the Muria of Bastar in Central India). Actually, it is on the very notion of sexuality that the Western view goes astray. In primitive and traditional societies, sexuality does not take on the value of an autonomous activity and a determining element of marriage, as it does in ours. Much more determining are considerations about the acquisition of allies and the sexual division of labor. This means that the social aspect is largely dominant over the "natural functions."

Yet another illusion: we think that the family ideology supposes society's very great concern to support and protect the family. "Everything shows rather that society mistrusts the family and contests its right to exist as a separate entity" (*VA* 61). The interest society shows for the family is thus in fact constantly turned toward concern for control over its functioning. The law of exogamy already shows that society does not intend to let the family close in on itself. In marriage, it is the *alliance* that is important, not the union of the individuals, not even merely the acquisition of a spouse; indeed, what is important is the possibility of ob taining brothers-in-law, in other words, allies. In short, "marriage is not, never has been, and cannot be a private affair" (*VA* 48).

One might thus, by extending these remarks by Lévi-Strauss, advance the hypothesis that "familialism" appears not when the family invades the social field but rather as a riposte to a situation in which it retires from that field, when other elements predominate in the definition of social ties. The family provides this tie under the guarantee of a law of nature (the biological reproduction of the group): this is what gives it its inestimable value. Society cannot easily do without this guarantee since it is a self-fulfilling legitimization. This is why, even in the West until very recently, relations of alliance between families were more important (especially, moreover, in groups more attached to tradition, such as aristocrats and peasants) than the social ties that could be produced through professional activity (trade and work relations), political activity (civic responsibility, membership in a party), or even the feeling of belonging to a nation. Until very recent times, all of our literature (from Balzac to Proust) was dominated by the narration of family ties (very overdetermined, of course, by the right to individual choice then established). We are obviously very far from a sociality that could be identified with kinship relations, but we are less so than we once thought (or claimed), and we have been so not as long as we supposed.

Chapter 4

Unconscious Categories and Universality of the Mind

In Lévi-Strauss's work, two concepts are constantly and explicitly used without truly being discussed or defined: *unconscious* and *mind*. This is not, however, what leads us to treat them together here; rather, we address them here because the distinction between these two concepts is really essential. It is not that each is the reverse of the other: their difference lies in their respective accents or perspectives on a single reality that we could define as the intelligibility of the natural and cultural aspects of the universe. The term "unconscious" thus marks the continual, inevitable presence of nature in culture, and "mind" the continual, inevitable presence of culture in nature. As we will see, this articulation will provide us with a wider view of the human sciences' claim to objectivity.

However, before entering into Lévi-Strauss's views on this subject, we must emphasize that the use of these concepts has often been considered by those who have encountered them in their own disciplines to be questionable or even inappropriate. First, anthropologists, accustomed to fieldwork and empirical observation, had reservations about notions with very wide theoretical implications. Psychologists were divided. Those marked by psychoanalysis understood something different by the term "unconscious," while those in other currents (behaviorism, gestalt theory, and so on) found the term "mind" to be an abstract entity, unrelated to observation. Philosophers could be irritated by the use of the term "mind" in a context and with a meaning in which they did not recognize their own tradition. Then again the very link between the two terms could seem unacceptable to them. As one of them put it: "The notion of the 'human mind' 'unconsciously' elaborating structures is so vague that perhaps it would be wiser not to look for its meaning" (Descombes 1980, 122). We will see later whether we really must give up so quickly. It is clear, however, that Lévi-Strauss's position is close to what is called *mentalism*. Let us get another opinion: "My own view is that such mentalism is one of the aspects of Lévi-Strauss's work which takes it beyond structuralism and which will outlast it" (Sperber 1985a, 57).

These differences in evaluation clearly show that we are before a central aspect of Lévi-Strauss's theoretical formulation, which thus requires more detailed explanation and discussion. What is important moreover is not so much to be able to find autonomous definitions for these notions or to submit them to a proper philosophical critique (which would require long, patient development). Instead here we must evaluate their coherency and determine how they are used in the anthropological argument (to which philosophers have most often given little attention). As we will see, there certainly are ambiguities, even awkwardness, in Lévi-Strauss's formulations, but we will also see that it would be even more clumsy to take advantage of these failings in an effort to avoid serious consideration of the content of the notions he advances (Rossi 1974). These notions are not, as has been suggested, a philosophical prosthesis added to the body of empirical research that it would be easy to remove. They are indeed, to the contrary, indispensable to setting the foundation for the method itself (thus they draw a clear line between the structural approach, and functionalism and evolutionism). However, Lévi-Strauss has never claimed anything but an indicative value for his theoretical choices. He never wrote a philosophical treatise and has often, as he admits himself, made unsophisticated use of notions for which a highly developed intellectual history already existed.

Unconscious Categories

In magic, as in religion and linguistics, it is the unconscious ideas which are the active ones.   —Mauss 1972b, 116

Lévi-Strauss constantly insists on the following methodological point: structures are not conscious. Must we conclude from this that it is possible, in this regard, to speak of the "structural unconscious"? This formulation can be found (for diametrically opposed reasons) in certain criticisms of structuralism (in which quotation marks appear like tweezers) and in the work of followers who are convinced, or at least claim to be so (they are more likely to use uppercase letters). It does not appear in Lévi-Strauss's writing. There is a good reason for this: it is a poorly formed expression. "Structural" modifies a method or some knowledge, not an object. The unconscious (supposing that such a noun is appropriate) could be called, in this respect, *structured* at the very most (it would be so "like a language" if we are to believe the famous adage). Yet it is something else — something much more interesting — to say that the structures are not conscious or that the unconscious is a "specific character of social facts" (*IMM* 34). It is already clear where the debate is situated: Does the term "unconscious" designate a *topos*? In other words, is it a noun, or is it only an aspect of a function (such as the symbolic function)? In short, is it only an adjective? This is no trivial question since the answer determines the very definition of the human mind and also of that which establishes the structural approach as an entirely renewed form of comparativism (indeed, if the same mind is at work everywhere, then it makes sense that formally identical solutions can be given to problems in entirely separate places and times).

Lévi-Strauss often uses the expression "unconscious categories," which he finds in Mauss (see *SA* 2:7), who in no way attempted to define its epistemological status. Lévi-Strauss also does not discuss it directly, but he insists on the point that structures are not conscious, and this insistence is probably because, in his view, that is why they can be approached scientifically. In fact, this insistence situates Lévi-Strauss not only in the heritage of Mauss's anthropology but also in that of Durkheim's sociology.

Both of these theorists had to face different (philosophical and psychological) versions of reduction of social facts to data of consciousness, which amounted to thinking about the collective as being produced from individuals. For Durkheim as for Mauss there are, to the contrary, immediate societal data, irreducible to conscious representations and individual behavior. Thus the transmission of traditions, the values given to attitudes (forms of courtesy, group aggressiveness, rumors, clothing styles, and so on), the influence accorded various institutions, the attachment to beliefs, and so on, depend neither on individual decisions nor on individual representations (not even through interaction of consciousnesses). "[T]he layer of individual consciousness is very thin" (Mauss 1972c, 10). Further on, Mauss adds in the same vein: "It is a long time now since Durkheim and I began teaching that communion and communication between men are possible only by symbols, by common signs, permanent ones, external to individual mental states which are quite simply sequential, by signs of groups of states subsequently taken for realities" (Mauss 1972c, 16). Unquestionably, this is the analysis Lévi-Strauss adopts and the explanation for the privileged position he gives to the linguistic approach, which has progressed only by taking this perspective seriously. However, contrary to what is generally asserted, it was not Saussure who was the inspiration here, but Boas. It was in the work of this great American anthropologist that Lévi-Strauss discovered an orientation for which Jakobson was later to provide an adequate methodology. As early as 1908, Boas wrote:

> [T]he essential difference between linguistic phenomena and other ethnological phenomena is, that the linguistic classifications never rise to consciousness, while in other ethnological phenomena, although the same unconscious origin prevails, these often rise into consciousness, and thus give rise to secondary reasoning and to reinterpretations. (Boas 1911, 67; quoted in *SA* 1:19)

However, one detail must be noted: Durkheim and Mauss criticized the illusions of consciousness, but they did not use the word "unconscious," at least not in its substantive form. Boas did not either. Actually, such use was not frequent at the time. Lévi-Strauss had the benefit of another heritage that was to allow him to formulate the same convictions differently. However, does not the substantivization of the adjective "unconscious" run the risk of hypostatizing that which was meant to designate only a characteristic of the collective?

First we may wonder about the use of this concept in a context dominated by Freudian reference. Moreover, Lévi-Strauss often takes a position regarding Freud, to recognize his debt to him (as in *Tristes tropiques* and in *Introduction to the Work of Marcel Mauss*), or to compare psychoanalysis to a shamanist cure (as in *Structural Anthropology*), or to challenge its originality (as in *The Jealous Potter*). We quickly see that between the unconscious of which Lévi-Strauss speaks and that with which Freud deals, there is little relation. We know that for Freud the unconscious is created by the "original repression." This hypothesis, which was developed to understand individual neuroses, was extended to the field of culture by Freud himself, but above all by his disciples. It supposes that human institutions result from a compromise between violent urges and a necessity for organization that brings about the order of law. In sum, what founds human society, what introduces into it differentiation and meaning, remains an operation that occurs entirely in the affective.

This affective genesis of the social is what Lévi-Strauss considers unacceptable. He does not deny the affective, emotions or sensations: to the contrary. However, according to him their role is not that of constituting the domain of intelligibility; in other words, it is not that of ordering the world through the treatment of sensible qualities that is evidenced in symbolic mechanisms constructed by primitive thought (as we will see in a later chapter). We must not, thus it seems, expect that Lévi-Strauss's notion of the unconscious has much in common with that of psychoanalysts. Yet, in a certain number of works, it is obvious that this notion is related to repression, to misrecognition, and thus to desire.

Must we thus envisage two competing, or at least simultaneous, theories of the unconscious in Lévi-Strauss's work? Or perhaps one followed the other? And if so, how can this succession be explained? Finally, what would be the consequences of this for the conception he proposes of the human mind? It is not the same to define the unconscious in terms of energies (forces, conflicts, refusals) and in terms of structures (positions, relations, system). And under the second definition, would not making the unconscious the seat of the categories be equivalent to the transcendental aspect of traditional philosophies? Unless it would be to define the level proper to symbolic thought as nothing other than that of "savage thought"?

Such are the principal issues that we shall try to clarify progressively. This clarification is all the more necessary since it has to do with highly controversial issues regarding which many philosophers, believing they finally have a subject that concerns them more than do arduous discussions of kinship or the classification of natural species, have thought they could, by isolating a few works, make their critical wisdom shine.

The Function of Illusion

We might ask whether Lévi-Strauss resorts to two parallel theories of the unconscious. According to one, the unconscious appears neutral, passive. The term simply qualifies data that are not accessible to conscious representation. We do not know simply because we *cannot* know. According to the other, the unconscious is active and conflictual in nature. It qualifies the unspoken goals shielded behind explicit representations. We do not know because we *do not want* to know. This conception is related to both the Freudian theory of repression and the Marxist criticism of ideology. In this form, the notion of the unconscious appears mainly in works of the first period (which ends in a way with *Structural Anthropology*, at the end of the 1950s).

This desire to not know manifests itself through a procedure of dissimulation or a production of illusion. A very good example of this is provided in *Tristes tropiques* regarding the Bororo, an example taken up again in two chapters (7 and 8) of *Structural Anthropology*. The Bororo seem to offer a remarkable example of what are called "dual organizations" (see above, the chapter on reciprocity). In such societies, all sorts of dualisms assert themselves at different levels (religious, sporting, economic, aesthetic). Such is the case among the Bororo: among them the most obvious dualism is that of two exogamous moieties, one living in the north part of the village, the Cera, the other in the south part, the Tugaré. Bororo myths present Cera heroes as the orderers of the civilized world, while Tugaré heroes are demiurges at the origin of the natural world. The latter were in power in earlier times but abandoned their power to the Cera. Thus the natural universe gave way to the world of social institutions. This is the initial harmonious representation of a necessary cosmological equilibrium of which the two moieties would be the terrestrial representatives. From this proceeds, according to Bororo sages, a whole set of services and exchanges, first among which are matrimonial alliances between the moieties and the obligation of each to bury the dead of the other. The myths help to reinforce this representation of a complementary society that is supportive and equitable. Now, Lévi-Strauss tells us, the reality is frankly less harmonious, for what appears neither in the myths nor in the rites is that each moiety is itself divided into three levels — superior, middle, and lower — and that matrimonial alliances can occur only between spouses of the same level. This is thus a very hierarchical society, with all the inequalities such a framework implies. This, however, cannot be admitted, no more than can be the reason women are excluded from funeral rituals, or other real unbalances completely erased in the narratives of origin and foundation:

> Despite, that is to say, all the appearances of institutionalized brotherhood, the Bororo village is made up in the last analysis of three groups, each of which always marries within its own numbers. Three societies which, all unknowingly, remain forever distinct and isolated, each imprisoned with its own vainglory, dissimulated even from its own self by misleading institutions. (*TT* 231)

This remark echoes the questions formulated in an earlier work: "Why do societies affected by a high degree of endogamy so urgently need to mystify themselves and see themselves as governed by exogamous institutions, classical in form, of whose existence they have no direct knowledge?" (*SA* 1:131).

This analysis, in its tone and expressions, seems to come straight out of the Marxist critique of ideology. ("I cannot, after all, dismiss the feeling that the dazzling metaphysical cotillion which I witnessed can be reduced, in the end, to a rather gruesome farce" [*TT* 229].) However, the inspiration is also partly Freudian since the desire for self-mystification is presented as itself unconscious ("all unknowingly") and also as following from a repression (a denial of reality in favor of an ideal representation; see also *SA* 2:80, where what is at issue is the "manner in which, through their myths, their rituals, and their religious representations, men try to hide or to justify the discrepancies between their society and the ideal image of it which they harbour").

This type of analysis of institutions and mythical representations increasingly tends to disappear in Lévi-Strauss's work, beginning in *The Savage Mind* (where a few traces still remain, probably linked to the debate with Sartre), but especially starting with *Mythologiques*. From that time on the accent is placed more on the neutral, objective aspect of the unconscious nature of the structures. There are several reasons for this change.

To begin with, we certainly could note a distance taken respecting at least two of the "three mistresses" that Lévi-Strauss recognized as responsible for his early theoretical initiation: Marxism and Psychoanalysis (in contrast, we see that he remains faithful to the third: Geology). However, this distancing must not be understood so much as his reaction to the questioning of an infatuation that was general (and that, concerning Marx and Freud, reached its acme in the 1960s and 1970s), but as the result of the author's own evolution. It seems increasingly clear that for Lévi-Strauss the appearance of a given form of institution is due less to a choice, however obscure, than to a process in which human initiative is very limited. To speak of self-mystification is still to suppose some sort of intention or will, but to whom can such actions be attributed? We cannot say they can be attributed to individuals since we are dealing with traditions and institutions, collective phenomena. Yet how could the group be attributed with a desire or will analogous to that of an individual subject, if not through linguistic convenience, a necessary metaphorical slide?

This is a classic problem, as we know. By moving closer and closer to physical, biological, and information sciences, Lévi-Strauss renounced the formulations that tended to make the group a sort of mega- or meta-subject. By the same token he gave up attributing it with behavior and representations ("mystification," "illusions") linked to such metaphysics of the collective subject. A major reason for this was that, in the observation of exotic societies, lucidity always belongs to the observer: his judgments refer to values that are first his own (let us understand this to mean those of his culture), and it is risky to decide that another refuses to consider certain objects without being able to evaluate one's own refusal, for one must be certain (and thus be able to demonstrate) that the other's refusal is not the inverse image of one's own. Thus it was necessary to leave the shaky terrain of obscure intentions and head toward the firmer ground of structural conditions. The unconscious nature of phenomena appears there not so much as a refusal to see, but as a specific feature of symbolic processes.

The Level of the Implicit

If, then, we make the exception of a very few works from the first period just mentioned, the unconscious of which Lévi-Strauss most often speaks is in no way an unconscious of repression: it is not the product of opposing forces. Its function is not to keep hidden something that could appear or be expressed only through a long process of recognition. So, how should we describe it? We could say that the term "unconscious" in his work can be considered to be a synonym of "implicit" or "virtual." Yet if Lévi-Strauss constantly resorts to the notion of unconscious rather than to any other, it must be that it allows him to emphasize an essential point, that the field of social structures cannot be identified with that of the representations developed by subjects. "Unconscious" primarily marks this anteriority and objectivity of structures. This said, we nonetheless may wonder why Lévi-Strauss considers it necessary to provide us with constant reminders. Biologists, physiologists, and especially physicists do not worry about asserting that the facts or processes they show escape consciousness. We are well aware that we have no access to these facts and processes except through the mediation of very elaborate knowledge (and instruments). To make this clear through a trivial example, we can say that consciousness of digestion cannot shed one iota of light on the nature of the biochemical transformations produced in the body during that process.

However, the human sciences precisely are not, from this point of view, in the privileged position of the exact sciences, for, on one hand, they must deliver themselves from illusions of consciousness (of consciousness supposed to be the provider of meaning), and on the other hand, they cannot ignore the fact that the object of their learning is the very subject of this learning and that, in consequence, objectivity is no longer assured of the same distance as in proper sciences. Under these conditions, what advantage is there in applying the notion of unconscious to phenomena?

If, in the universe of social facts, structures are called unconscious, it is only because at this level they are of a nature analogous to those of the physical universe. If they escape conscious representation, they do so not because of the subject's refusal but because they require mediation to be accessed. In this sense their unconscious nature could be called neutral: it belongs to the opacity of the world. It is indeed also because structures are not obvious, not given, that they necessarily must be represented by *models.*

We must thus make the following clarification: Lévi-Strauss does not think of the unconscious as a topos, and even less as a substance, but only as an aspect or characteristic of the activity of the mind. The unconscious defines no specific reality; it is only a quantifier that specifies a reality. Lévi-Strauss should not, thus, use the substantive form "the unconscious." When he does so, it is due more to acceptance of a vocabulary that has become common than to theoretical necessity. The way he uses it clearly demonstrates that the adjectival form is required. Therefore, following Lévi-Strauss in the discussions below, we too will succumb to convenience and use the substantive form, with these reservations.

Now, the reason Lévi-Strauss increasingly favors this conception of the unconscious over that depending on a dynamic of repression or illusion is probably that his theoretical efforts are directed essentially toward the internal conditions of knowledge rather than its social use. Thus what attracts his interest in a myth is the mechanism by which it is constructed and the myth's relation to other myths or other variants of the same myth in a transformational group (as we will see later). He is probably right to place the emphasis on this internal logic since it is what was primarily misunderstood in earlier research on myths. In fact, this is the same requirement that concerned him in the analysis of systems of kinship.

The priority given to theoretical models corresponds to that he gives (in his research, not in the facts) to communication structures over subordination structures. We can wonder whether it is possible to separate the study of structures from the conditions of their practice. As Augé notes,

"[T]he articulation of symbolic systems can only be thought in relation to the practices that set them going, and which in fact appeal, even in the case of the most anodyne among them, to all the registers of social life" (Augé 1980, 113). It is likely that Lévi-Strauss would bow to this requirement. He himself showed, regarding more than one example, how the conditions of practice allowed structure to be understood. However, he would add that so long as a good method of analysis of structures has not been perfected (which is indeed what was most lacking in anthropology), we cannot even understand the dynamic nature of practices.

In fact, we probably should say that the relation between "communication" and "subordination" in rituals and myths (or in facts about symbolism in general) can vary depending on the transformations a population undergoes. In the case of myths, a good example is provided by Lévi-Strauss ("How Myths Die," *SA* 2: chapter 14) regarding the changes certain narratives have undergone when passing from one population to another. In certain cases these transformations in no way alter the specificity of the myth, which is to maintain the plurality of schemas or "codes" (for example: cosmic, social, technical, ethical, and so on) that make up its layered structure and thus its symbolic richness. Contradictions experienced in reality are not dissimulated by myths but tend to be reduced progressively by a diversity of variants that are so many explorations of the logical possibilities that can be offered by the unconscious categories. Yet in other cases, when events remove structure, the myth tends to become nothing but a legitimizing narrative of the new social situation, and in such cases it seems to favor only the sociological code. This was the case of a narrative circulating among various northwestern Indian groups that the Cree, who were allied with the whites as early as the seventeenth century, turned into a story destined to justify their choice of collaboration with the newcomers. We could thus say, generally, that the function of dissimulation increases in proportion to the weakening of the structure: the myth loses the poetic function of speaking the world, of presenting its possible order. It is made to serve a cause. In fact, this is when we leave the universe of myth to enter into that of ideology and history. We will see later that this creates the conditions for the emergence of another type of narrative: the novel.

The Unconscious, Objectivity, Science

[M]uch of linguistic behavior lies on the level of unconscious thought.   —*SA* 1:56

To assert the unconscious nature of structures is the same as to state their nature as objective data, as observable phenomena that can thus be given a scientific approach. Why? What is the meaning of this supposed relation between the unconscious and objectivity? Boas had already formulated the answer to this question:

> The great advantage that linguistics offers...is the fact that, on the whole, the categories which are formed always remain unconscious and that for this reason the processes which lead to their formation can be followed without misleading and disturbing factors of secondary explanations, which are so common in ethnology, so much so that they generally obscure the real history of the development of ideas entirely. (Boas 1911, 70–71; quoted in *SA* 1:19–20)

The best example Lévi-Strauss gives of this is that of phonology: it reveals systems of differences and oppositions that are the conditions for the emergence of meaning in phonic matter, but as such they are never the object of conscious knowledge. More exactly, we must say that the process according to which these differences and oppositions are organized depends not on the speaker's choice but on constraints linked to language in its totality. This is indeed the way in which these phenomena are objective. Consciousness of these phenomena is not only excluded, but, even if it were possible, it would add nothing to their scientific consistency. We are in the presence of immanent intelligibility, like that of the kinship systems regulated by the principle of reciprocity of which Lévi-Strauss said, commenting on the marriage of cross-cousins: "This regulating principle can have a rational value without being rationally conceived" (*ESK* 101). This is probably the most pertinent formulation of this unconscious operation of the mind.

The unconscious nature of the symbolic system and of social phenomena also determines the approach to be taken, for the method of approach must be certain to evade the illusory information provided by conscious interpretations. In anthropology the problem is often posed specifically when the researcher is faced with an explanation given by the indigenous people themselves. This explanation may be perfectly pertinent, as it may also be a gloss or misleading rationalization. If structures are not conscious, then the only legitimate way to approach them should be analogous to that prevailing in experimental sciences, where the objectivity of the phenomena is postulated from the start. This means that the criterion of consciousness is, by hypothesis, eliminated.

When he identifies social structures with unconscious models, Lévi-Strauss explains that this is the only level on which we have a chance of grasping the truth about these phenomena. Thus we can say that the complex mechanisms of kinship structures; the transformation relations between several myths and between myths and rituals; and the relations of homology between human and animal groups, which is what we call "totemism" — all these are structures that escape the consciousness, the explicit knowledge, of users even though they most often have interpretations and explanations. (Such interpretations and explanations, in turn, constitute a subject matter that can be given structural analysis, as is done, for example, in the case of the Maori theory of the *hau,* meant to explain the imperative of reciprocity, and that of the Melanesian theory of *mana,* meant to explain the action of magical forces.)[1] Such interpretative models are not, moreover, to be confused with those other conscious models that are *norms* and that are also matter to be treated, not explanations of phenomena. These sorts of models, says Lévi-Strauss, "are by definition very poor ones, since they are not intended to explain the phenomena but to perpetuate them" (*SA* 1:281).

Here we return to the first remark, that the unconscious nature of the data studied by anthropology situates that data on the same side as that dealt with by any other science of observation. At this level, if the data are objective, they are so for all observers: we are before a fact analogous to a fact of nature; thus it is universal. This universality is precisely that of the human mind (of any time and any culture), the human mind of which Lévi-Strauss clearly intends to show the factual nature.

An Objective Intersubjectivity

The example of linguistics is generally what Lévi-Strauss advances when he wants to show how a discipline has succeeded in defining its object as situated beyond conscious representation. This is not without reason. "For it is linguistics and most particularly structural linguistics, which has since familiarized us with the idea that the fundamental phenomena of mental life, the phenomena that condition it and determine its most general forms, are located on the plane of unconscious thinking" (*IMM* 35).

The classical objection to such a presentation would thus be to ask: What communication is possible between subjects who do not, and cannot, know the conditions of possibility of their thought in the form of explicit, mastered knowledge? Lévi-Strauss's answer is precisely that communication is established at the very level of unconscious reality and that communication is not just between given people but between people of other times and places, since the unconscious activity in question is the symbolic framework of the human mind:

> The unconscious would thus be the mediating term between self and others. Going down into the givens of the unconscious, the extension of our understanding, if I may put it thus, is not a movement towards ourselves; we reach a level which seems strange to us, not because it harbours our most secret self, but (much more normally) because, without requiring us to move outside ourselves, it enables us to coincide with forms of activity which are both at once

ours and *other:* which are the condition of all the forms of mental life of all men at all times. (*IMM* 35)

The unconscious level of my thought is what does not properly belong to me. It is thus what I share with all others. It is what ensures the community of minds, or rather it is what makes it that there is mind, since mind is identified with the symbolic system. In this sense, this is a new version of universal subjectivity, neither postulated nor deduced, but induced from anthropological experience (we will see later that this hypothesis of the universality of the mind is one of the essential aspects of Lévi-Strauss's theoretical undertaking, from his research on kinship to that on myths).

In an extremely penetrating article titled "L'Esprit humain selon Claude Lévi-Strauss" (1966), Fleischmann, after having analyzed the pertinence and approved the use of the notion of mind, states, in contrast, serious reservations about that of the unconscious:

It would be an exaggeration to say that we find ourselves on sure footing since, from the beginning, we have felt ourselves to be trapped in the following dilemma: either I consciously understand others and, in this case, we will not meet; or else I give up my consciousness (if it is possible to do so) to meet the other in the terrain of the unconscious and, if this is the case, what do I understand? (Fleischmann 1966, 49)

We could object that, thus formulated, without any preliminary definition of the terms, this dilemma is very formal. Moreover, the author recognizes the dilemma Sartre advanced in *Being and Nothingness,* and he adds: "Curiously, the same arguments which prove to Sartre that no meeting is possible are used by Lévi-Strauss to prove the opposite" (Fleischmann 1966, 50). This is not really exact. Lévi-Strauss attempts not to situate the debate on the level of a *meeting* (an existential event) between two subjectivities but to establish the objective possibility of communication between subjects with the same mental equipment. This level of objectivity is not the object of a conscious representation, and this is what Sartre cannot accept, since he identifies consciousness and freedom, lumping into *bad faith* what consciousness has not recognized. For him the objective world remains in an undetermined, unintelligible exterior so long as the subject has not freely given it a meaning. To this we could object that this face-off between subjectivities is a philosophical artifact: between subjects there is always already something else, either, on the side of being, common membership in a given world, or, on the side of the subjects, the presence of a third party, the group, society, which is attested to by any form of speech or system of exchanged signs. These two levels of mediation are anterior to conscious representation.

Precisely for Lévi-Strauss, contrary to Sartre, there is no undetermined exterior, but an intelligibility proper to the objective (natural or social) world, and the human mind participates in this intelligibility, either in the explicit knowledge that is science or in the implicit knowledge that is that of symbolic systems. It is indeed the latter aspect that he calls "unconscious," not without the risk of a confusion with the Freudian concept. Later in his article, Fleischmann shows that he has allowed himself to be caught in this confusion since he includes in a single argument both sides of the notion in the work of Lévi-Strauss. As we hope to have shown, care must be taken to differentiate them. Lévi-Strauss himself does not always avoid a slide from one meaning to the other, and it would have been preferable to have not used the same term, or in any case to have avoided the substantive form.

Form and Content: Unconscious and Preconscious

[T]he unconscious activity of the mind consists in imposing forms upon content.   —*SA* 1:21

In order to hold this position strictly and rigorously, another condition is necessary: that the unconscious be made not a *content* but a *form*. We must add that this form has to be an "empty form" in which contents come to present themselves, a system for organizing data that do not belong to it. "As the organ of a specific function, the unconscious merely imposes structural laws upon inarticulated elements which originate elsewhere—impulses, emotions, representations, and memories" (*SA* 1:203). In opposition, what would be the meaning of an attempt to think of the unconscious in terms of content and not in terms of forms? Such thinking would amount to postulating a priori experience since it would be to suppose that figures, symbols, and images, in other words, data of experience and culture, are innate in the mind. ("[I]t is inconceivable that the content coming from experience should precede it" [*IMM* 37].) This is indeed the problem posed by Jung's archetypes. Such givens can only be acquired. They cannot be transmitted, except if we suppose the unverifiable hypothesis of the "hereditary character of an acquired unconscious" (*IMM* 37).

From this point of view, Lévi-Strauss proposes an original version of the distinction between the *unconscious* and the *preconscious*. It is original because, for classical psychology, the term "preconscious" designates what, from Freud on, has been called "unconscious." This notion was used only to designate states of an absence of attention ("to do something unconsciously") or of a loss of consciousness ("the wounded man was unconscious"). In the beginning, Freud himself (as J. Laplanche and J. B. Pontalis point out in their *Vocabulaire de la psychanalyse* [1967]) hesitated between the two terms before deciding on "unconscious," which was less ambiguous in his eyes, probably because it was little used and thus susceptible to better indicate the dynamic element, or process of repression. By choosing to use both terms concurrently, Lévi-Strauss constructed a new paradigm that no longer had anything to do with earlier uses. He did so in the following terms — the unconscious is an *empty form* that imposes *laws of structure:*

> The unconscious ceases to be the ultimate haven of individual pecu-liarities — the repository of a unique history which makes each of us an irreplaceable being. It is reducible to a function — the sym-bolic function, which no doubt is specifically human, and which is carried out according to the same laws among all men and actually corresponds to the aggregate of these laws. (*SA* 1:202–3)

As opposed to this, the preconscious is "the individual lexicon where each of us accumulates the vocabulary of his personal history" (*SA* 1:203). As we can see, the distinction between the unconscious and the preconscious is homologous to the Saussurian distinction between *langue* and *parole,* as it may be to the Chomskian distinction between compe-tence and performance. In fact, this is Lévi-Strauss's point of view, which is most apparent when he writes: "The notion of a collective unconscious appears to me to be, in effect, acceptable only on the condition that one seeks to discover in this unconscious only a set of logical constraints, thus of schemas" (Lévi-Strauss 1962c/a, 218).

This is why Lévi-Strauss rediscovers, though under another aspect, one of the fundamental characteristics that Freud attributed to the un-conscious: in other words, that it is ignorant of time. Yet here where Freud saw the atemporality of impulses, Lévi-Strauss designated the per-manence of a logical activity. "In relation to the event or anecdote, these structures — or, more accurately, these structural laws — are truly atem-poral" (*SA* 1:202). They are the same, always and everywhere, but also they always, and in every situation, function on specific contents that only a particular context reveals. From this context (the object of ethno-graphic description), the anthropologist attempts to reveal such structures by resorting to models.

Such unconscious mental activity in no way consists, as one critic wrote, in "application of the structures to the ever-diverse contents sup-plied by human experience" (Descombes 1980, 102). This formulation is very curious, for there is never a question of anthropologists applying structures to contents. At the very most it is possible for them only to reveal structures through analysis. In contrast, it is possible to apply a form to a subject, and thus to contents. However, as Lévi-Strauss demon-strates in all his work, a structure is precisely a constant relation between contents (a relation that can thus be formalized). There is therefore no question of *its being applied* to them.

Because savage thought operates in the symbolic mode, it cannot be described by applying its own operations to itself, as conceptual thought can be, by definition. Thus we see why, for Lévi-Strauss, there is an essential relation between the notions of unconscious and mind: the forms of activity of the former that interest anthropologists are essentially made up of kinship systems, "totemic" classifications, rituals, myths, arts and crafts, and so on. Savage thought is immanent in such symbolic systems. Here we are dealing with, as in the case of language, "non-reflexive wholes" that are perfectly intelligible and produce intelligibility through their operations (without the explicit definition and formalization of the latter).

To this necessarily unconscious nature of mental laws, the analysis of myths brings supplementary clarification. Myths, according to Lévi-Strauss, are especially interesting because they are detached from any practical function. They appear as a sort of pure mental activity. However, this activity is not that of a consciousness. Myths are not narratives in which themes express intentions, ideas, or meanings. Mythic thought is situated on an entirely different level, that of the layered system of multiple *mythemes* that are articulated, respond to one another, and are translated or inverted from one narrative to another within a transformational group. "Mythic thought" is not in the thinking subject; it is in the articulation of the syntagmatic order of narration and of the paradigmatic order of schemas that, depending on the case, simultaneously reveal a cosmology, a logic, a science, a morality, an aesthetic, and so on. Thus it is at the level of the system (which is unconscious, as in language) that the action takes place, not at the level of explicit statement (which is conscious, or at least intentional, as in speech). Thus we can better understand the famous passage in the introduction of *Mythologiques*:

> I therefore claim to show, not how men think in myths, but how myths operate in men's minds without their being aware of the fact.... And, as I have already suggested, it would perhaps be better to go still further and, disregarding the thinking subject completely, proceed as if the thinking process were taking place in the myths, in their reflection upon themselves and their interrelation. (*RC* 12)

This formulation, which has often been considered excessive, is problematic not because it would set aside the subject of the thought but rather because it plays on the alternation of two senses of the term "thought," which refers either to the act of representation (for example, the thought of Leibniz as the act of a thinking subject bearing that name) or to the set of statements of an author (Leibniz's thought is then the philosophy set out in his writings). To say that men think in myths refers to the first case, but to say that myths think themselves among themselves concerns the system of statements implicated in such narratives. This merely amounts to saying (as Lévi-Strauss often does) that myths have no author and that even if they did, their nature is to express a collective thought, a tradition shared by the group.

Logical Anteriority and the Repertory of Possibilities

The ethnologist's interest in the "unconscious categories of the mind" is precisely what, in the eyes of Lévi-Strauss, distinguishes him from the historian:

His [the ethnologist's] goal is to grasp, beyond the conscious and always shifting images which men hold, the complete range of unconscious possibilities. These are not unlimited, and the relationships of compatibility or incompatibility which each maintains with all the others provide a logical framework for historical developments which, while perhaps unpredictable, are never arbitrary. (*SA* 1:23)

We will see later that historians can also investigate constants that escape conscious representation and that they are not reduced to simply narrating series of events. They themselves increasingly become anthropologists of past societies. Yet perhaps they, unlike Lévi-Strauss, would not dare formulate the hypothesis of a repertory of unconscious possibilities, which exist in a finite number and which are brought into being in events through a function of a reciprocal compatibility criterion. A work like this (though there are others of the same sort) is probably the core of Lévi-Strauss's philosophical position and marks his kinship with Leibniz rather than with Kant. As stated earlier, Ricoeur defined Lévi-Strauss's structuralism as a Kantianism without a transcendental subject. We should say instead: a Leibnizianism without divine understanding.

Lévi-Strauss's deep conviction is that, behind the very great diversity of cultural expressions and of systems of organization and representation, there are a limited number of possible combinations of elements in accordance with which relations of kinship, logical classifications, expressions in arts and crafts, forms of ritual, and mythical narratives are ordered. Thus regarding similarities noted in the data on dual organizations in various, widely separated, regions of the world, Lévi-Strauss prefers not to have recourse to dubious diffusionist hypotheses but to set out the problem as follows: "From my point of view, it might just as well be a case of structural similarity between societies that have made related choices from the spectrum of institutional possibilities, whose range is probably not unlimited" (*SA* 1:133). This work thus implies that the notion of "possibilities" extends to all aspects of cultural activity: social institutions and art forms alike. Perhaps the most forceful assertion of this can be found in the chapter in *Tristes tropiques* devoted to the Caduveo:

> The ensemble of a people's customs has always its particular style; they form into systems. I am convinced that *the number of these systems is not unlimited* and that human societies, like individual human beings (at play, in their dreams, or in moments of delirium), never create *absolutely*: all they can do is choose certain combinations from a repertory of ideas which it should be possible to reconstitute. (*TT* 160; note the permanent nature of the phrase we have emphasized)

The idea of a repertory of possibilities is probably one of Lévi-Strauss's richest conceptions, but it is also the most risky to formulate. Here we find two important theses. The first amounts to saying that cultural manifestations, as expressions of the human mind, are like the elements of a language: the infinite variety of phenomena can be reduced to a small number of formative elements and rules of composition. This is a methodological thesis aimed at the analysis of cultural systems (language, kinship, rituals, myths: as with phonemes, there is ideally a very large, though finite, number of them, but each language uses only a limited number, in accordance with laws of compatibility).

The second thesis, grafted onto the first, consists in asserting that the set of cultural systems themselves amounts to shared elements that are fundamental givens of the human mind. Clearly this is a stronger thesis since we pass from the empirical to the transcendental. At this level, we cannot envisage contents (which would, as we have seen, suppose a priori experience), only forms, and this is indeed what Lévi-Strauss says when he remarks that the unconscious is an empty form, limited to providing structuring laws for the various contents of experience. This explains the discomfort that can be caused by the expression "ideal repertory," which seems to see the mind as a reservoir of elements that can be combined in various ways depending on the circumstances and conditions of compatibility (of compossibility, as Leibniz would have said). This presentation is rather static and too closely linked to the model of the initial Saussurian-type structuralism that favored the system of language. This model is obviously debatable if it leads to a preference for the virtuality of the constraints over the actuality of expressions. Lévi-Strauss's thesis is, to the contrary, much more understandable and also can be maintained without serious drawbacks within the framework of the Chomskian conception of the relation between competence and performance.

In fact, if (in spite of appearances) Lévi-Strauss's position is not Kantian, it is because the makeup of this table of possibilities springs not from a transcendental deduction but from a program of observation assigned to a truly general anthropology:

> For this one must make an inventory of all the customs which have been observed by oneself or others, the customs pictured in mythology, and the customs evoked by both children and grown-ups in their games. The dreams of individuals, whether healthy or sick, and psycho-pathological behavior should also be taken into account. With all this one could eventually establish a sort of periodical chart of chemical elements, analogous to that devised by Mendeleier. In this, all customs, whether real or merely possible, would be grouped by families, and all that would remain for us to do would be to recognize those which societies had, in point of fact, adopted. (*TT* 160)

Lévi-Strauss proposes to build this table on a true experimental foundation. Data are to be collected and compared, and from this abstractions are to be made, in other words, from this the mold can be constructed. "Starting from ethnographic experience, I have always aimed at drawing up an inventory of mental patterns, to reduce apparently arbitrary data to some kind of order, and to attain a level at which a kind of necessity becomes apparent, underlying the illusions of liberty" (*RC* 10). Let us add that these illusions are precisely those of consciousness and thus determine the other form of unconsciousness as repression (in sum, it would be a failure to recognize the unconscious anteriority of structures — or the limits of one's freedom — which produces the denial linked to the unconscious understood as repression).

In order to define this notion of "possibilities," Lévi-Strauss always resorts to the same formulations, almost word for word. Actually, this is the point of junction of the notion of unconsciousness and that of mind. We will now examine the latter more closely.

The Human Mind

In *The Savage Mind* we read, "[E]thnology is first of all psychology" (*SM* 131). This formulation was surprising at a time when the concept of psychology was identified primarily with the study of individual psychic states and behavior (to the point that, in order to consider collective aspects, the term "psychosociology" had to be coined). Moreover, psychology supposed that affective or emotional aspects were favored over the cognitive aspect. Now, when Lévi-Strauss speaks of psychology, it is clear that he is not referring to the term in this context, but that he understands this notion as did the most classical tradition: for him it is the study of the mental mechanism. Moreover, this is the definition to which cognitive psychology has returned today, as Sperber points out (Sperber

1985a, 102). As soon as we see this, Lévi-Strauss's formulation seems less surprising and the criticism according to which his position would be psychologism appears mistaken.

Obviously for Lévi-Strauss there is no question of approaching ethnological data from the point of view of individual subjectivity (which would lead only to universalizing the contents of a particular culture). Likewise, in opposition, transcendental categories are not to be defined (to do so would be to identify the mind with domesticated thought, in other words, with an *organon* of constituted reason). What he attempts to reach is a level of thought logically prior to the distinction between rational and irrational, between savage and domesticated, between natural and cultural (all these pairs of terms are, of course, not homologous).

That ethnology is a "psychology" means that it is, in the classical sense, *the study of the human mind,* but with the inclusion — and this is a modern addition — of its social and cultural manifestations. This means that ethnology cannot be content with collecting data and accumulating monographs on populations studied, but that it must ask more radical questions about the process of intelligibility that crosses the set of observable data. Ethnology is nothing other than the study of societies that present the greatest distance from our own, but other cases of instructive distances exist and should permit the development of a theory of mental structures and the apparatus of knowledge:

> The further a thought is from ours, the more we are condemned to see in it only essential properties, which are common to all thought. In consequence, ethnology can collaborate with child psychology and animal psychology, but only insofar as all three recognize that they are attempting, using different means, to grasp shared properties which in all likelihood do nothing but reflect the structure of the brain. (Lévi-Strauss 1962/ow, 217)[2]

By assigning to anthropology the ambition to be a *theory of man in general,* Lévi-Strauss could not avoid coming into conflict with many practicing in that discipline, for this ambition went against everything that had been done since the beginning of the century, in particular in English and American research. Such research aimed primarily to establish anthropology as an experimental discipline. This meant as a field discipline, the perhaps not unique, but essential, task of which was to observe and list data of all kinds from various cultures, with no claim to be able to establish identity between any of them, and even less to be able to suppose they have a common element. The transcultural constants that could possibly appear were to be treated with even greater circumspection.

This methodological prudence initially had a prophylactic nature: it was a question of protecting oneself, once and for all, from the generalizations and extrapolations that had crippled nineteenth-century anthropology and from which even the best of the "founding fathers" (Morgan, Lewis, Tylor) had not escaped. However, the theoretical ambitions of Lévi-Strauss have nothing in common with the generalizations of the preceding century. They too were intended to be strictly experimental and scientifically established. The point is to take seriously the very term "anthropology," which cannot be like the pure empiricism of ethnography. Indeed, it is a question of proposing a theory of humankind, *but exactly as a linguist proposes a theory of language or a physicist a theory of matter.*

In short, thus, what is proposed is a theory of humankind insofar as it is the object of specific knowledge (thus differentiated from other scientific domains) and of methodologically performed observation (and not of a priori consideration). Ethnography teaches us to consider the diversity of cultures and to study as carefully as possible what makes each one special. However, from this we cannot draw out the (both morally and scientifically inadmissible) argument that there is more than one humanity. Mental equipment is the same everywhere: we have identical abilities to perceive, feel, know, express verbally, organize socially, produce representations. The set of these abilities (attested to by social activities and cultural productions) is what Lévi-Strauss calls the human mind. Cultural diversity, far from posing a problem, permits understanding that identical competence necessarily produces different performances due to the original local conditions (the physical environment, relations with other cultures, and so on).

Lévi-Strauss's position is valuable because it does not posit this universality in an a priori manner (which would be gratuitous), and it does not suppose it as the sum of resemblances (which would amount to comparing contents without concerning oneself with their function or position in a system). What Lévi-Strauss proposes is to understand *that it is the models of organization of differences that resemble each other.* In short, universality appears in the inquiry as a necessary hypothesis.

In Lévi-Strauss's work, the universality of the human mind does not find its genesis first in a desire to give a sort of philosophical extension to his ethnological results (as Eco and Leach mistakenly claim). It is a hypothesis he considers necessary to the scientific inquiry itself. However, it must be noted here that speaking of the human mind no longer has anything to do with the tradition that considered it to be an individual faculty (which means that the human mind would be what is proper to each individual possessing reason). It is also unrelated to the more recent tradition that makes the human mind a sort of collective subject or reflexive entity of the totality (such as the Hegelian *Geist*). For Lévi-Strauss, to speak of the mind is to say that beyond cultural particularities and historical periods, all humans do indeed possess identical thinking

abilities (classification, representation, organization, and so on) and that
analogous circumstances (in other words, circumstances involving conditions and constraints of the same type) will result in formally identical
solutions. It is difficult to envision a serious philosophical objection that
could be raised against this.

Another misunderstanding must be avoided here. Lévi-Strauss in no
way identifies this mind with what was classically meant by "human
understanding." The mind of which he speaks is not the seat of abstract
categories that would form, as in Kant's work, a priori frameworks of
knowledge. It is a question of operations noted or recorded during the investigation of material data. An ethnologist thus proceeds in the direction
opposite to that of philosophers. "Instead of assuming a universal form
of human understanding, he prefers to study empirically collective forms
of understanding, whose properties have been solidified, as it were, and
are revealed to him in countless concrete representational systems" (*RC*
11). As we can see, to study constituted reason, to do the work of ob-
serving first, is to not adopt a static point of view: it is to see constituting
reason as generating empirical differences. These are what an ethnologist
always deals with (and ethnographical study must be as meticulous as
possible), but the mental effort must be equally great in order to avoid
remaining with an inventory of various facts, a catalogue of differences.
It is necessary to wonder about the regularities that occur between these
differences through places and times, which only the hypothesis of a
human mind that always has the same means and operations allows one
to understand.

For Lévi-Strauss it is also not a question of denying the individual
aspect of the question, in other words, the existence of the brain and
central nervous system as the unavoidable medium of all rational activity
and even simply of all human activity. However, this medium functions
only in a collective system that we have already encountered under the
name of "symbolic system" and that is simultaneously the framework
of language, institutions (kinship, social organizations), activities (techniques, rituals, arts), and systems of representation (logical classifications,
myths...).

Lévi-Strauss chose "mind" rather than "reason" probably because the
former's meaning is wider. From his point of view, we see clearly that it is
a question of simultaneously including the "savage mind" and "domesticated thought," simultaneously encompassing nonconscious mechanisms
and activities involving explicit knowledge. The mind can thus be identified by its capacities linked to the human brain and in its productions,
the complete set of which is called "culture." These two aspects cannot
be separated. The mind is a whole that can be considered only as given
from the start. The brain and the cultural system, the neuronal and the
symbolic, must be thought of at the same time.

The unconscious aspect is essential to this concept of the mind in that: (1) cultural mechanisms are "non-reflexive totalizations" (Lévi-Strauss says this of language, but this use can be generalized); and (2) the mind contains in itself a very large but limited number of latent possibilities, of which only a certain number are actualized in cultures. There is no better summary of this conception than this quote from 1949:

> If, as we believe to be the case, the unconscious activity of the mind consists in imposing forms upon content, and if these forms are fundamentally the same for all minds — ancient and modern, primitive and civilized... — it is necessary and sufficient to grasp the unconscious structure underlying each institution and each custom, in order to obtain a principle of interpretation valid for other institutions and other customs. (*SA* 1:21)

This leads us to the issue of universality.

The Universality of the Mind

For Lévi-Strauss, the issue of the universality of the mind is not primarily abstract or purely speculative. It appears in the process of his research as a necessary hypothesis. This is the case, in the very first place, with the incest prohibition. The fact that this prohibition (which institutes the universe of rules) is proven to be universal gives it the quality of a fact of nature. However, this is but the cornerstone of a universality that continues to appear in the field of culture, opened by this prohibition, which itself expresses only the universal nature of reciprocity: the gift/countergift relation in exogamous alliance, of which the preferential marriage of cross-cousins is, as we saw above, one of the most probative forms. This type of marriage does not exist in all societies, and it does not take the same form everywhere, but it appears in completely heterogenous, independent areas of civilization. Everywhere it offers the same logical solution to the same practical problem. Under its local diversity it points back to a "common base," a "global structure of kinship": precisely that which is postulated by the principle of reciprocity. In other words, for every woman received there is necessarily a woman owed: "[I]t is this general structure, of all the rules of kinship, which, second only to the incest prohibition, most nearly approaches universality" (*ESK* 124). Thus we see that the universality of which Lévi-Strauss speaks is first a factual universality: it appears concretely in the forms of organization of societies. It is not postulated as an essence or required as a value. It is because it imposes itself on the observer as a fact that it demands to be taken at a logical level and requires an explanation that goes beyond the relativity of local situations.

This geographical universality is what, in Lévi-Strauss's work, initially calls for the hypothesis of a structural universality. This necessarily leads to the question, What is the medium of such a universality? Why is it that the same solutions are applied to the same problems in very different places on the planet? Why is it that systems of transformation (such as Australian "totemic" systems of classification and the Amerindian myth variations) are present in widely separated areas? It is as if, at such a vast level, the system were intentional, as if it were the product of a conscious project, of a convention made between groups. Yet none of this is the case: much to the contrary. Must we thus say that we are dealing with a sort of transcendental reason (in that it is categorical and transindividual) or a subjectless objective reason (in that it appears in institutions but not in thematic knowledge)? What name should be given to this reason? To whom should it be attributed, or at least to what medium should it be assigned? For Lévi-Strauss, there is no possible response to these questions except that, in all cases considered, what we find is an identical organization of the human mind. So be it. But why speak of the "mind" rather than of humankind or society? This choice is not random, and we must understand that it is not so, for this is the point at which, without saying so explicitly, Lévi-Strauss departs from Maussian and Durkheimian "sociological" explanations. This sheds light on his remark: "Mauss still thinks it possible to develop a sociological theory of symbolism, whereas it is obvious that what is needed is a symbolic origin of society" (*IMM* 21).

The nineteenth century chose to designate "society" as the author of these operations, which are by nature collective. This is an analogical way to provide oneself with a subject without subjectivity, to create the hypostasis of what is outside or underneath individuality. From Comte and Durkheim to the present, the use of the term "society" has very often remained indebted to such presuppositions. This is the sort of hypostasis that Lévi-Strauss rejects, in spite of his professed faithfulness to his teachers. This rejection is first because such hypostasis disguises a pleonasm (for example, social institutions are produced by society) and mostly because the explanation then tends to become teleological (any institution or activity is the accomplishment of an end willed by the society).

Lévi-Strauss, in speaking of the human mind, proposes an answer of a new kind that allows us to avoid these difficulties. What he postulates is a system that is simultaneously individual (the brain) and collective (social institutions and cultural products). In Lévi-Strauss's work this hypothesis cannot be separated from his conception of symbolic systems and can be found at the horizon of the three main fields of his research: kinship, the logic of sensible qualities, and mythology. To speak of the universality of the mind is (1) to postulate a formal identity of cultures, rites, myths, beyond their very great variety of contents (it is thus to refuse, at precisely this level, cultural relativism); (2) to postulate the finite nature of the logical possibilities; and (3) to assert the anteriority of the logical over the functional. In this, Lévi-Strauss comes back to the same view as that reformer of comparativism, Dumézil, who wrote:

> At all times, the human mind has intervened in the sequences, on the fringe of sequences which imposed themselves on it, though it has often been stronger than them. The human mind is essentially organizational, systematic: it lives on simultaneous multiplicity — so that at any time, beyond secondary complexes which can be explained by successive historical additions, primary complexes exist which are perhaps more fundamental, more tenacious, in civilizations. (Dumézil 1952, 80)

Myths and the Structure of the Mind

To the universality of logical categories, or to that of certain forms of institutions, what is most important to add is the universality of the mythic systems (as we will see in more detail in a later chapter). In a well-known work in which he explains how myths refer to one another, how they form both a network and a system of transformation, Lévi-Strauss explains:

> And if it is now asked to what final meaning these mutually signi-ficative meanings are referring — since in the last resort and in their totality they must refer to something — the only reply to emerge from this study is that *myths signify the mind that evolves them by making use of the world of which it is itself a part. Thus there is simultaneous production of myths themselves, by the mind that generates them and, by the myths, of an image of the world which is already inherent in the structure of the mind.* (RC 341; emphasis added)

Regarding this work, J. Pouillon is right to note that Lévi-Strauss does not say "the mind which thinks them" but "the mind which causes them," for what is in question is not a position of subjectivity but an operation of which the mind — both as mental equipment and as symbolic system — is the producer. He writes:

> Myths are not freely constructed, and it is not to an active consciousness which is transparent to itself that they refer: they are determined not by productive, conscious thought — "the mind which thinks" — but by the unconscious structure of the mind — "the mind which causes." In other words, myths provide an image of the world not because through them free, conscious thought perceives it, but because they make manifest the "natural" functioning

of constrained, unconscious thought which is part of the world. (Pouillon 1966a, 105)

There could be no better statement of why it is at the unconscious level that the mind manifests its objective functioning, and thus why the two notions are, for Lévi-Strauss, necessarily related.

This also sheds light on what makes this "structure of the human mind" universal. In *Structural Anthropology*, Lévi-Strauss had already advanced the thesis that this structure is the same "for all minds — ancient and modern, primitive and civilized" (*SA* 1:21). This allows us to explain how it is that, beneath the historical and geographical diversity of the formulations, we find the same approaches and the same categories. We can also explain how formally identical myths appear in very different places on earth. Finally we must conclude that myths, in this case, inform us not only about the ways of thinking in a given society but about the very operation of the mind. "If all cultures develop very particular discourses which are remarkably homologous with respect to each other, as is the case with myths, it is valid to recognize in this, like Lévi-Strauss, the fruit of a single human mind. The human mind, or rather a mechanism proper to that mind, generates the structures of myths" (Sperber 1973, 66). This mind permits the explanation of the universality of a mythic thought through the diversity of its corpus. These two aspects can, according to Sperber, be seen as the competence/performance relation.

Consider the reversal: this form of thought, long held to be illogical or prelogical, is precisely that in which Lévi-Strauss finds the most constant (and still present) manifestation of the fundamental operations of thought. We can see how this also challenges all the pretensions to scientistic-type rationalism, but it also controverts the entire evolutionist perspective (but not the historical perspective, for there is indeed a history of knowledges, of their formulations and transformations, though there is no evolution in logical categories as such).

Anthropology truly fulfills its program by extending this far. This is, in any case, the task Lévi-Strauss assigns it. As in any science, here theoretical audacity is what makes the experimental procedure fertile.

If we were to summarize this discussion and evaluate Lévi-Strauss's recourse to the two concepts of the unconscious and the mind, it seems we could say the following.

The concept of the unconscious (progressively detached from its Freudian references) is first a descriptive concept: it allows us to say that something intelligible exists outside of explicit rational explanations and that it develops outside of the goals of the conscious subject. This hypothesis, which poses no problems in the natural sciences, seemed to the contrary to be difficult to advance in the social sciences and in the human sciences in general, where the question of subjectivity imposes itself. This

is why the example from linguistics was so important: in the phonological and syntactical rules of organization there appears an objective
rationality that not only is independent of the subject but more importantly imposes itself on the subject as a condition on its own speech. This
allows us to suppose that it is indeed at this level that one should look
for the categorical conditions of knowledge.

Thus the nonconscious nature of a process guarantees its objectivity,
and above all it shows that the intelligibility inherent to institutions, to
cultural facts, allows us to conceive of the continuity we suppose between
the individual level (the brain) and the collective level (which is both that
of the species and that of a given culture).

To speak of the human mind as an instance of intelligibility allows us
to maintain the point of view of a system without excluding the individual aspect, but above all it allows us to retain the collective point of
view while renouncing the sociologism of Durkheim (and even of Mauss),
which makes the collective the source and reason for the representations
and goals of individuals. In this way, Lévi-Strauss actually advanced toward a position we would call cognitivist today. The intelligibility that
there is in institutions and organizations comes not from the social as
such but from the fact that the collective system has the required content,
and it is because it has that content that the social is possible. This is
exactly what Lévi-Strauss tells us when he explains that one should not
look for a social origin of symbolism, but rather for a symbolic origin
of the social.

Chapter 5

Symbolic Thought

It might almost be said that in order to grasp Lévi-Strauss's approach from his first research on kinship to his most recent work on mythology, one must first understand what he means by symbolism: "Any culture can be considered as a combination of symbolic systems headed by language, the matrimonial rules, the economic relations, art, science and religion" (*IMM* 16). Thus it must be accepted that, for Lévi-Strauss, the concept of symbolism includes both the concept of system and that of structure. It also permits one to think through exchange, alliance, and the nature/culture relation. More importantly, it is the logical foundation of the categories brought out in *The Savage Mind,* and it is also what is presupposed in the set of formal operations demonstrated in the *Mythologiques.* It is therefore an essential concept. Moreover, it is such not only for comprehension of anthropological data but because it involves a whole view of the nature of the social, on one hand, and of the universality of logical categories, on the other hand. In other words, it involves a position on the nature of the human mind.

However, the reader may be perplexed at first: How and in what way can linguistic systems, kinship systems, economic relationships, art forms, scientific products, and religious expressions be called symbolic and thus put on the same level? Generally, it is relatively well understood how ritual gestures, the oriented layout of a village, dance costumes, pottery motifs, and the sexual division of labor can be called symbolic. But language? Rules of alliance? We must see what led Lévi-Strauss to propose this extension of the concept of symbolism to all cultural facts and discuss whether it is valid. We must also understand why, according to him, it is essentially as *systems* that symbolic data can be grasped. Does such exclusive insistence not risk the loss of the specificity of symbolism as opposed to other expressions of the mind (such as language, kinship, techniques, and so on)? It could be that symbolism, in which they are included, is but one of their dimensions.

Another difficulty must be considered: either the symbolic base, common to all cultural facts, is confused with culture itself and with the reality of the mind, and, in this case, it continues to be presupposed by modern activities of reason that would then only prolong or confirm its efficiency; or it is increasingly replaced by such reason, particularly by scientific activities (and indeed this is what Lévi-Strauss explained when he set out his *floating signifier* theory), and one might wonder if we should contemplate the fading away of the nature/culture opposition (for what would remain of a culture if the symbolism that initially defined it were to disappear?). This dilemma comes up in Lévi-Strauss's latest publications. Is it pertinent? We must try to determine this also.

First we must provide an exposition of this conception of symbolism in Lévi-Strauss's work. We must envisage all its consequences within his own definitions. In particular, we must discuss four successive problems around which this concept is organized: the first is related to the specific nature of symbolic representations and their mode of action; the second concerns the identification of symbolic order with culture; the third has to do with the systematic nature of symbolic data; the fourth deals with the problematic link between symbolism and science. Then, by confronting this approach with other points of view, we will be able to evaluate the paradox of this theory, which, seeming to lead to a sort of dead-end, surprises us by finding a way out. Its deliverance is not a new definition but the remarkable progress of the question brought out in the forms of symbolism discussed in *The Savage Mind* and *Mythologiques*. It is as if Lévi-Strauss were prisoner of his definitions as he built his theory about symbolism, which he did throughout his work, and were led to hold an increasingly uncomfortable position, from which he was rescued, without his complete awareness, by the work in which he explains symbolism most convincingly: *Mythologiques*. In short, while he did not explicitly recognize it, recourse to the musical model allowed him to achieve the most profound formulation of the theory of symbolism to which he had always referred.

The First Problem: The Inductive Property of Symbolism and the Passage from the Individual to the Collective

In "The Effectiveness of Symbols" (*SA* 1: chapter 10), Lévi-Strauss provides the clearest explanation for the change he effects on the notion of symbolism. The subject is an incantation gathered from the Cuna Indians of Panama. This incantation accompanies a shamanist ritual meant to aid a woman undergoing a painful childbirth. The incantation sets up a representation in which the body and organs are likened to sites (paths, gorges, mountains) evoking a whole affective geography, while the ailment itself and the pain appear as intense images. A whole plot unfolds in which the patient is led to take part in spirit. Her body is the scene of a dramatic battle between malevolent and tutelary spirits. The uterine world is represented by a drama peopled by menacing animals that have to be expelled: the body becomes the focal point of a cosmic reality.

Each figure and action is given minute description. In short, the patient is led to enter into a mythical world, to think of her body and sensations as a system of places and actors, to imagine a dramatic unfolding that involves conception and pregnancy, ending with the delivery in progress. She participates in this drama with her interior guests, tutelary spirits that first enter single file, then leave four by four, then all at the same time, as is required for the desired dilation. This whole imaging, these animals and characters — the expressions and actions of which are identified with the organs, sensations, states, and actions of the patient — can be called symbolic.

What is the *symbolic effectiveness* of this treatment? It is found on two levels simultaneously. One has to do with the very organization of symbolism (which differentiates it from signs or language, for example), the other with its social nature (thus it is shared with language and systems of signs in general).

Regarding the first aspect, in order to explain the possibility of representing organs and translating psychic states into animals and other characters, Lévi-Strauss speaks of an " '*inductive property*,' by which formally homologous structures, built out of different materials at different levels of life — organic processes, unconscious mind, rational thought — are related to one another" (*SA* 1:201; emphasis added). Indeed, this is something very special, proper to symbolism, and originating in this coalescence of figure and meaning, or rather in the fact that symbolism performs an intelligible operation directly on perceptible elements (we will see that this is exactly how Lévi-Strauss defines music and the narration of myths). Such an operation occurs at a level different from that of articulate language and conscious discourse. Psychoanalysis has very correctly understood the power of symbolism since the patient's statements, through free association and especially through transferal, enter into this inductive process, a process completely different from conscious knowledge (which would act instead as a screen).

Yet another aspect of the shamanist treatment is equally important and probably explains its success since the patient manages to overcome her pain and the delivery takes place:

> That the mythology of the shaman does not correspond to an objective reality does not matter. The sick woman believes in the myth and belongs to a society which believes in it. The tutelary spirits and malevolent spirits, the supernatural monsters and magical animals, are all part of a coherent system on which the native conception of the universe is founded. The sick woman accepts these mythical beings or, more accurately, she has never questioned their existence. What she does not accept are the incoherent and arbitrary pains, which are an alien element in her system but which the

shaman, calling upon myth, will re-integrate within a whole where everything is meaningful. (*SA* 1:197)

Here Lévi-Strauss clearly indicates what seems essential to him in this case: that the individual treatment was made up of a mobilization of representations that are collective. That the patient is led to construct an interior dramatization of the various images evoked, according to known forms of narrative and representation, means that she is able to meet the challenge through a whole social and cosmic world familiar to her; her body projects itself in this world, which is also interiorized in her. In short, there is symbolism only in this relation. Finally, the symbolic effectiveness of the shamanist treatment depends on this integration of the individual psyche in the representations provided by the group, and thus by tradition. (Likewise, in another work, "The Sorcerer and His Magic" [*SA* 1: chapter 9], Lévi-Strauss explains that a shaman is not called "great" because he cures; rather he cures because he is recognized as "great shaman": his effectiveness rests on belief and consensus.) It is as if the ailment consists in a break with the surrounding social world and as if the first task of treatment were to reintegrate the patient into the community. This is done through the mediation of symbolic representations, not only because they are by nature social and form a "coherent system" but because the steps of the treatment and the evocations that accompany them produce a very precise *ordering* of all the elements and figures evoked. The narration that summons them, arranges them, makes them act, and finally brings them back to their initial positions has the function of defining an order in time. "Both antecedent and subsequent events are carefully related" (*SA* 1:197). In effect, it is a matter of constructing a systematic whole. The recovery is considered successful only if the result is anticipated as the restitution of the former equilibrium. It must thus present the patient with "a resolution, that is, a situation wherein all the protagonists have resumed their places and returned to an order which is no longer threatened" (*SA* 1:197).

This text has thus demonstrated, by analyzing an example in detail, two aspects of symbolism: one amounts to the *inductive process;* the other is its *systematic and social nature.* Now it seems that, little by little, Lévi-Strauss was to favor the latter aspect to the point of identifying symbolism and system so much as to label symbolic all major manifestations of culture (kinship, language, art, economics, religion). This is the explanation that Lévi-Strauss takes up again in his *Introduction to the Work of Marcel Mauss:* "It is natural for society to express itself symbolically in its customs and its institutions; normal models of individual behavior are, on the contrary, *never symbolic in themselves:* they are the elements out of which a symbolic system, which can only be collective, builds itself" (*IMM* 12).

This is thus a strong affirmation of the identity of the symbolic and the social, which is Lévi-Strauss's central thesis. What should be understood by such a statement? Does one not run the risk of favoring only one aspect of symbolism? For to say that a symbolic element is such only through its membership in a system does not imply the converse: that all systems are symbolic.

It is clear here that by emphasizing the social nature of representation (and this aspect is indisputable in the example discussed), Lévi-Strauss did not take into account another aspect that, in his later research, was to become the principal issue: *What makes certain representations specifically symbolic* with respect to others that are not (though they are equally systematic and social) but that are, for example, of a realist, functional, technical, and so on, nature? Yet Lévi-Strauss's constant requirement was indeed to understand symbolism in itself without reducing it to the deformation or foreshadowing of something else.

In this case, is it legitimate to define symbolism essentially by its systematic and social nature? Is this definition more appropriate for symbolism than it is for any other knowledge or activity to which it might be applied? In symbolism there is a particular logic in the relations between the elements that brings into play other rules, other logics. This is true of magic, "totemism," mythic narratives, ritual practices, and so on. If these modes of behavior or language are symbolic, it is not only because they are collective but because they possess properties that are distinct from all known others. Indeed, without saying so directly, this is what Lévi-Strauss hoped to demonstrate in *The Savage Mind* and *Mythologiques*. Nonetheless, he did not renounce the notion of system, for it no longer seemed to him essential to go back over that given. Rather, the real problem is: Why did Lévi-Strauss not set out an explicit theory of this more complete, richer view of symbolism? Could it be that he developed it without gauging the degree to which he was remodeling his own views? The answer to this question is not without import: it sheds light on the methodological revolution effected in *Mythologiques* and explains why Lévi-Strauss ceased to stress the linguistic model and turned toward music.

However, before dealing with this point, we will look at the first approach, beginning with its origin, and analyze it and its various implications. This will give us insight into the reason the second approach proved necessary.

The Second Problem: Symbolism as Culture

It would be impossible to understand what led Lévi-Strauss to define the various expressions of culture (language, kinship, religion, and so on) as symbolic systems if one did not take into account the history of anthropology since the end of the nineteenth century, in other words since the work of its main "founding father," Lewis Morgan, and that of certain of his great English and American successors of the beginning of the twentieth century, such as Frazer and Malinowski. What, in Lévi-Strauss's view, is hardly acceptable regarding these authors (though their immense merit cannot be denied) is a utilitarian naturalism made commonplace through functionalist formulations. In contrast he recognizes people like Boas, Durkheim, Mauss, A. M. Hocart, and — in spite of some reservations — Radcliffe-Brown as masters. Let us briefly see why.

What bothers Lévi-Strauss about Morgan is his constant tendency to explain forms of social organization as responses to biological problems or to imperatives of subsistence. Sahlins has made this clear in *Culture and Practical Reason* (1976). In Morgan's work culture is presented as the social transposition of natural constraints: it simply marks the more complex nature of the human species among all living species. To this evolutionism, Malinowski adds a rigorous functionalism that can be summarized as two theses: (1) "every culture must satisfy the biological system of needs, such as those dictated by metabolism, reproduction, the physiological conditions of temperature" (Malinowski 1960, 171); and (2) "every cultural achievement that implies the use of artifacts and symbolism is an instrumental enhancement of human anatomy, and refers directly or indirectly to the satisfaction of a bodily need" (Malinowski 1960, 171).

The question that such assertions raise is: What leads Western observers to suppose that "primitive" people live as close as possible to physiological necessities, unless it is precisely the fact they are considered primitive? The criticism Sahlins makes of Morgan can also be applied to Malinowski when he writes that these explanations boil down to "the appreciation of the meaningful realities of other peoples' lives by the secondary rationalizations of our own" (Sahlins 1976, 73). Indeed it is among us (as Mauss had already pointed out) that this *Homo economicus* appears, the inceptive expressions of which are searched for among the savages. (We saw above how Frazer interpreted the reciprocal exchange of wives as a sort of rudimentary commerce.) This approach condemns us to understanding any culture as the sum of its responses to identical needs and to dissolving its singularity in the generality of a few functions. Sahlins explains: "Utilitarian functionalism is a functional blindness to the content and internal relations of the cultural object. The content is appreciated only for its instrumental effect, and its internal consistency is thus mystified as its external reality" (Sahlins 1976, 76). However, Malinowski's views could almost be considered moderate compared with the theories advanced by G. P. Murdock (who emphasized Morgan's positions) and J. Steward (who made culture simply an effect of the economic conditions and techniques of the environment, a thesis known as "cultural ecology").

Yet very early on (beginning at the end of the nineteenth century), Boas had suggested another perspective, along highly original lines. Boas came to anthropology from the physical sciences. While performing research on luminous coloring he managed to reveal the cultural factor in perception, then to generalize the importance of this factor in the relations people have to their environment and material conditions, until he finally claimed a sort of radical autonomy of the various cultures.

Lévi-Strauss has stated his debt to Boas in more than one work, in spite of what he has identified as "nominalism" in Boas's conception of the inability to compare cultures. This had to be remedied with a coherent theory of society, and this is indeed what he found in the work of Durkheim. In opposition to the "individualist" theories of Spencer and those of economists who postulated a rationality based on the needs of the individual, Durkheim asserted the primary, irreducible nature of the social fact. However, by separating social morphology and collective representation, Durkheim opened the way for a damaging dualism of society and culture. This is noted by Sahlins, who made the following remark (which could have been written by Lévi-Strauss): "Durkheim formulated a sociological theory of symbolization, but not a symbolic theory of society" (Sahlins 1976, 116). From this point of view, Mauss was more successful here, less in his explicit theorizing, though, than in the presuppositions of his analyses, such as those in *The Gift* and *Body Techniques*.

Yet what is the exact meaning of "a symbolic theory of society"? This is important to know since it is indeed what Lévi-Strauss intends to formulate. We probably now have a better understanding of its heritage, since such a theory defines itself first by what it rejects: utilitarian functionalism and biological ecologism. In short, for Lévi-Strauss, society and culture cannot be considered separately, and there can be no separation between natural surroundings and the products of the mind: the latter cannot be thought of as simple adaptations of the former. Thus to defend a symbolic theory of society is first to presuppose that society, while natural due to the beings that compose it, exists only as an institution and, as such, is other than natural. It might be called a spontaneous artifact, the environment for all artifacts, the source of their possibility. Furthermore, biological and material conditions are never raw materials on which the mind might work but data that are already structured and understandable and to which each culture, by selecting certain elements rather than others to make up an original combination, gives special meaning and style. *In short, there is no empirical level on top of which meaning would be added: meaning is there, from the beginning, in social life as culture.* Sahlins suggests that this issue must be pushed to the limit and that the distinction between infra- and superstructures must be abandoned, a distinction that Lévi-Strauss still accepts though he has corrected it by stating that the two levels are mediated by the "conceptual scheme" (*SM* 130). Sahlins's comments regarding this are the following: "Nor would the decoding of the scheme be confined to 'superstructure.' The general determinations of praxis are subject to the specific formulations of culture; that is, of an order that enjoys, by its own properties as a symbolic system, a fundamental autonomy" (Sahlins 1976, 56–57).

Let us reformulate the question: Exactly what does "symbolic" mean here, if not that as soon as there is human society another order exists? Though the material conditions obey their own mechanisms, this other order immediately recaptures and transforms them into something else. They become the lexicon of a syntax that they do not create but that is a fact of what Lévi-Strauss calls the human mind. This order can indeed be called symbolic if one accepts, like E. Ortigues, that all symbolism asserts itself in its radical otherness vis-à-vis all natural givens (Ortigues 1962). There is symbolism in and by the transformation of a purely useful, functional element into something that, in a specific culture, is valued and charged with meaning. This could concern, for example, clothing, food, objects, dwellings, tools, plants, animals, and so on. Thus the most immediate experience of things and situations is inseparable from representations that give them a symbolic status. Nonetheless, is it necessary to identify, as Sahlins does, symbolism and meaning (Sahlins 1976, 78) and to speak of "culture as a meaningful order" (Sahlins 1976, 86)? For to appeal to this equivalence (as Lévi-Strauss also tends to do) is to put oneself in the position of having to accept the corollary that all meaning is symbolic. We know that this is not so: what is meant may be simply informative or denotative (as in most situations of communication and thus in ordinary use of language).

Moreover, what is determining in symbolism is not only that one sees what is intelligible appear on the same level as sensible elements but above all that these elements are not primarily, as in the case of signs, supposed to deliver a message: they perform an *operation;* they ensure a performance (this can be said of the symbolic topology of a village, such as a Bororo village, which represents the world and makes up a plan of the organization of social life; likewise for the gestures and parts of a rite, the costumes of men and women, and so on).

In fact a symbolic system (as will be discussed in more detail later) organizes elements into an *operating mechanism*. In this respect it is probably the condition for a system of meaning, but it does not fuse with the latter. This operating aspect is responsible for the formal unity of logical symbolism (like that of mathematics) and of traditional symbolism. It also constitutes the originality of symbolism as opposed to discourse or any other system of meaning. What is important is not the meaning of the elements but their *position*. This is what makes their systematic nature determining. This is what Lévi-Strauss himself identified and designated as operating nature when he spoke of the "inductive property" of symbolism.

We have now reached another stage in our investigations and are faced with two requirements: (1) that symbolism must be distinguished from signification, and the consequences of this must be drawn out regarding the symbolic theory of society; and (2) that it is legitimate to consider all symbolisms as systems but not all systems as symbolic.

These are the two points we must now examine through reviewing Lévi-Strauss's arguments. By beginning with the second it will be easier to come to an agreement about the first.

The Third Problem: Symbolism as a System, toward Socio-logics

[T]he social is only real when integrated in a system.
— *IMM* 25

How is the social formed? was the traditional question. Without even reverting to the solutions of classical political thought, which imagined the genesis of society from isolated individuals or at most from families, modern anthropology has long continued to suppose that it was necessary, logically at least, to provide an explanation for the — primary, ungenerable — fact of the collective organization of human life. Once such an explanation was demonstrated, it would be easier to deduce its implications on many other levels: the collective nature of language, exchange, systems of signs, conventions, traditions, and so on. And thus on the level of symbolic expressions. This sort of perspective is indeed what dominates, according to Lévi-Strauss, the Saussurian conception of language: "Between 1900 and 1920 Ferdinand de Saussure and Antoine Meillet, the founders of modern linguistics, placed themselves determinedly under the wing of the anthropologists. Not until the 1920's did Marcel Mauss begin — to borrow a phrase from economics — to reverse this tendency" (*SA* 1:52). Yet this movement remained tentative: "Mauss still thinks it possible to develop a sociological theory of symbolism, whereas it is obvious that what is needed is a symbolic origin of society" (*IMM* 21). Lévi-Strauss completes this reversal when he writes: "The social phenomenon cannot be explained, and the existence of culture itself is unintelligible, if symbolism is not set up as an *a priori* requirement of sociological thought" (in Gurvitch and Moore 1945, 526). He adds: "[S]ociology cannot explain the genesis of symbolic thought, but has to take it for granted in man" (in Gurvitch and Moore 1945, 527).

Such assertions must be examined closely since they amount to saying that society can be conceived only in accordance with the system of
differences and oppositions that constitutes every symbolism (and if that
is true, then such a system could not emerge afterward as a product of
the social fact). However, we still must ask what permits one to call the
very organization of human society "symbolic." This seems to lead us
back to the debate presented above, but here we must be more precise.
Lévi-Strauss's response to this question would be: it is because human society exists only as an *institution*. This is what, for example, the analysis
of kinship data shows. Filiation and consanguinity can be traced back to
nature: they are links that are initially biologically self-evident, but marriage conforms to rules that prohibit, recommend, or prescribe. Alliance
is not part of nature's plan. At once, all kinship relations are redistributed
in accordance with this "artifice": relations of kinship and consanguinity
are no longer simply biological; from the start they are institutionally
marked by the assignment of names, positions, and statuses in a rule-
governed system of relations. This system is both the symbolic and the
social organization of humankind. Moreover, it is not separable from the
phenomenon of language (thus it is understandable that it was thought
possible to say that kinship is *like* a language, not of course in its function, but certainly, at some level, in its form). Symbolism is thus given
with the social, from the start, inseparably. Neither one can come before or after the other. At the very most one could, if required, admit the
logical priority of the symbolic system in that the formal system of the
relations is what makes the relations themselves conceivable.

Here there is clearly a kind of paradox in the formulation. Symbolism
is by definition what makes up and institutes culture: it should be placed
with rules, conventions, but at the same time it is presented as purely
factual, like that beyond which one cannot return. This de facto aspect
is what gives it a natural universality. This brings us right back to that
favored example, which is the original aspect of the incest prohibition:
that is, it is a rule (or convention) that possesses the characteristic of being universal (and as such identical to a law of nature). Thus symbolism,
as given a priori, is something of which we cannot imagine the genesis,
only expose the internal coherence. It contains the dual feature of *phusis*
and *nomos*, of nature and convention, the tension between which concerned Greek thought (here we are reminded of the dilemma formulated
in *Cratylus*).

It must thus be said that the social fact as a symbolic system is purely
cultural, but as a *fact*, precisely, it belongs to the natural order. This is
just what can be said about language, and it is also the issue underlying the debate on the "arbitrariness of the sign." As we see, Lévi-Strauss
thus offers an elegant solution to a very ancient dilemma. Moreover, this
allows us to reopen the eighteenth-century debate on the "original con-

tract" hypothesis, the question no longer being of how people form a society (just as it is not of discovering how language is born) but of how to understand this *fact* that, from the start, presents itself in the form of a *convention,* in other words, in the form of the symbolic system.

Lévi-Strauss had already stated about symbolism in general that which he was to say about structures in various fields of study (kinship, logical categories, mythology): the sufficient explanation for a system is in the system itself and not in the hypothetical events of its genesis (however, this is a problem we will have to reexamine later with respect to history). This claim can be made provided one is indeed referring to symbolism. The criterion advanced by Lévi-Strauss is first that of a rule, but inasmuch as the terms it governs make up a system.

This insistence on the systematic nature of symbolic facts is perfectly understandable if we consider that the symbolic function cannot be separated from the social instance of discourse, in other words, from a system of reciprocal recognition and accepted conventions. This is the aspect emphasized by Ortigues (1962, 60ff.), who reminds us how the very notion of symbol has its etymological roots in the image of an object broken in two: each partner keeps a piece, which fits the other, as testimony to the pact they have made.

A symbol thus cannot be defined simply as the coalescence of a figure and a meaning, for to consider such and such figure in itself is to separate it from others; it is to make it absolute; in short, it is precisely to tend toward the imaginary. To the contrary, the symbolic operation consists in grasping figures (or any other perceptible element endowed with meaning) not in themselves but in their reciprocal relations, in what differentiates them, places them in opposition, in short, in what organizes them into structures. Again, as Ortigues explains, this is what Dumézil understood so well when he showed, in his analysis of Indo-European pantheons, that we understand nothing of the figures of gods or of mythology in general if we venture to consider divinities individually, for if we do so, each of them seems to tend to absorb the others, to appropriate their functions. Dumézil calls this the imperialism of isolated representation, of the imaginary. Yet if we take the opposite approach and consider the divinities in their differential and oppositional relations, attributes are clarified and functions appear well defined (such as the three fundamentals of the Indo-European world: the sovereign function, the warrior function, and the fertility function; or, in Rome, Jupiter, Mars, and Quirinus). "A single term can be imaginary if we consider it absolutely and symbolic if we understand it as a differential value in correlation to other terms which reciprocally limit it" (Ortigues 1962, 194). One might thus ask what distinguishes the symbolic from discourse. Ortigues assigns it an intermediary position between the imaginary, the minimum threshold of opening, where the subject of representation is given; and discourse, the maximum threshold of completeness, which supposes simultaneously the system of language and recognition of the social rule. However, in this distribution, the symbolic's role is indeed, due to its power to differentiate, to bring the subject of representation toward discourse, in other words, toward the concept. (This is a very Hegelian perspective since symbolism would prepare the ground for the only instance of true thought: that of knowledge conscious of itself, which Lévi-Strauss would not accept, as we will see in the next chapter.)

To say that there is no symbolism but that which is social means that all symbolisms are systems and that the best model is logical symbolism. For Lévi-Strauss the only difficulty is that of recognition of a system behind the terms and thus of the social behind the individual. What he emphasizes in data on symbolism is (as in kinship data) the degree of the constraints the system brings to bear on the elements: the certitude (of which phonology provided the paradigm) that terms are values, which means they have only oppositional and differential meaning. Now, since symbolism does not arrive afterward (after society is constituted), since it is the form of the immanent expression of a world, an ordered world, the equation of symbolic system with social institution must thus be considered as given, as "original."

The necessity of understanding the terms in the systems of relations where they appear, which characterizes symbolic phenomena, has for Lévi-Strauss first essential implications for the way in which psychological information is approached, more specifically for the way in which the status of affectivity is defined. This issue is important because many theories see the origin of symbolism in the subject's urges or in shared emotions.

Far from the behavior of the group being the sum of individual sentiments, what must be said is that such sentiments are formed according to what is required by the group. "[E]ach man feels as a function of the way in which he is permitted or obliged to act. Customs are given as external norms before giving rise to internal sentiments, and these non-sentient norms determine the sentiments of individuals as well as the circumstances in which they may, or must, be displayed" (*T* 70). This could not be more Durkheimian or Maussian, as another remark also shows: "[T]he psychological formulation is only a translation, on to the level of individual psychical structure, of what is strictly speaking a sociological structure" (*IMM* 11–12).

Once more we find ourselves faced with the problems encountered above regarding the shamanist treatment, an issue dealt with again in *Introduction to the Work of Marcel Mauss,* where emphasis is placed on the social dimension of experiences such as trances, possession. The hypothesis is extended to pathological states (for, whatever their physiological substrata, their forms of expression remain socially defined).

Marginal or special behavior is then not a simple irregularity: we are dealing with individuals placed between different irreducible systems. "The group seeks and even requires of those individuals that they figuratively represent certain forms of compromise which are not realisable on the collective plane; that they simulate imaginary transitions, embody incompatible syntheses" (*IMM* 18). It is precisely through symbolic systems that these transitions (defined here exactly like the variations of a myth) are carried out. In other words, they are carried out through the elements of representation that simultaneously cause and suppose collective representations.

To call all cultural systems symbolic is probably a way of recognizing that the description of such a system is not exhausted by the inventory of its functions, that it is always also endowed with value. Thus kinship terms serve to classify and differentiate, but the positions they assign are also statuses and lead to attitudes. (We have seen this regarding maternal uncles, cross-cousins and parallel cousins, relations between brothers-in-law, the parents-in-law prohibition, and so on.) This clearly reveals how symbolic value is related to the system, but we also see clearly that the symbolic aspect is not defined by the system and that everything of a systematic nature cannot be called symbolic.

In fact, Lévi-Strauss establishes that the attributes of a symbolic system are (1) to be an intelligible system; (2) to be situated at the level of the unconscious; and (3) to have an intelligible aspect that springs from the differential and oppositional nature of the elements. Thus all systems exhibiting such traits are to be called "symbolic." This is so in the cases of language, kinship systems, rituals, myths, and so on. This also explains the temptation to call all cultural systems (kinship, art, ritual, mythology, and so on) "languages" because language is the best model of an intelligible unconscious system. In sum, for Lévi-Strauss, everything that is a system and has internal intelligibility is called "symbolic" — a term that therefore qualifies all cultural systems in opposition to natural systems. This assimilation is debatable, and Lévi-Strauss himself is led to question its presuppositions, as we will now see.

The Fourth Problem: Symbolism, Natural Codes, and Science

If symbolism is defined as the logico-social framework of our representations and behavior, if it is identified with all that is cultural or belongs to institutions, with all that denotes conventions, codes, then a difficulty arises: What about natural codes? Are they symbolic? If they are, then we can no longer say that symbolism merges with culture, or in any case, that would no longer be the central issue.

It is clear that for Lévi-Strauss, until *The Savage Mind,* there could be no question of speaking of a code other than as an element in the symbolic chain; in other words, a code could be spoken of only according to the hypothesis of an opposition of culture to nature. However, as soon as a code present in the biological order (such as the DNA code) appeared, a new problem arose. That meant that a code could exist at the level of nature, that a signifying chain could be given outside of any break supposing the emergence of the human world. This is a serious difficulty, for if we can speak of a code, even a language, without requiring the postulation of a rule being followed, the principle of reciprocity, for example, loses its pertinence, and at the same time we can wonder what happens to all that this principle explains (preferential marriage of cross-cousins, dual organizations, relations of alliance in general, in short, the whole system of kinship itself). The naturalism Lévi-Strauss criticized as incoherent in its utilitarian and functionalist versions seems to return clothed in the prestige of biology. How does Lévi-Strauss manage to overcome this new form of nature/culture dilemma?

Faced with the existence of codes given in nature, two theoretical reactions seem possible: either that of saying that the rule of nature extends very far into that of culture or that of asserting that the latter is manifest very early in that of nature. This means that rather than there being a passage between nature and culture, there is an overlapping. Lévi-Strauss vacillated for a time between these two positions until he finally headed toward a third, which has dominated his research since *The Savage Mind* — that of a continuity of the human mind that transcends the nature/culture opposition:

> [W]e shall perhaps discover that the interrelationship between nature and culture does not favour culture to the extent of being hierarchically superimposed on nature and irreducible to it. Rather, it takes the form of a synthetic duplication of mechanisms already in existence but which the animal kingdom shows only in disjointed form and dispersed variously among its members — a duplication, moreover, permitted by the emergence of certain cerebral structures which themselves belong to nature. (*ESK* xxx)

The same perspective is found in another text:

> Even if social phenomena must be provisionally isolated and treated as if they belonged to a specific level, we know very well that — de facto and even de jure — the emergence of culture remains a mystery to man. It will remain so as long as he does not succeed in determining, on the biological level, the modifications in the structure and functioning of the brain, of which culture was at once the natural result and the social model of apprehension. At the same

time, culture created the intersubjective milieu indispensable for the occurrence of transformations, both anatomical and physiological, but which can be neither defined nor studied with sole reference to the individual. (*SA* 2:14)

Many other remarks corroborate this vision: "[M]y thought . . . is itself an object. Being 'of this world,' it partakes of the same nature as the world" (*TT* 56). "As the mind too is a thing, the functioning of this thing teaches us something about the nature of things: even pure reflection is in the last analysis an internalization of the cosmos. It illustrates the structure of what lies outside in a symbolic form" (*SM* 248n.).

In Lévi-Strauss's eyes, advances in modern science require such a perspective. Biology, principally, teaches us that living beings are information systems regulated by programs. The intelligibility that the mind manifests in the natural world can be nothing other than that which it itself possesses. As it formulates itself and develops, it substitutes itself for that which symbolic thought proposes in the savage mode (in other words through treating secondary qualities). We are thus faced with the following situation: modern science has increasingly precise means of understanding the whole of the knowable world, while symbolic thought, which from the start gives a total meaning to the world, continues to give meaning to that which is not yet rationally explained: "[O]nly the history of the symbolic function can allow us to understand the intellectual condition of man, in which the universe is never charged with sufficient meaning and in which the mind always has more meanings available than there are objects to which to relate them" (*SA* 1:184).

Generally, symbolic thought provides evidence of the discrepancy it is trying to master by giving the unknown signified an undetermined signifier, which Lévi-Strauss proposes we call a "floating signifier" (this would be the function of *mana* among Melanesians or of any other term of the same sort elsewhere, such as "thing" in English). This would allow us to "acknowledge that the work of equalising of the signifier to fit the signified has been pursued more methodically and rigorously from the time when modern science was born" (*IMM* 62). Such equalizing is far from finished, and Lévi-Strauss thinks that the "floating signifier" function still has a long life ahead of it. Nonetheless, this presentation demonstrates an optimistic vision of science and assigns it a precise task regarding symbolic thought. One should be able to say that science takes over for such thought and, especially, relieves it of its duties. This would mean, at the limit (or, in any case, in principle), that symbolic thought could completely disappear in a universe where objective knowledge has responded to the totality of available signifiers.

It is thus understandable that a theory of "communication" could come to replace that of symbolism. Let us look at a fairly obvious example: in contemporary families, the incest prohibition (limited to the very tight circle of the biological group) is no longer relevant to the foundation and guarantee of marriage, since marriage is no longer primarily an alliance between two groups linked by the obligation of reciprocity. We are thus in an enlarged version of "complex kinship structures." We have passed from a mechanical order to a statistical one. Consequently, the opposition to nature, characteristic of symbolism, seems no longer necessary. The evolution of Lévi-Strauss's thought on this issue is expressed by the realization that the formation of a code is not necessarily linked to the nature/culture opposition; therefore, we can notice the tendency to replace the opposition of these terms with the idea of their continuity.

The problem is that this reversal of perspective occurs progressively and imperceptibly. So much so that the fact that he abandoned the first set of axioms was neither clear to nor recognized by Lévi-Strauss himself. Between that set and the next there is common ground that can give the impression that it was simply an inflection, for between the sphere of *symbolism* and that of *communication,* what is shared is the *code.* In the first case, it is conceivable only within the sphere of culture. In the second case, it appears as if a set of elements has simply been put in sequence and ordered, as is seen at the cellular level or in systems of animal communication. Yet is symbolism truly a question of a code? It could be that it is not and that Lévi-Strauss himself has gone beyond this position in spite of a terminology that remains unchanged.

General Review of the Issue

Until now we have tried to follow Lévi-Strauss in the area of his *explicit* definitions of symbolism and to show their principal aspects and implications from his point of view. It is time to go back to the questions we posed at the beginning of this chapter and to wonder whether the constant slide which led him to pull the notion of symbolism toward that of system, while it was pertinent, did not have undesirable implications. Did it not imply neglecting the mode of functioning proper to symbolism and giving it a meaning so general that its specificity was diluted? Yet — and this is a rather surprising situation — Lévi-Strauss has responded to such objections, though without fully realizing it. Rather he offers, without saying so, a completely different conception of symbolism, probably the richest conception that can be found in recent work in this domain.

Let us summarize briefly: that Lévi-Strauss went from the notion of efficiency to that of symbolic system is understandable given the requirements of his method. For him, faced with abundant anthropological material concerning forms of representation, classification, nomenclature, ritual, and mythological narratives, it was first a question of applying a few simple, efficient rules of interpretation. Simultaneously, it was also a question of supposing that beneath the profusion of images, figures, and themes (in short, beneath the infinite variety of contents) there was a logical framework of which the organizational principles could always be discovered. This is how Lévi-Strauss, like Dumézil regarding Indo-European mythology, gave himself the means to reduce arbitrariness to motivation. This supposed extremely precise knowledge of the data since, when the subject is culture, the integration of a detail into a system sup-poses first good knowledge of the context. Thus we see clearly where lie the requirements of the system, and, from this point of view, its valid-ity is unquestionable. The difficulty is that, along the way, Lévi-Strauss seems to have forgotten the notion of symbolic efficiency and has had the tendency in consequence to call symbolic everything that composes a system in culture: kinship, language, knowledge, techniques, religion. We may thus wonder if there is any human activity that is not symbolic, in which case "symbolic" would be a synonym for "cultural" and the concept would lose specificity. Lévi-Strauss pointed out this specificity in his analysis of the shamanist treatment as being defined by an "inductive property," but this promising notion disappears in his later works. Yet, though it might not be mentioned, it remains a force in all his research on "totemism," the "savage mind," and myths. Precisely, Lévi-Strauss con-tinues to think about symbolism in the framework of semiological theory and to demonstrate its effective functioning from a perspective that is in reality cognitive: this is the thesis argued by Sperber in *Rethinking Sym-bolism* (1975). Sperber, who, in more than one work, has stated frank reservations regarding Lévi-Strauss's analysis, here awards him remark-able praise as the author of "the richest and most intuitively satisfying interpretation ever given of mythology" (Sperber 1975, 6), but it is only to express regret that his conception of symbolism was not in agreement with his method of exposition.

Let us thus examine a few of the essential points of Sperber's analysis in order to attempt to resolve some of the difficulties so far encountered in Lévi-Strauss's formulations.

Sperber's principal thesis lies in this assertion: "Symbols are not signs. They are not paired with their interpretations in a code structure. Their interpretations are not meanings" (Sperber 1975, 85). Thus semiology, which deals with signs and their meanings, is not a theory appropriate to the analysis of symbolism. If it claims to be so, it will only reduce the symbolic phenomenon to a set of signs of which we must discover the message. Thus symbols would be deciphered by annulling, in a way, the specificity of symbolism and suspending the following obvious question: Why does symbolism exist if it can be reduced to something else? Lévi-Strauss precisely does not acquiesce to this sort of reductionism: to the contrary, as we will see later, he provides the most remarkable method for understanding the specificity of symbolic data. (Yet it is understandable why it is risky to speak of kinship or of a corpus of myths as a language. Neither one has the structure of a code, except metaphorically.)

If a symbolic system is not a system of meaning, not a code, then what is it? Sperber writes, "[S]ymbolism conceived in this way is not a means of encoding information, but a means of organizing it" (1975, 70). Elements appear in it in a system of homologies, oppositions, inversions. These operations cannot be the object of research into meaning, thus: "A symbolic opposition must not be replaced by an interpretation, but placed in an organisation of which it constitutes a crucial element" (Sperber 1975, 70). In short, symbolism is first an operating system, an instrument of organization. We do not ask what an instrument means, but what purpose it serves, what it allows to be produced. Symbolism produces order in a set of tangible elements, order that is intelligible from the perspective of the homologies, oppositions, and inversions that it brings into play. In sum, this is what Lévi-Strauss calls the "savage mind." It applies to the use of natural species to set up a system of differentiations in human society (what has been called "totemism"). Thus it also applies to rituals and, finally, to the schemas in mythical narratives. (For example, "The Story of Asdiwal" [*SA* 2: chapter 9] brings into play the oppositions of mountain and sea, hunting and fishing, winter and summer, close alliances and distant alliances, and so on, through which appear the more general categories of high and low, land and water, and so on.)

Faced with the data on symbolism, the traditional issues in semiology (like those in hermeneutics) consist in wondering: What does that mean? In short, what is the message of this code? Sperber points out that in fact semiologists have spent less energy trying to learn what symbolism means than they have trying to understand how it functions. This approach is the right one, but it is not what they claim to be doing. Thus there is a certain distortion between their advertised theory and their actual work. So, when we are dealing with various natural elements — moon, sun, fire, rain, or the many plants and animals — what is at stake is not knowledge of what they mean (an issue for those looking for a key to symbols or working on the hermeneutics of content) but knowledge of how such and such an element is used in a system. "Of the sun and the moon, the same thing can be said as of the countless natural beings mythically manipulated: Mythical thought does not seek to give them a meaning — it expresses itself through them" (*SA* 2:221). One should say instead that it functions thanks to them.

This is why a symbolic phenomenon cannot be affected except by another of the same order. The relations between them are those of *transformation*, which means that together they are like variations of a single schema, hence the variations of a myth or rite. It is thus clear how symbolism marks the strength of structure in relation to events: any new element tends to be integrated in a structure in the form of a variant. This is obvious when populations meet, as in the cases that ethnographers have been able to observe, but it is also true whenever one civilization borrows from another. Of this, history provides much testimony (such as the integration of Christian figures and narratives in the Indian world).

However, the immediate consequence of the fact that the relations between symbolic systems are relations of transformation is that any interpretation that is presented as a commentary on a symbolism cannot be metasymbolic but simply produces, most often unconsciously, a supplementary variation. In this way Lévi-Strauss sees the Freudian interpretation of the Oedipus myth as one of its latest influential variations in the modern era ("Therefore, not only Sophocles, but Freud himself, should be included among the recorded versions of the Oedipus myth on a par with earlier or seemingly more 'authentic' versions. . . . An important consequence follows. If a myth is made up of all its variants, structural analysis should take all of them into account" [*SA* 1:217]). Sperber provides a more general statement of this: "Exegesis, like unconscious representation, does not constitute the interpretation of the symbol, but one of its extensions, and must itself be symbolically interpreted" (Sperber 1975, 48).

Thus we can wonder what approach would not be immediately caught in the whirlpool of symbolism, what could avoid being an unconscious variation. While Lévi-Strauss did not consider it explicitly, this is the difficulty he always had to overcome. The issue is that of the "right distance" in the method of exposition. This is above all distance, which is what makes Lévi-Strauss's analysis of myth seem so disappointing. It certainly is disappointing regarding any demand for signification. Indeed, when, in contrast, someone like Ricoeur opposes the structural reading of myths to the reader's appropriation and adoption of the meaning, he is doing nothing other than asking to enter into the belief they presuppose — in other words, as Sperber says, to symbolically prolong the symbolism. This is perfectly legitimate within an existing tradition in which one takes part (which is indeed what Ricoeur claims). This could only, however, be a reductive, ethnocentric appropriation for any other tradition, except if one hopes to be its heir, but then one would be forced to take a syncretic position, not one of critical interpretation.

This is probably the reason why in *Mythologiques* Lévi-Strauss uses music as the expository and interpretive model. He requires a myth be read vertically first, according to its various codes, like a musical score. Most importantly he explains that myths, like music, cannot be transposed into something else: a myth explains itself in a variation as a musical theme explains itself in a development. "The myths are only translatable into each other in the same way as a melody is only translatable into another which retains a relationship of homology with it"

(*NM* 646). Myths and music are to be understood as symbolic mechanisms: they cannot be reduced to a meaning but must be received in their own particular order, defined by the operation produced by their forms. This is why those who study myths find themselves in a strange position. If they claim to comment on the subject of the myth, they enter into a process that symbolically prolongs the symbolism. They must thus restrict themselves to an exposition that reveals the systems of the myths, just as a conductor of an orchestra reads a score and undertakes to produce another performance of it. Thus it is a question not of discovering a meaning but of performing an operation. In the same way readers are invited to let themselves be "carried toward that music which is to be found in myth" (*RC* 32). What is at issue is a metaphor Lévi-Strauss uses as the most appropriate means for indicating something his semiological conception of myths did not allow him to formulate explicitly but that he had seen clearly in his work on shamanism: that symbolism is above all an inductive process and that the relations between the symbolic elements (or rather systems) are relations of transformation (we will see this more clearly in chapter 7).

These considerations regarding the primarily operational nature of symbolism allow us to come back to certain points mentioned earlier.

It is easier to understand the legitimacy of the concept of the unconscious, in the non-Freudian sense that Lévi-Strauss gives this term, as that which characterizes the transformational relations between symbolic elements: these relations are due to the constraints of a system, not to the intentions of a subject. It is also clear what defines the systematic nature of symbolism: it is to produce an order using heterogenous elements simply through the play of homologies, oppositions, and inversions. This produces a system of highly motivated relations between terms that seem perfectly arbitrary: this is, as we will see later, what Lévi-Strauss calls "intellectual *bricolage.*"

However, does calling symbolism systematic mean that it can only be collective? This can be said of the level of *unconscious mental activity*, in other words, of the level of competence, but not of that of performance. The production of an individual symbolism cannot be challenged. The real issue is that, since membership in a community is effected essentially on the symbolic level, there is strong pressure on everyone to adhere to shared representations (a pressure that comes from symbolism itself, one might say, rather than a sort of obscure will of the community or society).

There remains one issue on which a better understanding of symbolism can help to shed light. It is that of *floating signifiers*, which implies that the signifiers are inadequate for the signified. However, this hypothesis disappears if one ceases to think of the issue in terms of signification. In reality, facts pertaining to symbolism were assigned to the category of "signifiers," and then attempts were made to find out what they "signified." Undoubtedly, symbols and signs should not be identified with each other (though they often are in Lévi-Strauss's work). A term may appear undetermined from the point of view of meaning when it is perfectly determined from the point of view of function: "Savage thought does not distinguish the moment of observation and that of interpretation" (*SM* 223).

Perhaps this essential lesson should be taken from the symbolic functioning of thought: it is thought that operates on the same level as perception and that organizes the tangible world, the very world in which its action is performed. It can thus be said to be ordered precisely at a level of craftsmanship that maintains a delicate balance between the human and natural worlds.

To the contrary, in conceptual thought (which is indeed how this thought belongs to the domesticated world), logical tools separate themselves and become autonomous in that they exhibit their own functioning: their principles, rules, and procedures. Method is distinguished from result, which is why results are cumulative and lead to a technical universe that is no longer in symbiosis with the natural world but that develops like a prosthesis with respect to that world.

Symbolic thought, however, remains synthetic (as art still is today) and retains the simultaneity of all experience. It does not state what it thinks; it does not formalize its thought: it realizes it. It is operative, but in the totality of tangible objects (thus the analogy with logico-mathematical symbolism, which is operative in the domain of signs it gives itself by convention and which has thus the elegance of a work of art). In short, this is what Lévi-Strauss calls the *savage mind.*

Chapter 6

The Logic of Sensible Qualities

Every explanation is subject to the necessity of expressing an entire order of phenomena by combinations of a limited, and generally small, number of carefully determined variables.

— Valéry 1987, 185

[M]an has always been thinking equally well.

— *SA* 1:230

After many centuries of prejudices, it is not easy to state the simple observation (for it is indeed an observation, not a supposition) that there is not *formally* more rationality in the knowledge and techniques developed in the Western tradition than there is in the classifications and knowledge of societies we call "primitive." It is true that this assertion is not easily acceptable to thinkers who consider their science and its status to be special: this is perhaps (to speak like Freud) the last narcissistic wound inflicted on the certainties of Western man. In fact, such concern is not appropriate. That "man has always been thinking equally well" is excellent news: it should be cause for rejoicing for all reasonable beings and provide them with greater confidence in their fellow kind on all continents and at all times.

In fact, this amounts to a simple question: Are there any humanities that are totally heterogenous? For, whether one recognizes it or not, such heterogeneity is inevitably postulated as soon as one establishes a hierarchy of thinking *abilities*. If one accepts that humans are humans everywhere and that their humanity is universal, if such humanity distinguishes them from other species, then one must postulate that the capacities of the human mind are the same everywhere also. There are thus no heterogenous humanities. There are simply, from the point of view of knowledge and symbolic systems, very different ways to perform and manifest the operations of the mind.

What does this mean? Is it simply a question of asserting the inevitable diversity of cultures and ways of life? of benevolently recognizing their irreducible originality? Such benevolence risks hypocrisy and the loss of all scientific effectiveness. This is absolutely not the kind of approach

Lévi-Strauss invites us to take. The one he proposes, while asking us to recognize the universality of the "human mind," is that of understanding that at a deeper level—that of the abilities and operations of thought—the same logic is at work in savage systems of classification and in the most elaborate knowledge of our culture. In this, Lévi-Strauss makes anthropology take a considerable step. Not only is thought wholly at work in myths, rituals, and aesthetic productions of the various cultures studied, but to suppose the contrary would be to assert that we are faced with arbitrariness, imbecility, and, finally, nonhumanity.

It must still be shown how, by what means, according to what devices, and with what media "savage thought" performs its operations. This is what we must study in Lévi-Strauss's presentation of such thought. We will then be able to return to the importance of the rupture thus produced in the understanding of traditional societies.

The Neolithic Paradox and the Appearance of Modern Science

Science as we know it has, in fact, a relatively short history: it has been with us for only a few centuries (twenty-five to thirty, maximum). This is very little time, almost none with respect to the hundreds of thousands of years since the appearance of the human species or the tens of thousands since the beginning of the Neolithic Age. Lévi-Strauss considers these figures should be kept in mind, first to evaluate the degree to which, during the greatest part of its existence, humanity has thought in the "savage" mode (which thus, insofar as we are able to understand and reconstruct its processes, carries and maintains accessible the memory of such humanity). This should already lead us to be modest and to grasp the urgency of not allowing this heritage to be lost. Yet what should increase this modesty still more is consideration of another phenomenon, which Lévi-Strauss proposes we call the "Neolithic paradox."

The Neolithic is defined by the mastery of the major arts of civilization: pottery, weaving, agriculture, animal husbandry. The acquisition of these techniques is not a product of chance: it presupposes thousands of years of observation, experimentation, and control. Much more importantly, it also presupposes (as can be observed in many primitive societies today) disinterested curiosity, a taste for experimentation for its own sake, without any immediate utilitarian goal. In sum, with respect to both methods and mental attitudes, all the qualities required by modern science are already present. Moreover, the post-Neolithic development of metallurgy, with the complexity of the knowledge and techniques it requires, amply demonstrates the level of mastery humankind had acquired on the eve of such transformations.

The question that must be asked now is why this movement of discovery and development was interrupted. Why were there thousands of years of stagnation between the Neolithic and the beginnings of modern science? To this paradox, most historians of science and technology have responded by proposing endless hypotheses about either social and natural conditions, or internal and external stimuli. Lévi-Strauss does not even enter into this debate. For him, the answer is unquestionable:

There is only one solution to the paradox, namely, that there are two distinct modes of scientific thought. These are certainly not a function of different stages of development of the human mind but rather of two strategic levels at which nature is accessible to scientific enquiry: one roughly adapted to that of perception and the imagination: the other at a remove from it. It is as if the necessary connections which are the object of all science, neolithic or modern, could be arrived at by two different routes, one very close to, and the other more remote from, sensible intuition. (*SM* 15)

This is obviously a very important thesis. It appears provocative only to those who believe in a single line of evolution. It clearly indicates that *"savage thought" is not the past of modern science but another mode of apprehension of phenomena, which is parallel and rigorous in its order — that of sensible qualities.* Modern science proceeds thus from a late bifurcation. Savage thought and modern science are not situated on the same line, on which one would be the ancestor of the other: they are on two parallel lines and accomplish two tasks, which are formally comparable but profoundly divergent with respect to their presuppositions about the natural world.

Very often (and first in the *Mythologiques*), Lévi-Strauss emphasizes the degree to which the exercise of symbolic thought attains an astonishingly high level of formulation and complexity, the logic of which we are barely able to translate into our categories and instruments of formalization. Lévi-Strauss considers that his work is an initial, still modest, deciphering of this highly sophisticated system of thought. (He himself describes the Australian kinship systems as prodigiously sophisticated.) Yet we still must gain more precise understanding of the difference between the two lines, "one very close to, and the other more remote from, sensible intuition." It is a question of strategies of intervention. It is clear that the first strategy targets the maintenance of the human–nature homeostasis and that the distance taken by the second will continue to develop into a rupture, of which modernity's project of mastery seems to be the culmination.

Savage thought (and we will see later that it is in this respect very close to the knowledge conveyed by works of art) is thought that operates directly on the level of signs, thus before any dissociation of the intelligible from the sensible. This means that particular systems of signs are expressed in terms of others without any abstract, formal level of formulation such as that of concepts. We are thus on "a plane where logical properties, as attributes of things, will be manifested as directly as flavours or perfumes" (*RC* 14) — an excellent way to define symbolism and its particular way of operating, which is that of transformation between systems of secondary qualities. In short, savage thought, by remaining at its own level of intervention, which is that of the sensible, is no less logical and rigorous than domesticated thought. By proposing to show this, Lévi-Strauss simply embraces the ambition to "introduce these secondary qualities into the operations of truth" (*RC* 14).

"Intellectual *Bricolage*"

Yet how can we define this kind of operation, which lacks the reflexive form, the formalized expression, and the rigorous progressiveness of rational knowledge? How can we define a form of thought that, by taking analogical reasoning as its principal recourse, builds ordered sets by mobilizing all the homologies that can be observed between the various fields of experience?

Lévi-Strauss answers these questions in the first chapter of *The Savage Mind*. There he sets out a notion that might seem curious and that (not without misunderstandings) has often attracted readers: it is that of "intellectual *bricolage*." Thus the pages where it is presented must be reread attentively. We may find it questionable, but at least we will have established clearly its defining elements and the field in which it might be applied. Now, first, why does Lévi-Strauss resort to this notion, the analogical value of which seems rather outlandish? The reason can be found in these lines:

> The characteristic feature of mythical thought is that it expresses itself by means of a heterogenous repertoire which, even if extensive, is nevertheless limited. It has to use this repertoire, however, whatever the task in hand, because it has nothing else at its disposal. Mythical thought is therefore a kind of intellectual "bricolage" — which explains the relation which can be perceived between the two. (*SM* 17)

Note that the issue at stake here is specifically that of mythic thought as a particular aspect of the savage mind, which has many other aspects as well (such as systems of classification, naming, computation, and so on). As we will see when we discuss the *Mythologiques*, mythical narratives have the peculiar feature of virtually systematically scanning all possibilities of narrative transformation and of the combination of elements employed, as if their etiological value was secondary to this sort of free exercise of thought that appears in the proliferation of variants. Yet, even if the natural world offers a virtually unlimited variety of elements as bases for such narratives, it is still the case that, for a given motif in a myth, the choice is restricted. Elements that have been used already are indeed picked up again and treated once more: this authorizes the analogy with *bricolage,* except for the problem of which version of the myth came before it was reworked.... But first let us see how Lévi-Strauss argued for the validity of this analogy. His argument is entirely based on the engineer/*bricoleur* opposition. What, thus, characterizes engineers, or rather their activities?

Their activities are not separable from modern science, from at least four points of view: (1) the *project,* not so much the global project, is that of a systematic transformation of nature, as the always specific, directed program of a work site that supposes the use and coordination of elements in view of a clearly defined result; (2) the *method* supposes theoretical knowledge and very great professionalism, and its aim is to arrive at the desired result using the simplest, least expensive means; (3) the *elements* are always specific (basic materials or objects already produced) and organized in view of obtaining a specific effect; and (4) the *results* are limited and reproducible.

With respect to this, *bricolage* does not have the framework of a coherent project (for the *bricoleur* it is always a question of an occasional, limited intervention); it does not entail specific knowledge (a *bricoleur* is an amateur); it has no specific elements (a *bricoleur* reuses and modifies the use of the materials he finds, which were meant to belong to other entities); finally, the results are uncertain, never identical, and thus difficult to reproduce.

Given these points, the analogy remains to be established: mythic thought is to science what the activity of a *bricoleur* is to that of an engineer. This provides us with the following oppositions: where science proceeds by *concepts,* mythic thought proceeds by *signs;* where science sees no limit to its renewed investigation of phenomena, mythic thought is restricted to returning to and to reusing elements that are already known and marked.

We may thus wonder where lies the *knowledge* of savage thought, as it is viewed here in the form of mythic thought. In this case as in that of science, says Lévi-Strauss, the world is ordered; phenomena are organized. The signs by which this level is defined are halfway between concepts and perceptions: in them there is always knowledge (which rests in their referential value), but it is organized out of the concrete, colorful substratum. Thus, animals, plants, meteorological phenomena, and so on, staged by the mythical narrative, are always chosen from details and characteristics that are very precisely observed and classified (exactly as in the case of "totemic" classifications). The mythical narrative remains absurd if this level has not been identified first (as we will see later regarding the issue of infrastructures).

In the minds of those who find it surprising, this analysis of *bricolage* could sow a seed of doubt regarding the pertinence of savage classifications. How could they be valid if such indifference is to be observed concerning the terms themselves?

Here we must understand a point that will be decisive in the analysis of myths. *Lévi-Strauss does not in fact say that the contents are indifferent: all his work shows precisely the opposite.* He simply says that the terms have no meaning taken in isolation: "[T]he same characteristics could have been given a different meaning.... Arbitrary as it seems when only its individual terms are considered, the system becomes coherent when it is seen as a whole set.... The terms never have any intrinsic significance. Their meaning is one of 'position'" (*SM* 54–55).

What, then, about *contents*? If the terms make up a system, if they lend themselves to a structural reading, it is due to very concrete, very special determinations (which, depending on the case, may be colors, odors, figurative elements, dimensions in space, sounds, not to mention all the varieties of animals and plants) that lend themselves to the play of oppositions, symmetry, and any other operation that contrasts elements or places them in series. We will run into this issue again, as the central issue in *Totemism,* not as: Why all these animals? but as: Why that animal rather than this animal? Why such and such pair of elements? The answer (as we will see later) is in the details, in the perception of properties or features that organize and construct a system of differences and oppositions.

Thus if we place it in opposition to the activity of an engineer, this activity is appropriately called *bricolage.* The savage mind "plays" with the given world, not in the sense of gratuitous play — for its constructions are motivated as all symbolic systems are in an internal way — but in the sense in which it does not aim to master the natural world in its entirety (for the control targeted by magic remains occasional, most often linked to ritual practices). The only drawback to the notion of *bricolage* is that it implies that the *bricoleur* works with the leftovers of the engineer and thus comes after him. Lévi-Strauss has demonstrated precisely that savage thought is to be placed neither before nor after modern science: it follows another path. The analogy is thus not quite rigorous. It indicates at the very most a manner, that which consists in making do with what is at hand, in organizing sensible contingencies into coherent systems using properties that lend themselves to the expression of logical relations. It thus constructs its structures out of events. It manufactures crystals from debris, just as a kaleidoscope (a frequent comparison used by Lévi-Strauss) can be used to produce as many symmetrical images as one desires from pieces of shapes and fragments of colors that themselves are not symmetrical.

The entire world of daily experience is mobilized, and this demonstrates the importance of ethnographic data. This will now be the subject of our discussion.

Infrastructures

The final reason for differences between myths which all belong to a single *genre* lies in the infrastructures, in the sense of the relations which each society maintains with its environment.   — in RB 40

The savage mind works through ordering the natural world. However, the natural world is not the world in general: it is very concretely the one that is experienced by the people who live in it. It is thus a landscape, a climate, seasons, stars, animals, plants, and also foods, techniques, tools, and so on. The series of fundamental oppositions on which the other classifications are based are first constructed from these givens, in their very great diversity.

From this point of view, we can consider the set of natural conditions and techniques (at all levels) as the infrastructure of symbolic thought, in other words, as the material with which it is provided and from which it operates. However, we must also note that the material conditions in no way constitute a causal system or, if one prefers, a determinism. Put differently, the logic of the symbolism cannot be deduced from the properties of these natural elements. In contrast, observed properties (sizes, colors, flavors, positions in space, forms, periodicity, and so on) are so many available features that could intervene in a construction of thought: "[M]an's relations with his natural environment remain objects of thought: man never perceives them passively; having reduced them to concepts, he compounds them in order to arrive at a system which is never determined in advance: the same situation can always be systematized in various ways" (*SM* 95).

As Lévi-Strauss explains again, infrastructures are like cards dealt to players: the distribution is imposed, yet from there each player produces a series of plays that are unforeseen and unforeseeable. By adding up the constraints due to the nature of the cards available, the rules imposed, and the talent of the various players, one can be certain (from the point of view of statistical probability) that with the same deal there will never be the same game twice.

However, to speak of infrastructures, and thus of superstructures, as Sahlins notes, is perhaps not to use an adequate terminology. Lévi-Strauss abandoned this dualism, as can be seen in a work such as "Structuralism and Ecology" (*VA*, chapter 7). He no longer presents material givens as the conditions or framework of forms of thought. Such forms are already operating at the level of such givens, which are not inert or undetermined: they already have form. Thus the perceiving body already orders the exterior world. We know, for example, that vision is not the passive reception of objects that would be photographically recorded on the retina, but that it is made possible though a coding of distinctive features that allows them to be recognized as objects. The activity of thought deals with a prestructured subject. "Structural arrangements are not a pure product of mental operations; the sense organs also function structurally; and beyond us, there are analogous structures in atoms, molecules, cells, and organisms" (*VA* 117). Yet the activity of thought can be recognized in that it can connect and articulate the various codings that precede it and operate with more general categories, such as inclusion and exclusion, symmetry and equivalence, presence and absence, and so on. The setting, the particular conditions, is used to define an original lexicon according to which forms of thought mark themselves and make up the unique style and contingency of a culture.

Magic and Determinism

Savage systems of classification are based on extremely precise observations: it is a precision that is all the more indispensable since it rests on the play of oppositions founded on details that are often minute and of which the differential value and stable nature have had to be recognized. Thus, in this approach, just as in that of the sciences of our tradition, there is observation, identification of the objectivity of phenomena, and recognition of their reciprocal action. In short, there is indeed what we call "determinism." One might object that this is going too far. Should this judgment not be tempered by the observation of the very numerous behaviors, most often rituals, that belong to what we call *magic?* Is this not the amply demonstrated proof of a complete misunderstanding of the proper notion of determinism?

After all, between technical activity, which is based on knowledge of the nature of phenomena and which evaluates itself on verifiable results obtained through this knowledge, and magical action, which is most often devoid of empirical effectiveness, it seems there is no cause for hesitation. Usually we state this difference in terms of objectivity, on one side, and subjectivity, on the other. In the first case, phenomena would be taken into account in their own order: they interact independently of our consciousness or our desire. In the second case, magic would be nothing but the projection onto the physical world of the agent's desire to obtain such and such result.

This is, in any case, how we usually present magic rituals, and we generally consider this presentation all the more honest since, very often, it is indeed veracity that seems to be lacking in the actions of the officiant of the ritual or the sorcerer: tricks and frauds meant to give a helping hand to a recalcitrant process (the essay in *Structural Anthropology* titled "The Sorcerer and His Magic" gives some surprising examples of this). This point of view, even when it is not meant to be depreciating, nonetheless remains necessarily exterior and amounts to completely ignoring the manner in which the ritual is understood by those who perform it. In fact, the whole perspective is reversed — for the agent of magic action, it is activity with a utilitarian goal and a controllable yield that claims to interfere in the physical world:

> Magical operations, on the other hand, appear to him as additions to the objective order of the universe: they present the same necessity to those performing them as the sequence of natural causes, in which the agent believes himself simply to be inserting supplementary links through his rites. He therefore supposes that he observes them from outside and as if they did not emanate from himself. (*SM* 221)

If the rite continues the natural action, it becomes clear how the idea of fraud loses its meaning: it is but one more link in the series of physical causes.

Certainly one could still object that, *in the end,* modern knowledge and its requirements are the correct ones. However, this is not what is presently at issue: the question is whether or not the savage mind comprehends something like determinism. We must thus note that the point on which it was considered to be in most complete ignorance of determinism is precisely the one where its assertion of determinism is most marked, since *magic, through its rites, amounts to including human actions themselves in the order of natural phenomena.*

Formally, the attitude is the same. The difference is rather in the results and the internal logic of these results. It is what Wittgenstein expressed very well when he wrote: "Simple though it may sound, we can express the difference between science and magic if we say that in science there is progress, but not in magic. There is nothing in magic to show the direction of any development" (Wittgenstein 1979, 13e). This connects exactly with the difference Lévi-Strauss sees between science and *bricolage,* between domesticated thought and savage thought.

Thought Itself or Disinterested Knowledge

In this inquiry into the logic of the sensible, Lévi-Strauss intends — as in all his work — to give anthropology back the ambition of its conception. Yet, even if this is one of its undeniable effects, it is not a question of simply restoring esteem for the rigor, precision, and complexity of the forms of thought of "primitive" societies (we are now well aware of the degree to which criteria of archaism are strained by evolutionist prejudices). It is a more radical question of identifying original forms of thought in which, in a specific way, all of thought operates. To put it differently, it is a question of bringing out how, from social and technological conditions in which the links with the natural world remain full of immediate intimacy and solidarity, the mind, which in its possibilities has no age or place, gives itself the means to construct a complete understanding of the world with which it is provided. This is how we must understand "this 'savage mind.'... [I]n this book [that is, *The Savage Mind*] it is neither the mind of savages nor that of primitive or archaic humanity, but rather mind in its untamed state as distinct from mind cultivated or domesticated for the purpose of yielding a return" (*SM* 219). This is an important remark since it defines an expression that could be misunderstood.

What is to be understood by domesticated thought?

The notion of domestication in anthropology concerns the process of human control of a certain number of animal and vegetable species, marking the development of pastoral and agricultural activities (and thus the process is most often, though not necessarily, linked to the establishment of a sedentary way of life). The most remarkable aspect of this process is the effort to submit nature to methods of which humankind is the exclusive beneficiary (without this necessarily implying detriment to nature itself). We can say that here we see the constitution of a world that is essentially anthropocentered. Domestication is already the establishment of a *project*: it is the coordination of knowledge and planned action for a determined goal regarding the world as a whole. This is the project that science and its modern techniques have brought to completion, and it is in this respect that we can call such thought domesticated. Such thought singles out and orders with a goal of mastery, while "savage thought" receives the world in its profusion of qualities. This does not mean there is confusion or approximation. To the contrary: savage thought classifies and orders no less than the other, but according to other procedures and other ends. We cannot say that it renounces acting on the world (the case of magic, and more importantly its techniques, is proof to the contrary), yet this action (be it mechanical or symbolic) remains essentially caught in a system of articulation and reciprocity with the natural world.

It would be false and absurd to say that savage societies have remained distant from this process since the "arts of civilization" are part of it. However, and this is precisely what can be called the "paradox of the Neolithic," this mastery never tended to disrupt the ecosystem. The difference with respect to the other approach is situated in the very forms of representation of the natural world. One aims to formalize discrete quantities, thus making possible mechanical action on phenomena. The other performs an ordering of the world at the level of sensible qualities treated not as essences but as symbolic values. In the latter case, there are thus as many systems of representation as there are cultures, yet everywhere we find the same "intellectual techniques," such as analogy, homology, inversion, symmetry, and so on.

If thus we had to compare the two approaches *from the angle of their disinterested nature,* we would have to say that it is indeed savage thought that comes out on top since the other is, as Lévi-Strauss says, constituted "with an eye to the yield." One of the traditional arguments against "primitive" thought consists in asserting that knowledge in such thought is acquired essentially for its practical utility. Savages would not consider it worthwhile to classify animal and plant species except in proportion to their possible use. Beyond this end, there would be no quest for knowledge. This is the functionalist thesis focused on the notion of *need.* Malinowski states it with a condescension that, given the time he spent in the field, seems rather misplaced: "The road from the wilderness to the savage's belly and consequently to his mind is very short, and for him the world is an indiscriminate background against which there stand out the useful, primarily the edible, species of animals and plants" (cited in *T* 57). Lévi-Strauss's first step is to expose the falseness of this judgment and demonstrate that, to the contrary, what is astonishing in indigenous systems of classification is the wealth of the inventories, which very largely overflow the boundaries of the criteria of utility. Totemic animals are not chosen because they are "good to eat" but primarily because they are "good to think." Moreover, what is striking in these classifications is their ability to fulfill purely intellectual requirements. For these societies, no less than for ours, what is important is to assign a logical order to observed data and, more fundamentally, to construct an order of the world in general.

One might object that this emphasis on the very speculative, disinterested nature of forms of savage thought totally neglects another aspect that has always leapt out at observers (from ancient travelers to present-day ethnologists): their religious nature, their integration in a sacred representation. Lévi-Strauss replies that these two problems are in fact related, but perhaps not in the way most often imagined. The question is indeed about the nature of the process of making things sacred. Quoting the aphorism (reported by A. C. Fletcher) of a Pawnee sage, "All sacred things must have their place," Lévi-Strauss continues: "[B]eing in their place is what makes them sacred for if they were taken out of their place, even in thought, the entire order of the universe would be destroyed" (*SM* 10).

At the same time, the extreme precision, which appears to us to be obsessive, of certain rituals ceases to seem absurd or to be able to be interpreted in terms of exorcism. The detail of the ritual gains its whole meaning as a dramatic representation of an ordering of the world, an organization of its elements in a given situation. This is what happens among the Pawnee: the crossing of a waterway is transformed into a ceremony meant to stabilize the order of things (which such an action threatens to disturb). Each part of the progression (first contact, immersion of the feet, immersion of the whole body) is accompanied with the invocation of a new element encountered (water, wind, stones, and so on). The ordered enumeration and the invocation cannot be separated. It is as if the requirement of order (its production and maintenance) were so great that it is indeed what gives rise to the ceremonial, even to its impressive, sublime nature.

Beyond Totemism

Savage thought is a classificatory thought, as are all types of thought. How does it operate? The data related to what has been called "totemism" can give us a remarkable demonstration of this. But why speak of totemism here? Why did Lévi-Strauss himself consider his short work *Totemism* as the introduction to *The Savage Mind?* Is there a relation between this old question and the idea of a logic of sensible qualities? Lévi-Strauss would answer: to bring the first question back into the second is all that is required for the demonstration. Totemism then appears as a false problem, and its contradictions resolve themselves when it is understood that it consisted of classificatory procedures and of methods of naming and organizing human groups through reference to natural species. However, let us go back a little.

Ever since the term "totemism" was introduced in the eighteenth century and the theory was explicitly formulated by McLennan in 1870, this issue has remained a "bone of contention" in anthropology. Was it necessary to resolve it, or was it not wiser to set it to the side? The choice between these two attitudes seems to divide the ambitious from the more modest. What was the totemism thesis? It could be summarized as follows: a group or an individual is identified with an animal that then becomes sacred and is the object of alimentary or other prohibitions for those who carry its name.

The catch is that very little data fit this definition. For certain "totemic" groups, the animal or plant is the object of no prohibition; in other cases there are prohibitions with no totem to justify them; finally, it must be added that in many cases totems are not animals, plants, or real beings, and they can be insignificant objects (cords, chevrons, leathers, for example): we are far from identification with the sacred animal and the strong affective charge it supposes.

Before so many contradictions with respect to the original definition or, if one prefers, before such heterogenous data and the difficulty in assembling them into a coherent theory, many anthropologists have considered it wiser not to persist. They have suggested setting the problem aside (without daring, however, to say that it is poorly formulated), for how could one hold Frazer's *Totemism and Exogamy,* published in 1910, to be null and void? Yet as early as 1919, Van Gennep concluded in an update on the issue that it would soon disappear. Indeed, since 1920 most of the treatises and manuals in anthropology have, little by little, eliminated from their accounts not only the issue but the very term "totemism." However, this did not stop a pleiad of prestigious anthropologists from attempting to meet the challenge and to propose an explanation of what seemed to have become unexplainable.

The important chapter 4 of *Totemism,* "Toward the Intellect," shows us, through a brief examination of three series of works, the dissolution of the very idea of totemism and the emergence of the structural hypothesis among very well-known English and American anthropologists, some of whom were closely linked to functionalist positions: Fortes and Firth, Radcliffe-Brown, and E. E. Evans-Pritchard.

In his work on the Tallensi, Fortes shows that this ethnic group (living in the North of present-day Ghana) observes alimentary prohibitions that are shared over a wide area by other groups in the region. These prohibitions target birds such as canaries, turtledoves, domestic chickens; reptiles such as crocodiles, snakes, turtles; certain fish; large grasshoppers; monkeys; wild pigs; ruminants such as goats and sheep; carnivores such as cats, dogs, leopards; and so on. We are forced to recognize that the functionalist hypothesis is no help here because this list is so heterogenous. Some of these animals have no economic interest (they are not edible); other very offensive ones have no particular meaning from the point of view of danger and its avoidance. Fortes's conclusion is: "The totemic animals of the Tallensi thus comprise neither a zoological nor a utilitarian nor a magical class. All that can be said of them is that they are all generally fairly common domestic or wild creatures" (cited in *T* 73).

Two questions appear unavoidable when faced with these facts: (1) Why is there animal symbolism? (2) Why are certain animals chosen rather than others, in other words, why this symbolism rather than another? Meticulous study of these prohibitions reveals to Fortes that some of them are individual, others collective. Among the latter, some are related to specific places. In this way a relation is recognized between certain sacred species, certain clans, and certain territories. The relation between ancestors, unpredictable and capable of harm, and certain carnivorous animals, for example, becomes clearer. Fortes considers that generally animals are apt (unlike plants and ordinary objects) to symbolize human behavior and that of spirits. The use of different types corresponds to differences in our behavior and in our social and moral codes.

Firth proposes the same sort of hypothesis in his study on Polynesian totemism, where he also wonders why animals win out over plants and other elements:

[T]he tendency is then for the more mobile species, endowed with locomotion and versatility of movement, and often with other striking characteristics in the matter of shape, color, ferocity, or peculiar cries, to be represented in greater measure in the list of media which serve as outlet for supernatural beings. (cited in *T* 75)

In spite of their incomplete nature (Why accord less value to nonanimal "totems"?) these approaches of Fortes and Firth already have the merit, in Lévi-Strauss's view, of shedding light on at least two essential aspects of the issue: (*a*) that the denominations are neither indifferent nor arbitrary; and (*b*) that the connection with the eponym is not that of identification or contiguity, but of *resemblance*.

The difficulty then lies in knowing how to situate this resemblance. There is an abundance of examples where such direct correspondence does not exist. Lévi-Strauss concludes from this: "All these facts lead one to search for a connection on a far more general level, a procedure which the authors we have been discussing could scarcely object to, since the connection which they themselves suggest is purely inferential" (*T* 76).

The second problem is what to do with nonanimal totems and even animals other than carnivores that lend themselves poorly, in the analyses of Fortes and Firth, to resemblance with ancestors. Their theory is thus pertinent only for societies in which the cult of ancestors is developed: it remains inoperative in other cases and thus cannot be universalized.

Finally, Fortes and Firth conceive of the resemblance between animals and ancestors very empirically, in other words, as correspondences between qualities identified in each of the beings compared. This is the point at which, for Lévi-Strauss, the essential weakness of their method is situated. These two authors tend, in effect, to place what is signified (strength, cruelty, kindness, and so on) in parallel, when the problem to be solved is why an animal (or plant, or any other) series is placed in parallel with a social series. In other words: *How is it that a series of differences matches another series of differences?* To frame the question in this way is to understand that *"it is not the resemblances, but the differences which resemble each other"* (*T* 77). What is significant is what differs in each series. The series of differences identified in the natural world are then used as a "code" to institute and designate differences in the human world:

The resemblance presupposed by so-called totemic representations is *between these two systems of differences*. Firth and Fortes have taken a great step in passing from a point of view centered on *subjective utility* to one of *objective analogy*. But this progress, having been made, it remains to effect the passage from *external analogy* to *internal homology*. (*T* 77–78)

Going back to an article by Evans-Pritchard will allow us to advance along this path. In his famous study on the Nuer, Evans-Pritchard notes that regarding "totemic" designations of that population, no criterion of utility could be relevant since the list of such designations is so heterogeneous. Many edible animals do not appear on it, and a host of surprising elements (cords, chevrons, leather, and even illnesses) do appear on it, in contrast. "The facts of Nuer totemism do not, therefore, support the contention of those who see in totemism chiefly, or even merely, a ritualization of empirical interests" (quoted in *T* 78).

We are now on the right track: what we call totemism is simply a particular case (which has been deformed and made fantastic by Western observers) of a general procedure in savage societies, which consists in representing the differences in society (or even prompting them if necessary) by means of differences identified in the natural world. An animal that is said to be "totemic" is thus not an animal that would be the object of a mysterious identification between it and a given individual or a given group: an animal is first a "conceptual tool," for as an organism it is a system in itself, and as an individual it is a member of a species. It is thus perfectly apt to be used to signify the unity of a multiplicity and the multiplicity of a unit. It is a tool that gains flexibility from the fact that each animal can be the medium for a number of levels of category: for example, it belongs to several subspecies; it passes through a number of states; it exhibits a number of appearances. This is the case among the Osage Indians: it is never a question of an eagle in general, but of a golden eagle, a spotted eagle, a bald eagle; it is considered to be young, adult, old; to be red, spotted, white. "This three-dimensional matrix, a genuine system *by means of* a creature, and not the creature itself, constitutes the object of thought and furnishes the conceptual tool" (*SM* 149).

Totemism, which was simply the name of an anthropological illusion, covered instead a real problem of classification that, thus solved, becomes the best introduction to the operation of the "savage mind."

Unity and Multiplicity:
Species as a Logical Operator

It is also now clearer why recourse is so frequent to zoological and botanical classifications: they are made up of *species,* or very large sets that can contain a virtually unlimited number of individuals, but these individuals are themselves organisms. Differentiation operates in extension toward a system of definitions and in comprehension toward a system of functions.

"The notion of species thus possesses an internal dynamic: being a collection poised between two systems, the species is the operator which allows (and even makes obligatory) the passage from the unity of a multiplicity to the diversity of a unity" (*SM* 136). Better yet, this operator allows the maintenance of a constant passage between the continuous and the discontinuous, or between the system, which incorporates a collection, and the lexicon, which, in accordance with the dichotomies, defines the properties.

To classify is to establish general characteristics, to identify constants. One might think that, for these reasons, *proper nouns* would escape this enterprise since they represent, in principle, the line at which the classification stops. In general, proper nouns are considered to be kinds of deictic words: they are used to designate an individual, to identify that individual in his or her specificity, without telling us anything about him or her. Naming begins where meaning ends.

However, this tendency of proper nouns to be empty of meaning, which develops in our societies (though it is much less prevalent than it appears, as we will see below), does not exist in savage societies, for "we have conceived of the forms of thought with which we have been concerned as totalizing thoughts, which exhaust reality by means of a finite number of given classes, and have the fundamental property of being *transformable* into each other" (*SM* 172). Without renouncing its own necessity, which is to be a science of the concrete, such a form of thought could not leave a fringe of the real outside its intelligibility: "[E]ither everything, or nothing, makes sense" (*SM* 173). We can thus expect that proper nouns, like the others, are caught in the system of meaning. In other terms: the arbitrary is reduced as much as possible in favor of the motivated.

There are thus rules for forming proper nouns. They are as diverse as cultures themselves, but they exist everywhere. Their principle is simple: "[J]ust as an individual is part of the group, so an individual name is 'part' of the collective appellation" (*SM* 174). Many examples could be given to show that always and everywhere *to name is to classify*. Thus among the Dogons, studied by G. Dieterlen, there is a precise method for attributing proper nouns in function of the position of the individual in a genealogical and mythical series. This method entails that each name is linked to a sex, a line, the structure of the group of relatives, an order of birth (for example: twin or born after twins, or boy born after one or two girls, or the inverse, or boy born between two girls, or the inverse, and so on).

The case of proper nouns seems thus to extend further, into a domain where it was not expected: the ordering activity ensured by the mind. We would be tempted to suppose that nothing, or almost nothing, is left to chance. The question is then whether ethnologists do not risk discovering system in savage (most often implicit) classifications that, in reality, contain far less rigor. In other words, they may risk reducing the zones of the arbitrary and the contingent by introducing an excess of motivation. There is indeed a danger of this. Here there are similarities with kinship systems. Many arrangements become necessary due to variations in concrete situations (natural accidents, wars, demographic changes, confrontations with other civilizations, and so on). Whatever the system, we are always dealing with living beings that tend to adapt themselves. However, such an irruption of history in system, of event in structure, shows that while the system is never safe from contingency, it also tends to reconstitute itself unceasingly and to integrate new, disparate elements within itself, to find in those events the pertinent features, sufficient analogies, to allow homologies to be made between the natural order and the social order. However, this work must be made clear in ethnographic data through conclusive checks (correspondences between autonomous series), so that the structures that appear will indeed be those of the domain under consideration and not those that could very randomly be attributed to them by an observer desiring to discover order and who would perform, using whatever materials were at hand, an involuntary "intellectual *bricolage*" just when claiming to propose a critical analysis. Not everything is structured, reminds Lévi-Strauss: such areas of indetermination are also what ensures the mind its relaxation and allows it to play with its own instruments.

Just as *Totemism* is presented by its author as an introduction to *The Savage Mind,* the latter work in turn appears to be the best introduction to the *Mythologiques,* since mythical narrative supposes and displays, from beginning to end, this logic of sensible qualities (eagle hunting among the Hidatsa, presented in chapter 2 of *The Savage Mind,* already provides a remarkable example of this).

It is difficult not to recognize that Lévi-Strauss caused, with the publication of *The Savage Mind,* a remarkable and profound change in the approach to societies called "primitive." From then on it was impossible to be content with making inventories of forms of organization, practices, rites, myths, to conclude simply that human cultures are extremely diverse. Such benevolent relativism amounts to eluding the only pertinent question: Are these forms of expression of human life and knowledge partial, limited, and thus — the inevitable corollary — inferior? Or must we recognize that everywhere and always the human mind exercises all its means, manifests all its resources and requirements, by using in an original way — in other words in a given culture — the entire variety of available media? We know that the answer to the second question must be in the affirmative because it can be demonstrated.

After this survey of the various types of operations of "savage thought," a number of conclusions can be drawn with certainty.

First, there is the extraordinary ability to differentiate, classify, and organize that is available to a form of thinking performed at the level of sensible qualities and for which an animal can become in itself a very complex, very complete conceptual tool (such as the eagle among the Osage, mentioned above). It can be said that all perceptions function directly as concepts: all of the elements of sensible experience (without excluding the contributions of any of the five senses) become material for classification. Logical activity is not isolated and formulated (or formalized) for itself; it is nonetheless equally present, in a complex, rigorous way, in all the operations performed directly with these elements.

The other question is more difficult. It places us before a sort of enigma that can be formulated thus: Why is there this imperious necessity — which is constant and universal — to differentiate, to oppose, and so to classify? Lévi-Strauss shows clearly how this requirement is accomplished. He is probably the first to have attempted to do so in such a novel, masterly way. However, the explanation of the reason for this need is certainly a difficulty of another order. Here there is the danger of being tempted to resort to a final meaning and to pass a definitive judgment on humankind. Anthropologists know very well that nothing is more relative to a culture than this sort of response, except if one situates the cause in the natural order itself: for example, in the brain. However, the case of the incest prohibition has clearly shown that in human societies there are rules with a universality analogous to that of nature and that nonetheless, as social facts, are necessarily situated on the level of culture. We are thus forced to resort to the canonical formula of conjecture: "[I]t is as if..." Yes, it is as if society exists only through the ordering of the world, which in turn becomes a means of formulating an ordering of human groups, a means of "coding" their relations. This is indeed what Lévi-Strauss means when he speaks of a symbolic origin of society.

One question still remains: What is this savage thought with respect to ours, which Lévi-Strauss defines as domesticated? Ricoeur characterizes it as a "thought which does not think itself" (Ricoeur 1969, 37), thus indicating its insufficiency and marking as an indirect consequence the fundamental requirement of Western thought that, since Greek philosophy, has unceasingly formalized its own approaches. It is certain that when Lévi-Strauss analyzes the operations of savage thought, he does so using thought that thinks itself. But it is precisely to recognize that the one that does not think itself (in this it is symbolic) is no less wholly thought. It does not state what it does, yet it does it: this innocence is the source of its beauty — like an art that does not know itself as art — and perhaps it is no less the source of its fragility.

Chapter 7

The Analysis of Myths

[W]e may be able to show that the same logical processes operate in myth as in science, and that man has always been thinking
equally well.   — *SA* 1:230

The human mind...in myth employs all its faculties simultaneously.   — in RB 52

Lévi-Strauss published his great tetralogy, the *Mythologiques*, between
1964 and 1971. Since then his interest in myths has not flagged, as his
many publications show, in particular *La Voie des masques* (1975)[1] and
La Potière jalouse (1985).[2] In fact, this interest appeared relatively early
in his teaching (such as in the 1952–53 courses on Zuni emergence myths
at the École des Hautes Études), as well as in his writing: as early as
1955, the article "The Structural Study of Myth" (originally published in
English and republished in *SA* 1: chapter 11) constituted a true program,
the suggestions and intuitions of which have never been repudiated, only
refined and above all enriched.

From the start, this article specifies how its author's approach differs from the approaches that have generally prevailed in the analysis of
myths. They can be summarized as follows:

- for certain approaches (with philosophical or psychological tendencies), myths are the expression of fundamental human emotions and
  the dramatization of their conflicts;

- for others (with symbolist tendencies), myths are the metaphorical
  translation of natural phenomena (meteorological, astronomical)
  that are difficult to explain;

- for still others (with sociological tendencies), myths reflect the structures of the society and offer, in the imaginary, a solution to
  problems that cannot be resolved in reality.

In every case, mythical narrative is taken to be a discourse that says
something other than what it seems to say, a discourse that is unable to
articulate its subject as successfully as other discursive forms (such as that

of the commentary itself on myth) or that does not even know what it says (it is then a symptom, an involuntary utterance the message of which is engulfed in its disguises). All these reductionist analyses of myths unwarily adopt the point of view that considers myth to be an archaic genre, a naive discourse, proceeding by pictures and fables. These analyses consider myths to be waiting for their conceptual translation. This is the kind of presupposition that Lévi-Strauss wants to try to set aside from the beginning. For him, myths must be taken as they present themselves, not so that they can be translated into another form of discourse, but to show that myths say very well, very completely, what they say. The problem for us (we who are from another civilization, with another education) is to understand how myths can be simultaneously a narrative about origins, a sociology, a cosmology, a logic, an ethic, an art of living, and a free play of thought. They are the very exercise of "savage thought." Their internal unity and logical coherency are thus not situated on the sides of plausibility or reference. They must be approached differently, and this is what Lévi-Strauss proposes.

In fact, what strikes any reader of myths is the apparently absurd or gratuitous nature of the episodes and details. To want to reduce this absurdity or gratuitousness by interpreting the figures or images, by deciphering the contents considered in themselves, would be to refer them to a meaning that would be prior to or beyond the narrative. This is what symbolists tend to do by searching for universal keys such as archetypes (thus Jung and Eliade) or, very differently, what functionalists attempt to do by looking for what use or need the myth fulfills.

Lévi-Strauss breaks with these approaches. First, he posits the hypothesis that myths from the same cultural area make up a system (as a language is said to do). The search for the interpretation must take place on this level: in the reciprocal relations of narratives and their variants. Next, he reminds us that myths are narratives that have their own rules, rules that extend beyond the specific context of a given culture. Myths not only provide information about one type of society: they tell us about the very processes of their production. In fact, what Lévi-Strauss proposes is a radical change in the method of approaching mythical narratives. The key is to understand the process of formation of such narratives, a process that essentially follows laws of transformation. It includes operations such as permutation, substitution, inversion, symmetry, and so on. The narrative is, in a way, a dramatization of these logical operations. Each of them corresponds to a variant or variation. Thus the existence of different versions of a narrative is far from being a difficulty (as was thought by mythologists who searched for the "correct" or "true" version). To the contrary, it is the system of their transformations that interests mythologists and allows them to reconstitute, or rather to display, the logical operation developed in the narrative. The narrative does not, for all that,

lose its referential value (in other words its relation to the social and natural surroundings), but this value can be read differently: in the system
of relations and not in isolated contents.

It is indeed remarkable that today our use of "myth" is most often in
the singular ("the Oedipus myth," "the myth of Sisyphus," "the myth of
Don Juan," "the Aryan myth," and so on). This notion of myth, centered
on the images or fantasies of a tradition, has virtually nothing to do with
the myths of which Lévi-Strauss speaks. Precisely when he reminded us
(in *SA* 2:65) of the three fundamental rules to observe in the analysis of
myths, his definition was virtually the contrary of what most commen-
tators do. These rules can be summarized: (1) Do not reduce a mythical
narrative to only one of its levels. (2) Do not isolate a myth from the
other myths with which it is in a relation of transformation. (3) Do not
isolate a group of myths from the other groups of myths to which it is
connected.

Now, when in our literary and philosophical traditions we occasionally refer to myths (such as those mentioned above), we do so to indicate
or reconstruct an exemplary figure or to develop an argument around
that figure. The mythical figure becomes the emblem of an idea or thesis.
What we call a "myth" is nothing but the revival of a known figure in a
cultural imagination. In reality, what is produced is an allegory or para-
ble. This form of narrative or myth-poetry can be very instructive for
understanding the critic's universe of fiction or for informing us about
the imaginary of the time, but it is never an analysis of the mythical narrative in the context of the culture in which it was developed and from
which it has been arbitrarily detached.

The First Period: The Linguistic Model

The revolution that Lévi-Strauss proposes in his analysis of myths seems
at first to be analogous to the one he caused in the domain of kinship.
Here again he refers to the linguistic model, at least in his analyses prior
to the *Mythologiques*. This is a choice that was later partially questioned
by Lévi-Strauss himself and that has occasioned a certain number of criticisms. However, before we analyze these later occurrences, it is important
to understand the nature of this initial approach.

It was a question of asking linguistics to provide not schemas that
could be transcribed directly but a methodological orientation. This request seemed all the more reasonable since between the problems of
traditional linguistics and those of the interpretation of myths there was
a very precise resemblance. Traditional linguistics (let us understand by
this: that of philosophical reflection since the Antiquity) searched for a
relation between sound and meaning. This quest was destined to failure because the same sounds are found to be associated with different

meanings in different languages. The methodological revolution was accomplished the day the problem was phrased differently, when it was understood that there could be no meaning in sounds taken in isolation, only in the laws of their combination. The same applies to myths, explains Lévi-Strauss: themes and figures have no meaning by themselves (it is thus vain to try to find in them an archetypal or universal meaning). Here again meaning is to be found in the laws of combination and composition of the elements. Of course this does not mean a pure and simple transposition of linguistic methodology to mythology: it means a model that allows terms to be situated in systems of relations.

Just as in the domain of kinship, the system has to be thought of as a system; in other words, the priority (which does not mean anteriority) of relations over terms has to be considered. In the case of myths, the narrative must be considered to be made up of constitutive units the pertinence of which is determined by the system. Yet how should such units be defined? What system is in question?

Mythical narrative, as a fact of language, is submitted as such to common linguistic analysis and on this level reveals nothing more than any linguistic statement. However, the sentence, which is the largest unit for which linguistics can state rules, is to the contrary precisely the smallest unit for which discourse analysis can consider combinations. The highest level of the first becomes the lowest level of the second. In short, it is not the sentence that must be treated by the mythologist as is the phoneme by the linguist: as an oppositive, relative, and negative entity. However, *sentence* must be understood here as the indication of a threshold, as a discursive unit. This discursive unit must be a unit proper to the genre in question here: the narrative or, more precisely, the mythical narrative. Lévi-Strauss proposes we call this minimal narrative unit, which defines the level to which the other levels may be reduced, a *mytheme*. *A mytheme is thus no more identified with a sentence than it is with a word:* it is not a linguistic entity, but it has the logical form of such an entity. It is not a meaning or a theme, yet it is not separable from the figures that people the narrative. It is inseparable from both of them, and this is indeed what makes it difficult to analyze. It cannot be isolated as an object: it can be identified in combinations and transformations insofar as it is the recurring element in them. Its existence is logical rather than thematic; it rests in the operation and play of relations:

> In any hypothesis, one would be wrong to put the mytheme in the same category as the word or the sentence — entities whose meaning or meanings can be defined, albeit ideally (for the very meaning of a word varies with the context), and arranged in a dictionary. The elementary units of mythical discourse certainly consist of words and sentences which — in this particular use and without

overextending the analogy — are, however, more in the category of phonemes: meaningless units that are opposed within a system, where they create meanings precisely because of this opposition. (*VA* 145)

The analogy between the mytheme and the phoneme is thus purely methodological. In his analysis of myths, Lévi-Strauss has in no way attempted to isolate mythemes in order to then reveal their combinations. The effect would have been artificial, considering the plasticity of the narratives and the wealth of their metamorphoses. This difference between the method advertised and the method used was probably an indication of a difficulty that had not been resolved. Many, occasionally very severe, criticisms have emphasized this.

Thus T. Pavel (1988), after formulating a general challenge to Lévi-Strauss's recourse to Saussurian linguistics (though the inspiration came most often from Jakobson), criticizes the assimilation of mythemes to phonemes, pointing out that while sounds taken in isolation have no meaning, the same is not true of segments of narrative. Why was the phoneme given priority over another linguistic element on a more complex level? "Does the analysis of myths need a phonology, or would it benefit more from a morphology, a syntax, perhaps a lexicon?" (Pavel 1988, 49).

Such criticism is suggestive, yet we must note that it is based on only the 1955 article ("The Structural Study of Myth") and overlooks the developments made in the *Mythologiques,* a work that contains an increasingly complex integration of levels of analysis (the logic of qualities, the logic of forms, the logic of propositions). Taking the phoneme as the model could present a risk insofar as this unit is not only oppositive and relative but above all *negative:* in short, it has no content of its own. It would seem absurd to say the same of the mytheme, except that what we are forgetting here is that the analysis is not situated on the linguistic level, but on another: that of mythical discourse. Lévi-Strauss does not say that the mytheme is empty of *linguistic meaning:* he asserts exactly the opposite (everyone understands sentences like "His head rolled and became a comet," and "The hero climbed up the tree and could not get back down"). Lévi-Strauss says only that a narrative segment or a pertinent feature of a myth provides us with no information outside of the system in which it appears and the relations of transformation in which it is caught. From this point of view its status is *analogous* to that of the phoneme. This analogy makes it possible to radicalize the method in relation to previous approaches. This is the level at which the relation to phonology is established and to which it is limited. For the rest, we see clearly that other resources of linguistic disciplines are used: morphology, syntax and even — yes! — lexicon, as desired by Pavel, who seems to be in ignorance of the 1960 article "Structure and Form," written about the publication in English of *Morphologie du conte* by V. Propp (and reprinted in *SA* 2: chapter 8). In this article, Lévi-Strauss once more reminds us that *structuralism is not a formalism* (even though formal analysis holds an essential position in it, which is obviously in no way contradictory). What is proper to the formalist approach is that it renders content insignificant. What is proper to structural analysis, to the contrary, is that it takes the greatest possible account of the context, of material details specific to each culture (thus a bird will not be a bird in general, but a given type of bird, from a given land, identified by a behavior, a cry, a size, a plumage, a feeding behavior, a way of making nests, a seasonal return, and so on, and contrasted or placed in continuity with other birds or animals in virtue of often minute details that are carefully identified by a given culture). In short, far from ignoring content, structural analysis demonstrates that structure must be understood as the establishment of relations through the basis of the recurrence of pertinent features that are so many specific contents.

This amounts to saying that the syntax is always understood as operating in a definite lexicon. Any lexicon (like any context) is local, empirical, nondeducible (thus the following modest note: "It is currently accepted that language is structural at the phonological stage. We are gradually becoming convinced that it is also structural at the level of the grammar, but less convinced about the vocabulary stage" [*SA* 2:141]). The first task of the mythologist is thus to meticulously establish the ethnographical documentation at all levels (those of the physical environment, social organization, technological conditions, and so on), in short to perform the inventory of what makes up the elements of the lexicon of the mythical narrative. This is what the formalist approach does not do:

> The error of formalism is thus twofold. By restricting itself exclusively to the rules which govern the grouping of propositions, it loses sight of the fact that no language exists in which the vocabulary can be deduced from the syntax. The study of any linguistic system requires the cooperation of the grammarian and the philologist. This means that in the matter of oral tradition the morphology is sterile unless direct or indirect ethnographic observation comes to render it fertile. Imagining that the two tasks can be dissociated, and that the grammatical study can be undertaken first and the lexical study postponed until later, one is condemned to produce nothing but an anaemic grammar and a lexicon in which anecdotes replace definitions. (*SA* 2:141)

Structural analysis simultaneously treats syntax and lexicon, does not dissociate the study of rules from that of contents, and articulates the details proper to each context, while identifying general logical procedures. Thus in its use of the linguistic model structural analysis far from neglects the lexicon: rather, such analysis is notable precisely for the extreme importance it accords to the lexicon. The criticisms on this point are thus entirely unfounded.

Another objection regarding this recourse to the linguistic model deals with a more global aspect and could appear to be more serious. It consists in asking, as Sperber (1975) does, and as might be asked of any language, whether one could envisage a grammar of myths. Now, what defines a grammar is the ability to virtually engender, from the rules that define it, all the sentences in a language without exterior input. Myths, to the contrary, are generated out of each other. The input is exterior and forms thus an infinite, nondenumerable set: "The device that would generate myths depends on an external stimulus; it is thus similar to cognitive devices and opposed to semiological devices: it is an interpretative, not a generative, system" (Sperber 1975, 82–83).

In another work (1985b) the same author notes that the linguistic terminology used regarding myths is purely metaphorical:

Taken literally, most of these metaphors are either meaningless or hopelessly paradoxical. If, for instance, the myths studied in *Mythologiques* belong to a single "language," then each American Indian society has access to only a small fragment of that language. Nobody (except possibly Lévi-Strauss himself) could be said to be even remotely fluent in it. What kind of a language is that? (Sperber 1985b, 82–83)

We could point out that by resorting to the term "language" to designate the mythical whole, Lévi-Strauss was thinking more of language as a system and thus as a virtual mechanism mobilized and actualized by each discourse. Even so the situation has not been improved since it is not a relation of this type that is supposed between myths but — and this is a much more interesting approach — a relation of transformation. This is indeed the reason, as Sperber justly points out, that Lévi-Strauss's great originality, which entirely revitalized the issues of myths and symbolism, lies in the fact that he passed beyond the attempt to establish meanings. "This is one achievement which Lévi-Strauss not only does not claim but explicitly *dis*claims" (Sperber 1985b, 84).

In reality, Lévi-Strauss sensed the difficulties related to using the linguistic model and the concept of meaning. He himself did not formulate the reasons for these difficulties explicitly, but he found a way around them by resorting to another model: music. However, it seems that he provided a remarkable solution to a problem without having truly been aware of its elements or, therefore, sufficiently formulated the solution. This explains the veiled nature of certain formulations, which are extraordinarily intuitive yet unsatisfactory in their methodological formulation. We will examine this later.

The Function of Myth and the Mind in Liberty

[T]here is nothing more abstract than myths.
— in GC 55

According to Lévi-Strauss, mythical activity is a little like the judgment of taste according to Kant: it is free and, at the limit, gratuitous. It "has no obvious practical function" (*RC* 10). Most traditional interpretations of myths look above all for the etiological elements, which are certainly to be taken into account, but which cannot limit the interpretation of a myth. In a myth it is as if the mind were testing itself behind closed doors, as if it were examining its logical possibilities through play, as if it could oppose its own determinism to that which tends to be imposed by the exterior world. Here we come to what is generally one of the essential contributions of the structural approach: to have been able to show us and remind us about the nature and meaning of an *internal constraint*. We can use this term to designate the logic that is obeyed by any set of elements governed by a law of structure, in other words, any system. From this point of view, Lévi-Strauss had a good model in the phonology of Trubetzkoy. He developed his own demonstration with the analysis of kinship relations and broadened and completed it with the analysis of myths.

To speak of internal constraints means that, independent of the exterior conditions, the relations between the terms are distributed, organized, and transformed according to purely logical requirements (opposition, inversion, symmetry, negation, and so on). There is then separation with respect to the referent, entrance into a new "space," defined by what Lévi-Strauss calls the "laws of the human mind."

This autonomy of the mythical field might not be visible to an observer who remains in a single culture and knows only a very limited number of myths. What such an observer will, in contrast, find very obvious is the importance of contextual data provided by ethnography. On an initial level, these data are essential, and Lévi-Strauss himself devotes a major part of his studies to them (moreover, it is ignorance of context that he reproaches of formalist studies and symbolist approaches). In short, when context is taken into account, the "internal syntagmatic chain" appears essentially determined by the "external paradigmatic set" (*HA* 356).

In contrast, the greater the number of myths studied, the more clearly the multidimensionality of the mythical field appears. Mythologists then become aware of another phenomenon:

On the one hand, the paradigmatic relationships internal to the field increase in number much more rapidly than the external relationships, which indeed reach a ceiling, as soon as all the available ethnographical information has been assembled and utilized, so that the context of each myth consists more and more of other myths and less and less of the customs, beliefs and rites of the particular population from which the myth in question derives. (*HA* 356)

This text is important in several respects. It allows us to see that the mythical universe is made autonomous due to an internalization of the paradigmatic level, but this process would not be possible without another (to which we will return later): that all myths are transformations of other myths or other groups of myths. Thus we can make sense of the assertion that myths are experiments in logical possibilities.

These reflections on the free play of the mind in mythical activity should lead to the conclusion that myths do not, and cannot, have a function. Yet Lévi-Strauss explicitly says the contrary: the function of myths is to reduce — or at least to attempt to reduce — oppositions encountered in reality, of which some can be overcome, but others cannot: "[M]ythical thought always progresses from the awareness of oppositions toward their resolution" (*SA* 1:224). In other words, mythical speculations "do not seek to depict what is real, but to justify the shortcomings of reality, since the extreme positions are only *imagined* in order to show that they are *untenable*" (*SA* 2: "The Story of Asdiwal," 173).

How does myth intervene in these contradictions? This is precisely where the narrative play and logical subtleties begin:

[S]ince the purpose of myth is to provide a logical model capable of overcoming a contradiction (an impossible achievement if, as it happens, the contradiction is real), a theoretically infinite number of slates [i.e. variants] will be generated, each one slightly different from the others. Thus, myth grows spiral-wise until the intellectual impulse which has produced it is exhausted. Its *growth* is a continual process, whereas its *structure* remains discontinuous. (*SA* 1:229)

We saw above that Lévi-Strauss rejects the sociological thesis that would make myth merely an imaginary solution to real contradictions perceived in society or the surrounding universe. We must wonder thus what is the original status of this *mediation* function. For, on one hand, a myth is not the simple reflection of the society where it is encountered; on the other hand, the elements that enter into its images (animals, plants, landscapes, meteorological phenomena, foods, technical instruments, and so on) refer to an infrastructure of which there must be precise knowledge (which is why, says Lévi-Strauss, mythologists must also be botanists,

zoologists, meteorologists, geologists, and so on, as much as they are ethnologists and sociologists). Such knowledge is so true and so important
that it is the empirical basis from which variations (and variants) of a
single myth in different geographical areas can be understood. This fact
is largely proven concerning the transformations that go from tropical
America (in the South) to temperate America (in the North).

Yet, whatever its importance, this empirical foundation does not permit an explanation of myth. The elements of social reality, like those of
the natural world, are taken as terms in a lexicon. Their status is that of
"the instrument of meaning, not its object" (*HA* 341). "Of the sun and
the moon, the same thing can be said as of the countless natural beings
mythically manipulated. Mythical thought does not seek to give them
a meaning — it expresses itself through them" (*SA* 2:221). We should,
moreover, say that it manifests itself rather than that it expresses itself,
as is generally the case with symbolic systems. "The myth is certainly related to given facts, but not as a *re-presentation* of them. The relationship
is of a dialectic kind, and the institutions described in the myths can be
the very opposite of real institutions" (*SA* 2:172).

A good example of this is provided in the study "Four Winnebago
Myths" (in *SA* 2: chapter 10). Lévi-Strauss takes up the analysis of these
myths, which were collected and presented by Paul Radin. He shows that
the fourth, which seems to be atypical in relation to the first three, is in
fact a transformation of the others (we will see the importance of this
concept below). However, what interests us here is that in the fourth
narrative, a social situation appears that does not correspond to Winnebago society. Ethnologists are tempted to suppose that such a situation
could have existed in the past and that this myth refers to that time. Such
a hypothesis is wholly undocumented and so remains unverifiable. But,
wonders Lévi-Strauss, is it necessary? Does it not entail misunderstanding the inventive ability that is proper to myths? "It does not follow that
whenever a social pattern is alluded to in a myth this pattern must correspond to something real and attributable to the past if, under direct
scrutiny, the present fails to offer an equivalent" (*SA* 2:203–4). In myths,
the mind plays freely, but such play is neither gratuitous nor arbitrary. If
a myth features a social situation that corresponds to nothing real or that
at least contradicts that of the society from which it comes, it does not
do so in order to deny or idealize that reality. Its purpose is to offer, in
the series of versions, a variant that replies very precisely to the others
by inverting their values. Thus in the fourth Winnebago myth in question
"the so-called stratified society should be interpreted not as a sociological
vestige, but as a projection on some imaginary social order of a logical
structure wherein all the elements are given both in opposition and in
correlation" (*SA* 2:207).

A hypothesis of this type was new in the analysis of myths: Lévi-

Strauss was probably the first to propose it systematically and to demonstrate its validity. In isolation it might have appeared debatable, but when many examples are given its remarkable pertinence is shown. First it has the advantage of delivering us from an exhausting search for causes (that which required that each myth deal with an empirical referent) and an all-encompassing semiology (which had to find a meaning proper to each narrative). However, a new problem arises with the discovery of the free play of combinative possibilities revealed by certain variants: What could be the source of these combinations if it is not the human mind itself? This, thus, is the ultimate goal of the study in the *Mythologiques*.

Another way of approaching this problem would be to show, with respect to various examples, how, beginning with a given version of a myth, variants multiply, not arbitrarily, but as so many attempts to explore that myth's logical possibilities. This is the case in "The Story of Asdiwal." This myth of the Tsimshian of the Northwest Coast of North America (British Columbia) is presented and analyzed in detail in *Structural Anthropology*, volume 2 (chapter 9), and it is taken up again in *The View from Afar* under the title "From Mythical Possibility to Social Existence" (chapter 11). Other than the three known Tsimshian versions, there is one version from an aristocratic Kwakiutl group that differs with respect to the others in very notable ways. We are indeed faced with a group of transformations the analysis of which would allow us to see the situation to which the myth responds. This situation seems to be the contradiction felt between the high world (mountains and celestial space, hunting areas) and the low world (the marine and underwater world, fishing areas). The function of the hero, through the facts about him and his actions, is to manifest this contradiction and possibly provide a solution.

In two of the Tsimshian versions, the hero fails to overcome the contradiction (each world leaves him longing for the other, and he ends his career transformed into a rock). The myth stages the impossibility of living harmoniously in these two universes: they remain antithetical extremes. However, a third Tsimshian version offers a sort of solution: the hero goes to live on the coast, halfway between the two worlds. The contradiction is not resolved, it is evaded with "neither one nor the other." The movement stops with an antihero who renounces a quest judged vain. This is indeed also a failure.

The Kwakiutl version (or, more precisely, that of the noble house of Naxnaxula) is entirely different. This version seems at first to be a mixture of the preceding ones, but in fact another logic clearly organizes its episodes and constructs the solution. Here the purpose of the myth is to found, through the success of the hero, the family's claims to status and thus its hegemony. It does this by taking up the structure of the third Tsimshian version and inverting it. Instead of conceiving a disjunction and thus a neutralization of terms (neither mountain nor sea), it proposes a synthesis. Just as the hero succeeds in the synthesis of kinship and alliance by being simultaneously the chief of his mother's tribe and of that of his wife, he succeeds in the synthesis of mountain and sea by remaining a hunter, but a "sea hunter."

In these narratives it is as if myths had the special faculty of being able to explore all the possibilities or all the variations of a scenario or situation. It seems, in certain cases, that they are explored purely gratuitously, as if rejected possibilities and those not actualized in the social reality nonetheless had to appear as available or, conversely, as impossible to realize. Each case must be evaluated independently, but the process always remains surprising:

> [M]ythical thinking proves mysteriously prolific. It never seems satisfied with offering one single response to a problem: once formulated, this response enters into a play of transformations in which all other possible responses emerge together or successively. The same concepts, rearranged, exchange, contradict, or invert their values and their functions, until the resources of this new combinatorics are dissipated or simply exhausted. (*VA* 172)

While it is true that a myth, in a given place, has a precise relation to the sociological situation (kinship relations, interethnic relations), this is not a simple, though perhaps disguised or inverted, representation of that situation. It plays with it in a way by presenting a range of alternatives that indicate all sorts of other possibilities that have been abandoned or that simply cannot be made real. In this sense, a myth, or rather its many variants, escapes all functionalist or finalist explications. This, however, in no way diminishes its ability to convey the situation experienced: myths do this regularly, and their success can be identified in what Lévi-Strauss calls the "sociological code." However, this is only one of the aspects of mythical narrative. Myths never limit themselves to a single level of reality. They tell much more in every case by simultaneously integrating cosmic, religious, topographical, meteorological, and other elements.

Analogical Reasoning

Most often mythical characters seem, at first sight, incomprehensible either with respect to what they represent or in regard to the nature of their actions. However, some are even more enigmatic than the others. Any search for meaning on an immediate level dealing with the isolated content of the figure is doomed to failure. What Lévi-Strauss shows is that the choice of figure (one type of animal, for example, rather than another) can be understood only if we consider the logical operation performed by mythical thought. The answer appears as the end of an analogical line of thought that develops a perfectly coherent play of mediations and substitutions. This seems the only approach that could possibly resolve, for example, the enigma of the character called the *trick-ster* — the deceiver — present in most North American mythologies. Why is this character generally incarnated in the coyote and the crow?

The coyote eats carrion. It is thus related to predators that consume the flesh of animals, but it does not kill what it eats, which brings it closer to producers of vegetable food. The crow is perceived as a garden preda-tor. It is thus to the plant world as the coyote is to the animal world. However, the chain continues since the herbivore can be considered to be a collector of vegetable food while becoming itself food for carnivores. In short, on one end of the system there are those who feed themselves by killing (hunting animals), and on the other end there are those who feed themselves without killing (herbivorous animals). Between the two extremes there is the series of carrion-eaters and predators that are me-diations (they steal food — either flesh or vegetable — that they have not killed or produced). This series corresponds to that of the set: war, hunt-ing, agriculture; which is itself caught in the life/death opposition. The trickster figures make the passage between these two terms possible: they permit the conception of a paradoxical relation (life carries death, and death makes life possible). This is not the object of a direct statement (such as the one just made here as a commentary): this thought oper-ates in a dramatization — the mythical narrative — in which the trickster character may play a central role, depending on whether this tension is to be resolved or simply pointed out. The figures can be understood only in their reciprocal positions and in the movement of the progressive media-tion that they perform between the two extremes of the dilemma. These extremes are not incorporated into the theme as such, but implied in the interlocking of analogies of the style: what *A* is to *B*, *C* is to *D*, and so on. This is indeed how "mythical thought always progresses from the awareness of oppositions toward their resolution" (*SA* 1:224).

The expression "awareness" is not perhaps the most appropriate ex-cept if it is taken in the broad sense of experience or of taking into account. The logic that is active at the level of mythical figures is not a logic that is explicitly recognized or developed as a theme. It is not the object of a discourse on its own operation. It remains immanent in the figures and operations through which it occurs. In short, it is symbolic.

The same might be said of any set of mythological narratives. In this way we can follow the transformations of cooking fire in the *Mytholo-giques*. Why was this angle of approach chosen for speaking of the Indian myths of the two Americas? This could appear unusual to philosophers and mythologists used to considering mythologies essentially from the an-gle of divinities and their actions. Lévi-Strauss, however, wonders what world such narratives produce with what elements, with what data, since this type of narrative does not essentially (or does not at all) tend to organize the episodes of a plausible action, but rather to organize a universe by favoring elements that can make up so many semantic layers in the unfolding of the narrative. The narrative links these blocks of representations (these "parcels of relations"), the lexicon of which is provided by natural or cultural sensible data.

Why was the culinary universe and its categories chosen as the source of the lexical reference to be used to approach an entire set of myths from the two Americas? For the general reason (the givens of which vary from culture to culture) that cooking, through the mastery of fire that it supposes and through its many different ways of altering what is natural to produce the cultural, is capable of being the medium and means of formulating a multitude of formal relations at the level of sensible elements. Thus from the *raw* two essential states of food are possible: the *cooked,* which is its cultural transformation, and the *rotten,* which is its natural transformation. On this fundamental triangle all sorts of intermediary states can be placed, such as the *boiled* and the *roasted,* for example. Both of these belong to cooking and thus to culture, but because roasting leaves the interior of the meat relatively raw and can be done on a naked flame, it remains closer to the natural point. In contrast, boiling produces a complete cooking and supposes the mediation of a utensil that can contain water; thus it is closer to the cultural point. Moreover, boiling produces the paradox of cooking the food using water, which is the contrary of fire. There would, therefore, seem to be good reasons to guess that the boiled appears everywhere as the more elaborate state, indicating more refined values than the roasted. However, to assert this would be to give in to the formalist temptation, for although the opposition of the roasted to the boiled is indeed that of least to most elaborate (as is shown by numerous ethnographic examples), it could also be that the relation is inverted under another consideration: the boiled could be placed on the side of endo-cooking (affinity with the interior, the concave, intimacy: boiled food would then be like a stew, home cooking, cooking by wives and mothers), while roasted food would belong to exo-cooking, that of open, public festivities, banquets, and would connote the world of men. In this case the roasted would be placed on the side of culture and prestige, while the boiled would display affinity with the rotten due to its liquid element and the process of mixing (thus *olla podrida* in Spanish, or "putrefied pot," which designates the contents of a pot of meat and vegetables). In sum, what remains stable is the roasted/boiled opposition, but the values attached to each term can be nuanced or even inverted. This cannot be deduced: only ethnographic study can establish it case by case (various examples of this are given in *OTM* 482ff.).

We can imagine now how the system can become more complicated if, in addition to the preceding ways of cooking, we consider others such as smoking, grilling, frying, marinating, drying, steaming, baking, braising. For suddenly all sorts of categories come into play at once, making systems of oppositions, homologies, symmetries, and so on, possible. Smoking, for example, is related to roasting (the meat is cooked over a fire), but it differs in the use of a wooden grill (thus the mediation of a utensil) and in the layer of air between the fire and the food. Thus, in relation to roasting, we already have differential features marked by the oppositions *near/far* and *fast/slow*. In contrast, the existence of a utensil and the depth of the cooking links smoking to boiling, though the utensil — the wooden grill (in most Indian cultures) — must be destroyed. We therefore have the following system: the boiled is related to the rotten (thus to the perishable), but the utensil remains; the smoked is a food that will last, but in exchange the utensil must be perishable. "It would seem as if the prolonged enjoyment of a cultural product involved, sometimes on the level of ritual and sometimes on that of myth, a corresponding concession in favor of nature: when the result is long-lasting, the means must be precarious, and vice-versa" (*OTM* 489). Thus in the cooking system there is a relation between nature and culture, lasting and immediate, near and far, which, added to all the different ways of cooking, permits a considerable number of combinations and thus of expressions of the logical modalities of thought. These are the possibilities that mythical narratives use and integrate as "codes" throughout their narration. According to Lévi-Strauss, the set of these possibilities can be reduced to a matrix which can be represented by a triangle on which the principal differences are situated (*OTM* 490; see figure 7).

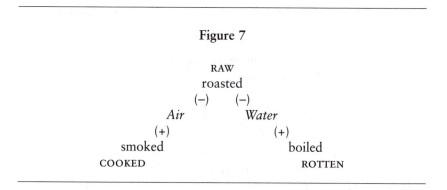

Figure 7

RAW
roasted
(–)   (–)
Air   *Water*
(+)   (+)
smoked   boiled
COOKED   ROTTEN

No specific myth presents the table of the elements in this way. Depending on the context, each myth plays on some of these oppositions by linking them to other terms in different semantic registers. Yet it is remarkable that we always find this play of mediation between systems of oppositions with two or more extremes.

The myth's manner of searching for a middle solution by staging elements that are themselves susceptible to being mediators can be illustrated strikingly by a whole set of narratives presented under the title "The Canoe Journey of the Moon and the Sun" in the third part of *The Origin of Table Manners.*

In order to see how the canoe, the sun and the moon, and, finally, the voyage itself can function as logical and semantic operators, we must, as Lévi-Strauss reminds us, take precise account of the ethnographic data (in other words, we must compile the lexicon). From this point of view, attention must be paid to the fact that the seats in the canoe are assigned very carefully. The use of this kind of boat requires at least two passengers: one in the back responsible for the helm, and another responsible for paddling but who, for reasons of balance, necessarily must sit at the front. When navigating, neither passenger may move toward the front or back or lean to the side without the risk of capsizing the canoe. They are thus associated and linked by a necessary distance: neither too close, nor too far away. Moreover, generally, the task of the helmsman, which requires little energy, is given to the weakest of the two (or of the group): a woman or an old man, while the other passenger or passengers must be more robust. These elements will serve as media to portray oppositions, correlations, incompatibilities, extreme positions, and their intermediate solution. The two necessarily distanced positions in the canoe will thus be appropriate as those of the sun and the moon, in their reciprocal dependency, their distance, their common movement. Better yet, the cooking fire often carried by Indians during their voyages is placed in the center of the boat, thus apt as a symbol of a successful mediation between the sun's excessive heat and its nocturnal absence. The canoe becomes a mental operator capable of carrying in narratives a multitude of oppositions and mediations between extremes such as those of close or distant alliance, hot and cold, day and night, masculine and feminine, irreversible time and periodicity, and so on:

> By being too close to each other, the sun and the moon would create a rotten or burnt world, or both these effects together; by being too far apart, they would endanger the regular alternation of day and night and thus bring about either the long night, a world in which everything would be inverted, or the long day which would lead to chaos. The canoe solves the dilemma: the sun and moon embark together, but the complementary functions allocated to the two passengers, one paddling in the front of the boat and the other steering at the back, force them to choose between the bow and the stern, and to remain separate. (*OTM* 181–82)

Thus the myth exposes a thought and actualizes it.

The Second Period: The Musical Model

It has sometimes been said that with the *Mythologiques*, Lévi-Strauss passed from the linguistic model, which had prevailed until then, to a musical model. This is only partially true since the linguistic model still remains pertinent on the *methodological* level: mythemes are given a status analogous to that of phonemes. In other words, they are rendered purely differential, oppositional, semantically empty minimal units. Lévi-Strauss seems first to ask music to provide him with an *expository* model, and he explains his choice in the introduction (the "Overture") of the *Mythologiques* and comes back to it in his general conclusion (the "Finale," obviously). Moreover, in the first volume of the *Mythologiques*, Lévi-Strauss chose to give the various parts or moments of his exposition the names of musical genres ("The 'Good Manners' Sonata," "Fugue of the Five Senses," "A Short Symphony"), but he abandons this procedure in the following volumes since it proves excessive to simulate in explicatory discourse a form of language belonging to a specific art. Yet this form of exposition increasingly reveals itself to be something else that Lévi-Strauss clearly felt but seems not to have identified clearly: it is also a form of analysis, or rather what renders inoperative, or even illegitimate, the traditional form of analysis. The whole question is how a metalanguage can intervene in, or with respect to, a symbolic process. Can it dissect such a process without necessarily missing it or expose it without necessarily being a part of it? Outside? Inside? We will see how Lévi-Strauss struggled with this dilemma and how he asked music to provide an *analogon,* as a form of solution.

This expository model is justified first by the synchrony/diachrony opposition. Mythical narratives, like polyphonic pieces, must first be given a linear reading (the succession of narrative sequences in one case, the melodic sequence in the other), and then they must be read from top to bottom (the semantic levels of the myth; the harmonic levels in the musical composition). This analogy regarding the relation of the simultaneity of the levels, already pointed out in the 1955 article, is perhaps not the most interesting. There is another much more important relation regarding language and time.

Myths, like music, can be called languages precisely in that they ensure communication between those who hear them (which supposes — an initial condition of any language — that signs are stable within a given community). The analogy ends there since, unlike language, neither of them is able to give rise to a signified that is neither separate from nor confused with the signifier. Music seizes the listener in and by sound. Myths produce their effects through analogous means. Now, what does this mean?

A narrative, like a musical performance, exists only in a temporal succession. Music, through the treatment of sounds, which are chosen and used in accordance with tonal scales, unceasingly mobilizes physiological rhythms in the listener, creating expectations, pauses, tensions, and their resolutions. This directly perceivable action is simultaneously the intelligible operation of music. Unlike in the case of spoken language, no signified detaches itself to allow itself to be translated into another code.

In what way does mythical narrative pertain to this model? It cannot be from the angle of its membership in ordinary language (of which it upsets neither the syntax nor the lexicon). Thus it can be only from another level, which makes language enter into another system or dimension. The hearing of a myth, like that of a piece of music, occurs in irreversible time and yet "transmutes the segment devoted to listening to it into a synchronic totality, enclosed within itself" (RC 16). However, this temporal similarity (which begins with physiological rhythms) is twinned with another, which is that of uniting the intelligible and the perceivable. On the very level of the dramatization of animal and human figures and in the articulation of a diversity of natural elements, myths state a cosmology, an ethic, an aesthetic, and so on. Traveling through the narrative sequences, overflowing them, this simultaneity of schemas offers itself to the listener as a thought system immanent in the events and images evoked. This immediate, complete capturing as sensation and knowledge is what likens myths to music. Between these two forms, however, there is a fundamental difference in application:

> Just as music makes the individual conscious of his physiological rootedness, mythology makes him aware of his roots in society. The former hits us in the guts; the latter, we might say, appeals to our group instinct. And to do this, they make use of those extraordinarily subtle cultural mechanisms: musical instruments and mythic patterns. (RC 28)

Therefore, it is important to understand this recourse to the musical model if we hope to grasp the coherency of the approach proposed and its application by Lévi-Strauss, who finally gives a clear reason for it when he says that what is proper to both myth and music is that they cannot be transposed into another system of meaning. Music's "peculiar quality is to express what can be said in no other way" (RC 31), but can it be put into relation with myths that are stated in common language? At what level can isomorphism be discerned? This level can be only the metalinguistic, that of the narrative system. Only on this level does a myth operate on time in a way identical to the way music does. What is proper to this sort of operation is that it *is not substitutable*; it exists only as performance. In other words, it exists only for its addressee and during its accomplishment:

In both instances the same reversal of the relation between transmitter and receiver can be observed, since in the last resort the latter discovers its own meaning through the message from the former: music has its being in me, and I listen to myself through it. Thus the myth and the musical work are like conductors of an orchestra, whose audience becomes the silent performers. (*RC* 17)

The question we might ask here would be then: Does this not also apply to the reception of any work of art, to the perception of a painting or to the reading of a novel? Wherein lies the difference? What is it that music among the arts and myths among genres of discourse have in particular that sets them apart in their domains and makes them resemble each other?

It is as if in the case of myths, unlike in the cases of problems in kinship or "totemic" classification, something was bothering Lévi-Strauss in the exposition of the logical system that underlies their activity; as if, in this case, unlike in previous domains of research, there was an irremediable loss linked to the analysis; as if the disclosure of the internal architecture of myths and their functioning was necessarily done at the price of their direct enjoyment. This is why (yet is it paradox, modesty or lucidity?) the "Overture" of *Mythologiques* ends with an invitation to the reader to forget the book about to be read and with the hope that, beyond it, the reader will be "carried toward that music which is to be found in myth" (*RC* 32). However, this necessarily will be by gaining on one level and losing on another: what is gained is the "secret meaning" of such narratives (this formulation sounds bizarrely "hermeneutic"), and what is lost is "the power and majesty that cause such a violent emotional response when it [the secret meaning] is experienced in its original state, hidden away in the depths of a forest of images and signs and still fresh with a bewitching enchantment, *since in that form at least nobody can claim to understand it*" (*RC* 32; emphasis added).

However, this explanation put forward in the "Overture" is probably insufficient. The "Finale" proposes another that, without repudiating the first, modifies and completes it in an original way (and without a doubt the years spent reading and recording hundreds of myths caused the author to change his view). It is no longer only a question of opposing analysis to performance: it is a question of asserting that myths, like music, cannot be translated into a code other than their own. This is probably a consequence of the importance gained by the concept of transformation: "The myths are only translatable into each other in the same way as a melody is only translatable into another which retains a relationship of homology with it" (*NM* 646). Now, by presenting myths (and their systems) in this manner, Lévi-Strauss was doing nothing other than defining them as a symbolic process, which (as we saw in chapter 5) is essentially characterized by its operative power. A myth (or rather a group of myths) organizes elements, constructs an order. It has no meaning in itself; it is at most what makes a meaning possible through the arrangement it produces:

> A myth proposes a grid, definable only by its rules of construction. For the participants in the culture to which the myth belongs, this grid confers a meaning not on the myth itself but on everything else: that is, on the images of the world, of the society, and of its history, of which the members of the group are more or less aware, as well as on the images of the questions with which these various objects confront the participants. In general, these scattered givens fail to link up and usually collide with one another. The matrix of intelligibility supplied by myth allows us to articulate those givens in a coherent system. (*VA* 145–46)

The discovery of this performative aspect of mythical narrative is clearly what led Lévi-Strauss to emphasize the analogy of myth and music and to suggest the self-effacement of mythologists before their subject, as if he had understood that the exegesis of a myth cannot be done, that the only task possible is that of reconstructing its operating mechanism. This also explains the recourse not to a discipline like linguistics but to an art like music.

Transformation Groups and the Canonical Formula

> Properly speaking, there is never any original: every myth is by its very nature a translation.   —*NM* 644

Ever since his 1955 article (see above), Lévi-Strauss has proposed a general formula of the structure of myths, which he has unceasingly confirmed and verified in his later research (even though he has made very little explicit use of it, as has been pointed out).
The presentation of this formula is in the following terms:

> [E]very myth (considered as the aggregate of all its variants) corresponds to a formula of the following type:

$$\text{F}x\ (a) : \text{F}y\ (b) :: \text{F}x\ (b) : \text{F}a\text{-}1\ (y)$$

> Here, with two terms, *a* and *b*, being given as well as two functions, *x* and *y*, of these terms, it is assumed that a relation of equivalence exists between two situations defined respectively by an inversion of *terms* and *relations*, under two conditions: (1) that one term be replaced by its opposite (in the above formula *a* and *a-1*); (2) that an inversion be made between the *function value* and the *term value* of two elements (above, *y* and *a*). (*SA* 1:228)

When he presented this formula in 1955, Lévi-Strauss had already done a certain amount of specific research on myths, but he was far from having performed the survey that is that of the *Mythologiques*. The hypothesis was daring. Was this audacity profitable? Yes, if we accept not only that Lévi-Strauss was not forced to belie his formula but that, at many crucial points in his research, his formula was what allowed him to find a way through certain impasses (apparent incoherencies or insufficiencies in the available narratives). The canonical formula allowed the deduction of the probable existence of versions matching the succession of transformations already known — a "transcendental deduction," as Lévi-Strauss says, which is most often confirmed by empirical documentation.

A good example of the pertinence and fecundity of the method, as well as of the use of the canonical formula, is provided in *The Jealous Potter*. The cycle of myths analyzed in this work begins with a Jivaro narrative in which there is a woman named Aôho who has two husbands: Sun and Moon. The former, who is warm and powerful, mocks the other, who is cold and weak. Moon is offended, flees to the sky using a vine, blows out Sun, and cuts the vine by which the wife, carrying a basket of clay, is attempting to reach him. The clay falls here and there on the earth, and, as she is falling, the wife metamorphoses into a bird, the Goatsucker (Aôho), of which she is the namesake and whose plaintive cry is heard at each new moon from then on.

What this narrative (even in its summary form) reveals is primarily a relation, which is incomprehensible at first sight, between conjugal conflict, clay for pottery, and the bird, Goatsucker. More specifically, we should say that we are dealing with four terms:

• two concerning attitudes and functions: jealousy and pottery;

• two concerning characters: wife and Goatsucker.

Lévi-Strauss proposes the application of the canonical formula in which a and b designate characters, and x and y designate functions;

$$\text{thus, } Fx\,(a) : Fy\,(b) :: Fx\,(b) : Fa\text{-}1\,(y)$$
$$\text{becomes here: } Fj\,(g) : Fp\,(w) :: Fj\,(w) : Fg\text{-}1\,(p)$$

where j $(=x)$ = "jealousy"; p $(=y)$ = "pottery"; g $(=a)$ = "Goatsucker"; and w $(=b)$ = "woman."

This can be read in the following way: "the function 'jealous' of the Goatsucker is to the function 'pottery' of the woman as the function 'jealous' of the woman is to the function 'inverted Goatsucker' of the 'pottery'" (see *JP* 57–58). Of course light must be shed on the relation between jealousy and pottery, but we can already see that, in the fourth element of the formula, there is an inversion of the value between the term and the function. This transformation leads to the hypothesis that there are other narratives in which there appears a character who is the inverted figure of the Goatsucker. Indeed, such is the case of the Ovenbird, a bird that appears in the myths of other populations and that presents all the characteristics opposite to those of the Goatsucker: it is diurnal; it has a joyful cry; it builds nests; and so on. These narratives of the inversion, in consequence, gain meaning only in relation to those that they inverse and of which they are the logical closure.

In the relation of pottery to jealousy we see the appearance, in other myths, of the figures of the sloth, the howler monkey, and the frog, as well as the themes of excrement, the head that flies and turns into the moon, and the body that transforms into a meteor. Without entering into the details of these narratives, let us go directly to the explanation of what links these figures before we reconsider their transformations:

> Every art imposes form on matter, but, among the so-called arts of civilization, pottery is probably the one in which the transformation is most direct, involving the smallest number of intermediate stages between the raw material and the product, which comes from the craftsman's hands already formed, even before it undergoes firing. (*JP* 177)

In very many civilizations, Lévi-Strauss notes, the work of the demiurge is compared to that of the potter. "But imposing a form on matter does not mean simply imposing a discipline. The raw material, pulled out of the limitless range of potentialities, is lessened by the fact that, of all these potentialities, only a few will be realized: all demiurges, from Prometheus to Mukat, have jealous natures" (*JP* 178). This control exercised over matter, like the extremely delicate nature of the manufacturing and fir-ing techniques, creates around pottery attitudes and rites of exclusion of which "jealousy" is the narrative equivalent. If woman becomes the agent par excellence, it is because, when pregnant, she is identified with a vessel both by her appearance and her activity. Suddenly there is a whole series of transformations dealing with the relations between the container and the content, the unformed and the transformed, nature and culture, which come into play in the mythical narratives dealing with pottery. We have thus a symmetry between cultural transformations of clay:

clay $\Rightarrow$ extraction $\Rightarrow$ modeling $\Rightarrow$ firing $\Rightarrow$ vessel (container);

and the natural transformations of food:

food (contents) $\Rightarrow$ cooking $\Rightarrow$ digestion $\Rightarrow$ ejection $\Rightarrow$ excrement.

Narrative series in which the various mythical figures (incontinent howling monkey, sloth stricken with retention, and so on) appear are situated on these two lines as so many transformations of the schema container/content, for which pottery is the model:

Any myth or sequence in a myth would remain incomprehensible if each myth were not opposable to other versions of the same myth or to apparently different myths, each sequence opposable to other sequences in the same or other myths, and especially those whose logical framework and concrete content, down to the smallest details, seem to contradict them. (*WM* 56)

In fact, the notion of transformation and of transformation group allows comparison to be revindicated, but only a comparison very different from classical comparativism. What Lévi-Strauss proposes we compare are neither common themes (a given star, animal, or type of character) nor even similar narrative arguments. Such similarities exist; identifying them produces nothing but the observation of a common lexicon: "The task I have undertaken is quite different; it consists in proving that myths *which are not alike*, or in which the similarities seem at first sight to be accidental, can nevertheless display an identical structure and belong to the same group of transformations" (*OTM* 200).

The concept of *transformation* is undoubtedly Lévi-Strauss's most original and powerful contribution to the study of mythical narratives. There are several reasons for this. The first is that it points out that a myth is first a narrative (before becoming a thematic or figurative nucleus), but a narrative of a particular type: the linking of the sequences on the syntagmatic line can be understood only through the articulation of the schemas (or "codes") that form the system of reference on the paradigmatic level. The second reason is that it explains that the proliferation of variants and versions is in no way a corruption of a supposedly original or legitimate version. A myth always belongs to a group of transformations the variants of which are different responses to different contextual situations and explorations of logical possibilities that transcend those contexts.

Myth and Rite

To perhaps the same extent as myths, rites offer a rich domain for savage thought. Can it not be said that their modes of organization, their symbols, and their unfolding are governed by determinate logics and exhibit, *in actu*, categories of the mind? Such are the thoughts of those who regret that Lévi-Strauss showed only a fragmentary interest in this important aspect of anthropological reality. He was not, however, oblivious to the relation classically supposed between myth and rite. Moreover, he explained his position at various points in his work and in certain very enlightening passages. (*Anthropology and Myth* provides testimony of the research done on this subject for a number of courses taught during the 1950s and 1960s.) He tackles the problem in his earliest theoretical works on myths, such as "Structure and Dialectics" (*SA* 1: chapter 12). From the beginning of the latter study (which appeared in English first, in 1956), Lévi-Strauss proposes a change to the methodology of the approach to data on rituals, in particular regarding the relations of such data to mythical narratives.

The traditional presupposition was that between myth and rite there was a homology, in the form of a term-to-term correspondence. Thus the former would say on the representative level what the latter would mean on that of action. Correspondence of this sort probably exists, notes Lévi-Strauss (who admits that he himself overestimated it in his first research), but it is rare. Generally, the relations between myth and rite are more complex: they mobilize the same type of logical operations as those that can be seen within the mythological systems themselves. What does this mean? It means, for example, that the protagonists, symbols, and procedures of a ritual can present themselves, within a single culture, as so many correlational, inverted elements of a mythical narrative. However, Lévi-Strauss points out, the application of the method in this form also risks being disappointing; in other words, it risks leaving important elements of the myth or rite unexplained. This hypothesis must be defined and extended. In this work from 1956, we then see Lévi-Strauss prefigure what will be his constant approach in the *Mythologiques:* to search for the solution to a sequence (of a rite or myth), gathered in a given cultural and geographical zone, in the variants offered by a neighboring area.

Thus beginning with a myth gathered from Pawnee Indians (from the plains of North America) concerning the origin of shamanist powers, Lévi-Strauss shows that the series of oppositions around which the narrative is organized has no direct or inverted equivalent in any ritual of those same Pawnee. From this one might simply conclude that this is a myth to which no rite offers a reply. This, however, would be to give up too quickly, for there are, in other neighboring groups with which the Pawnee are linked geographically, culturally, and historically (such as the Blackfoot, the Mandan, and the Hidatsa), shamanist initiation rituals that are indeed, point for point, the inverted materialization of the Pawnee narrative.

We thus find that all elements can be taken into account precisely because we no longer hold the hypothesis of a simple homology — such as a symmetry. Instead we endorse a system of permutations in which semantic values remain the same while symbols are inverted. This is how Lévi-Strauss conceives of a dialectical relation between structures, the complex relation, mediated by inversions and transformations, that occurs between myth and rite. Such an approach is not a sort of theoretical bid for power to introduce rationality in what, at first sight, seems to be devoid of it (for we could find the demonstration almost too neat due to the degree to which it illuminates an internal logic in the sets studied). However, two considerations allow the validity of the method to be confirmed:

- The permutations and transformations identified operate within a coherent cultural whole. It can thus be seen to be legitimate "to compare myth and ritual, not only within the confines of one and the same society, but also with the beliefs and practices of neighbouring societies" (*SA* 1:240), and to consider that "the affinity [such as that of which linguists speak] can be seen not only in the diffusion of certain structural properties outside their area of origin or in their rejection, which impedes this propagation. The affinity may also be demonstrated by antithesis, which generates structures presenting the character of answers, cures, excuses, or even remorse" (*SA* 1:241).

- The arguments are always based on the consideration of precise details the meaning and function of which have been confirmed by their recurrence and repetition in various series (sociological, cosmological, technological, or other, depending on the case). There is thus the possibility of an external control that would satisfy the requirements of objectivity. It would be incorrect therefore to consider the method to be purely formal: the logical movement that it displays is always articulated according to the nature of the contents, but the latter do not signify in themselves, only through the play of oppositions and differences that places them in specific paradigms.

Another remarkable example of the transformational relations between myth and rite is given in *The Raw and the Cooked,* where we see how the Sherente perform in a ritual the symbolic staging of a mediation between earth and sky that the Central and Eastern Ge express in the form of a mythical narrative (*RC* 292ff.). In the Sherente rite, an officiant climbs to the top of a pole and remains there until he has obtained, on the one hand, some fire from the sun, fire that will allow extinguished home fires to be relit, and, on the other hand, the promise that rain will be sent. This corresponds to two modes of limited communication between the sky and the earth, which are in danger of joining in a conflagration due to the sun's hostility toward humankind. Here we find the schema of the Bororo reference myth (M1) and its variants: the narrative of the seeker of bird nests who climbs to the top of a tree and remains a prisoner there until the unconnected extremes of the sky and the earth find a balanced conjunction through the mediation of cooking fire.

Thus we see that Lévi-Strauss does not say that the rite is a translation into action of the myth that would be the rite's projection in narrative.

Between groups in the same cultural area, the relations are of transformation (thus they can be relations of inversion as well as of symmetry). Yet
the choice of form is not arbitrary. This is a point of capital importance,
for the mythical universe and the ritual universe are not of the same nature: "[I]t is a serious mistake to make mythology and ritual seem so
much alike as to be one and the same — as suggested by certain British
and American anthropologists" (VA 191). The reflections devoted to this
problem in the last pages of The Naked Man are very instructive. Lévi-
Strauss notes that we have often confused the problems by taking a ritual
to include a mythical narrative, or elements of a mythical narrative, that
may accompany it (which is what Lévi-Strauss calls "implicit mythology"). Now, what is of moment regarding ritual is to understand that it
is specifically made up of actions, to the point that the utterances themselves become equivalent to actions. From this point of view, two formal
operations define ritual: fragmentation (the many phases of a single action or operation, excessively detailed citations of all sorts of elements
as veritable taxonomic indexes, and so on) and repetition (of actions, utterances). These are the two aspects in which ritual profoundly differs
from myth:

> [W]hile myth resolutely turns away from the continuous to seg-
> ment and break down the world by means of distinctions, contrasts
> and oppositions, ritual moves in the opposite direction: starting
> from the discrete units that are imposed upon it by this preliminary
> conceptualization of reality, it strives to get back to the continu-
> ous, although the initial break with lived experience effected by the
> mythic thought makes the task forever impossible. (NM 679)

It is as if myth and ritual fulfilled two diametrically opposed requirements and were by this very fact capable of being — though are not
necessarily — complementary. Rather what should be said is that ritual
seems to want to erase what myth produces and establishes. Lévi-Strauss
sees a good example of this in the existence of two categories of Roman
divinities, as identified by Dumézil: on one side, there are the major mythical gods assuming the tripartition of the world, and, on the other, there
is the multitude of minor divinities brought into action in complex phases
of rituals to which control of the various aspects of ordinary existence is
assigned. "Ritual, by fragmenting operations and repeating them unwear-
ingly in infinite detail, takes upon itself the laborious task of patching up
holes and stopping gaps, and it thus encourages the illusion that it is possible to run counter to myth, and to move back from the discontinuous
to the continuous" (NM 674).

Ritual never ceases to bring back together what myth has broken
apart. This is what creates its obsessive nature. Is this to say that its function is to ward off an anxiety felt in the face of reality, as some have

supposed? According to Lévi-Strauss, to make such a claim would be to confuse causes and effects. Anxiety is not primordial. Rather it is the result of the fragmentation performed by taxonomic thinking. "Ritual is not a reaction to life; it is a reaction to what thought has made of life. It is not a direct response to the world; it is a response to the way man thinks of the world. What, in the last resort, ritual seeks to overcome is not the resistance of the world to man, but the resistance of man's thought to man himself" (*NM* 681).

Lévi-Strauss had already given a good example of this in *The Savage Mind,* when he opposed the totemic system to that of sacrifice. Totemism (or at least what it is agreed that this inappropriate term means) postulates, as we have seen, a global set of relations between a cultural series and a natural series. The differences identified between the species are used to express (or rather to institute) differences between social groups or between individuals, which would be impossible to discern from the point of view of species. Thus the operation is essentially that of classification: "[T]he system's sole reality consists in a network of differentiation between terms posited as discontinuous" (*SM* 223). It is thus strange that some have supposed (as have so many historians of religion) that totemism was at the origin of sacrifice, which operates in a diametrically opposed manner. Sacrifice aims, through a series of mediations, to reduce the distance between two terms posited as completely unconnected — the divinity and the officiant; in short, it aims to make possible a continuity that was considered impossible initially. The victim taken from the natural species swings, at the moment of its destruction, into the field of the divine, calling for grace to be granted to humankind: the irreversibility of the renouncement is supposed to inspire the irreversibility of the divine answer. Thus sacrifice establishes a continuity between terms that are initially separate. This is also the aim of rites (of which sacrifice is only one aspect) and probably of the other forms of religious life.

Limits to Interpretation

[M]yths do not admit of discussion, they must always be accepted *as they are.* —*HA* 121

Within any community, the category of myth excludes all dialogue: the members of the group do not contest its myths, but transform them while believing that they are repeating them. —*NM* 655

One thing necessarily strikes every reader of the analysis done by Lévi-Strauss regarding myths: it is a sort of *restraint in interpretation.* Some would see in this a deliberate desire to efface himself with respect to the narrative and to leave it up to the reader to complement a commentary that is merely sketched. What is certain is that, compared to the abundance of suggestions and glosses that mythical texts usually inspire, Lévi-Strauss's analysis is surprisingly sober, even terse. This is not due only to strict fidelity to the structural method insofar as it simply aims to bring out sequences of transformations after having identified the pairs of oppositions, homologies, equivalences, symmetries, and inversions. There is more to it than that. Its rationale lies elsewhere, probably in the fact that for Lévi-Strauss an interpretation that deals with content would not be an analysis at all, but rather an extension of the myth. Such an interpretation would propose yet another version of the myth. This is precisely, he says, what psychoanalysis, for example, does regarding the Oedipus myth. The Freudian interpretation is its modern version, the most recent one. Thus it remains on the same level as the object: it does not ensure the distanced position required by science. There is not really any harm in prolonging a myth or adding new versions to it. Simply, the prolongation of the myth must not be confused with its analysis.

We cannot simply say, as do some well-intentioned critics, that structural analysis is a sort of initial approach that identifies the logical system or narrative framework of a myth, allowing hermeneutics to then intervene, on these sound foundations, to propose a reading that would link the old text up with the reader's current experience. This supposed hierarchy of approaches rests on a misunderstanding. The structural approach (or at least Lévi-Strauss's approach) and that of hermeneutics are profoundly incompatible, not due to lack of goodwill but simply because the former considers the latter to belong to the same level as the myth, and the latter does not see that the structural approach does not refuse to interpret content: for the structural approach it is methodologically impossible to do so. For Lévi-Strauss, interpreting is limited to bringing out pertinent features and their relations, variants, and transformations and thus to understanding how a set of myths establishes the representation of a given world and attempts to provide answers to questions, not in the form of statements but within the very play of such representations.

Understanding myths, not in isolation but from within the corpus they form, endeavoring to establish their relations while meticulously refraining from saying what they mean "for me," the method that assigns to the mythologist the function of a scrupulous cartographer who ingeniously multiplies perspectives and sections is probably the most sure way to avoid mythologizing on myths.

Interpretative restraint is necessarily required when we no longer attempt to find in a myth (or in a set of myths) an ultimate meaning or to define a level of reference that would be that of truth. A mythical narrative may thus bring into play several "codes": sociological, technological, economic, cosmological, sensory, meteorological, astronomical, and so on. If, through the study of these various transformations, we conclude that a myth "in the end" attempts to make sense of, for example, conflicts between brothers-in-law in a given social structure (and this is only one of the many examples possible), what have we done? We have reduced all levels of expression to nothing but the translation of a single one of them, which is then found to be the one that, due to its etiological value, would carry the meaning and the truth of the mythical narrative.

Lévi-Strauss's great originality, the profound innovation provided by his method, is to have rejected such simplification, not, however, in principle but due to the teaching provided by the myths themselves. All these levels inter-express themselves in each other (as Leibniz would say), translate themselves in each other. A myth does not carry an intention (to deliver a given message through a given metaphor, to reflect it from level to level) but provides in the linearity of the narrative and the diversity of the codes an *analogon* of the simultaneity of the levels and the totality of the networks.

Myths, Novels, History

What is specific to myths (this plural is indispensable) is that they possess the ability to analyze themselves, but instead of doing so as a critical language that discusses an object, they analyze themselves by transforming themselves, in other words by specifying and developing themselves in other myths. Each myth clarifies each point in its narration in another point in another narration (thus the role of redundancy and of that of commutation). By doing so, each myth satisfies the requirement of saturation without leaving the level to which it properly belongs. We might wonder if (without misusing language) we can call these developments, ramifications, extensions, and so on, "analyses." Could the same not be said, in that case, of novels or of any richly narrative literary form? In what way are myths unique in their mode of functioning?

It is the apparent absurdity of myths, the seemingly preposterous nature of the characters and the episodes, that should put us on the right track, for meaning is not to be found in a plausible element that would refer (as in a novel) to a world already possessing order and truth. The "meaning" of a myth is built out of the double play of the various codes on the paradigmatic line and the episodes, themes, and variations on the syntagmatic line: it is immanent in the logic that governs the entire system. In the case of a novel, there is a general meaning that is ensured outside of the work, so the novel has no need to concern itself with such meaning. It develops on this certainty, on this given, and refers back to it at all times.

Myths, to the contrary, precisely because they organize the world, seem absurd. As Lévi-Strauss explains, myth has no meaning in itself precisely because it gives meaning to everything else. The function of its narrative units is not that of reproducing a unit that is already given or that of reinforcing its structures: it is that of producing such a unit, to such an extent that characters and episodes mean nothing by themselves, only through the positions of which they are the logical representations. Actions primarily obey this necessity, which may contradict all require-ments of empirical plausibility. What is proper to mythical thought is the integration of all elements of reality from each of its segments. Thus kinship relations, such as those of brothers-in-law (takers and givers of spouses), may be at the same time a tension between heaven and earth, the high and the low, the near and the far. Likewise, matrimonial union may be echoed in the oppositions of proper and excessive distance, day and night, dry and wet, air and water, and so on. Between these extremes appear mediating terms, such as, often, woman or cooking fire; or what might be called professional mediators, such as twins, the trickster, or the messiah. It is precisely because myth is the most complete and integrated expression of thought in oral traditions that it tends to be most strongly structured. Transmission is performed through transformations, through operations of inversion and symmetry that maintain the integrity of the structure.

However, when in a given region the mythical structure is weak-ened, we also see the predominance of "history": narrations of successive events as an explanation of the present reality. In other words, the chronological code wins out over the cosmological code, which is an-other way of saying that explanation through the generation of series on a single line is substituted for explanation through the construction of a system of homologies between the human world and the natural world. Lévi-Strauss says that "the structure deteriorates into seriality" (*OTM* 129): others would say that this is where history begins. (We will discuss this opposition in more detail in the next chapter.)

We henceforth see that the problems of relations between individuals and groups predominate. Simultaneously the natural elements and their coding values become less powerful in the narrative. The social becomes omnipresent, and faced with it the rest of reality tends to fade away. In savage societies, narrative must make sense of all aspects of reality simultaneously. It must be, at once, a cosmology, knowledge of social classifications, knowledge of the order of natural data, everyday wisdom, and so on. This is why the least history in it also becomes an event in the world, or rather why it is translated as such. In other words, it is reversed in the metaphorical relation of the natural to the social: it is an immobile event, or rather, the reabsorption of the event in the structure.

The apparently unconnected nature of mythical narrative (facts, ac-tions, and events appear in succession without any causal link appearing between the sequences, without certain facts or events following from others) demonstrates that myths are indifferent to chronological causality, an indifference that would make a modern novel intolerable. It is clear why. The sequences of a myth are determined by the symbolic values of the elements that appear in it. The actions themselves are part of this logical system that makes up the intelligibility of the myth. Novels, to the contrary, as rich as their systems of connotations may be, primarily target *the ordered, plausible establishment of actions* because chronological causality is what is most important to them *in a world already ordered.* The narrative element in myths introduces time into the system; narration in novels introduces system into time. In the former case the unity of the world is given in a synchronic whole of representations, and narrative appears as the necessary submission of an exposition linked to the sequential nature of discourse. In the latter case the unity of the world is conceivable only if human action appears in it as a final reason: here the narrative in the form of a chronological succession assumes the function of linking time to itself by establishing a continuum of events through the production of series on a single line.

We know what science has told us and continues to tell us about the cosmos, its transformations, the multitude of phenomena that make up the physical world. For us, this knowledge is a given, even though its mastery is not always within our abilities (and even among the learned it always remains limited to a restricted domain). In any case, our narratives need not take care of that, and moreover they do not. All that remains open to them is the social and the intimate. The history of the novel over the last two centuries is testimony to this narrowing of the narrative field. Between Balzac and Proust, between Dickens and Joyce, the slide from the social to the intimate can be seen clearly, until the narrative itself appears as an artifact and the only possible narrative becomes the statement of the impossibility of narrative. A period of the world has perhaps ended. We no longer know what remains to be told, and this is probably what has been meant metaphorically by "the end of history," . . . or of the story.

Chapter 8

The Lesson of the Work of Art

It could be that since Sophocles we have all become tattooed savages. But there is something in Art other than the correctness of the lines and the polish of the surfaces. The plasticity of style is not as great as the whole idea.... We have too many things and not enough forms. —Flaubert, in Bollème 1990, 111

[A]rt constitutes to the highest degree that take-over of nature by culture which is essentially the type of phenomenon studied by anthropologists. —in GC 107

In the very pursuit of their inquiries, anthropologists necessarily find themselves confronted with the existence of plastic and graphic works of art by the people being studied. They cannot, for example, separate the analysis of a rite from that of the costumes and masks (when such are used) with which that rite is associated, but everyday objects (pottery, clothing, tools), the canonical forms of which are often linked to specific symbolic representations, are even more compelling. Data concerning these productions (materials, motifs, circumstances, uses, and so on) may be gathered from a purely ethnographical point of view. However, beyond such indispensable study, a wider question cannot be avoided: that of the meaning and function of such invention of forms in a society.

This is the type of question Lévi-Strauss asks. The interest in such inquiries lies in the fact that they permit us to escape the horizon of obviousness drawn by a history of art that takes for granted the very fact of the existence of the work of art and the use of aesthetic concepts that, since classical antiquity, belong above all to a very specific tradition: that of the West. Anthropologists, while they cannot claim to be exempt from this, may at least relativize the point of view inherited from their culture by putting it into relation with other perspectives, by using them to provide varying perspectives on each other, by describing (even though such description may be in the anthropologist's own language) entirely different experiences. It is clear, for example, that arts called "primitive" are not representational or imitative arts but arts that favor certain features by organizing them as systems of signs. At the same time this contrast may be the starting point for the deepening of an entire inquiry into figurative and nonfigurative expression. This, however, is only one of the approaches Lévi-Strauss proposes for defining forms of art very different from our own. Another method would be to wonder about the relative roles of the model, material, and addressee, or, more generally, about the system of echoes that exists between aesthetic forms and the other aspects of a culture. However, beyond this, and due to analyses of this properly anthropological domain, Lévi-Strauss holds a view on contemporary art that is most often very critical and reserved. He has often been reproached for an excessive rejection of modernity. We must thus see what, in his eyes, justifies a severity that, in spite of the decades, has never weakened.

The Work of Art:
Structure of the Object and Knowledge

If we had to define the function of art according to Lévi-Strauss, we could say without hesitation that it is primarily a function of knowledge.[1] Such a function is obvious in the case of science, which proceeds by constructing models capable of accounting for the structure of the object. However, this object is placed at a distance and, in a way, cleaned of its sensible qualities so that it may be apprehended: it is pulled completely on to the side of formal models. This is entirely mediated knowledge.

Art also provides access to knowledge of the structure of the object, but from the standpoint of sensible qualities. Thanks to this, it maintains the immediate relation that underlies and envelops all perception. As we see, aesthetic knowledge is closely related to the approach of the "savage mind," of which it is perhaps the ultimate use in our civilization. What constitutes this knowledge? To see this, we must compare it with what occurs in language. A linguistic sign reveals nothing immediately about the object it names. There is no homology between the signifier and the signified. In art, in contrast, the homology exists. In short, "the work of art, in signifying the object, succeeds in creating a structure of signification which is in relation to the structure of the object" (in GC 89).

We might wonder if such an operation does not take place in ordinary perception, if it is not simply the most obvious cognitive function of such an operation. To this Lévi-Strauss would answer that the specific effect of a work of art is to isolate, articulate, and manifest features of the object that normally remain implicit or imperceptible. This is what he calls the "signifying function of the work" that is performed so well in "primitive" art (and so poorly in a certain art of representation that would limit itself to providing a copy of the object, as we will see below).

In sum, the signifying function is identified in Lévi-Strauss's work with the cognitive function. This appears in the nature/culture relation that is produced in a work of art. There is a passage from one to the other that

> is particularly well exemplified in art... to the extent that the pro-motion of an object to the rank of sign, if it is successful, must bring out certain fundamental properties which are common both to the sign and the object, i.e. a structure which is evident in the sign and which is normally latent in the object, but which suddenly emerges thanks to its plastic or poetic representation, and which furthermore allows a transition to be made to all sorts of different objects. (In GC 124–25)

In a work of art nature is transformed into a system of signs, and this transformation is the revelation of the structure of things. It is thus not surprising that this revelation of the properties of the object is for Lévi-Strauss also a disclosure of the "structure and functioning of the human mind" (in GC 125). We come full circle: there is objectivity in the work of art insofar as it displays properties of the object (it is thus not a gratuitous play of signs); however, the subjectivity that asserts itself there is not that of an individual psyche: it belongs to the universality of the cognitive function and displays its laws.

Lévi-Strauss's most explicit formulation of the knowledge function of artistic activity is probably that found in the first chapter of *The Savage Mind*. It is defined as follows: "[A]rt lies halfway between scientific knowledge and mythical or magical thought" (*SM* 22). In the preceding pages Lévi-Strauss has just defined the difference between science and *bricolage* (which is presented as an approach analogous to that of mythical thought). This difference is also that of structure and event. Science aims at knowledge of structure by distancing that of the event. In contrast, it can produce the event since it generates changes in the world. Myth-ical or magical thought, to the contrary, groups together and organizes elements of the world by isolating pertinent features here and there: it introduces or discovers a logic and a necessity in what seemed purely ac-cidental. In short, it produces structure using the event (which is the very way *bricolage* operates).

In what way is art half-way between these two approaches? Art's start-ing point is the world and objects given in all their diversity (it thus "*bricoles*" like mythical thought). Yet at the same time it grasps the object under very precise formal conditions. It produces a purpose-free artifact of the object. It aims to attain it in its truth, which is a cognitive act: in this it belongs on the side of science (though it does not belong to the same sort of knowledge; therefore, its originality must be specified).

In order to make clear the simultaneity of art's double apprehension, Lévi-Strauss proposes a theory that he calls the *small-scale model:*

Now, the question arises whether the small-scale model or minia-
ture, which is also the "masterpiece" of the journeyman, may not in
fact be the universal type of the work of art. All miniatures seem to
have intrinsic aesthetic quality — and from what should they draw
this constant virtue if not from the dimensions themselves? — and
conversely the vast majority of works of art are small-scale. (*SM* 23)

(An immediate objection to this might be the number of cases that seem to
contradict this thesis, but we will see how this criticism can be answered.)
    Lévi-Strauss gives the example of a lace collar in a painting by Clouet.
The faithful, thread-by-thread reproduction of the lace can be seen in this
work, yet even though the texture is rigorously respected, what is produced does not resemble a manufactured fabric. The object is deformed
by perspective, by shadows, and is given only partially. Nonetheless, the
eye grasps it as a whole: it immediately corrects and recognizes the complete form. Better yet, it comprehends it in its relation to the whole
garment; it matches it to the face, the colors, and the tones of the portrait, including the social standing of the subject. In short, an immediate
synthesis occurs in which there is an integration of much contingent data,
all that which can be condensed under the category of *event*. In this, the
work of art performs a sort of complete understanding of the object by
targeting the synthesis of its properties and circumstances. In this way all
works of art are "small-scale models."
    Why "small-scale"? Is this expression appropriate? Can it be applied
to a palace or a church? or a statue that is larger than life-size? There is
first the problem of a change in scale, and in particular we must discover
in relation to what the change is performed. The characters painted on
the Sistine Chapel are, in themselves, larger than life, but they do not appear to be so when seen from the distance at which they are to be viewed.
Moreover, it is the whole scene that is presented as a reduced copy with
respect to the cosmic referent. The same can be said of a temple that
presents itself as a *compendium mundi* or even of an equestrian statue,
for example, of which "we may ask whether the aesthetic effect... derives
from its enlargement of a man to the size of a rock or whether it is not
rather due to the fact that it restores what is at first from a distance seen
as a rock to the proportions of a man" (*SM* 23). However, this reduction
in scale is not the only one: a work of art adds many others to it with
respect to properties that are either simulated (such as depth in painting)
or abandoned (odors, tactile sensations, colors — in engraving).
    In short, the small-scale model is indeed a permanent, essential feature
of works of art, and Lévi-Strauss's aesthetic theory is certainly original
for having pointed it out. The notion of the small-scale model brings together three essential aspects of the work of art by allowing such a work
to be conceived of simultaneously as an artifact (thus as an experiment on

the object), as a reproduction (thus faithful to the object), and as a transformation (thus as an emphasizing of central aspects of the object). This
is how this reduction presents itself as "a sort of reversal in the process
of understanding" (SM 23). How so? In that it allows us not to proceed
from the parts to the whole but to receive the whole from the start by offering us a "homologue of the thing." "And even if this is an illusion, the
point of the procedure is to create or sustain the illusion, which gratifies
the intelligence and gives rise to a sense of pleasure which can already be
called aesthetic on these grounds alone" (SM 24).

   This analysis of the work of art could seem to favor the representative function if Lévi-Strauss did not take into account another aspect
which, in his eyes, is just as essential: the fact that it is specifically a
work, in other words something that has been produced. As such, a
small-scale model presents richer characteristics: "They are therefore not
just projections or passive homologues of the object: they constitute a
real experiment with it" (SM 24; emphasis added). Its structure has been
experienced, deeply recognized in the process of its composition. What
is proper to this experiment is not only that it provides access to a
unique occurrence, for production constantly requires choices and thus
exclusions. The object produced also carries all the possibles that were rejected. These possibles are what the spectator's eye adds to the work, and
thus the creation of the work continues in the spectator. (This is along
the lines of what Montaigne wrote: "I have read in Titus Livius a number of things which peradventure others never read, in whom Plutarke
haply read a hundred more, than ever I could read, and which perhaps
the author himselfe did never intend to set downe" [1910, 163]).

   In what way is art knowledge? This was the initial question. We can
answer that it is knowledge in that it performs an immediate synthesis of
the properties of the object (properties that science aims to isolate analyt-
ically) and the material givens of its apprehension (colors, smells, tastes,
tones, perspectives, and so on). This immediate synthesis, this integration
of structure and event, this giving of the intelligible in the sensible, this
offered whole (like a small-scale model), is what makes such knowledge
a pleasure, an aesthetic pleasure.

   This theory of the small-scale model is thus related, in its aspects —
condensation, experimentation — to two traditional definitions of the
work of art as a compendium mundi and an experimentum mundi. However, we must take care when using Lévi-Strauss's modern formulation:
while there is indeed something of the small-scale model in the work of
art, the reverse is not necessarily true. A model (of a car, rocket, building, or city), as charming as it may be, is nonetheless not a work of art. It
reveals only one of its subject's possibilities. Let us agree that it is related
to the work of art because: (1) the change in scale effects the distancing
that opens the eye to detached contemplation; and (2) this operation is,

due to its very precision, a discovery and display of the structure of the object. However, it must be pointed out to Lévi-Strauss that the work of art does something else, of a different order. Through the features it chooses, through its way of changing their position, transforming them, and recomposing them, it is distanced from imitative faithfulness. Over and above possibles, it provides a view of what was unexpected, what remained even unimaginable. This surprise is what creates the very event in the structure, or even the event *of* the structure. This, in consequence, crosses beyond the field of perception. This distortion or nonconformity is what is striking in arts called "primitive" and is perhaps what, in all art, beyond the plausible, attains truth and makes the work something greater than a production: it makes it an invention.

At this point, an uncertainty might cross the mind of the reader of Lévi-Strauss. Is the notion of a small-scale model really generalizable? Should it not be reserved uniquely for representative arts? Such arts, as we shall soon see, have a profound relation to mastery and possession. Now, this is precisely what haunts the small-scale model, as Lévi-Strauss explicitly recognizes: "[T]his quantitative transposition extends and diversifies our power over a homologue of the thing, and by means of it the latter can be grasped and apprehended at a glance" (*SM* 23). Can this be said of primitive arts or of art from earliest times or more generally of nonfigurative arts? These are forms of art that intend not to represent but to "signify." We will now explore this issue.

Signifying and Representing

The opposition between signifying and representing is probably the cornerstone of Lévi-Strauss's aesthetic thought. It is the key to all his evaluations of contemporary art. When asked by Georges Charbonnier about what, in the eyes of an ethnologist, might characterize the art of societies called "primitive," he answered that it is an art that in no case (except in later, and thus "modern," forms) attempts to provide an imitative representation (a "facsimile") of the object but that isolates some of its features, reinforces them, and puts them into relation with others. In short, it institutes the object as system of signs. Because this art aims to signify, it does not attempt to be figurative or to represent. In this sense, works of art have a status analogous to that of language in one very specific respect (and in that respect only). A language is possible only on the condition that there is very great stability of the rules and signs of which it is composed. Without this stability, communication would not be ensured (or, as in the case of jargon or secret language, communication would be possible for only a minority within the group). The art of "primitive" societies, due to the permanence of its canons and the enduring nature of its distinctive features, can be perceived and recognized by all members of the group. Like language, art, seen in one of its aspects, is a system of signs (which makes communication possible), but contrary to language, there is in this type of sign a material relation between the signifier and the signified. There is a *mimèsis* of the object in the forms that represent it. The comparison with language (and Lévi-Strauss places heavy emphasis on this) is pertinent only with respect to this relation, for with respect to the rest there is no common measure between the work of art and the linguistic sign. Thus the bald assertion that art is a language, which has been made by a number of semiologists, is an abuse of language, and even simply false.

What characterizes a representative art? According to Lévi-Strauss, it is that it is an art that aims to obtain a sort of copy of the object. This slightly hasty definition can probably be traced to the Platonic notion of *mimèsis,* but less clearly to that of Aristotle, which is more nuanced and richer, since *mimèsis* appears there not as an imitation so much as a production. We shall see that this nuance contains perhaps some of the difficulties in Lévi-Strauss's position. For him, the *mimèsis* of representative art (which asserted itself in Greece beginning in the fifth century and that reappeared in Italy in the quattrocento, and then in Europe in general) is unique in that it targets a sort of appropriation of the object. The represented world is a world possessed in effigy, mastered in its double:

> For Renaissance artists, painting was perhaps an instrument of knowledge but it was also an instrument of possession, and we must not forget, when we are dealing with Renaissance painting, that it was only possible because of the immense fortunes which were being amassed in Florence and elsewhere, and that rich Italian merchants looked upon painters as agents, who allowed them to confirm their possession of all that was beautiful and desirable in the world. (In GC 133)

Curiously, Western art thus performs something analogous to magic, itself a counterpart to science and technique, which provide true mastery.

Lévi-Strauss considers that this representative capacity is in proportion to the artist's mastery of the available means. This is another original point in his analysis. The necessity of restricting oneself to signifying features is imposed largely by the recalcitrance of materials and the limitations of tools. The objective technical contingencies of a given culture or a given period are what demand stylized expression. In contrast, more advanced, complex technology tends to "render" the object as it appears. (Something analogous occurs in the oral tradition, which retains only the features most likely to favor memorization, hence the highly structured nature of narratives transmitted in this way.) If, thus, the work is able to signify, it is because "in art, the artist is never completely in control of his materials and technical processes. . . . If he were, he would achieve a complete imitation of nature" (in GC 108). This is a rather original thesis that opens up interesting perspectives on the problems of contemporary art, but which Lévi-Strauss seems not to have envisaged. Perhaps he has his reasons.

Lévi-Strauss tells us two different things regarding the art of representation: first that it is related to the symbolic appropriation of the world (this is consistent with his criticism of the West's desire for mastery and its anthropocentrism); then that this art is linked to the development of the technical means of reproduction and grows with them. It would thus be interesting to see how these two phenomena are related. Now, in the signification/representation opposition we see clearly that for Lévi-Strauss, true art lies on the side of the former. Yet the theory of the small-scale model (which is given a perfectly positive, general value) applies first to the art of representation (which is constantly challenged, as we have seen). Representation would thus be excellent in certain cases, but in others it would be utterly suspect.

Here we are unquestionably touching on a difficulty, even a paradox, in Lévi-Strauss's analyses and, at the same time, on what determines his extremely reserved evaluation of the main currents in modern art. For, contrary to all expectations, his criticism of cubism is severe (Picasso would be nothing but a "dead-end"), while his praise for Ingres (as for all those whose figurative paintings are *minutely detailed*) may seem surprising. Does this mean that, finally, he takes the side of representation and the most classical forms of art? Some have been too quick to assert this. We will see that the representation/signification opposition is more complex than it first seems. For Lévi-Strauss, neither of these terms provides, in itself, a guarantee. He asks: Representing *in what way?* Signifying *what* for *whom?* In other words, he refuses to sidestep the issues of the referent, the context, and the addressee. He thus endorses the need for a semantic approach and reiterates his rejection of all formalist complacency. This can be seen more clearly by analyzing the way in which he proposes to think of the relation between art and society.

Art and Society

When he claims to be solitary, the artist lulls himself in a perhaps fruitful illusion, but the privilege he grants himself is not real. When he thinks he is expressing himself spontaneously, creating an original work, he is answering other past or present, actual or potential, creators. Whether one knows it or not, one never walks alone along the path of creativity.   — WM 148

If the relation of art to society is primarily a question of semantics, it is because it is not sufficient to postulate the necessary signification of a work of art for the group. What also must be done, taking things from the other end, is show in a precise manner how a type of society expresses itself (even if it is in an inverted or idealized way) in determinate plastic forms. That such a relation exists is a shared certainty that, since Hegel, has concerned all those who have attempted to develop an aesthetic theory. Explanations have oscillated between a search for the causality of representations and one for a causality of the material conditions. Lévi-Strauss does not enter into this debate, which is a legacy left by his predecessors, probably because he resolutely places himself outside of all causalist views. The only such reference he accepts in this domain is to that of the work of Erwin Panofsky (in whom he recognizes an authentic structuralist). How, thus, does he phrase the question himself? He very explicitly does so, from an anthropological point of view, at three points in his work: in the chapter on the Caduveo in *Tristes tropiques,* in the chapter in *Structural Anthropology* titled "Split Representation in the Art of Asia and America," and finally in the whole of *The Way of Masks* (to limit ourselves to the most explicit statements).

The chapter on Caduveo art is significantly titled "An Indigenous Society and Its Style." It begins with a remark in which we clearly recognize the method and theoretical hypothesis of Lévi-Strauss:

> The ensemble of a people's customs has always its particular style; they form into systems. I am convinced that the number of these systems is not unlimited and that human societies, like individual human beings (at play, in their dreams, or in moments of delirium), never create *absolutely:* all they can do is to choose certain combinations from a repertory of ideas which it should be possible to reconstitute. (*TT* 160)

Indeed, Lévi-Strauss imagines producing a sort of "periodic table like that of the chemical elements." We would see here, in the actual data, combinations corresponding to the table of possibles. This is a very Leibnizian formulation as we have already pointed out in this study. However, this Leibnizianism does not stop here: we will find it again in the relation of mutual expression between art and society that defines, here, the Caduveo style. To see this, we must take a rapid glance at the ethnographic data on this population.

As the author explains, the Caduveo belong to the last representatives of a larger group, the Mbaya-Guaicuru, which was characterized by an extremely hierarchical social organization. It was a caste society, dominated by nobles who were themselves divided into great hereditary nobles and ennobled individuals. The former were also divided into an older and a younger branch. Next came warriors, who could become noble through initiation, and finally Chamacoco slaves and Guana serfs, of which the latter were divided into three castes like their masters. The nobles could be recognized by paintings on their bodies, from which all hair was removed (in this respect, Europeans appeared to them to be of very low extraction). They also wore costumes made up of large pieces of leather decorated with geometric motifs in highly contrasting colors, which caused them to be compared to the characters on our playing cards.

The Caduveo are the most direct heirs of the graphic art of the Mbaya (who have now disappeared), which is "a graphic art which is quite un-like almost anything which has come down to us from pre-Columbian America" (*TT* 184). This art and its practice are marked by a whole series of dualisms. The first is due to the fact that men sculpt wood and draw on various surfaces (zebu horns used as cups) using as their themes *figurative* motifs (people, animals, foliage); while women paint and draw only *abstract* motifs on bodies and pottery. This feminine art also presents a dualism between angular and geometrical motifs, mainly present in borders, and curvilinear motifs (arabesques, curls, spirals). To this is added a figure/background opposition (in which the relations can be inverted) in interlacing designs of heraldic nature:

> The Caduveo decorative style therefore presents us with a whole series of complexities. There is in the first place a dualism which is projected on to successive planes, as in a hall of mirrors: men and women, painting and sculpture, figurative drawing and abstraction, angle and curve, geometry and arabesque, neck and belly, symmetry and asymmetry, line and surface, border and motif, piece and field, pattern and background. (*TT* 191)

This dualism, which can be read in the result, can be observed in the action of composition, which seems to be performed without prior plan-ning: "[T]he primary themes are first decomposed, then reconstituted as secondary themes which use fragments taken from the first as elements of a provisional unity, and then these secondary themes are juxtaposed in such a way that the original unity re-emerges as if it had been conjured back into existence" (*TT* 191).

The idea of a similarity with playing cards thus finds its explanation. Each painting, like each card, has both a *function* (that of being an ob-ject that is used in a dialogue or duel between two partners) and a *role* (that of holding a status in the series). The former is fulfilled by sym-metry, the latter by asymmetry: reciprocity and differentiation. How can these two aspects be expressed simultaneously in order to resolve this contradiction? The solution, which is a compromise, is to be found in the adoption of a symmetry, but on an oblique axis, and without identical elements on each side.

At this point Lévi-Strauss introduces the question of the relation be-tween art and society. He asks: "What, therefore, is the purpose of

Caduveo art?" (*TT* 195). Generally, it is used, as in the case of face paintings, to display the *civilized body* in contrast with the purely natural body, in short to celebrate "human dignity." Yet more specifically it marks the differences in status in this society, which is attentive to etiquette and recognition of rank to the extent that caste endogamy gives rise to the preference for adopting enemies or strangers rather than risking a misalliance with a group considered inferior. What conclusion can be drawn about this concerning the style of painting described above? To answer this question, we must take a detour to other ethnic groups, such as the Bororo, belonging to the same culture. Among them also we find hereditary endogamous classes (with three levels: upper, middle, and lower), but here the moiety system (the obligation to take one's spouse from the other moiety, the obligation of each moiety to ensure the burial of members of the other, and so on), in being superimposed on the class system, tends to efface (or provide the illusion of effacing) the reality of the hierarchies. The egalitarian, complementary representation of the two groups (attested to by myths) allows the asymmetry of one system to be compensated by the symmetry of the other. This solution is represented concretely in the very topology of a Bororo village, which is constructed like a Caduveo drawing.

This then is the answer to the question: it is as if the Bororo had resolved on the level of social organization the contradiction created between symmetry and asymmetry, reciprocity and hierarchy, and as if the Caduveo, not having known how, or not having been able to bring themselves — *noblesse oblige* — to adopt this solution, were nonetheless led to express it symbolically: "Not in a direct form, which would have clashed with their prejudices, but in a transposed, and seemingly innocuous, form: in their art" (*TT* 196–97). In this way a style, even to the point of its most specific forms, expresses a society not through the circulation of a single signifier (as is supposed by thematic criticism) but in a structural homology that brings out constants present across various domains of expression. This way of seeing the relation between forms of art and society would be called by Lévi-Strauss himself *dialectical*, which means, in his work, that the relation is not direct, does not follow from a reflective causality, but, as we have seen regarding myths, brings analogical reasoning into play.

Are these analyses concerning exotic societies still pertinent when we turn to modern societies? How, in the latter, is the relation between forms of art and society presented? This question is, as we might expect, extremely complex, and Lévi-Strauss does not claim to provide an exhaustive answer to it. He proposes only a certain number of scattered remarks that allow an orientation to be defined. Essentially, what appears is that the venture of modern art seems to him to have begun very poorly, burdened with regrettable misunderstandings. Moreover, the avant-garde, which has proliferated during the last century and a half, is evidence above all of a deep rupture in the former relation between art and society because it also refers to a rupture with the natural world. In short, what it prides itself on as a sign of its renewing force appears to him, to the contrary, as the signal of a decline and the loss of a dimension essential to any work of art worthy of the name.

Impressionism's Dead End and
the False Promise of Cubism

To such pessimism we might object that modern art began rather well, at least if we consider that its birth was simultaneous with the appearance of impressionist painting. The latter asserts itself first as a break with the previous academic, highly "rhetorical" art, which, in Lévi-Strauss's terms, is art that is the prisoner of its formulas and conventions (even of its recipes), an art that consists of an anaemic discourse on its own history. Such painting is nothing but an imitation of painting at both the level of code and that of theme. Thus does impressionism not appear to be the return to freshness, light, open air, and landscape? This is what has been said time and time again, and it is also what the impressionist painters themselves explicitly targeted. Yet on this seemingly accepted point, Lévi-Strauss insists on bringing us back down to earth.

First, impressionism produces no break with respect to representation. Certainly it does not refer to an object in the same way that previous painting did, yet it also remains within mimetic reproduction. It wants to remain faithful to reality by claiming to see it better, to give it back its rights. In this respect, as we have seen, this style of painting remains the means of appropriation that has been, for Lévi-Strauss, the criterion of Western art since the quattrocento. "The 'possessive-representative' aspect survives intact in Impressionism, and the Impressionist revolution is superficial and only skin-deep, whatever incidental importance it may have for us" (in GC 70).

Why such severity? Mainly because impressionism resigned itself to banality and the fait accompli of industrial civilization. Certainly, previous painting could be reproached for using a favored nature, for systematically representing "sublime countryside" (mountains, waterfalls, cool valleys, ancient trees, wild lakes...). Yet it was also true that such nature was present and accessible everywhere. Impressionism, in contrast, seems to say: let us take the world as it has become. Thus the impressionists' "sudden predilection for humble, suburban landscapes or the often unattractive countryside near towns — a field, say, or a single line of trees" (in GC 71).

We could object that this is precisely where lies the interest of the turn taken by modern art: to have understood that it is not the beautiful subject that creates the beauty of the work but the form itself (be it pictorial, musical, narrative, or other). In short, the style is not in the conventional value of the thing represented. Lévi-Strauss does not challenge — to the contrary — this new requirement, which is a liberation with respect to academicism. Nonetheless, in his eyes impressionism did not live up to the hope it inspired, and this failure was twofold: it failed with respect to the object and with respect to its method.

With respect to the *object,* first because it endorses, in spite of appearances, the dominating advent of urban and mechanical civilization, impressionism holds that "mankind must be taught to be satisfied with the small change of nature, which is all that is left to them of the great Nature which has now been lost forever.... In Impressionism, there is this didactic purpose, an attempt to act as the guide of civilization" (in GC 72).

With respect to its method next, impressionism, in spite of its claims, far from letting things speak for themselves, far from reinstating their immediacy, is rather the endorsement of subjectivity. It aims to record states and instants of perception. It does not attempt to attain the essence of the object (as "primitive" art succeeds in doing by renouncing representation). Thus this severe remark: "Impressionism gave up too quickly when it accepted the idea that the sole ambition of painting is to grasp what the theoreticians of the era called the physiognomy of things — that is, their subjective aspect — as opposed to an objectivity that aims to apprehend their nature" (*VA* 249). (We might object: Is this not an approach to knowledge? To which Lévi-Strauss would reply that knowledge depends not on variable states of perception but on the categories of the mind insofar as the mind is in accordance with the structure of the object.)

We might have thought that cubism would succeed where impressionism failed. Having renounced representation from the start, it indeed seems to return to the "signifying function" of the work, analogous to that which can be seen in the "primitive" arts (which were explicit inspiration for cubism). However, this analogy remains superficial for, as we have seen, this signifying function in traditional societies is due to the fact that the work of art is shared, like a language, by all members of the group. There communication takes place at the semantic level, while cubist works of art remain experiments on forms (as interesting as they may be for understanding what is occurring in modernity). In cubism representation certainly is overtaken in favor of the sign, but it is a sign that remains empty, that is given like a simulacrum, like a form without content, a signifier deprived of a signified. This leads Lévi-Strauss to conclude: "Cubism, on its own, cannot recreate the collective function of the work of art" (in GC 73). "[T]he signs have nothing more than the formal function of a sign-system: actually, and sociologically speaking, they do not operate as a means of communication within a given group" (in GC 78).

We could object that removing the semantics from the sign, giving it the status of a simulacrum, is essentially ironical, that it could not be otherwise as soon as the traditional relations defining an *ethnic community* are dissolved. The work of art can do nothing more than mirror this fragmentation for us, and, from then on, the relations between art and society are reversed. The group is no longer in charge of providing a semantic content for the work: it is rather the work that creates a community around itself. This is how art was envisaged by Kant, who in fact reformulated the problem of the work of art from the starting point of its reception, in other words, from a theory of *taste*. This is a very clear indication that we are in the presence of an individualization not only of the creator but above all of the spectator, reinforced by the private acquisition of works. The community of taste, a network of individuals, is nothing like an ethnic community. The artist now comes from nowhere and addresses anybody. We could of course deplore this (as Lévi-Strauss manifestly does), but we must recognize that this is necessarily the point from which all modern forms of creation must consider the work of art and its destiny.

However, we have to admit that the proliferation of "manners" among the moderns is made more understandable. Picasso provides the most striking example of this (with what we call his "periods," but there were many who followed him: Braque, Gris, Miró, and in music, Stravinsky). In these changes there was something of a scanning of traditions and thus a sort of indifference to them all.

This explains the danger of denying one academicism only to fall into another. That of the preimpressionist period was an "academicism of the signified": the subjects of the works (scenes, objects, characters) were defined by a tradition that had fixed their conventions. Now, however, the danger is that of an "academicism of the signifier" that can be defined as "an almost obsessional consumption of all the sign-systems which have been, or still are, in use in the human race, anywhere and everywhere, ever since men have had a form of artistic expression" (in GC 72).

Modernity and Excess of Culture

For Lévi-Strauss, a work of art is primarily, as we have already noted, a means of access to knowledge. This means the work is unique, complete in itself: it has the property of being conveyed by sensible experience, to require it as such, to magnify all its possibilities. It institutes a specific, deep relation with the natural world, and thus culture constantly finds new resources in it. Each period confronts this necessity and invents a style for this experience.

However, since the break introduced by cubism, modern art has tended to be a commentary on itself. Culture has closed itself up in its own productions (just as the historical world generally tends to become self-referential). This deviation, this forgetfulness, even this decadence, is seen by Lévi-Strauss to be exhibited in a striking manner in the work of Picasso: "This is a work which, rather than contributing an original message, gives itself over to a sort of breaking down of the code of painting, a secondhand interpretation, much more an admirable discourse on pictorial discourse than a discourse about the world" (SA 2:277).

We might have expected, he also notes, that cubism, through the kind of disarticulation/reconstruction that it inflicts on the perceived object, would have had the ambition of recovering "a truer image of reality behind the world" (SA 2:278). Yet this is in no way its aspiration. What cubism develops (and especially, following it, all the plastic experiments of the avant-gardes) is a breaking into pieces, a very conscious, systematic dismantling of forms. The illusion inherent in such an approach is that it is possible to produce a work of art through the learned mastery of its laws. The artist is no longer guided by an experience of the world, but by a theory. This is an illusion because "the real problem posed by artistic creation lies in the impossibility of thinking through the outcome ahead of time" (SA 2:278). Thus we fall back on ready-made formulas, on recipes analogous to those of a "rhetoric." (Lévi-Strauss alludes to the excess of this linguistic technique developed by Renaissance rhetoricians.) In short, by cutting itself off from experience of the world, the work of art settles into artifice. It becomes knowledge about knowledge, not about an object itself. "The future of art — if it has one — requires rather a getting in touch with nature again, in its raw state, which is, strictly speaking, impossible; but there can at least be, let us say, an effort in that direction" (SA 2:278). This demand for the "raw state" could appear a bit naive if Lévi-Strauss did not explain himself on this point. He notes that many of his structuralist colleagues seem to have found inspiration in abstract art. In his own case, he considers that the inspiration has come rather from the sight of stones, flowers, butterflies, and birds (moreover, in Tristes tropiques he emphasizes the role played in his vocation by the sight of geological differences in landscapes). From this he draws the conclusion: "There are then, at the origin of structuralist thought, two very different stimulations: the former more humanist — as I would put it — the latter oriented toward nature" (SA 2:278). Humanist? He later explains that by this he means the major current "which claimed to set up mankind as a separate kingdom" (SA 2:280). This sheds light on his critical intentions, for we find here one of the most constant warnings of an anthropologist who watches, in mourning, as humanity closes itself in on its own productions. With often disastrous results, Western civilization has, since the Renaissance, developed a project of domination aimed at reducing the natural world to the role of matter to be transformed, without the consequences of such violence ever being evaluated (except by a few original individuals who have been aware of the dangers). Modern art is testimony to this regrettable position. ("How many men between God and me!" exclaimed Rousseau [1911, 261]; Lévi-Strauss could write: so much culture between the world and us!)

Yet there is perhaps an aspect that is even more serious: it is not only nature that is endangered; it is also, and for the same reasons, other civilizations. The danger is essentially due to the fact that presently the dominant feature of Western civilization is that it is parasitical. The break with the natural world, by cutting off the necessary, profound source of all creation, forces the West to turn toward cultures that are still alive, to mine them for what is increasingly lacking in it: sensations, energy, works. In order to explain the creative impotence with which our civilization is afflicted, Lévi-Strauss briefly and forcefully (*SA* 2:281ff.) proposes a fairly disturbing hypothesis in the form of a metaphor, that of the virus, an organism that comes late in evolution because it can live only on other, much more highly developed, organisms that are already autonomous. The virus is a form of life that is relatively modest: it is little more than a genetic code. Yet it has the formidable power to impose itself on other living things, "forcing their cells to betray their characteristic formula in order to obey its own and to manufacture beings like itself" (*SA* 2:282). Such would be, transposed onto another plane, the essence of Western civilization. We have not heeded Descartes's clear exposition of our civilization's special nature, which "consists essentially of a method which, because of its intellectual nature, is not suited to generating other civilizations of flesh and blood, but one which can impose its formula on them and force them to become like it" (*SA* 2:282–83).

According to Lévi-Strauss, all of Western civilization has entered into this parasitical or viral model. Thus the tendency to look for a reality that it no longer creates, either *elsewhere,* in other cultures that are still alive, or *before,* in its own past as preserved in museums. It therefore may be that our culture will survive only by imitating itself (which would result in increasing numbers of "neo" movements) or by bringing other cultures into a carnival of the most eclectic forms. Or perhaps, to the contrary, it could propose to declare its illness through narration or dramatization of the form as such, emptied of all content. This analysis has many points in common with what Nietzsche diagnosed almost a century earlier as "European nihilism." One might even think he was the author of the following judgment by Lévi-Strauss:

> In comparison with these civilizations — whose living art expresses their corporeal quality because it relates to very intense beliefs and, in its conception as much as in its execution, to a certain state of

equilibrium between man and nature — does our civilization correspond to an animal or viral type? Had one to choose in favour of
the latter hypothesis, it could be foretold that . . . the morbid hunger
which drives us to gulp down all forms of past and present art in
order to elaborate our own will experience a growing difficulty in
satisfying itself. (*SA* 2:283)

Representation beyond Itself:
The Model, the Materials, the User

A sort of contradiction seems to slide into Lévi-Strauss's theory of the
work of art. On one hand, impressionism is reproached for remaining a
prisoner of figurative expression (and thus of possessive representation);
on the other hand, we are told that abstract art, since cubism, revels
in manipulating empty signs. This is a double dead-end that leaves little hope for contemporary art. The crisis springs from society itself: it
no longer carries the semantic function (what linguistics calls the "message") that is the content of the works of a community and period (which
we saw above with respect to Caduveo art).

Is there really no hope? It would not be strictly accurate to say
so. Lévi-Strauss considers that we have buried *figurative expression* too
quickly and that it requires complete rethinking. Thus we must look to
early and modern painters for whom representation is so extremely precise and fine (the Flemish school, Ingres, and, closer to us, Anita Albus)
that we could say that an excess of representation saves from representation. However, this is probably badly phrased. We must ask how
what appears as a copy or illusory double of reality in the work of some
becomes a masterpiece in the work of others:

> [I]t seems to me that Ingres's secret is that he could give the illu-
> sion of a fac-simile (we need only think of his Cashmere shawls
> reproduced with all the most minute details of design and shades
> of colour) while at the same time the apparent fac-simile reveals a
> signification which goes far beyond perception and even extends to
> the structure of the object of perception. (In GC 90)

In the same spirit, Anita Albus is praised for the figurative rigor of her
paintings: "[I]nstead of asking the object to be something different from
what it is, she assiduously renders with minute precision the weave and
drape of a textile or the veins and grain of old wood. We see them as we
no longer realized or had forgotten that we could see them" (*VA* 342).
In short we are no longer dealing in any way with the privilege of subjective states (which is what impressionism wanted to convey) but with
minute attention to the properties of the object (whether it is to be found
in nature or produced by man), and, moreover, we see respect for its

"physical integrity" (*VA* 253). In this way figurative painting goes back to what Lévi-Strauss considers to be its very vocation: to be a source of knowledge or, rather, to be knowledge in action.

We must thus accept that the representational function of the work, its membership in *mimèsis,* is not necessarily related to possessiveness or mastery, as Lévi-Strauss claims a little too hastily when he compares Western art with primitive art. These assertions, which may be correct from a certain point of view, are no longer so when the field of the question is extended. It seems therefore that two sets of problems of representation — we could say an opposition between good and bad *mimèsis* — exist side by side in Lévi-Strauss's work, and neither their articulations nor their limits can be defined. This is probably due to the fact that he has been too summary in his reduction of the notion of *mimèsis* to that of *copy* (a position that could be called Platonic), when it also includes that of *production* (as is clear in Aristotle's work). In the Aristotelian formula *he technè mimeitai tèn phusin,* it must be understood that art imitates not only *natura naturata* but *natura naturans.* It does not limit itself to providing images of beings produced by *phusis:* it continues the operation. Seeing *mimèsis* in this way allows us to relativize the representation/signification opposition, as well as that of figurative and nonfigurative expression. This dimension is what Lévi-Strauss rediscovers — apparently without clearly evaluating it — in representation as figurative expression, and which legitimates his notion of the small-scale model. In short, we can say that he finally moves his notion of representation from Plato (*mimèsis* as a copy or twin) to Aristotle (*mimèsis* as *poièsis*).

Nonetheless, the difficulties Lévi-Strauss raises could be solved by the distinction he himself proposes between three terms: *model, materials, user,* in chapter 1 of *The Savage Mind* (a work produced after Georges Charbonnier's *Conversations with Claude Lévi-Strauss,* in which there are clear contradictions). The way these three terms are related would allow us to see that the favor accorded to representation in the Western tradition (at least until recently) is perhaps not, as has been repeated too often, linked exclusively to a form of thought and culture. It would be rather an assertion of a possibility that we encounter everywhere and that exists in conjunction with others, while circumstances may bring it out or conceal it. When the *model* is favored, the result is representative art, that which has dominated in the West since the quattrocento (but which is also found elsewhere); when the *materials* are asserted, the execution of the work is in favor, which results in "primitive" or, in the West, "early period" art (which thus matches the "signifying" function); finally, when the *user* is targeted, it corresponds primarily to applied arts. In fact, these three aspects are always related, and each of them is present within the others as a recessive feature under the dominant trait.

It is clear, for example, that the relation to the materials and to the user is almost entirely erased ("internalized" in Lévi-Strauss's terms) in the last five centuries of Western painting. How can this situation be explained? The answer is more simple than it seems. It is due to the fact that, on one hand, technological problems have been resolved or are supposed to have been (it is thus not a question of placing value on the material, and even less of being subject to its constraints) and, on the other hand, the work targets no utilitarian function (as could a tapestry, garment, vase, and so on). Conversely, all possibility is concentrated on the motif or the subject (the "occasion" in Lévi-Strauss's terms) and tends to favor it unconditionally. "Freed from the contingent both with regard to execution and purpose professional painting can, then, bring it to bear upon the occasion of the work, and indeed if this account is correct it is bound to do so" (*SM* 28).

This hypothesis is extremely interesting in that it proposes a structural, not a genealogical or ideological, explication of the hegemony of representative arts in the West. In other words, it is not so much a crippling, enigmatic tendency proper to a form of thought (which some call the "metaphysical tradition") as it is a three-term system in which the background position of two of the terms leads necessarily to the promotion of the third. Why? What reason is there for the reciprocal relation of the three elements? For Lévi-Strauss, it is a mutation linked to transformations in technical mastery. Any change in the means redistributes the cards, for the means determine the material possibilities of the forms (which does not prevent the forms from following their own logic within the limits of the means of expression available to them).

The hegemony of representation should be seen thus as an effect and not as a cause. Moreover, it is in no way particularly negative or positive: it is simply the indication of a constant relation between technical means and aesthetic expression that can affect any culture or tradition of thought. We can thus see it in a latent state in other cultures and identify the first signs of it in domains where technical enfranchisement occurs. A philosophy of representation follows, rather than precedes or creates, such transformations.

The relevance of such hypotheses is confirmed when we consider the opposite aspect, which is that of *applied arts*. Here the execution of the work must make itself clearer since the object is produced for a use. The work is thus entirely turned toward its addressee. Function predominates and renders representation minimal. In fact, no dominant form can ignore the others without loss. Scholarly painting that turns in upon itself falls into the academicism of facsimile, which is probably the source of two modern reactions (which Lévi-Strauss understands poorly but which his analyses make comprehensible): that of placing the materials on the forefront once more (this could be the meaning of nonfigurative works) and that of eliminating technical mastery from the execution (which unfortunately leads to the loss of *skill*, which Lévi-Strauss rightly deplores). Applied arts, when they target only functionalism, lose all aesthetic character: what is missing is the integration of the *model* aspect without which the object is deprived of the minimum of autonomy that designates it for disinterested contemplation.

However, certain arts, notes Lévi-Strauss, have managed to achieve a kind of balance between the various elements: "In so far as early art, primitive art and the 'primitive' periods of professional painting are the only ones which do not date, they owe it to the dedication of the accidental to the service of execution and so to the use, which they try to make complete, of the raw datum as the empirical material of something meaningful" (*SM* 29). We thus see that the relation between the before and the after in the transformation of forms is not so much the result of a historical causality as the product of a new combination in which the event will be determining as a catalyst but will have no effect on the result. All history of art conscious of the gratuitousness of continuist hypotheses should return to this modesty. There is no logic of the succession of forms but a logic of the variations of their relations.

We can go further in this research by wondering about an art in which the material presents, in its treatment, radically different problems from those of visual arts: music.

Musical Knowledge:
Excess of Nature or Lack of Nature

The primary interest — but not the only one — of an art like music is that it is delivered from the hypothesis of representation from the beginning. This is due to the fact that its relation to nature is the inverse of that of painting and other visual arts. Painting finds in nature a raw material that it transforms: it encounters objects that are already colored (thus the natural references in designations: lemon yellow, midnight blue, cherry red, and so on). Of course, these facts can be specified culturally, and the abstract designation of colors (blue, red, ...) can be removed from their various substrata. Nonetheless, an initial level of articulation is given before any production of forms.

We are in the inverse situation with respect to sounds: they do not exist in a natural state (except in a limited manner in the songs of birds, but we know that even in this case we are dealing with recognition codes within each species). The sounds used in music exist only precoded and preselected in the systems of tonal scales: their material is cultural from the beginning. However, these scales are not arbitrary. They are based on physical and physiological properties and are legitimized in this way. Music seems thus to be able (and this would be the source of its uniqueness) to return to nature what it first took away.

If we accept this analysis, then the two dominant forms in contemporary music pose problems analogous to those posed by postimpressionist painting. First there is the case of what has been called ("by antiphrase," according to Lévi-Strauss) *musique concrète,* which, as we know, directly questions the very idea of sound, which is supposed to be the product of an artifice since the tonal hierarchy rests on conventions. *Musique concrète* intends to take as its starting point all sorts of sounds captured in the natural or technical environment, "raw sounds," as they are called. The musical operation consists in reworking them, deforming them, even rendering them unrecognizable. What is done in reality? asks Lévi-Strauss. We act as if the sounds were an initial level of articulation, which is not the case since we can identify in them no system of simple relations that would allow us to develop a second level of articulation. In short, we are dealing with something that is at the very most an accumulation of deformed noises, pseudosounds, which is interesting as an acoustic experience but has nothing to do with music, except through an abuse of language.

The problem posed by "serial music" seems to be the opposite, but it is much more serious because here the question of sound is not evaded. To the contrary, it is radicalized. Such music accepts (because it knows that without it, it would no longer be music) the traditional definition of sounds, but it proposes to eliminate the tonal scales, in a sort of leveling, in a sort of in-principle nondifferentiation of sounds, to which only the methodologies (as Boulez says) developed by each composer will be able to provide relations in the *hic* and *nunc* of a work. We begin with previously developed sounds, transmitted by tradition, and submit them to a formal treatment detached from all anchoring in "natural" experience. This is even an explicit goal of this type of music. In this way it is indeed situated on the extreme opposite to that of *musique concrète.* However, while the latter gives itself an illusory nature, serial music settles into a formalism that links it to attempts in abstract painting, and, like such painting, it operates on desemanticized signs. What does this mean? That the very hypothesis of a general listening community is set aside, for there is communication only through stability of signs and codes within a society. Since each composer is free to create his own code, there is community only for those who know the rules. This results in as many schools as composers (and thus a corresponding number of conflicts over territory and influence, as is the case in all avant-gardes). What traditional music ensured was, to the contrary, a common return to sources in the "natural" (let us read physical and psychological) anchoring of tonal scales.

What Lévi-Strauss wants to warn us about, in opposition to all formalist approaches, is that one cannot forget or evade the corporal nature (or the corporeality, as Merleau-Ponty would say) of the perceiving subject with impunity. Any language, like any culture, performs a coding of natural data: thus the double circulation of phonemes and morphemes; thus, in another domain, the rules of alliance changing the biological necessity of union into a cultural fact; thus the integration of colors in forms; thus, again, that of sounds in tonal scales. However, if forms become autonomous and reproduce from the starting point of themselves, a culture then comes face-to-face with its own products. It is indeed in this that the kinship of abstract paintings with serial music becomes apparent. Contrary to what we might have thought, and to what some have said, the structural approach has no particular complicity with this "modernity." Lévi-Strauss notes this with a certain humor: "However, by virtue of its theoretical presuppositions, the serialist school is at the opposite pole from structuralism and stands in a relation to it comparable to that which used to exist between free thought and religion — with the difference, however, that structural thought now defends the cause of materialism" (*RC* 27). This materialism is in no way a naturalism. Nature in Lévi-Strauss's work is not an initial state or the simple totality of beings: it is what, in experience, appears as the extreme of the given, the untransformed, which is always grasped — in a complementary or conflicting mode — with the developed, the transformed. It is thus always a term in a relation.

It is precisely because it believes in an original, immediate, raw nature that the music that calls itself *concrète* has produced nothing concrete. Symmetrically, it is because it disconnected itself from the natural anchoring of sounds that serial music has closed itself into a purely idiomatic coding. Lévi-Strauss concludes abruptly: "Whatever the gulf between *musique concrète* and serial music in respect of intelligence, the question arises whether both are not deceived by the utopian ideal of the day: one concentrates on matter, the other on form; but both are trying to construct a system of signs on a single level of articulation" (*RC* 24).

Of Aesthetic Emotion

If art has, in Lévi-Strauss's view, a knowledge function, does the priority granted to the cognitive element amount to total neglect of the other phenomenon constantly recognized with respect to aesthetic perception: that of the pleasure that accompanies it? We might be tempted to think so unless, in fact, the two things are related.

According to Lévi-Strauss, the aesthetic emotion is due to the access that is provided to the structure of the object. The shaping performed by the work of art is due primarily to the grouping of features it arranges in a meaningful way, due to an *ordering* that is, as we have seen, halfway between the *bricolage* order of myth and the rigorous order of science. There is generally an aesthetic pleasure in any operation of this type. This is why, in *The Savage Mind*, Lévi-Strauss could quote G. G. Simpson (1961): "taxonomy, which is ordering par excellence, has eminent aesthetic value" (*SM* 13). Myths that are also an intelligible dramatization of the world (at many levels) possess this cognitive value and, by this very fact, seduce: "Myths — and this is perhaps their most essential property — are beautiful objects which move you" (Backès-Clément 1970, 205).

The aesthetic emotion is thus directly linked to the cognitive value of works of art, and, reciprocally, an aesthetic emotion always accompanies the act of knowing. It is thus appropriate to wonder what is, from the aesthetic point of view itself, the difference between perception of the work of art and that of the object of science. We could answer, still following Lévi-Strauss, that in the former case the aesthetic emotion is due to the fact that intelligibility is given from the start, before any analysis, and that in the latter case it is the result of analysis. The work of art (as shown by the small-scale model theory) presents itself as a homologue of the object. The whole is grasped before the parts. The intellectual operation here is metaphorical. In science, in contrast, a whole is made up by the construction of parts: the operation is thus metonymic. Yet there is still more: science reduces the (accidental, singular, nonreproducible) event in favor of structure. The work of art, to the contrary, attains the structure in the event: it grasps the object in its circumstances, in its specific states of space and time. Thus it maintains the object in the whole of its being, in the profusion of its possibles: "The aesthetic emotion is the result of this union between the structural order and the order of events, which is brought about within a thing created by man and so also in effect by the observer who discovers the possibility of such a union through the work of art" (*SM* 25).

We thus see more clearly the deep kinship that exists between the knowledge offered by a work of art and that which is established by "savage thought." The latter apprehends the world and organizes its elements from the starting point of sensible experience. The work of art does nothing different in that it constructs an artifact that is the homologue of the object. Science proceeds in the opposite way: instead of systematizing the sensible qualities provided to perception, it searches for the formal properties linked to the structure of the subject. At least this has been its constant approach for centuries. However, today it begins to reintegrate into its perspective the knowledge of the concrete world on which it initially turned its back. In short, if a little science distances the sensible world, a lot brings it back.

We can thus grant a sort of advantage to the knowledge conveyed by the work of art and by "savage thought." Both provide immediate access to an intelligibility that science obtains only after a laborious journey — though we must admit that the angle of attack is not the same. Science's approach is determined by a virtually unlimited ability to intervene in the natural world, of which complete "domestication" is the goal.

Chapter 9

Time in Societies and the Question of History

> One does not perform a good structural analysis if one has not first
> done a good historical analysis. —Lévi-Strauss 1966/ow

Regarding history, it seems that many misunderstandings have accumulated between Lévi-Strauss and some of his readers. Each time Lévi-Strauss
has to deal with the deficiencies of evolutionist or diffusionist analyses,
his criticism is directed toward what he places under the general heading
of "the historical point of view." This assimilation runs the risk of being
detrimental in that it primarily targets conjectural history. We would be
wrong to conclude from this that Lévi-Strauss rejects history as a discipline and as a legitimate perspective on an object. The discipline called
"history" does not necessarily (or even does not at all) imply support for a
teleological or even a historicist vision. Much of Lévi-Strauss's criticism is
also directed toward purely narrative history or against the "History" hy-
postatized by certain philosophies. A few historians, with whom he could
only be in agreement on methods and principles, have taken such remarks
to be a challenge to their discipline. This misunderstanding has been gradually reduced, however, and the development of *historical anthropology*
has only reinforced collaboration and mutual respect.

We must define the terms of this debate.

It seems obvious, even banal, to say that the problems do not remain
the same when we speak of history as the reality of changes or as a discipline that has such reality as its object. Now, it is precisely the original
way in which Lévi-Strauss poses the problem that shows that the issues
concerning the former aspect immediately reflect on the latter. In other
words, we can say that the issue of the historical approach cannot be
separated from a culture in which a cumulative representation of time is
dominant. At once all the other problems linked to this paradigm enter the
debate. Thus we see: synchrony and diachrony, structure and event, historical narrative and mythical narrative, evolution and system, continuity
and discontinuity, and so on. All of this must be taken into account.

We must, thus, return to the fundamental problem: What is a historical society? What is a historical point of view on a society? What are the conditions and limits of such a point of view? When is historical analysis not only not pertinent but, in any case, impossible? Conversely, when and why is it legitimate?

History and Anthropology

And a little history — since such, unfortunately, is the lot of the anthropologist — is better than no history at all.   — *SA* 1:12

How can historical methods be used on societies in which written documents, records in general, are lacking? If, in the absence of such documents, we nonetheless claim to have recourse to history, it will not be to history as a rigorous discipline (which necessarily presupposes the treatment of documents accumulated over time, available to critical evaluation and thus to contradiction). Instead we would be referring to nothing but a representation of time as a causal series. We would then necessarily be led to suppose very general geneses and genealogies, which could not be verified and which in consequence would be most often imaginary.

This is the problem facing anthropology when the object it adopts is societies without writing. It does not reject history in principle: it simply cannot ask history to proceed in a terrain where its materials do not exist. Is this to say that such material, in the case of such societies, is always, everywhere, completely missing? If not, what attitude should anthropology adopt? It can be defined in this way: "One does not perform a good structural analysis if one has not first done a good historical analysis. If we do not do a good historical analysis in the domain of ethnographic data, it is not because we consider it beneath us, it is because, unfortunately, it is beyond us" (Lévi-Strauss 1966/ow). This statement summarizes what may be, in the eyes of Lévi-Strauss, the relations between anthropology and history.

Given the antihistoricist prejudices ascribed to structuralism, we might be surprised by such a strong statement of the necessity for historical inquiry. What does it mean? It means that, even from the point of view of the system, it is never useless to know about the transformations that have affected a society. Thus a fusion between two groups may explain certain forms of dual organization (without, nonetheless, explaining their principle) or shed light on certain anomalies in kinship structures. A migration may allow us to see why the mythology of a population includes, for example, animals that do not correspond to the local zoology. Such information is, for Lévi-Strauss, extremely precious and in no way hinders the construction of a structural model. Whatever the empirical reasons for the appearance of a given element in the system, what is important is the way in which this element enters into relation with others. Yet this relation itself — by which the structure is defined — always remains concretely marked by its conditions of appearance.

Before coming to the details of this demonstration, we must note that in the eyes of the anthropologist no information should be considered irrelevant to the understanding of forms of social organization, mythical representations, rituals, and so on. We must thus have precise data on the geography, climate, animals, plants, techniques, and so on, but also, of course, on the history of the society, when sufficient elements are available, including those on hand in the oral tradition. Even when there is little or nothing at the purely local level, the anthropologist cannot ignore information that can be provided by macro-history, that which deals, for example, with the demographic changes of a region or continent, as attested to by archaeology.

Thus, for Lévi-Strauss, it is very important to have plausible hypotheses available on waves of peopling as well as on the various movements of populations in both Americas in order to understand the unity of the mythic corpus of those continents. This unity is shown by hypothetico-deductive means, in other words, solely by the structural analysis of myths. Thus we now know, principally through the use of carbon 14 dating, that the beginning of the peopling of America goes back several tens of thousands of years. The northwest region of North America, the myths of which make up the greatest part of those treated in *The Naked Man* (*Mythologiques*, vol. 4) and in *The Way of Masks* and a large number of those treated in *The Jealous Potter*, presents specific aspects that can be accounted for by archaeological inventories of periods of peopling, establishment, and migration:

> One is therefore tempted to see in the Salish and Penutian peoples evidence of ancient waves of migration which left some representations confined between the mountains and the ocean, while the remainder, passing to the east of the Rockies, went on into South America long before the advent of the Athapaskans, the Sioux and the Algonkin. According to this hypothesis, the close relationship observed between myths of a northern region of North America and those of tropical America would seem less strange. (*AM* 51)

Whenever possible, historical information — at any level — should not be ignored by any anthropologist who hopes to make sense of the *present* state of a society. If the meaningful relations the anthropologist brings out on the synchronic level appear confirmed by empirical genealogies, there is thus supplementary proof of the validity of the deductive method, and it guarantees the reliability of this method for situations in which such proof is not available.

Anthropologists, like historians, refuse to draw any conclusions on what is not supported by precise data and verifiable material. Thus they are obliged to confine their hypotheses to the only document that is available: a given present society with its forms of organization, modes of activity, and systems of representation. We might say that this is a living record (since its forms have been maintained for centuries), but without traces of material memory (since the absence of writing and monuments makes chronological coding impossible). It is, of course, highly probable that the present state is the result of a transformation (or of a series of transformations), due either to the effects of social events (migrations, scissions, fusions, wars, and so on) or to the effects of natural events (changes in climate, floods, growing scarcity of resources, and so on). Yet if nothing allows material proof to be brought, anthropologists must, following proper scientific method, limit themselves to what they can verify: to present data and their internal coherency. Nothing prevents them from making hypotheses on probable transformations (as we saw above) from the starting point of distortions in this coherency and anomalies in the referent, but such hypotheses must deal with precise elements, particular facts, which can be discussed case by case.

Clearly this has nothing to do with evolutionist-type generalizations that assign laws of transformation to traditional societies. This historicist teleology, which could be called an *excess* of history, matches, on the opposite extreme, another naturalist teleology in which, to the contrary, we see a *lack* of history. This is the case of the functionalist perspective that long dominated in British and American anthropology associated with names as prestigious as Malinowski and Radcliffe-Brown. For them the preference for synchrony suffers no exceptions. Functionalists postulate that all social forms and activities correspond to a *present* goal, which amounts to ignoring the fact that we are often dealing with the remnants of former institutions. They thus sentence themselves, according to Lévi-Strauss,

> to misjudge the present because only the study of historical development permits the weighing and evaluation of the interrelationships among the components of present-day society. *And a little history* — since such, unfortunately, is the lot of the anthropologist — *is better than no history at all.* . . . For to say that a society functions is a truism; but to say that everything in a society functions is an absurdity. (*SA* 1:12–13; emphasis added)

If we ask why functionalists are made uncomfortable by historical information and why structuralists, to the contrary, hold it to be important, the answer is simple: what, in various cultures and different groups within a single culture, interests functionalists are *resemblances,* for functionalists can use them to infer the permanence or even the universality of a *need.* History then appears as a superficial factor of disturbance, for the same functions become apparent through the identity of the needs that all refer, finally, to an identical human nature.

Structuralism's discourse is diametrically opposed to this. What interest structuralists are the differences: they are what is meaningful because
they establish the terms between which relations are formed, and identities themselves are conceivable only between sets of relations, in other
words, between structures. As Lévi-Strauss says, it is *"the differences
which resemble each other"* (*T* 77). History is thus interesting as a gen-
erator of differences: structural sets are always local, singular, and, in a
way, unique. By history we must understand at once cultural diversity
and appearance of changes in a given culture. Yet structuralists, no less
than functionalists, claim to attain universality, and while Lévi-Strauss
does not speak of human nature, he always refers to a human *mind*
of which the laws would be constant in space and time. Precisely this
universality does not have to do with needs or content, for needs, a biological minimum (nourishment, protection, reproduction, and so on),
concern the behavior of the species and provide no specific information on the plurality of societies. Most tellingly, we know that needs are
par excellence what, in its expression, are most strongly affected by cultural variations. Content (such as themes in myths) is not universalizable
either: its meaning changes depending on the system in which it is integrated. This thus disqualifies Jung's and Eliade's "archetypes," as we
showed above regarding symbolism and myths. We also saw, during the
discussion of the notion of the human mind, that the idea of universality cannot be envisaged except at a very abstract level: that of laws of
structure, categories, and principles. Nonetheless, their effects are always
made clear through specific situations and objects.

In the end, there are at least two reasons the purely historical approach
in anthropology cannot be very fertile, and while these reasons appear
very different, they are in fact closely linked. The first seems simple: it is
that it is difficult to perform a historical inquiry in the absence of documents, vestiges, archives, and monuments, and this is indeed the case of
societies without writing, which are also generally societies in which the
interest in accumulating long-lasting testimony of their culture does not
appear. The reason for this "choice," this "indifference" toward history,
must be explained.

The second reason is that when documented history exists, it is, most
often, recent, born of contact between indigenous communities and Western civilization (missionaries, explorers, traders, colonial administrators).
The history told is that of the changes provoked by such contact. It
seems that there is thus a progression of history as change, but this is
precisely because, under the effect of such contact, these traditional societies undergo rapid evolution. Of course, in this case, and with these
reservations, history becomes important: it allows us to understand dise-
quilibriums and distortions between earlier formulas that are still claimed
and present realities that are highly modified with respect to tradition

(but it remains that the new formula, in turn, can become a system, can perform an original *bricolage,* and find in another mode its internal coherency, even if it is fragile or unrecognizable).

Limits to Historical Explanation

[S]pecial prestige seems to attach to the temporal dimension, as if diachrony were to establish a kind of intelligibility not merely superior to that provided by synchrony, but above all more specifically human. — *SM* 256

Anthropology has at least this in common with history (as a discipline): it devotes itself to the study of other societies. Thus both these disciplines are assured a degree of distance with respect to their object. This, compared with other social sciences, is a kind of advantage. Now, how are they different? Their difference lies in the fact that the societies studied by historians are distant in time, while those studied by anthropologists are distant in space.

These are, on an initial approximation, a similarity and a difference that are easy to identify (though there are studies of immediate history about the very recent past and anthropological inquiries into our own societies). The question we must ask is: In the name of what could history annex ethnology in its explanation? In other words, in what way could intelligibility in historical time be supposed to be greater than intelligibility through the social present, through the present structures of the societies under consideration? Lévi-Strauss does not consider this difficult to determine. The reason is that we postulate that all history is cumulative; thus we implicitly take our society in its present state as the term of reference from which we study the past. To this initial presupposition is added a second: we take it for granted that "primitive" societies represent an earlier stage in our own development. They are thus present societies that have remained in the past. In this respect they fall under the historical perspective. Immediately diversity in space is reduced to diversity in time, and since it is accepted that the beginnings are clarified and explained by what follows them, it becomes thus "natural" to look to our societies for the justification of those we consider to have remained at the origins. We were what they still are: they will become what we already are.

Such is, for Lévi-Strauss, the highly debatable link forged between historical knowledge and historicist ideology. The critical requirement is first to break this link, to return the discipline of history to its task, which is that of objective analysis and not that of the self-legitimization of a specific society. Now, it is to this critical effort that anthropology, as Lévi-Strauss understands it, can make an effective contribution. It can do so first through its *dépaysement* technique, which he establishes as the first stage of his method. Next comes the fact that his method takes spatial diversity seriously: savage societies are in time like ours; simply, the solution they have developed with respect to the necessity of living together and the use of the natural world is entirely different from that developed by so-called historical societies. As soon as historical reduction is rejected, diversity becomes problematical and truly instructive.

The lesson for historians themselves is of capital importance, for they are required no less than to grasp the specificity of blocks of the past of a single society or to understand a number of different societies, in a single slice of time, and to comprehend the different temporalities of institutions and forms of expression of a given time. In short, historians must learn to think of history in the plural, to recognize series and discontinuities, and, like anthropologists, they also must learn to enumerate discontinuous sets, which means reasoning not from creation and causality but through homologies and isomorphisms.

We thus see that if we reject the hypothesis of a unique, privileged history constituting a referent for all societies, we must look elsewhere for what could make up the unity and identity of humanity. We must wonder what is shared, what is universally recognizable in all societies at all times. Lévi-Strauss does not speak of "man" because that is precisely what he must define. He also does not write of the "subject," a concept that has a very definite philosophical history. He speaks of the human mind, which (as we saw in chapter 4) designates neither a substance nor a moral category but rather an activity the medium for which is necessarily the brain and the central nervous system but the expression of which implies all cultural activities. Understood in this way, this concept is valid for all past and present societies.

History and System

An historical explanation, an explanation as a hypothesis of the development, is only *one* kind of summary of the data — of their synopsis. We can equally well see the data in their relations to one another and make a summary of them in a general picture without putting it in the form of a hypothesis regarding the temporal development.   — Wittgenstein 1979, 8e

There is thus a sort of fundamental antipathy between history and systems of classification.   — *SM* 232

We must thus return to the question at a more radical level and ask under what conditions the representation of time called history gains explanatory value. In fact, Lévi-Strauss considers that societies have two fundamental possibilities for self-explanation: either (1) the use of "finite groups" to order the world; or (2) chronological identification.

In the first case (which all of *The Savage Mind* demonstrates), we put order into the human world by drawing homologies between it and series identified in the natural world (series that may be animal, vegetable, or other). The variety of natural species and the diversity of their properties then become means of formulating differences and classes in the human species, which itself appears unique and homogenous. The human world is constantly referred to the natural world as the source of the principle and image of its order. Time cannot enter into this "coding." To the contrary, time is not a factor since the relation between the two sets is supposed to be constant or even immutable.

In the second case, we are dealing with a society that is defined by history. In other words, the intelligibility of the human world is ensured through divisions of the temporal continuum. Instead of two homologous series in opposition, we have the indefinite succession of series made up of segments of time. Each of the segments becomes an "originating series" in relation to a "descendant series." In the first case we have a finite system, while in the second case we have an evolving series capable of accommodating an unlimited number of terms.

In order to understand the relations between history and system, we can study an example given (to another end) in *The Elementary Structures of Kinship*. This example deals with the explanation of the, sometimes accidental, origin of dual organizations in certain societies. Lévi-Strauss gives the example of two New Guinea tribes that progressively became mixed by bringing their villages nearer each other or by forming two distinct groups within the same villages. We thus call "history" the specific reasons that caused the modifications to the previous situation, but does this history allow us to understand the present situation? *In other words, can the sum of the causes of the change account for the reality observed?* This is certainly how we would be inclined to see the explanation today. Lévi-Strauss, without entering into this discussion at this point in his work, makes only this capital remark: "The reasons for each particular migration are to be found in demographic, political, economic or seasonal circumstances. Nevertheless, the general result gives proof of *integrating forces* which are independent of such conditions, and under the influence of which *history has tended towards system*" (*ESK* 77; emphasis added).

Another interesting example is provided with respect to the Indians of the plains of North America, where the peopling has been greatly modified since the sixteenth century due to several major migrations as well as the violent decline caused by the arrival of the Europeans and the resulting epidemics. Assembled together in a limited territory, the survivors, which included members of the Mandan and Hidatsa tribes, were led to bring their traditions together. The result is that, in spite of great dissimilarity,

> everything transpires as if the Mandan and the Hidatsa had suc-
> ceeded in organizing the differences in their beliefs and practices
> into a system. One could almost believe that each tribe — aware
> of the corresponding effort of the other tribe — has made the ef-
> fort to preserve and cultivate the oppositions and to combine the
> antagonistic forces in order to form a balanced whole. (*SA* 2:240)

From this we may advance the remark: there is history insofar as external elements upset the system. History is always a sign of such unbalance,
such irruption. However, when integrating forces are dominant, history
tends toward zero; in other words, history tends "toward system." This
logic, which can be identified at the level of social organization, can be
verified equally well in representative systems such as myths when events
manage to modify the context. The system, far from disintegrating, tends
to the contrary to adapt its framework to integrate the unexpected:

> The system has only to be disturbed at one particular point for it
> immediately to seek to re-establish its equilibrium by reacting in
> its totality, and it does so by means of a mythology which may be
> causally linked to history in each of its parts, but which taken in
> its entirety, resists the course of history and constantly readjusts its
> own mythological grid so that this grid offers the least resistance
> to the flow of events which, as experience proves, is rarely strong
> enough to break it up and sweep it away. (*NM* 610)

This necessarily leads to the issue we must now treat.

Structure and Event

The history/system relation constantly ties in with that of structure/event.
Lévi-Strauss proposes a theoretical case (which could correspond to many
cases encountered in the concrete) of a society organized into three "totemic" clans: the Bear, the Eagle, and the Tortoise. Here it is easy to see a
three-part division: land, sky, water. This is the structure. Let us suppose
an event: a demographic change causes the Bear clan to disappear. The
system resists history by re-creating the third partner differently: there is
now the Eagle clan and two Tortoise clans (Yellow Tortoise and Gray
Tortoise). The system has been saved, but the symbolic arrangement no
longer has the same values, for there is now a sky/water opposition and a
day/night opposition (corresponding to the colors yellow and gray). This
means that the system has four terms. There are thus two binary oppositions instead of the previous tripartition. "It can be seen therefore that
demographic evolution can shatter the structure but that if the structural

orientation survives the shock it has, after each upheaval, several means of re-establishing a system, which may not be identical with the other one but is at least formally of the same type" (*SM* 68). The structure's resistance is moreover not limited to the social organization: it is manifested at all levels of reality, particularly in those of religious activities (such as rites) and symbolic representations (such as myths). The new clan division will necessarily be reflected in these levels, but not immediately (thus the strange, sometimes paradoxical, relations between a society and its representations). This lag and the desired adjustment are simultaneously marks of the event on the structure and what displays the strength of structural regulation over historical change and the manner in which the system resists time. This is where we find the strength of *bricolage*, the art of constantly grasping the element in the accidental that can form a class to order dissimilar elements and transform debris into crystals. However, it is indeed because the savage mind does not expect special intelligibility from a succession of events (nothing moreover provides any guarantee that the supposition that such events are ordered will ensure a future result) but expects it only from a *hic* and *nunc* ordering of the elements present. Historical thought gambles on the fact that there is intelligibility in a succession of events (which obliges it to suppose a causal continuum), while for savage thought the event is, to the contrary, what endangers an intelligibility that can be given only in the structure and thus that must always return to it.

This does not mean, of course, that nothing happens in savage society. There life is as full as ours of surprising events of which people speak and of which there are long-lasting memories. This is not what is at issue. Simply, events are integrated into the available systems of representation. This is the price of reducing the danger of disorder carried by events. To the contrary, in societies of rapid change, events no longer pose this sort of problem. This is precisely what chronological coding allows, for such coding, by situating the event on a specific line, removes it from disorder without having to eliminate it in the structure. Chronological coding permits time to be represented not as natural (the time of biological rhythms, seasons, the cosmos) but as organized and cultural. Thus it is not only no longer necessary for the structure to absorb the event, but perhaps not possible. We must even say that events dominate structure. In this case, "what happens" becomes (unlike mythical systems) the always renewed material of narratives and also introduces the tension between the old and the new in tradition. Events win out over structure because they inaugurate or reorient a tradition. Thus history is indeed the essential means of signifying the unity and identity of a society. Structure is nonetheless not annulled, for it is still what selects items in the flow of events, what makes the event appear as such. In short, it is what leaves aside certain elements and favors others. By establishing transformations produced in time, history teaches us nothing except what are the current elements in a system. It explains *how* a given element traveled through time, *but it cannot account for the present coherency of a system*. If a datum is maintained over a number of periods of time, if it resists numerous transformations, it is because that datum has a reason for being that exists at each of these times and that is thus something other than mere transmission. Let us call this coherency, at each moment or period, "structure." We could thus say not only that it resists events (understood as what varies) but, much more, that it is what creates events since the fact that it resists is what ensures that there is continuity, in other words, that there is a homogenous class of events over time.

We are provided with a good example of this by the phenomenon of "split representation" (to use Boas's formula). What is this? It is a troubling observation (see *SA* 2: chapter 13) made by many specialists of the surprising kinship that exists between the arts of civilizations that are very distant in space and time: the Northwest Coast of America (eighteenth and nineteenth centuries), South America (Caduveo, nineteenth and twentieth centuries), China (first and second millenniums B.C.), the Amur region (prehistoric period), New Zealand (Maori, from the fourteenth to eighteenth centuries). In each of these different cases we find works presenting the following features: representation of a being seen from the front by two profiles, dislocation of details, intense stylization of features, symbolic expression of the attributes of an individual, and so on. The resemblances noted have led partisans of diffusion to make daring, but unverifiable, theories about the movement of populations between these various areas. However, the problem is the following: even supposing that we were able to prove diffusion and borrowing, we would still have to explain *why these elements have resisted while so many others have disappeared*. "Why should a cultural trait that has been borrowed or diffused through a long historical period remain intact? Stability is no less mysterious than change.... External connections can explain transmission, but only internal connections can account for persistence" (*SA* 1:258). In the case in question, Lévi-Strauss shows that we can identify the internal connections as a constant relation between the plastic element and the graphic element, between the support (vase, box, mask, face) and the decoration, and more profoundly yet that the observed dualism is a constant feature of extremely hierarchical societies (as is confirmed by the examples in question). We thus return here to the argument suggested above. Showing how something is transmitted does not explain its present raison d'être: to the contrary, the reason for its existence is the explanation why the feature in question was transmitted. In short, establishing a continuity or exposing a process would be but to demonstrate the reinvention of a structure, to demonstrate a constant relation between elements submitted to identical material conditions.

Societies That "Refuse History"

It is as if the goal of traditional systems of classification were to annul time or, and this amounts to the same thing, constantly to bring time back to the present of the system. Nothing that happens can or should — in principle — escape the comprehension offered by the relation of the two series, in other words by the interpretation of cultural facts in natural images and facts. However, this is not a simple representative activity. This "nonhistorical" mode of existence supposes, first, institutions, regulations, which tend to prevent the appearance of imbalances, tensions by which the irreversible would be introduced into the experience of the group. Thus the importance of the regulation of alliances, exchanges, powers, and so on. To annul time is first to annul what can cause enduring change to the homeostases.

What does this "refusal of history" by savage societies mean? It does not mean, of course, that the temporal dimension is absent. Like all others, such societies are caught in time and subject to change. This is not a subject for debate, except to raise illusionary problems. We could say that the question is posed in the following manner: How can such societies, while caught like all others in the movement of time, avoid chronological coding? For there is indeed a *before* and an *after* for them. How can this relation be prevented from being an interpretive framework for the entire life of the society (as it is for us)?

The response of savage societies can be presented thus: what comes after is supposed to have to be the rigorously faithful image of what came before, which is itself situated *outside of time,* in the natural series. The time of the ancestors is that which coincides with the formation of beings: living species, plants, stars, and so on. Thus time introduces nothing but the regular repetition of this earlier state. Mythical narrative is the putting into form of this nonhistorical repetition. This is why the very possibility of history is unceasingly intercepted by the system. Everything that occurs is immediately coded in the spatial system of nature/culture homologies. In this sense, history does not take place. The structure annuls the event before it occurs.

It is clear that the principal effect of such a system is the resorption of all change. It is not that nothing changes (it would be false and naive to affirm so) but that what changes is integrated as a supplementary feature in the structure: every variation becomes a variable of it. This, generally, means that societies conceive of their coherency, their unity, their validity, as an art of persevering in their condition. Maintaining an identity means simultaneously maintaining balances achieved in human-nature relations, in social relations, in relations with other groups, in the system of production and circulation of goods, and so on. This requirement of enduring identity is what inspires strategies that annul temporal variations:

These societies exist in time like all the others, and with the same title to it, but unlike us, they refuse to belong to history and they try very hard to inhibit, within themselves, whatever would constitute the faint promise of a historical development. . . . Our Western societies are made for change; it is the principle of their structure and of their organization. The societies called "primitive" appear to us to be such mostly because they have been conceived by their members to endure. (*SA* 2:321–22)

This resistance to change, this "refusal of history" appears not only in the logic of institutions: it is at the roots of the *mythological system,* a true "machine for suppressing time." This Lévi-Straussian formulation finds its commentary in this remark:

If taken to its logical conclusion, the analysis of the myths reaches a point where history cancels itself out. . . . [A]ll the Indian peoples of both North and South America seem to have conceived of their myths for one purpose only: to come to terms with history and, on the level of the system, to re-establish a state of equilibrium capable of acting as a shock-absorber for the disturbances caused by real-life events. (*NM* 607)

Indeed, there are numerous examples that show the existence of reworkings of traditional versions of certain myths in order to integrate in them events such as migrations, wars, and famines that have made lasting marks on a group or its environment.

The predominance of the historical perspective in the West must itself be situated in this alternative. History is essential to us precisely because we define ourselves by *change.* We give change a positive value (we oppose it to immobility and closure). In this way the historical perspective appears to us to be superior and incites us to think in hierarchical terms of the difference between so-called historical humanity and that which is not. Placed on the line of historical time, this difference appears as the relation between an earlier stage (the "primitive") and an accomplishment ("civilized" or "developed" society). To this teleology, which is also ethnocentricism, we cannot reply with a simple argument of openness and tolerance with respect to other societies. Ecumenical relativism (on the theme that all cultures are equally respectable and each is accomplished in its style, and so on) is even less effective. Clearly, what is required is to understand the alternative represented by historical explanation versus explanation through finite groups, and not to suppose that the former holds the keys to the interpretation of the latter, for this general hypothesis on the representation of time has immediate effects on the level of method. It is indeed this certainty of the prevalence of historical time that constitutes the basis for the legitimacy of evolutionist and diffusionist hypotheses in anthropology. Although Lévi-Strauss does not deny that there very frequently are evolutions and diffusions (he himself gives examples of them), he rejects such occurrences as general principles for explaining variations. Variations can be explained only case by case, using unquestionable documentation.

It would, however, not be sufficient to confine ourselves to such examples of the abuse of history. It is possible to envisage others in which, to the contrary, knowledge is linked to a history understood as a transmission of tradition and an active use of memory. This is the point of view that Ricoeur, for example, forcefully asserts in his dialogue with structural anthropology (and with Lévi-Strauss in particular). For Ricoeur, the biblical tradition, for example, is a constant return to the meaning in the present of experience, an internalization of writings and reappropriation of the past in the freshness of the historical present. According to him, Lévi-Strauss gives himself particularly favorable conditions for his thesis by restricting himself to the study of societies without writing and even to the study of the most savage among them.

This cannot be denied, but this is precisely where the dividing line lies, for there is a preliminary issue that Ricoeur does not raise: for history to make sense, it is initially necessary that a society enter into another experience of time. In short, through writing, the urban phenomenon, and social stratification, it enters into a process of cumulative change. This was the case of the Semitic and Indo-European peoples, who provided the bulk of the heritage of Western civilization. Comprehension through structure or through history is not only a question of method. In the case of savage societies, it is clear that the synchronic approach is pertinent and that the historical approach is so only in a very limited manner. Likewise, the representation of time as history necessarily gives rise to historical knowledge, but, as we have seen, nothing prevents us from situating savage societies historically when documents permit us to do so and, as we will see, nothing forbids us to identify structural constants in historical experience.

The Beginnings of History in Societies "without History"

We might ask: Are there societies that have always been fated to history and others that are destined to reject it? If history is linked to a cumulative representation of time, and if this representation is possible only from the starting point of a rupture in the homeostatic closure, nothing prevents us from thinking that many sorts of internal processes could make this rupture possible. Lévi-Strauss himself gives several examples of this in the domain of kinship (a fundamental domain in the societies under consideration since in it is concentrated the essential of social relations).

Thus, when, with respect to restricted exchange, Lévi-Strauss compares the solutions offered, on one hand, by marriage between cross-cousins and, on the other hand, by dual organizations, he first notes that the former solution is not necessarily prior to the latter and adds: "The two institutions are in contrast, one being crystallized, the other flexible. The question of chronology is completely foreign to this distinction" (*ESK* 102–3). Marriage between cross-cousins, because it operates on relations between individuals (in opposition to dualist organizations that involve classes), "acts deeper down in the social structure, and so is more sheltered from historical transformations" (*ESK* 103). Many observations show that marriage between cross-cousins appears as a recourse when the group wants to protect itself or turns in on itself. Inversely, any other solution indicates the beginnings of a departure from the protective enclosure of short-term reciprocity.

In generalized exchange, which supposes a system that is more open and has more flexible solidarities, reciprocity, as we have seen, operates on the long term and implies confidence in the responses of the partners to such exchange. "The belief is the basis of trust, and confidence opens credit. In the final analysis, the whole system exists only because the group adopting it is prepared, in the broadest meaning of the term, *to speculate*" (*ESK* 265). However, this speculation (which the demographic size of the group makes reasonable since opportunities are sufficiently numerous) creates the need to give oneself guarantees: polygamy is the most obvious form of this because it increases the circle of allies. Yet such monopolization of spouses engenders an inequality of situations, as in the case of the Katchin in Burma. Generalized exchange, which seems to suppose equality, can create inequality and orient a society toward feudal forms and the appearance of a central power that is already state-like. This provides one of the conditions for the appearance of cumulative time. As we can see, the possibility for it is manifested through a strictly internal process.

Other examples allow even better evaluation of the nature of this possibility. Take the case of feudal Japan as it appears in a great literary work of the eleventh century, the *Genji Monogatari*. In this work, court society is described, and we see cross-cousin marriage lose esteem in favor of distant alliances:

> The former brings security but also monotony: from one generation to the next, the same or similar unions are repeated, and the familial and social structure is simply reproduced. On the other hand, while a match between distant relatives is subject to risk and adventure, it also permits speculation: it creates unprecedented alliances, and new coalitions stir up the dynamics of history. (*VA* 74)

History — or at least its beginnings — would thus be a gamble on time, the very form of risk and of the pleasure that we find linked to it (the work describes traditional marriage as "boring"). The society thus enters into a process of transformations, but it is interesting to note that if the dynasty is threatened, the group closes in on itself and returns to marriage with cross-cousins.

This logic of closing-in can be observed in a symmetrical, inverse example from Fiji. Distant alliance did indeed occur there, only to be immediately translated or disguised as close alliance, in that the new spouses lost their distant characteristics through a naming operation: "The husband and wife became, nominally, each other's cross-cousin, and all the kinship terms changed accordingly. Each spouse's siblings became the cross-cousins of the other spouse, and each set of parents-in-law became cross-uncle and cross-aunt" (*VA* 77–78). Here there is an attempt to conjure away the danger of novelty and the possibility of history by transforming strangers into close relatives.

We might ask why what is favored in Japan was rejected in Fiji. Is the difference in choice linked to demographic size? to the state of technology and material production? to forms of religion? or to a specific combination of these factors and perhaps yet others? It is difficult for anthropologists to give an answer to this, but to have been able to identify the elements of the problem is already no small achievement.

The Elements of a Structural History

[T]he idea of a structural history contains nothing which could shock the historian.   —*SA* 2:16

The expression "structural history" may seem strange when we have made obvious the antinomy of structure and event and have favored the analysis of synchronic systems. Yet historical research, insofar as it attempts to understand the totality of the social fact with respect to a given period, deals first and foremost with recurring events and constants. Generally, as soon as history stops being that of events, it tends to be structural in that it brings out the deeper layers, which are thus more stable, slower phenomena. There is a slowing of the structures that, under the acceleration of events, provides, over time, an *analogon* of the synchronic. In sum, the more distance taken by the perspective, the more clearly stabilities appear. This is the lesson of long-term history, as has been demonstrated by F. Braudel, who saw in the way kinship structures resist time, as shown by Lévi-Strauss, a perfect example of observable phenomena recurring over centuries.

Nonetheless, these considerations do not exhaust the idea of a structural history. In order to see what Lévi-Strauss means by this expression, we must show how two epistemological questions are involved in it: that of the synchrony/diachrony relation and that of causality. Likewise, two methodological questions must be asked: How is the analysis of structures valuable, on the one hand, for a "regressive history," and how does it open the way, on the other hand, for a prospective history?

Synchrony and Diachrony

The attempt has often been made to characterize the structural method by the priority given to the synchronic element over the diachronic element. Such an approach is certainly not wrong, but it runs the risk of considerably simplifying the relations between these two aspects in the work of Lévi-Strauss. For him, the diachronic is not to be confused with the historical perspective. It can be a dimension internal to the structure, as is the case for the relations between generations in kinship systems, for the movement of reciprocity in alliances with very long cycles, or for moments in mythical narrative.

In fact, this question is linked to the more general one of the relation between structure and process. Structural anthropology, by choosing as its models Saussurian linguistics and Trubetzkoy's phonology, made a clear choice in favor of the synchronic approach over the diachronic approach. Lévi-Strauss summarizes this by saying that it chooses the analysis of *structures* rather than that of *processes*.

> The claim to undertake jointly the study of processes and that of structures implies, at least in anthropology, a naive philosophy which does not take into account the conditions under which we operate. Structures appear only through observation performed from outside. Inversely, such observation is always incapable of grasping the processes which are not analytical objects, but the specific way in which a temporality is experienced by a subject. (Lévi-Strauss 1962c/a, 44)

The definition Lévi-Strauss gives here of the concept of *process* is very limiting and corresponds, in short, to what could be in his eyes that of phenomenology ("the processes which are not analytical objects but the specific way in which a temporality is experienced by a subject" [Lévi-Strauss 1962c/a, 44]). It is thus all the more interesting to note that he gives a different extension to the concept of diachrony: he refuses to identify it with the historical dynamic, just as he refrains from reducing the synchronic to the static.

In fact, there is a concept that Lévi-Strauss uses constantly and that could play here the role of a mediating term between synchrony and diachrony: *transformation*. In chapter 3 of *The Savage Mind*, Lévi-Strauss discusses Frazer's explanation of "totemic" institutions, some of which Frazer presents as primitive, others as derived. Lévi-Strauss shows that they simply hold transformational relations to one another, in other words that some "totemic" institutions are symmetrical, inverted versions of others. This amounts to establishing a synchrony where a genealogy was supposed to have been found. Likewise, Lévi-Strauss shows that the kinship systems and totemic institutions of the Aranda and the Arabama (in Australia) become intelligible if we see that they are in a relation of transformation. However, we saw earlier how neighboring peoples (such as the Mandan and the Hidatsa of Upper Missouri) could inverse their rites and myths and how sets of myths compose groups of transformation (this is indeed the essence of Lévi-Strauss's approach to explaining the production of variants). Yet this notion, which seems to indicate structure's ability to impose itself on process, nevertheless implies relations of succession. This means two things: first, that the causality is dependent not on events but on logic; second, that from the structure we can read an order of succession that is nonetheless not a genealogy. Here, clarification is required.

Causality

All structural approaches necessarily imply that a position has been taken on causal explanation. Why? At least because structural analysis gives itself objects that are sets of elements grasped synchronically in their reciprocal relations. It is thus difficult to establish relations (even if they exist) of cause and effect between these elements, since such research would favor the relation between an antecedent and a consequent, thus the genetic explanation. Time is perhaps the very form of this relation: "A logical opposition is projected in time in the form of a relation of cause and effect" (*RC* 183).

As soon as structural analysis renounces the genetic point of view, it must limit itself to establishing homologies between the various series in which the constants that it has listed appear. Is this an abandonment of explanation? Or is it to the contrary the best way of making explanation possible? Let us take the case of marriage between cross-cousins (described in chapter 2). Many explanations have consisted in looking at the past of each society for a reason, so that this form of alliance could be seen as the remainder of institutions that have disappeared. The same operation has been repeated for the prohibition on parallel cousins. We also know that genealogies of the same type have been proposed to account for the incest prohibition. There are thus as many explanations as there are histories, and if some are comparable, they are so due to luck rather than to logic. To the contrary, the structural explanation consists of showing that these prescriptions and prohibitions form a single complex; that the same logic of reciprocity is responsible for exogamy and, simultaneously, prohibits union between a man and his sister or daughter; and that cross-cousins are the simplest, most obvious form of membership in different lines and can thus be in an exogamous relation, while, to the contrary, parallel cousins necessarily belong to the same line.

We discover an analogous problem when we consider the connection between appellations and attitudes. To explain, for example, the latent hostility between father and son, and the confidence between nephew and maternal uncle; or the distance imposed between brothers and sisters, and tenderness between spouses, as facts having to do with a tradition for which, in each case, we must try to reconstitute the heritage, is to suppose that these facts are autonomous (the problem of the nephews and the problem of the spouses would thus be considered unrelated), and it is also to suppose that giving them a genealogy is in itself enlightening. "Each detail of terminology and each special marriage rule is associated with a specific custom as either its consequence or its survival. We thus meet with a chaos of discontinuity" (*SA* 1:35). Instead, we must demonstrate that all these relations are linked, that we are in the presence of a system with four terms in which it appears that "the relation between maternal uncle and nephew is to the relation between brother and sister as the relation between father and son is to that between husband and wife. Thus if we know one pair of relations, it is always possible to infer the other" (*SA* 1:42).

We can now speak of causality if we want, but in the sense of an interdependence of terms, of a reciprocal implication of positions. In short, we are dealing with what Lévi-Strauss calls "concomitant variations" instead of what were previously presented as inductive correlations. Genealogies can describe successions of states — supposing there have been changes — but they cannot account for the present coherency of a system that alone makes them understandable. In the final analysis, this can be reduced to the epistemological rule that one does not explain a fact by a fact: one explains it by a law.

This leads us to the methodological considerations, or, in other words, what may be the practice of a structural history. In the first place, such history could consist of what has been called "regressive history," which would consist of examining the present state of an institution or a whole society to decipher the transformations that indicate where structure has been distorted by events. This method is very helpful primarily when the past cannot be accessed through direct documentation. It consists of asking what events must be supposed to account for the existence of a given element in a specific structural system, when such presence appears inexplicable in such a system.

Lévi-Strauss gives us a striking example of this in an essay entitled "Social Structures of Central and Eastern Brazil" (*SA* 1: chapter 7). In this work, while discussing Sherente forms of marriage and dual organizations, he notes an entire series of anomalies that leads him to reconstitute a historical evolution permitting identification of the following stages: the existence of three patrilineal, patrilocal lines; the appearance of two matrilineal moieties; the creation of a fourth patrilocal line (mythicized in the present as a "tribe captured formerly"). This explains a conflict between a kinship rule and a residence rule, leading the moieties toward patrilineal kinship and to the transformation of lines into associations. In short, the present structure contains in its contradictions, in their imprint, the memory of the succession of accumulated events. The succession is not what makes the present situation intelligible: it is the intelligibility of the structure that allows us to understand the succession.

We could object that the example is of course favorable in the case of small societies ordered on mechanical, rather than statistical, models. However, other examples can be given in response, such as that of plastic forms. Let us look at the essay titled "The Serpent with Fish inside His Body" (*SA* 1: chapter 14). There Lévi-Strauss discusses the studies published by Alfred Métraux that brought out surprising parallels between oral traditions of Chaco today and narratives of the Andean region recorded in old documents. One of the narratives concerns a supernatural serpent named Lik, whose tail is filled with fish and who is alternately dangerous and helpful. Lévi-Strauss identifies this exact motif on vases, one from Nazca and the other from Pacasmayo. What is interesting is to find in contemporary oral traditions glosses on these ancient pieces. These correspondences between elements distant in time (several centuries) and in space (the Andes and Chaco) give an idea of the possible fruitfulness of the intersection of the approaches of archaeology and ethnology. Through its incredible stability, a present-day oral tradition can provide a very ancient document: "We can no longer doubt that the key to so many heretofore incomprehensible motifs is directly accessible in myths and tales which are still current. One would be mistaken to neglect these means which enable us to gain access to the past" (*SA* 1:272). Here again, the present of the structure carries in itself the key to the tradition and the traces of a transformation in time. Lévi-Strauss gives many examples of such traces of history in myths: the hypotheses he proposes from the basis of variants alone confirm research undertaken by historians and archaeologists (see the examples given in *From Honey to Ashes* with respect to the former relations between the Bororo, the Ge, and the Tacana). This method, which reveals itself to be very valuable in the case of societies without writing, loses none of its pertinence when written documents exist.

Yet the notion of structural history is not limited to the task of reconstitution alone. It comes to completion, in Lévi-Strauss's view, in a sort of "calculation" of the possibilities of events, in a *prospective history*. Let us return to the whole of the passage cited earlier:

[T]he idea of a structural history contains nothing which could shock the historian... [T]here is no contradiction in a history of symbols and signs engendering unforeseeable developments, even though it brings into play structural combinations in a limited number. In a kaleidoscope, the combination of identical elements always yields new results. (*SA* 2:16)

We return here to a set of problems discussed regarding the issue of the unconscious and with respect to which we noted that the only way to consider this combination acceptable is to establish empirically that it is valid. This is indeed what Lévi-Strauss proposes (through "making an inventory of all recorded customs" [*TT* 178]).

Nonetheless, as seductive as it is, this hypothesis sees events as cases of the system, which amounts to thinking of time, in the framework of games theory, like a selection of moves, just as we can conceive of speech as the performance of language. Yet perhaps this perspective should be reversed and the system should be seen as the whole of the limits of each case and as existing only in the virtual of their realization. In this way events belong to what is irreversible. Moreover, Lévi-Strauss comes close to this position when he proposes to set aside all teleology favoring a determinate history. Abilities are the same everywhere. This situation is compared by Lévi-Strauss to the "possibles" that are in a seed and that only a certain number of external factors — thus events — will allow to develop, to emerge from their "dormancy":

The same is true of civilizations. Those which we term primitive do not differ from the others in their mental equipment but only by virtue of the fact that nothing in any mental equipment ordains that it should display its resources at a given time or utilize them in a certain direction. The fact that, on one occasion in human history and in one place, there occurred a pattern of development which we see, perhaps arbitrarily, as being the cause of subsequent events — although we cannot be sure of this since there is not and never will be any term of comparison — does not give us authority to transmute one historical occurrence, which can have no meaning beyond its actual happening at that place and in that time, into a proof that such a development should be demandable in all places and at all times. If such were the case, it would be too easy to conclude that, wherever such an evolution has not taken place, its absence is to be explained by inferiority or inadequacy of societies or individuals. (*HA* 474)

The history that Lévi-Strauss criticizes is without a doubt primarily pure history of events and conjectural history. Such criticisms in no way target the work of the *new history*, that which, in France for example, has come out of the Annales school and of which Braudel has probably been one of the most remarkable representatives in recent decades. However, it is true that, in this case, we see history become simultaneously demographic, economic, geographic, and so on. In short, the only dimension that now distinguishes history from these disciplines is that it deals with past segments of time and thus has available only limited documentation, requiring a highly developed deductive ability. We could therefore say that historians are anthropologists who choose as their field of research segments of time (going from very short to very long periods) and whose informants are various types of documents (writings, monuments, tools, works of art, and so on) left by a given society or group of societies.

In the final analysis, we can consider that the structural method has led the historical approach to ask itself a certain number of fundamental questions that it tended to avoid. First, it obliged it to recognize that if certain societies (those called "primitive") can only with difficulty — apart from exceptional circumstances — become the object of historical analysis, this does not mean that they must be situated before our history or that we should postulate an evolution of which our society would be the end. Yet we probably, even unconsciously, continue to consider them to be an image of our past. They would thus be waiting for their true temporality: that in which we are already immersed. In short, they are in the "not yet." The historical dimension is supposed to provide them with the meaning they are lacking. Such is the general — implicit or explicit — conception of historical thought respecting traditional societies (we need only think of Hegel's condescending pages on the "dark continent ... ").

The structural approach answers: these societies are intelligible in another way, which is in keeping with their mode of being. This is the intelligibility that appears in forms of social organization (like kinship), forms of representation (like myths), and systems of symbolization (like rituals). The meaning is found wholly in this synchronic set precisely because this set operates with a view to its own permanence. Society explains itself through the mediation of series given in nature (as is shown by the demonstration in *The Savage Mind*). Events of diachrony are constantly placed in relation to this stable referent and annulled in it. Change is unthinkable because the institutions themselves are ordered so as to reject it. We are thus not simply where history is lacking: we are in a logic where the very possibility of history (as a cumulative process) is set aside.

This is probably the fundamental consideration that makes it possible to ask in a relevant way the question of the legitimacy of the historical approach. We see better that such an approach is inseparable from the general conditions of the representation of time in a given society. For ours, precisely, which is a society of *change*, diachronic causality is determining, and for that reason the historical explanation is unavoidable. However, the condition for this is precisely that we not give ourselves a naive conception of this causality under the form of continuist or teleo-logical representations. History is itself made up of many temporalities, of series with their own genealogies that exist side by side or that inter-sect, echo one another, and sometimes merge. Between these "blocks of history" can appear, at certain times, constants the persistence of which allows us to sketch the outlines of an era. At this point, the structural approach can be fertile for historical research. It allows us to better de-fine the horizontal solidarities between different fields and to see that the points of rupture are no less meaningful than the continuities.

Concluding Remarks

The Moral Issue

We could conclude by reviewing the theoretical assessment of Lévi-Strauss's work and of structuralism in general. However, to do so would risk simply adding notes to the remarks made in the introduction. Instead we propose to move to another terrain and give closer attention to a problem that is only touched on at various points in this book: that of the moral implications of anthropological work and the definition of the obligations incumbent on the civilization that produces such work.

As we have seen, due to the special nature of their work, anthropologists are necessarily led to reflect on the origins of their knowledge and on the relation this knowledge has to the peoples studied. We said (in chapter 1) that here the moral issue was part of the epistemological question. However, this question is perhaps not limited to an attitude with respect to other people and other cultures. Faced with the last savage cultures that can be encountered, anthropologists, who come from the civilizations with the most highly developed technology, are always led to wonder about a subject that concerns the future of the human species in general and about the way in which various cultures have treated, and still treat, the natural world: its equilibrium, diversity, integrity. To such musings, it does not seem difficult to answer that the most (technically) advanced civilizations have long been engaged in a process of violence and destruction. This is probably the point at which we might speak of Lévi-Strauss's Rousseauism. Yet there is a nuance. Rousseau wrote at the dawn of the industrial revolution and his diagnosis dealt mostly with the erosion of the social bond. Today, after two centuries of industrial development and with apparent understanding of the prediction addressed to the reader of the second *Discours* ("the dread of those who will have the unhappiness to live after you" [1964, 104]), Lévi-Strauss is primarily concerned by threats to the natural environment. For him, this is where the most urgent ethical issue of our time is situated. (This is also the one formulated, for example, by Michel Serres in *Le Contrat naturel* [1995].) Now, let us see Lévi-Strauss's arguments.

Prolegomena to an Ethic of the Living

If there is one thing of which Western humanist thought believes it should be proud, it is to have promoted and been able to make globally accepted a conception of a human as a moral being. This is also, in Lévi-Strauss's view, perhaps its greatest defect, at least when such insistence on the universality of humanity becomes exclusive. It may seem paradoxical to challenge the vision that led to the modern conception of human rights. Indeed, it is not a question of denying it, but it must be seen clearly that it developed only at the expense of a misunderstanding — even an exclusion — of what can define humanity in a more complete, fundamental manner: the fact that a human being is a *living being*. This does not amount to rejecting a human being's definition as a moral being — to the contrary. It simply shows the enormous immorality that may be harbored by excessive privileges accorded to humanity at the expense of other living species. At the same time it provides an exact definition of the broader, more radical level of ethical requirement: "[I]f man possesses rights as a living being, then it follows immediately that these recognized rights of humanity as a species will encounter their natural limits in the rights of other species. Thus the rights of mankind stop whenever and wherever their exercise imperils the existence of another species" (*VA* 282). Lévi-Strauss does not say that humankind should stop gaining its subsistence from other living beings, for from this point of view all species are in a dependent relation. He simply says that this process can never legitimate the disappearance of any species. Thus the formulation of what we might call the *categorical imperative of an ethic of the living*: "The right to life, and to the free development of the living species still represented on the earth, is the only right that can be called inalienable — for the simple reason that the disappearance of any species leaves us with an irreplaceable void in the system of creation" (*VA* 282). This imperative can be called categorical in that its principle is not conditional but a priori: it calls for *absolute respect* for the integrity of the natural world. The just moral definition of humankind thus is first the *recognition of the rights of what cannot demand rights*. The more powerless nature becomes with respect to humanity, the more humankind is obliged, categorically and imperatively, to change humanity's excess of virtual power into rights since, precisely, it alone can transform into rights what was until now primarily a regulation of life. Rights intervene to correct what has been done. The moral requirement is not to conceive of humankind exclusively as a moral being. To conceive of people as living beings is the most profound moral requirement insofar as we take seriously their existence as members of a species in the universe and in the future of the natural world.

The Content of Freedoms Is Always Local

No doubt can be cast on the necessity of formulating and asserting human rights. Who could challenge the validity of the fundamental rights of respect for the individual and of freedom of opinion, expression, and movement of all human beings? Yet such universalism requires closer examination since it takes no context into account: it defines freedom in a sort of homogenous, unlocated, unreal space. It presupposes a general humanity, without specific traditions, customs, memories. This amounts to ignoring the fact that human beings are always among other human beings, either in long-standing communities and traditions or in more restricted or more flexible groups that (as in modern metropolises) display their own manners and tastes, in short their own ecological-cultural niche. This is what creates pleasure in living: uniqueness and style, no less than weights and restrictions, provide content to freedom. An ethnologist knows this better than anyone and thus has more claim than anyone else to validity when writing:

> By providing freedom with a supposedly rational foundation, one condemns it to eliminating this rich content and to sapping its own strength. For the attachment to freedoms is all the greater in that the rights that freedom is asked to protect have a basis that is in part irrational: they consist of those minute privileges, those possibly ludicrous inequalities that, without infringing upon the general equality, allow individuals to find the nearest anchorage. True liberty is that of long habit, of preferences — in a word, of customs: that is, as France's experience since 1789 has proved, a form of freedom implacably opposed by all the theoretical ideas proclaimed as rational. (*VA* 287)

This denunciation of an abstract universalism and, conversely, defense and illustration of the local is certainly one of the two most frequently appearing points in Lévi-Strauss's recent work. He goes so far, in "Race and Culture" (*VA*), as to not shrink from asserting that a group's or culture's protection of its difference necessarily occurs through a certain form of refusal of other groups and cultures. This might appear shocking in the face of the now widespread naive moralism of cultural altruism, perhaps mainly because such stealthy assimilation compensates and allows us to be excused for the more violent assimilation performed by our ancestors. Yet ethnologists know that such recognition can be fatal to the cultures that are its objects: "For one cannot fully enjoy the other, identify with him, and yet at the same time remain different. When integral communication with the other is achieved completely, it sooner or later spells doom for both his and my creativity" (*VA* 24). Just as population genetics teaches us that isolated populations paradoxically contain the maximum number of genetic stocks offering the greatest possibilities of transformation, cultures have created and developed their traditions and their arts only in a certain degree of separation from other cultures. Of course, contacts and exchanges are clear everywhere in the relations between civilizations. Historians unceasingly show this, but what is omitted is that such borrowings establish original traditions and styles only insofar as the culture that receives simultaneously refuses to let itself become assimilated and even, to a certain degree, rejects the values and representations of the culture from which it borrowed. Yet earlier in "Race and History," Lévi-Strauss made this principle clear: the coalition of cultures creates their strength, and their reciprocal fertilization enables them to develop and survive.

Lévi-Strauss in no way rejects this principle. It is simply that, twenty years later, he sees that he had underestimated the need for a certain distance, or rather that, as he discovered in the study of myths and the Indian wisdom carried in them, one must always establish the correct distance. "The great creative eras were those in which communication had become adequate for mutual stimulation by remote partners, yet was not so frequent or so rapid as to endanger the indispensable obstacles between individuals and groups or to reduce them to the point where overly facile exchanges might equalize and nullify their diversity" (*VA* 24). Lévi-Strauss considers that it indeed could be that racism initially springs from fear linked to the risk of loss of identity, to excessive proximity, of which the physical features of the other are then used as a criterion for rejection because they are what is most obvious (all sorts of rationalizations then come to aid this primary, basic fact).

What is urgent is thus not to welcome and mix but to recognize oneself in one's differences and to firmly maintain this difference. We may even be led to admit also that between cultures there are incompatible features and that there is neither necessary complementarity nor joyful unity.

The Quarrel regarding Humanism

In the 1950s and 1960s, it was asked whether structuralism is a humanism. Perhaps it has no less claim to such a title than does the existentialism for which Sartre then asserted this quality. A number of times when Lévi-Strauss was under attack from critics who reproached him for dehumanizing his object, he reacted by showing that his approach was, more than any other, respectful of the uniqueness of beings and that anthropology was closer than any other human science to being the accomplishment of the humanist project. However, the term "humanism" has taken on two very different meanings of which we must give an explanation, for all the ungrounded debates on this subject are due to the

fact that the two meanings have been amalgamated. Yet it is not difficult
to see that Lévi-Strauss has not confused them.

There is no problem in defending humanism if what is understood
by it is the heritage of what appeared under this label beginning in the
Renaissance: the rediscovery of writings from antiquity, the opening of
knowledge to new disciplines, the autonomy of research from religious
authority, the formulation of a new universality founded on the reasonable nature of all human beings. More precisely, Lévi-Strauss shows (see
"The Three Humanisms" in *SA* 2:271–74) how anthropology belongs
specifically to this current of which the essential part is, in his view, the
recognition of the following necessity: "[N]o civilization can define itself
if it does not have at its disposal some other civilizations for comparison" (*SA* 2:272). The study of the literature, religion, and society of
antiquity was, for the people of the Renaissance, a formidable effort in
putting their own culture into perspective. It was a sort of *dépaysement*
in time, but also a remarkable appropriation of a past of which the memory consisted only in writings. The next major experience (the second
humanism) was linked to the discovery and study of great non-European
civilizations, which were, however, contemporary this time, such as those
of the Middle East (the Muslim world) and the Far East (mainly India and China). These are the civilizations that strongly affected thought
from the seventeenth century on and that, in the nineteenth century, gave
rise to new institutions in knowledge (history, philology, linguistics, comparative religious studies). What the twentieth century has seen develop
(which is the third humanism) is an interest in civilizations that were
held until now to be "inferior" and were thus called "primitive." Ethnology has been able to teach us that such nonliterate civilizations are
nonetheless accomplished and refined, having developed, in their symbolic productions, their ways of life, their systems of classification, and
their myths, forms of thought just as complete and sophisticated as those
of other civilizations, but from a different perspective on the natural
world and social organization. Even with respect to its method, anthropology has more claim than any other form of knowledge to be able to
say that nothing human is foreign to it. The humanism that Lévi-Strauss
calls "democratic" (in contrast with the two others, of which the first
is called "aristocratic" and the second "bourgeois") is by far the most
open, the most truly universalist, since it aims to grasp the intelligibility of the differences even to the slightest manifestations of forms of
life and culture. This is the goal of structural anthropology, and *from
this point of view* it can unhesitatingly call itself eminently "humanist." It is also in this respect that it necessarily concurs with an ethic
of tolerance while simultaneously insisting on the requirement that local identities be asserted (which were identified above as the content of
freedoms).

However, next to this scientific and ethical humanism, there lies a much more debatable humanism, which could be called metaphysical or, more precisely, ideological. What is at stake is less the assertion of the openness of knowledge and cultures, or the proclamation of the respect due to human beings as such, than the provision of humanity with a hegemonic status with respect to other beings. This humanism cannot be separated from a conception of knowledge as mastery that also began developing in the Renaissance and that found in Cartesianism its most explicit expression. This tradition is the one Lévi-Strauss criticizes when he speaks of "this type of imprisonment which man increasingly imposes on himself from within his own human nature" and of the "great, supposedly humanist current which claimed to set up mankind as a separate kingdom. This current seems to me to represent one of the greatest obstacles in the way of the progress of philosophical thought" (*SA* 2:280).

Here we recognize one of the most constant criticisms of Lévi-Strauss when he tries to define the cultural sources of Western violence against other civilizations. In this he feels close to Rousseau, and it is specifically in the article he devotes to Rousseau that we can read this stern observation:

> We started by cutting man off from nature and establishing him in an absolute reign. We believed ourselves to have thus erased his most unassailable characteristic: that he is first a living being. Remaining blind to this common property, we gave free reign to all excesses. Never better than after the last four centuries of his history could Western man understand that, while assuming the right to impose a radical separation of humanity and animality, while granting to one . . . all that he denied the other, he initiated a vicious circle. The one boundary, constantly pushed back, would be used to separate men from other men and to claim — to the profit of even smaller minorities — the privilege of a humanism, corrupted at birth by taking self-interest as its principle and its notion. (*SA* 2:41)

The Lesson of the Savages

Anthropocentric humanism is, in fact, the negation of ethical humanism — understood in its deepest sense — which necessarily includes respect not only for human beings themselves but for the whole of the given world. This is the humanism that we have always been taught by those we call "savages." It is among them that we find "those vast systems of rites and beliefs that may strike us as ridiculous superstitions but help to keep a human group in harmony with the natural environment" (*VA* 14). It is also among them that we find "the idea that human beings, animals and plants share a common stock of life, so that any human abuse of any species is tantamount to lowering the life expectancies of human beings themselves" (*VA* 14). In this, Lévi-Strauss sees the testimony of "a wisely conceived humanism, which does not center on man but gives him a reasonable place within nature, rather than letting him make himself its master and plunderer, without regard for even the most obvious needs and interests of later generations" (*VA* 14).

This is what we learn from the ethics of myths, writes Lévi-Strauss at the end of *The Origin of Table Manners:*

> In the present century, when man is actively destroying countless living forms, often wiping out so many societies whose wealth and diversity had, from time immemorial, constituted the better part of his inheritance, it has probably never been more necessary to proclaim, as do the myths, that sound humanism does not begin with oneself, but puts the world before life, life before man, and respect for others before self-interest: and that no species, not even our own, can take the fact of having been on this earth for one or two million years — since in any case, man's stay here will one day come to an end — as an excuse for appropriating the world as if it were a thing and behaving on it with neither decency nor discretion. (*OTM* 508)

This would be the admirable lesson of the savages, and it is, in the eyes of the anthropologist, the expression of the highest degree of civilization.

We could certainly, as has been done more than once, criticize Lévi-Strauss for a lack of a sense of modernity, for holding a position very withdrawn from the promises of the hyper-technical world that is developing before our eyes. In response to this he incessantly asks, like Rousseau, the only question he considers crucial: In what way is this development good not only for humanity but for all living things and the whole of the living world?

To a journalist from a French daily who asked him, among a few others, what testimony of our era he would choose to include in a capsule that would be buried somewhere in Paris and addressed to archaeologists of the year 3000, Claude Lévi-Strauss answered:

> I will put in your time-vault documents relative to the last "primitive" societies, on the verge of disappearance: specimens of vegetable and animal species soon to be destroyed by man; samples of air and water not yet polluted by industrial wastes; notices and illustrations of sites soon to be ravaged by civil war or military installations.... Better to leave them some evidence of so many things that the misdeeds of our generation and the next will have forever deprived them of knowing: the purity of the elements, the

diversity of beings, the grace of nature, and the decency of man. (*SA* 2:286–87)

It is the most humble peoples and civilizations that have provided the anthropologist with this lesson in wisdom for the next millennium. It will remain indispensable long after the last savage is no more than a memory in our museums and libraries.

Chronology

Note: Most of the information contained in this chronology comes from *Tristes tropiques* (abbreviation: *TT*) and especially from the interviews granted to Didier Eribon which have been published as *Conversations with Claude Lévi-Strauss* (abbreviation: *CCLS*). Lévi-Strauss agreed to check the precision of the information given here himself, and he was also kind enough to provide precious complementary information.

1908

Birth of Claude Lévi-Strauss in Brussels, on November 28, of French parents: Raymond Lévi-Strauss and Emma Lévy. His father was a painter, specializing in portraits.

1909

Return of family to Paris. Secondary school studies (up to the *baccalauréat*) at Lycée Janson-de-Sailly, in Paris.

1924–25

Read Marx ("I was immediately fascinated by Marx" [*CCLS* 8]). This study was begun under the influence of a Belgian family friend and socialist militant, who oriented Claude Lévi-Strauss toward the French socialist party (the SFIO). Lévi-Strauss was later to become the secretary-general of the Fédération des Étudiants Socialistes.

1926

Entrance into the preliminary course to prepare for admission to the École Normale Supérieure (one of the most prestigious universities in the French system). In the end, Lévi-Strauss abandoned the project of applying for this institution.

1927

Entrance into the Paris Faculty of Law, and at the same time into studies in philosophy at the Sorbonne. His professors were, among others,

---

I have included the abbreviations for the English translations of works by Lévi-Strauss whenever the original French versions are mentioned in the chronology. By referring to the list of abbreviations, which begins on p. ix of the book, the reader will be able to find the publication information for both versions. *Trans.*

Léon Brunschvicg, Georges Dumas, Jean Laporte, Léon Robin, Louis Bréhier (all of whom were then well-known representatives of scientific rationalism), and Célestin Bouglé (a specialist of castes in India). It was under the direction of the latter that Claude Lévi-Strauss prepared his master's thesis on the philosophical postulates of historical materialism. He was awarded his *licence* in law.

1928

Preparation for the examination for the *agrégation* in philosophy (the *agrégation* is one of the highest degrees in France and provides tenure valid in all French public schools). Among those preparing with him: Maurice Merleau-Ponty and Simone de Beauvoir ("...very young, with a fresh, bright complexion, like a little peasant girl. She had a crisp but sweet side to her, like a rosy apple" [*CCLS* 12]).

Lévi-Strauss met the philosopher and writer Paul Nizan, one of Sartre's close friends, at Nizan's marriage to one of Lévi-Strauss's younger cousins. "Paul Nizan told me he himself had been drawn to anthropology. That encouraged me.... Of course I had read *Aden-Arabie* [1932], which I admired" (*CCLS* 17).

1931

Awarded the *agrégation* in philosophy. Among those who also passed that year: Ferdinand Alquié (who was to become a very well-known specialist on Descartes) and Simone Weil (whose philosophical, political, and religious destiny was exceptional).

1932

Military service. Marriage to Dina Dreyfus. First teaching position, in October, at Mont-de-Marsan lycée in the Southwest of France. Lévi-Strauss was a socialist candidate in the cantonal elections in that area, but during the campaign a minor car accident put an end to those political aspirations.

1933

Assigned to the lycée in Laon (in the Northeast): "I began to tire of it [teaching]. And above all, I wanted to travel, to see the world" (*CCLS* 14). Read Robert H. Lowie's *Primitive Society* (1920). It was a revelation:

[I]nstead of notions borrowed from books and at once metamorphosed into philosophical concepts I was confronted with an account of first-hand experience. The observer, moreover, had been so committed as to keep intact the full meaning of his experience. My mind escaped from the closed circuit which was what the practice of academic philosophy amounted to: made free in the open air, it breathed deeply and took on new strength. Like a townsman let loose in the mountains, I made myself drunk with the open spaces and my astonished eye could hardly take in the wealth and variety of the scene. (*TT* 63)

1934

"My career was initiated one Sunday morning in the autumn of 1934. At nine o'clock the telephone rang. It was Célestin Bouglé, who was then the Director of the École Normale Supérieure" (*TT* 49). Bouglé, director of Lévi-Strauss's master's thesis in philosophy (see above) and aware of his interest in ethnology, proposed that Lévi-Strauss apply for a position in sociology at the University of São Paulo in Brazil; the university had just been created under the responsibility of a French university mission headed by the psychiatrist George Dumas. Lévi-Strauss met with the latter, whose courses he had attended in the past, and Dumas decided to hire him.

1935

Embarked for Brazil from Marseilles in February, via Barcelona, Cadiz, Algiers, Casablanca, and Dakar. He landed in Santos. On the boat he wrote the famous "sunset" passage (*TT,* chapter 7); he later said that it was the only completed fragment of what was meant to be a novel.

He took up his position at the University of São Paulo. He taught sociology there until 1938. It was expected that he would base his teaching essentially on the heritage of Comte and Durkheim. A French colleague in sociology considered him to be too unfaithful to Comte and so attempted to force him to leave. ("I arrived as an avowed anti-Durkheimian and the enemy of any attempt to put sociology to metaphysical uses" [*TT* 63].) He was maintained in his position thanks in part to the solidarity of the two other members of the French mission: Pierre Monbeig and, especially, Fernand Braudel, whose work was already authoritative.

Instead of returning to France at the end of the first university year, Lévi-Strauss and his wife undertook, for the Paris Musée de l'Homme and the city of São Paulo, an expedition into the interior of Brazil, in the Mato Grosso. This was to be the occasion of his first study of the Caduveo and Bororo Indians. "I felt I was reliving the adventures of the first sixteenth-century explorers. I was discovering the New World for myself. Everything seemed mythical: the scenery, the plants, the animals" (*CCLS* 21).

This first expedition, the narration of which takes up a great deal of *Tristes tropiques,* was in a way Lévi-Strauss's "ethnographic baptism." In this way he initiated himself into a discipline for which he never received any university training or professional preparation.

1936

Returned to France during the winter of 1936–37. (Winter in Europe corresponds to summer in the Southern Hemisphere and thus to holidays for Brazilian universities.) The Musée de l'Homme organized the exhibition of the ethnographic collection brought back by Lévi-Strauss and his wife, Dina Dreyfus. This collection included ceramics and painted skins from the Caduveo, as well as costumes, weapons, and utensils from Bororo country.

At this time Lévi-Strauss published an article on the Bororo that attracted the attention of the ethnologists Alfred Métraux and Robert H. Lowie (see _CCLS_ 24). This was to be a determining moment for his career as an Americanist.

"A year had passed since my visit to the Bororo; and, during that year all the conditions required to make an anthropologist of me had been fulfilled. Lévy-Bruhl, Mauss and Rivet had given me their blessing — even if only after the event" (_TT_ 235). Lévi-Strauss had very briefly met the first two, who dominated French ethnology, before his departure for Brazil.

1937

In Paris, prepared for a new expedition to Brazil. Thanks to the impact of his articles and the exhibition, he obtained funding for a second expedition from the Musée de l'Homme and the Direction de la Recherche Scientifique.

1938

Returned to Brazil in the beginning of the year and made the material arrangements for the expedition, which was to last several months. His goal was to cross the region situated to the west of the Mato Grosso, between Cuiabá and the Rio Madeira. This region remained one of the least documented in Brazil. In Cuiabá he recruited men and bought draught animals for the expedition (fifteen mules, thirty oxen, and fifteen caravaneers and herdsmen). The scientific mission included four people: his wife, Dina Dreyfus; himself; Luis de Castro Fara (from the National Museum of Rio de Janeiro); and a medical doctor, Jehan Vellard.

The expedition left Cuiabá in June and traveled to Nambikwara country, where it remained until September. Lévi-Strauss duly pursued his ethnographic studies (related in his publication _La Vie familiale et sociale des Indiens Nambikwara_ [1948], the essentials of which are taken up again in _Tristes tropiques_). "I had been looking for a society reduced to its simplest expression. The society of the Nambikwara had been reduced to the point at which I found nothing but human beings" (_TT_ 310).

In September the expedition continued further to the north. In October it arrived in Pimento Bueno. Lévi-Strauss and his associates decided to leave most of their caravan there and to perform a preliminary survey from the river with two men and four paddlers. They met a group of Mundé Indians with whom they spent one week.

On their return to Pimento Bueno, they learned of the existence of a group of Tupi-Kawahib. They decided to visit them and were accompanied by a Tupi-Kawahib who had left his group many years earlier and was willing to act as an interpreter.

After several days traveling by pirogue on the Machado, they made it to the village and began their study. "In this way, day after day, I would try to reconstruct from its last fragments a culture which had fascinated Europe, and one which, on the right bank of the upper Machado, might well disappear on the very day of my departure" (*TT* 355). (Indeed, those Indians were soon to leave their village in the company of the interpreter.)

Due to a serious accident involving a member of the Brazilian group who had to be evacuated as rapidly as possible, Lévi-Strauss remained alone with the Indians. He was to be reunited with his companions after a few weeks and passed through Bolivia on his way back to Cuaibá to liquidate the expedition's supplies and equipment.

1939

Returned to France in the beginning of the year. Installed the collections brought back from Brazil in the Musée de l'Homme. He and his wife separated.

Because France had entered the war, he was mobilized and assigned to the Ministère des PTT (Department of post and telecommunications), in the telegram censorship department. He remained there a few months before he succeeded in being assigned as a liaison officer, for which he received training.

1940

Forced withdrawal of his unit to the Bordeaux region in the face of the advances of the German army. The withdrawal ended in Béziers, a city close to the Spanish border, and he met up with his parents in the Cévennes, in the southern Massif Central. He offered his services as a philosophy professor to the national education administration in Montpellier; he was demobilized.

It was at this time that he read another work in ethnology that was to play a determining role in the orientation of his intellectual interests. It was the book on kinship systems in China that Marcel Granet had published the preceding year: *Catégories matrimoniales et relations de proximité dans la Chine ancienne* (Granet 1939).

In September, "utterly oblivious" (*CCLS* 26), in other words, without considering the threat to himself as a Jew, he went to Vichy, where the government of Maréchal Pétain was sitting, to contact the Department of National Education in order to request that he be allowed to occupy the position he had been granted at Lycée Henri IV in Paris. In the department a civil servant explained to him the enormous risk he was running and refused to send him to Paris. "I was unaware of the danger.... [T]he die was probably cast at that time" (CCLS 26). He returned to his parents' home in the Cévennes and was named professor of philosophy at the lycée in Montpellier. However, after three weeks he was dismissed in accordance with the racial laws of the Vichy government.

He was contacted by post from the United States and invited to take advantage of the plan to save European scientists and thinkers that had been set up by the Rockefeller Foundation. One of his relatives, who was already living in the United States, actively worked on having him brought over. Moreover, Robert Lowie, Max Ascoli, and the ethnologist Alfred Métraux, who lived in the United States, obtained an invitation for him from the New School for Social Research in New York.

Claude Lévi-Strauss would have liked to return to Brazil to continue his fieldwork, but due to new Brazilian regulations, he could not be granted a visa.

1941

Decided to leave for New York and obtained an exit visa to travel to the United States. In February he found a boat in Marseilles that would take him across. On the boat he discovered a certain number of well-known people such as Anna Seghers, Victor Serge, and André Breton ("I introduced myself and we hit it off" [CCLS 28]).

After putting in at various ports, the boat landed its passengers at Martinique, in the French Antilles.

After a few administrative problems, Lévi-Strauss reached Puerto Rico on board a Swedish banana boat.

In Puerto Rico, he was thought suspect by the American authorities since they considered his papers were not in order. His trunk of ethnographic documents was (as it had been in Martinique) judged strange, and he was placed under house arrest. He obtained permission to visit the ethnologist and politician Jacques Soustelle, who was stopping over on the island. The latter (who had known Lévi-Strauss since 1936) was on an official mission in the name of General de Gaulle and spoke to the American authorities in Lévi-Strauss's favor. This resulted in his being able to leave for New York aboard a regular boat.

He made his home in New York in a Greenwich Village studio apartment, on Eleventh Street. Much later he was to learn that one of his neighbors in the same building was Claude Shannon, the founder of cybernetics.

He wrote *Family and Social Life of the Nambikwara* in English ("to learn the language," he says in CCLS 48). (It was published in French in 1948 as a complementary thesis.)

He saw André Breton again and met a number of other famous exiles: Yves Tanguy, Marcel Duchamp, Max Ernst, Alexander Calder, André Masson, Pierre Lazareff, Georges Duthuit, Denis de Rougement, Wilfredo Lam, and other people linked to them such as Leonora Carrington, Dorothea Tanning, Patrick Waldberg, and Peggy Gugenheim.

He worked occasionally as a speaker at the OWI, the Office of War Information.

Lévi-Strauss developed a strong friendship with Max Ernst. Both of them were passionately interested in Native American art and bought pieces (mainly from the northwest coast of North America) from antique shops in New York.

He saw the ethnologist Alfred Métraux again and met two of the masters of American ethnology: Robert Lowie and A. L. Kroeber.

He took up his position at the New School for Social Research and started teaching courses there. (He was asked to provide a course on contemporary sociology in Latin America.)

He introduced himself to Franz Boas, who, though he had been retired for almost thirty years, kept his office at Columbia University. ("He was the great man of American anthropology and had enormous prestige. He was one of these nineteenth-century titans, the likes of which are no more to be found" [*CCLS* 36]). A few weeks later Boas died suddenly during a luncheon with Lévi-Strauss, Dr. Paul Rivet (director of the Paris Musée de l'Homme), Ruth Benedict, Ralph Linton, and a few others.

1942

Gave (in French) courses in ethnology at the New York École Libre des Hautes Études, which had just been founded by French and francophone intellectuals such as the philosophers and writers Jacques Maritain, Henri Focillon, Jean Perrin, Henri Grégoire, and Alexandre Koyré.

Koyré introduced Lévi-Strauss to a famous linguist of Russian origin, Roman Jakobson. Intellectually, it was a decisive meeting: "At the time I was a kind of naïve structuralist, a structuralist without knowing it. Jakobson revealed to me the existence of a body of doctrine that had already been formed within a discipline, linguistics, with which I was unacquainted. For me it was a revelation" (*CCLS* 41). It was also the beginning of an exceptional friendship: "A friendship of forty years without a break. It is a bond that never weakened, and, for me, an admiration that never ended" (*CCLS* 41). Jakobson gave a series of lectures at the École Libre ("a marvel") that was to be published much later in France under the title *Six leçons sur le son et le sens* (1976; with a preface by Lévi-Strauss [the English translation, *Six Lectures on Sound and Meaning*, was published in 1978. *Trans.*]). Jakobson also attended Lévi-Strauss's classes, in particular those that he gave on kinship and that were to lead to his 1948 doctoral thesis.

1943

Devoted his free time to reading ethnological works in the New York Public Library. "I realized early on that I was a library man, not a fieldworker" (*CCLS* 44).

He began writing his doctoral thesis, *Les Structures élémentaires de la parenté*.

1944

Taught during the summer session at Barnard College in New York.

He was then called back to France by the Direction des Relations Culturelles.

In December he embarked on a ship in an American marine convoy.

1945

In January, reached France via London, which was still being bombed.

In Paris, as secretary of the New York École Libre des Hautes Études, he occupied an office in the Direction des Relations Culturelles, where he was responsible for advising people wishing to go to the United States. At that time he met Maurice Merleau-Ponty, who was one of the candidates for such a voyage.

He was named director of the cultural center attached to the French embassy in Washington, with residence in New York, where he went in the spring. (He remained there until the end of 1947.)

He married Rose-Marie Ullmo after his divorce from Dina Dreyfus. From this new marriage a son, Laurent, was to be born.

As director of the cultural center he met, among others, Jean-Paul Sartre ("[H]e didn't need me to organize his stay" [*CCLS* 48]), Simone de Beauvoir, Albert Camus, Jules Romains, Jean Delay, and Gaston Berger.

1947

Returned to France at the end of the year.

1948

Was named maître de recherches at the CNRS (Centre National de la Recherche Scientifique) for a few months and assistant director at the Musée de l'Homme, thanks to the support of Dr. Paul Rivet.

He met the ethnologist and writer Michel Leiris, who was working at the Musée de l'Homme ("I didn't know his work and read it with delight" [*CCLS* 53]).

His book *La Vie familiale et sociale des Indiens Nambikwara* was published in Paris by the Société des Américanistes.

At the Sorbonne he defended his thesis, which was titled *Les Structures élémentaires de la parenté* (typed version).

The jury was chaired by Georges Davy (sociologist and dean of the Sorbonne). The other members were Émile Benvéniste (linguist and Indian specialist), Albert Bayet (sociologist), and Jean Escarra (jurist and sinologist); while Marcel Griaule (ethnologist and African specialist) took responsibility for evaluating his complementary thesis on the Nambikwara.

He met Jacques Lacan at Alexandre Koyré's home. "We were very close for a number of years.... We hardly ever talked about psychoanalysis or philosophy; instead it was usually art and literature. His knowledge was vast" (*CCLS* 73).

It was to be at Lacan's home that he would meet his future wife, Monique Roman.

1949

Publication of *Les Structures élémentaires de la parenté* (*ESK*) at the Presses Universitaires de France. This work immediately brought Lévi-Strauss to the attention of specialists (in particular British and American specialists), but it was also received in wider circles. Thus, Simone de Beauvoir, who was writing *The Second Sex* (1953), gave a very favorable review of it in *Les Temps modernes* (Beauvoir 1949). Georges Bataille also wrote a very detailed article on it, which was republished in *L'Érotisme* (Bataille 1957).

Forty years later, *Les Structures élémentaires de la parenté* was considered by its author to be "far too ambitious" (*CCLS* 102), but he added: "It was challenged from the first and still is. But the fact that it is an almost obligatory reference in any discussion of the problem is very consoling to me" (*CCLS* 102).

At that time, Lévi-Strauss was asked to present his candidature to the Collège de France (one of the most prestigious French research and teaching institutions). This first attempt failed probably because of very sharp conflicts between the leanings of those who were already members, on one hand, and due to opposition from the director, on the other.

1950

Was sent by UNESCO to India and Pakistan (then divided between two territories, the West and the East; the latter was to become what is Bangladesh today).

He failed a second time to gain entrance into the Collège de France, in spite of the support of Émile Benvéniste, Georges Dumézil (who had just been accepted), and Marcel Bataillon (the future director).

With Dumézil's support, he was elected director of studies at the prestigious École Pratique des Hautes Études, in the fifth section, religious studies. His chair was in the area of Religions Comparées des Peuples Non Civilisés (Comparative Religions of Uncivilized Peoples). This

chair was created in 1888 and had been occupied in turn by Léon Mar-
iller, Marcel Mauss, and Maurice Leenhardt. Lévi-Strauss managed (in
1954) to have it renamed Religions Comparées des Peuples sans Écriture
(Comparative Religions of Peoples without Writing).

1952

Publication of "Race et histoire," an essay written the previous year at
the request of the International Council of Social Sciences (a nongovern-
mental association under the aegis of UNESCO). Certain reactions were
very violent, such as that of the essayist Roger Caillois, who rejected
the great esteem Lévi-Strauss holds for "primitive" civilizations. Caillois
pointed out the proven superiority of the West. Lévi-Strauss answered
him in "Diogène couché" (1955a/a), an article with a sharp, sometimes
even stinging, tone, published in the journal managed by Jean-Paul Sartre,
Les Temps modernes.

1953

Elected secretary-general of the International Council of Social Sciences.
      Clyde Kluckholn, professor of anthropology at Harvard, asked Tal-
cott Parsons, then visiting Paris, to suggest to Lévi-Strauss a tenured
professorship at that university. Lévi-Strauss preferred to decline that
prestigious offer. ("I had no desire to start life as an exile again"
[*CCLS 55*].)

1954

Married Monique Roman after his divorce from Rose-Marie Ullmo.
In 1957 they were to have a son, Matthieu.

1955

Publication of *Tristes tropiques* (*TT*). This book was written in four
months. "It seemed that I was interrupting my work by an intermission
that had to be as short as possible" (*CCLS 58*).
      He wrote this story of the genesis of an ethnological vocation, of his
expeditions in central Brazil, and of a few other trips at the request of the
ethnologist Jean Malaurie, who had just created the collection Terre humaine at Plon. This work, unanimously applauded by the critics, was an
overnight success in bookstores. It is probably the book that ensured its
author would become known to a wide public. The Académie Goncourt
jury publicly expressed its regret at not being able to award him its
prize (the most prestigious French literary award), which was reserved
for works of fiction. (It is amusing to note that the title itself was meant
for a novel of which only the famous "sunset" pages remain.)

Well-known writers such as Michel Leiris, Georges Bataille, Maurice Blanchot, Mircea Eliade, Pierre Mac Orlan, Raymond Aron, Claude Roy, René Etiemble, and many others published admiring reviews of *Tristes tropiques*. In contrast, Dr. Paul Rivet, director of the Musée de l'Homme, closed his door to Lévi-Strauss, and Alfred Métraux said amicably that he was becoming "unbuttoned." It is clear that the sudden fame also irritated British and American anthropologists who were very attached to university reserve, as Edmund Leach admitted.

In the *Journal of American Folklore*, Lévi-Strauss published, in English, an article that was to become famous: "The Structural Study of Myth." (This article was reprinted in *Anthropologie structurale [SA]* in 1958.)

1958

Publication of *Anthropologie structurale (SA)*. The choice of adjective in the title was to contribute to making Lévi-Strauss seen as the leader of the structuralist current. "[T]he vogue for structuralism unleashed all manner of unfortunate results. The term was besmirched; illegitimate, sometimes ridiculous applications were made of it. There was nothing I could do" *(CCLS 68)*.

1959

Elected to the Collège de France in the chair of social anthropology. In fact, it was the first chair with this title, since that of Marcel Mauss had been called "sociology."

His election was due largely to action taken by his friend, the philosopher Maurice Merleau-Ponty ("[H]e devoted three months of his life to it, and he was not to live much longer" *[CCLS 60]*).

In the Collège de France, Lévi-Strauss found himself reunited with some of those who had already played important roles in his career, such as Fernand Braudel, Émile Benveniste, and Georges Dumézil.

1960

Gave (on January 5) his inaugural lecture at the Collège de France.

He founded the Laboratoire d'Anthropologie Sociale at that institution. Through UNESCO, the laboratory received one of the twenty-five copies of the *Human Relations Area Files,* produced by Yale University.

1961

Creation of *L'Homme: Revue française d'anthropologie*. The goal was for French ethnology to have a journal comparable to *Man* in Great Britain and *American Anthropologist* in the United States.

Georges Charbonnier's *Entretiens avec Claude Lévi-Strauss (GC)* came out. It is the transcription of radio interviews transmitted on Radio France-Culture from October to December 1959.

1962

Publication of *Le Totémisme aujourd'hui* (*T*) and *La Pensée sauvage* (*SM*).

These two books gave rise to a very important debate, as much among philosophers as among anthropologists, in France and elsewhere.

1964

Publication of *Le Cru et le cuit* (*RC*), the first volume of *Mythologiques*.

1966

Received (in Chicago) the Gold Medal from the Viking Fund for Anthropology (this medal is awarded by an international vote of members of the ethnological profession).

1967

Publication of *Du miel aux cendres* (*HA*), the second volume of *Mythologiques*.

1968

Publication of *L'Origine des manières de table* (*OTM*), the third volume of *Mythologiques*.

Lévi-Strauss received the Gold Medal from the Centre National de la Recherche Scientifique (CNRS).

The "events of May" for him? "For me, May 1968 was symptomatic of yet another step downward in the deterioration of the university, which began a long time ago. . . . I don't believe that May 1968 destroyed the university but rather that May 1968 took place because the university was destroying itself" (*CCLS* 80).

1969–70

Devoted himself entirely to finishing his work on myths.

1971

Publication of *L'Homme nu* (*NM*), the fourth and last volume of *Mythologiques*. "I began to lean toward mythology in 1950 and I completed my mythology series in 1970. For twenty years, I would get up at dawn, drunk with myths — truly I lived in another world" (*CCLS* 133).

"Race et culture" was published. It is the text of a conference given under UNESCO's auspices and a sort of complement to the 1952 essay "Race et histoire." Like the latter, it was controversial.

1973

Election to the Académie Française. His candidature surprised his friends; thus it was to them above all, he said, that he addressed his reception speech, which was intended to point out the anthropological interest of that very old institution.

Roger Caillois, his old adversary, was charged with welcoming him with a speech. His discourse was friendly at first but rather acid and even unpleasant at the end: twenty years later, the quarrel over "Race et histoire" was not yet entirely buried.

That same 1952 essay was republished in a volume of articles that appeared that year: *Anthropologie structurale deux (SA 2)*.

In Amsterdam he received the Erasmus Prize.

Traveled to British Columbia, Canada (in 1973 and 1974).

1975

Publication of *La Voie des masques* (WM).

He gave a lecture in Ottawa.

1977

Publication of *Discours pour la réception d'Alain Peyrefitte*, a speech made to welcome Alain Peyrefitte to the Académie Française.

He gave, in English, five radio addresses in the framework of the Canadian Broadcasting Corporation's "Massey Lectures."

He went to Japan at the invitation of the Japan Foundation.

1978

Publication of *Myth and Meaning*, the text resulting from the "Massey Lectures" given the preceding year.

1979

Publication, by Plon, of a new edition of *La Voie des masques* (WM), which had been revised and had additional material included.

Gallimard published the *Discours de la réception de Georges Dumézil à l'Académie Française et réponse de Claude Lévi-Strauss*, a speech made to welcome Georges Dumézil to the Académie Française.

Schocken Books, New York, published *Myth and Meaning*, the text of the "Massey Lectures" given in 1977.

He went to Mexico.

He made a second trip to Japan, at the invitation of the Suntory Foundation.

1981

Traveled to South Korea, at the invitation of the Korean Studies Academy, in order to participate in a seminar devoted to his work.

1982

Retired. He stopped teaching at the Collège de France but remained a member of the Laboratoire d'Anthropologie Sociale.

1983

Publication of *Le Regard éloigné* (*VA*), a collection of articles published between 1971 and 1983, with the single exception of one earlier article, "La Famille," which dates from 1956.

Third trip to Japan at the invitation of the Japan Productivity Center.

1984

Voyage to Israel, where he presided over an international symposium on art as a means of communication.

He undertook a speaking tour of some of the campuses of the University of California: Berkeley, Davis, San Francisco, Los Angeles.

Paroles données (*AM*) was published.

1985

Publication of *La Potière jalouse* (*JP*), a new study dealing with a set of myths from both Americas that provides a sort of complement to *Mythologiques*. He returned to Brazil for the first time since 1939. His stay was very short; he was one of the guests of the president of France, François Mitterand, who was on an official visit.

1986

Fourth trip to Japan at the invitation of the Ishizaka Foundation.

1988

Fifth trip to Japan, organized by the Centre de Recherche pour les Études Japonaises.

On the occasion of his eightieth birthday, a volume of interviews granted to Didier Eribon, *De Près et de loin* (*CCLS*), was published.

1989

At the initiative of Jean Guiart, an exhibition was organized at the Musée de l'Homme in Paris. It was titled *Les Amériques de Claude Lévi-Strauss* and included some of the pieces Lévi-Strauss brought back from Brazil in 1936 (Bororo, Caduveo) plus a certain number of others concerning Northwest Coast populations (Tlingit, Haida, Kwakiutl, Bella Bella, Salish, and so on).

An anthology of his various articles on art was published on this occasion under the title *Des symboles et leurs doubles*. For this anthology, which also includes a foreword by Jean Guiart, Lévi-Strauss wrote a preface and a short piece on Bill Reid (the great contemporary Haida sculptor, many of whose pieces are shown and who is presented in a study by his wife, Martine Reid).

1991

Publication of *Histoire de Lynx*, a work that continued his exploration of indigenous North American myths.

1993

Publication of *Regarder, écouter, lire*, reflections on painting, music, and poetry.

1995

Publication of *Saudades do Brazil*, in which were published for the first time virtually all the photographs taken by Lévi-Strauss during his research expeditions in Brazil between 1935 and 1938.

1998

Lévi-Strauss's ninetieth birthday.

Notes

Introduction

1. This translation is by L. Scott-Fox and J. M. Harding, the translators of Descombes 1980. — *Trans.*
2. This translation is by L. Scott-Fox and J. M. Harding, the translators of Descombes 1980. — *Trans.*

1. The Anthropologist, the West and the Others

1. The term *dépaysement,* used in the section's title, is often left in French in translations of Lévi-Strauss's work since the closest English equivalent, "estrangement," connotes rejection on the part of the one estranged. *Dépaysement* implies only the milder negative connotation of the discomfort felt by an individual in an unfamiliar environment. — *Trans.*

2. The Movement of Reciprocity

1. The term *bricolage* has no precise English equivalent and is usually left in French in English translations of Lévi-Strauss's work. It means creating by using whatever materials are available. — *Trans.*

3. Structures of Kinship

1. The translation of this passage in *Structural Anthropology* (p. 300) is rather free. In order to make this quotation comprehensible in this context, a more literal translation has been provided. The French original can be found on page 331 of Lévi-Strauss's *Anthropologie structurale.* — *Trans.*
2. There is a small, but important, error in the translation of this passage as it appears in *Elementary Systems of Kinship.* I have substituted "the husband's" for "her husband's." — *Trans.*

4. Unconscious Categories and Universality of the Mind

1. Umberto Eco (1968) has harsh criticism regarding this discussion of the *hau* and the necessity Lévi-Strauss postulates of supposing "unconscious mental structures" in order to understand the logic of gift/countergift. According to Eco, this hypothesis is an unnecessary philosophical addition that is even more regrettable since Lévi-Strauss's analysis of reciprocity seems to him to be perfectly convincing; further, bringing in unconscious mental structures would be to claim to give a universal value to a demonstration that is not the only one possible. "It

is in this passage from method to ontology that there is 'ideological' degeneracy of the discipline" (Eco 1968, 347). What then is the solution Eco proposes to anthropology in the *hau* example? It is to accept the logic proposed by the indigenous people as different from and complementary to our own. In this way we would be able to compare all sorts of different logics and shed light on isomorphisms thanks to the structuralist method. Perhaps. Yet, on one hand, the explanation of reciprocity also has its source in an indigenous logic and, on the other hand, the case of the *hau* is special because it is a gloss to be treated as such and not as an explanation of gift/countergift. This is even more clear in the case of myths that seem absurd on the syntagmatic level so long as the paradigmatic levels and their transformations have not been revealed: any indigenous (or other) gloss would only add to known versions. To bring out the isomorphisms, as Eco requests, is precisely to suppose common mental structures between indigenous thought and any other thought; otherwise no one would understand any one and comparison would be wholly inconceivable. This does not amount, as Eco says, to postulating a "universal thought" (Eco 1968, 347), and it does not reduce "the diversity of thought to a single thought" (Eco 1968, 347): it is only the postulation of a mental mechanism common to the various cultural expressions of thought. Because he did not understand this, the author (who is so often brilliant and perceptive) of *La Struttura assente* was able to come to this utterly bizarre conclusion: "An immobile, eternal discovery, situated at the very roots of Culture, Structure, which was only a tool, has become a Hypostatic Principle" (Eco 1968, 348). If there is hypostasis here, it is indeed in these notions adorned with capitals that seem to condense the vision of a neo-Platonist gnostic but have nothing to do with Lévi-Strauss's analysis of kinship and myth systems.

2. E. Leach must have been unaware of these positions (which are, however, reaffirmed frequently) when he wrote in the preface of *L'Unité de l'homme* (1980): "All readers of the present articles will immediately notice my debt to Lévi-Strauss, but I do not follow him when he writes as if cultural phenomena were the expression of an abstraction, the 'human mind,' which manages, in one way or another, to operate purposefully and independently of the biochemical functioning of human brains" (Leach 1980, 9 [while the other articles in *L'Unité de l'homme* can be found in English, the preface seems to have been published only in French — Trans.). Later in the work, the chapter titled "The Legitimacy of Solomon" (originally published as Leach 1966) begins with an ironical review of the various possible meanings of the term "mind" in Lévi-Strauss's writing, which ends up seeing in the term a "ghost in the machine" (to use Ryle's famous expression) or, to the contrary, a new version of Hegel's *Geist*. Finally, Leach admits that he does not understand Lévi-Strauss's use of this concept. Indeed, we have to agree with him there.

7. The Analysis of Myths

1. *The Way of Masks* appeared in English in 1982. — *Trans.*
2. *The Jealous Potter* appeared in English in 1988. — *Trans.*

8. The Lesson of the Work of Art

1. This is a point on which J. M. Merquior justly insists in his book on *L'Esthétique de Lévi-Strauss* (1977). It is also the only real point of explicit convergence with the analysis proposed in the present chapter.

Bibliography

The ambitions of the present bibliography are limited.

First, a number of general bibliographies of Lévi-Strauss's works and of the structuralist current will be given.

Second, a complete list of Lévi-Strauss's books and a listing of some of his major articles will be presented.

Third, a list of the principal books, parts of books, and journal articles dealing directly with Lévi-Strauss's work is provided.

Fourth, some books and articles that have been published in relation to the structuralist current and that still retain a certain relevance are listed.

The final section lists other works that are cited in the text.

General Bibliographies

Bibliographies of Works by and about Lévi-Strauss

Hénaff, Marcel. 1991. *Claude Lévi-Strauss.* Paris: Editions Belfond. This is the French original of the present book. In addition to the bibliography, the French edition contains an analysis (sometimes chapter-by-chapter when the book is a collection of articles) of each of Lévi-Strauss's books.

Lapointe, F. H., and C. C. Lapointe. 1977. *Claude Lévi-Strauss and His Critics: An International Bibliography of Criticism (1950–1976).* New York: Garland Publications. This bibliography is, in a way, and in spite of a few shortcomings, the principal reference catalog of publications by and on Lévi-Strauss. Its major failing is that it has not been updated since 1977.

Nordquist, Joan. 1987. *Claude Lévi-Strauss: A Bibliography.* Santa Cruz: University of California at Santa Cruz. This bibliography, published in the Santa Cruz Bibliographic Series, aims to provide an exhaustive list of English-language publications by and on Lévi-Strauss (up to 1987).

Many other bibliographies have been compiled by the authors of various works on Lévi-Strauss, but they were published before the three works mentioned above and contain virtually the same lists. Thus they have been left aside.

266

Bibliography

Bibliographies on the Structuralist Current

The following are two bibliographies dealing with the structuralist current in general:

Harari, José. 1971. *Structuralists and Structuralisms: A Selected Bibliography of French Contemporary Thought (1960–1970)*. Ithaca, N.Y.: Diacritics.

Miller, Joan. 1981. *French Structuralism: A Multidisciplinary Bibliography*. New York: Garland Publications.

Publications by Claude Lévi-Strauss

Books

The following is the canonical list of books that was established by Lévi-Strauss himself and that appears, for example, at the beginning of his most recently published book, with the exceptions of *Myth and Meaning* (1979b), which has not been published in French, and *Introduction to the Work of Marcel Mauss* (1987), which was published in French in Marcel Mauss's *Sociologie et anthropologie* (1950).

1948   *La Vie familiale et sociale des Indiens Nambikwara*. Paris: Société des Américanistes.

1949   *Les Structures élementaires de la parenté*. Paris: Presses Universitaires de France. Rev. ed., La Haye: Mouton, 1967. Published in English as *The Elementary Structures of Kinship,* ed. Rodney Needham, trans. James Harle Bell, John Richard von Sturmer, and Rodney Needham (Boston: Beacon Press, 1969).

1955   *Tristes tropiques*. Paris: Plon. 2d. ed., 1973. Published in English as *Tristes Tropiques,* trans. John and Doreen Weightman (New York: Atheneum, 1975).

1958   *Anthropologie structurale*. Paris: Plon. Published in English as *Structural Anthropology,* trans. Claire Jacobson and Brooke Grundfest Schoepf (New York: Basic Books, 1963).

1961   *Entretiens avec Claude Lévi-Strauss*. Ed. Georges Charbonnier. Paris: Plon. Published in English as *Conversations with Claude Lévi-Strauss,* ed. Georges Charbonnier, trans. John and Doreen Weightman (London: Jonathan Cape, 1969).

1962a   *La Pensée sauvage*. Paris: Plon. Published in English as *The Savage Mind,* trans. George Weidenfeld and Nicolson Ltd. (Chicago: University of Chicago Press, 1966).

1962b *Le Totémisme aujourd'hui.* Paris: Presses Universitaires de France. Published in English as *Totemism,* trans. R. Needham (Boston: Beacon Press, 1963).

1964 *Le Cru et le cuit.* Vol. 1 of *Mythologiques.* Paris: Plon. Published in English as *The Raw and the Cooked,* vol. 1. of *Mythologiques,* trans. John and Doreen Weightman (New York: Harper and Row, 1969).

1966 *Du miel au cendres.* Vol. 2 of *Mythologiques.* Paris: Plon. Published in English as *From Honey to Ashes,* vol. 2 of *Mythologiques,* trans. John and Doreen Weightman (New York: Harper and Row, 1973).

1968 *L'Origine des manières de table.* Vol. 3 of *Mythologiques.* Paris: Plon. Published in English as *The Origin of Table Manners,* vol. 3 of *Mythologiques,* trans. John and Doreen Weightman (New York: Harper and Row, 1978).

1971 *L'Homme nu.* Vol. 4 of *Mythologiques.* Paris: Plon. Published in English as *The Naked Man,* vol. 4 of *Mythologiques,* trans. John and Doreen Weightman (New York: Harper and Row, 1981).

1973 *Anthropologie structurale.* Vol. 2. Paris: Plon. Published in English as *Structural Anthropology,* vol. 2, trans. Monique Layton (New York: Basic Books, 1976).

1975 *La Voie des masques.* Geneva: Éditions d'art Skira. Revised edition with additions published in 1979.

1977 *Discours de réception d'Alain Peyrefitte à l'Académie française et réponse de Claude Lévi-Strauss.* Paris: Gallimard.

1978 *Myth and Meaning.* Toronto: University of Toronto Press. Also published by Schocken Books in 1979.

1979a *Discours de réception de Georges Dumézil à l'Académie française et réponse de Claude Lévi-Strauss.* Paris: Gallimard.

1979b *Myth and Meaning.* New York: Schocken Books. Also published in 1978 by the University of Toronto Press.

1979c *La Voie des masques.* Rev. ed. Paris: Plon. Published in English as *The Way of Masks,* trans. Sylvia Modelski (Seattle: University of Washington Press, 1982).

1983 *Le Regard éloigné.* Paris: Plon. Published in English as *The View from Afar,* trans. Joachim Neugroschel and Phoebe Hoss (New York: Basic Books, 1985).

1984   *Paroles données.* Paris: Plon. Published in English as *Anthropology and Myth*, trans. Roy Willis (Oxford: Blackwell, 1987).

1985   *La Potière jalouse.* Paris: Plon. Published in English as *The Jealous Potter,* trans. Bénédicte Chorier (Chicago: University of Chicago Press, 1988).

1987   *Introduction to the Work of Marcel Mauss.* Trans. Felicity Baker. London: Routledge and Kegan Paul. Originally published in Marcel Mauss, *Sociologie et anthropologie* (Paris: Presses Universitaires de France, 1950).

1988   *De près et de loin.* Paris: Éditions Odile Jacob. Published in English as *Conversations with Claude Lévi-Strauss,* trans. Paula Wissing (Chicago: University of Chicago Press, 1991).

1989   *Des symboles et leurs doubles.* Paris: Plon.

1991   *Histoire de Lynx.* Paris: Plon. Published in English as *The Story of Lynx,* trans. Catherine Tihanyi (Chicago: University of Chicago Press, 1995).

1994a   *Regarder, écouter, lire.* Paris: Plon. Published in English as *Look, Listen, Read,* trans. Brian C. J. Singer (New York: Basic Books, 1997).

1994b   *Saudades do Brazil.* Paris: Plon. Published in English as *Saudades do Brazil,* trans. Sylvia Modelski (Seattle: University of Washington Press, 1995).

Articles

Most of Lévi-Strauss's articles have been republished in various books. The following list gives only the most influential of the articles that have not been republished.

1943   "Guerre et commerce chez les Indiens d'Amérique du Sud." *Renaissance* 1, nos. 1–2) (New York: École Libre des Hautes Études): 122–39.

1944   "Reciprocity and Hierarchy." *American Anthropologist* 46, no. 2:266–68.

1945   "French Sociology." In *Twentieth Century Sociology,* ed. G. Gurvitch and E. Moore. New York: Philosophical Library, 503–37.

1948a   "The Nambicuara." In *Handbook of South American Indians,* ed. J. Steward. Washington, D.C.: Bureau of American Ethnology, Smithsonian Institution, 3:361–69.

1948b "The Tribes of the Upper Xingu River." In *Handbook of South American Indians*, ed. J. Steward. Washington, D.C.: Bureau of American Ethnology, Smithsonian Institution, 3:321–48.

1950a "Marcel Mauss." *Cahiers internationaux de sociologie* 8:72–112.

1950b "The Use of Wild Plants in Tropical South America." In *Handbook of South American Indians*, ed. J. Steward. Washington, D.C.: Bureau of American Ethnology, Smithsonian Institution, 3:465–86.

1952a "Le Père Noël supplicié." *Les Temps modernes* 77 (7th year): 1572–90.

1952b "Race et histoire." In *La Question raciale devant la science moderne*. Paris: UNESCO. (Reprinted in *Anthropologie structurale*, vol. 2 [Paris: Plon, 1973].) Published in English as "Race and History," in *Structural Anthropology*, trans. Claire Jacobson and Brooke Grundrest Schoepf (New York: Basic Books, 1963).

1953 "Panorama of Ethnology 1950–1952." *Diogenes* 2:69–92.

1955a "Diogène couché." *Les Temps modernes* 110:1187–1220.

1955b "The Mathematics of Man." *International Social Science Bulletin* 6, no. 4:581–90.

1957 "The Principle of Reciprocity: The Essence of Life." In *Sociological Theory: A Book of Readings*, ed. L. Coser and B. Rosenberg. New York: Macmillan, 74–84.

1959 "Marcel Mauss." *Encyclopedia Britannica* 14:1133a.

1961 "Le Métier d'ethnologue." *Les Annales: Revue mensuelle des lettres françaises*. N.s. 129 (July): 5–17.

1962a "The Bear and the Barber." Henry Myers Memorial Lecture. Reprinted in *The Journal of the Royal Anthropological Institute* 18, no. 1 (1963): 1–11.

1962b " 'Les Chats' de Charles Baudelaire." *L'Homme* 2:202–21. (In collaboration with Roman Jakobson.)

1962c "Les Limites de la notion de structure en ethnologie." In *Sens et usages du terme structure*, ed. R. Bastide. The Hague: Mouton.

1963 "Réponses à quelques questions." *Esprit* 322 (November): 628–53.

1964   "Reciprocity: The Essence of Social Life." In *The Family: Its
        Structures and Functions,* ed. R. L. Coser. New York: San
        Martin's Press, 36–48.

1983   "Histoire et ethnologie." *Annales* 38, no. 6 (November–
        December): 1217–31.

1987   "De la fidélité au texte." *L'Homme* 27, no. 1:117–40.

1988   "Exode sur *Exode.*" *L'Homme* 28, nos. 106–7 (April–
        September): 13–23.

Publications Dealing with Lévi-Strauss's Work

Books Focusing on Lévi-Strauss's Work

The following list is restricted to selected books in which the authors have
explicitly adopted the task of setting out and discussing Lévi-Strauss's
research. Note that most of them were published around 1970.

Badcock, C. R. 1975. *Lévi-Strauss: Structuralism and Sociological The-
    ory.* London: Hutchison.
Bellour, Raymond, and Catherine Clément, eds. 1979. *Lévi-Strauss.*
    Paris: Gallimard. (Includes essays by B. Pingaud, J. Pouillon, P. Clas-
    tres, R. Barthes, J. F. Lyotard, C. Lévi-Strauss, L. De Heusch,
    A. Glucksmann, C. Ramnoux, J. Le Goff and P. Vidal-Naquet,
    B. Bucher, M. Zéraffa, and C. Clément.)
Boon, James. 1971. *From Symbolism to Structuralism: Lévi-Strauss in a
    Literary Tradition.* Oxford: Basil Blackwell; New York: Harper and
    Row, 1972.
Clarke, Simon. 1981. *The Foundations of Structuralism: A Critique
    of Lévi-Strauss and the Structuralist Movement.* Brighton, England:
    Harvester Press.
Clément, Catherine. 1970. *Lévi-Strauss ou la structure et le malheur.*
    Paris: Seghers. 2d. ed., 1974.
Courtès, Joseph. 1973. *Lévi-Strauss et les contraintes de la pensée
    mythique: Une Lecture sémiotique des Mythologiques.* Paris: Mame.
Delruelle, Edouard. 1989. *Lévi-Strauss et la philosophie.* Brussels: Édi-
    tions Universitaires.
Gardner, Howard. 1973. *The Quest for Mind: Piaget, Lévi-Strauss and
    the Structuralist Movement.* New York: Knopf.
Gasché, Rodolphe. 1973. *Die hybride Wissenschaft: Zur Mutation des
    Wissenschaftsbegriffs bei Émile Durkheim und im Strukturalismus
    von Claude Lévi-Strauss.* Texte Metzler, 26. Stuttgart: Metzler.

Hammel, Eugene. 1972. *The Myth of Structural Analysis: Lévi-Strauss and the Three Bears*. Reading, Mass.: Addison-Wesley.

Hayes, Nelson E., and Tanya Hayes, eds. 1970. *Claude Lévi-Strauss: The Anthropologist as Hero*. Cambridge, Mass.: M.I.T. Press. (Includes essays by S. de Gramont, H. S. Hughs, E. Leach, F. Huxley, H. Nutini, B. Scholte, D. Maybury-Lewis, C. M. Turnbull, R. F. Murphy, G. Steiner, S. Sontag, P. Caws, R. L. Zimmerman, and L. Abel.)

Josselin de Jong, J. P. B. de. 1952. *Lévi-Strauss's Theory on Kinship and Marriage*. Mededelingen van het Rijksmuseum voor Volkenkunde, 10. Leiden: Brill.

Korn, Francis. 1973. *Elementary Structures Reconsidered: Lévi-Strauss on Kinship*. Berkeley: University of California Press.

Korn, Francis, and Rodney Needham. 1969. *Lévi-Strauss on the Elementary Structures of Kinship: A Concordance to Pagination*. London: Royal Anthropological Institute.

Leach, Edmund R. 1970. *Lévi-Strauss*. London: Fontana/Collins.

Lepenies, Wolf, and Hans H. Ritter, eds. 1970. *Orte des Wilden Denkens: Zur Anthropologie von Claude Lévi-Strauss*. Frankfurt: Suhrkamp. (Includes essays by W. Lepenies, E. Leach, E. Fleischmann, H. Ritter, H. Nagel, R. Gasché, and J. Derrida.)

Merquior, José Guilherme. 1977. *L'Esthétique de Lévi-Strauss*. Paris: Presses Universitaires de France.

Montes, Santiago. 1971. *Claude Lévi-Strauss: Un Neuvo discurso del méthodo*. San Salvador: Ministerio de Educación.

Moore, Tim. 1971. *Lévi-Strauss and the Cultural Sciences*. Occasional Studies, 4. Birmingham, England: University Centre for Contemporary Cultural Studies.

Nutini, Hugo, and Ira Buchler, eds. 1970. *The Anthropology of Claude Lévi-Strauss*. New York: Appelton-Century-Crofts.

Pace, David. 1985. *Claude Lévi-Strauss: The Bearer of Ashes*. London: Routledge and Kegan Paul.

Paz, Octavio. 1969. *Claude Lévi-Strauss o el nuevo festin de Esopo*. 2d ed. Serie del Dolador. Mexico City: J. Mortiz. Published in English as *Claude Lévi-Strauss. An Introduction*, trans. J. S. Bernstein and Maxine Bernstein (Ithaca, N.Y.: Cornell University Press, 1970).

Pouillon, Jean, and Pierre Maranda, eds. 1970. *Echanges et comunicacions: Mélanges offerts à Claude Lévi-Strauss à l'occasion de son 60e anniversaire*. The Hague: Mouton.

Rossi, Ino, ed. 1974. *The Unconscious in Culture: The Structuralism of Claude Lévi-Strauss in Perspective*. New York: E. P. Dutton. (Contributors include I. Rossi, G. Mounin, M. Dubin, J. Maquet, A. Kasakoff, J. W. Adams, N. Ross Crumrine, B. J. Macklin, Shin-po Kang, E. Schwimmer, J. Pouwer, A. Wilden, Y. Simonis, S. Diamond, L. Krader, L. Rosen, and B. Scholte.)

Scholte, Bob. 1973. "The Structural Anthropology of Claude Lévi-Strauss." In *Handbook of Social and Cultural Anthropology,* ed. J. Honigmann. Chicago: Rand McNally, 637–716.

Scubla, Lucien. 1988. *Lire Lévi-Strauss.* Paris: Éditions Odile Jacob.

Shalvey, Thomas. 1979. *Claude Lévi-Strauss, Social Psychotherapy, and the Collective Unconscious.* Amherst: University of Massachusetts Press.

Simonis, Yvan. 1968. *Claude Lévi-Strauss ou la passion de l'inceste: Introduction au structuralisme.* Paris: Aubier-Montaigne. 2d ed. in "Champs" Collection (Paris: Flammarion, 1980).

Sperber, Dan. 1973. *Le Structuralisme en anthropologie.* Paris: Seuil. Previously published in F. Wahl, ed., *Qu'est-ce que le structuralisme?* (Paris: Seuil, 1968).

Journal Numbers Focusing on Lévi-Strauss's Work and Structuralism in General

Annales (Économies–Sociétés–Civilisations) 6 (19th year) (November–December 1964): 1085–1115. (Articles by R. Barthes, R. Pividal, and E. Leach.)

Anthropologica 20, nos. 1–2 (1978). Volume title: *Mélanges offerts à Claude Lévi-Strauss à l'occasion de son 70e anniversaire de naissance.*

L'Arc 26 (1965). Volume title: *Claude Lévi-Strauss.* (Articles by B. Pingaud, G. Genette, L. de Heusch, J. Pouillon, C. Deliège; notes by J. Guiart, J. C. Gardin, and P. Clastres.)

Cahiers pour l'Analyse 4 (1966). Volume title: *Lévi-Strauss dans le XVIIIe siècle.*

Esprit 322 (November 1963). Volume title: *La Pensée sauvage et le structuralisme.* (Articles by J. Cuisenier, N. Ruwet, M. Gaboriau, P. Ricoeur, followed by a discussion between these authors and Lévi-Strauss.)

Esprit 360 (May 1967). Volume title: *Structuralismes: Idéologie et méthode.* (Articles by J.-M. Domenach, J. Cuisenier, Y. Bertherat, J. Conhil, M. Dufrenne, P. Ricoeur, P. Burgelin, and J. Ladrière.)

Esprit 402 (1971). Volume title: *Le Mythe aujourd'hui.* (Articles by R. Barthes, I. Calvino, C. Rabant, M. Dufrenne, C. Ramnoux, C. Lévi-Strauss, P. Boyer, and so on.)

Magazine Littéraire 223 (October 1985). Volume title: *Claude Lévi-Strauss.*

Magazine Littéraire 311. (June 1993). Volume title: *Claude Lévi-Strauss.*

Revue Internationale de Philosophie 73–74 (1965). Volume title: *La Notion de structure.* (Articles by G. Granger, A. Martinet, N. Mouloud, P. Francastel, and E. Paci.)

Les Temps modernes 246 (1966). Volume title: *Problèmes de structuralisme.* (Articles by J. Pouillon, M. Barbut, A. J. Greimas, M. Godelier, P. Bourdieu, P. Macherey, J. Ehrmann.)

Yale French Studies 36–37 (1966). Volume title: *Structuralism.* (Articles by A. Martinet, C. Lévi-Strauss, M. Riffaterre, H. W. Scheffler, J. Lacan, J. Ehrmann, P. Lewis, G. Hartman, V. L. Rippere, E. Barber, A. R. Maxwell, A. G. Wilden, T. Todorov, S. Nodelman, and J. Miel.)

Articles and Parts of Books concerning Lévi-Strauss's Work and Structural Analysis

The studies included here are various. Some are very specific regarding anthropological research; others are more general and deal with epistemological, philosophical, aesthetic, historical, or other aspects of Lévi-Strauss's work.

Augé, Marc. 1979. *Symbole, fonction, histoire.* Paris: Hachette. Published in English as *The Anthropological Circle: Symbol, Function, History,* trans. Martin Thom (Cambridge: Cambridge University Press, 1980).

Bailey, A. M. 1985. "The Making of History: Dialectics of Temporality and Structure in Modern French Social Theory." *Critique of Anthropology* 5, no. 1:7–31.

Barnes, John. 1971. *Three Styles in the Study of Kinship.* Berkeley: University of California Press.

Barthes, Roland. 1962. "Sociologie et socio-logique: A propos de deux ouvrages récents de Claude Lévi-Strauss." *Information sur les sciences Sociales* 2, no. 4 (1962): 114–22.

———. 1964a. "L'Activité structuraliste." In *Essais critiques.* Paris: Seuil.

———. 1964b. "Les Sciences humaines et l'oeuvre de Lévi-Strauss." *Annales (Économies–Sociétés–Civilisations)* 6 (19th year; (November–December).

Bastide, Roger, ed. 1962. *Sens et usage de la notion de structure dans les sciences humaines.* The Hague: Mouton.

Bataille, Georges. 1957. "L'Énigme de l'inceste." In *L'Erotisme.* Paris: Minuit.

Beauvoir, Simone de. 1949. Review of *Les structures élémentaires de la parenté.* In *Les Temps modernes* 49 (November): 943–49.

Benvéniste, Emile. 1962. "La Notion de structure en linguistique." In *Sens et usage de la notion de structure dans les sciences humaines,* ed. R. Bastide. The Hague: Mouton.

Blanchot, Maurice. 1956. "L'Homme au point zéro." *La Nouvelle revue française* (April).

Boon, James. 1970. "Lévi-Strauss and 'Narrative.'" *Man* 5, no. 4:702–3.

Boudon, Raymond. 1968. *A quoi sert la notion de structure?* Paris: Gallimard.

Bourdieu, Pierre. 1968. "Structuralism and Theory of Sociological Knowledge." *Social Research* 35:681–705.

Caroll, M. P. 1980. 1979. "Lévi-Strauss on Art: A Reconsideration." *Anthropologica* 21, no. 2:177–88. Continued under the same title in *Anthropologica* 22, no. 2 (1980): 203–14.

Champagne, Roland. 1987. *Claude Lévi-Strauss.* Boston: Twayne Publishers.

Clarke, S. 1977. "Lévi-Strauss's Structural Analysis of Myth." *Sociological Review* 25, no. 4:303–6.

Cohen, Percy. 1969. "Theories of Myth." *Man* 4, no. 3:337–53.

Conley, Tom. 1975. "The Sunset of Myth: Lévi-Strauss in the Arenas." In *20th Century French Fiction,* ed. George Stambolian. New Brunswick, N.J.: Rutgers University Press.

Cook, Albert. 1980. *Myth and Language.* Bloomington: Indiana University Press.

Culler, Jonathan. 1973. "The Linguistic Basis of Structuralism." In *Structuralism: An Introduction,* ed. David Robey. Oxford: Clarendon Press, 20–36.

———. 1975. "Mythologic Logic." In *Structuralist Poetics: Structuralism, Linguistics, and the Study of Literature.* Ithaca, N.Y.: Cornell University Press, 40–54.

Deleuze, Gilles. 1973. "Qu'est-ce que le structuralisme?" In *Histoire de la philosophie,* vol. 8. ed. François Châtelet. Paris: Librairie Hachette.

Derrida, Jacques. 1967a. "La Structure, le signe, le jeu dans le discours des sciences humaines." In *L'Écriture et la différence.* Paris: Seuil, 409–28. Published in English as *Writing and Difference,* trans. Alan Bass (Chicago: University of Chicago Press, 1978).

———. 1967b. "La Violence de la lettre: De Lévi-Strauss à Rousseau." In *De la grammatologie.* Paris: Minuit, 149–234. Published in English in *Of Grammatology,* trans. Gayatri Chakravorty Spivak (Baltimore: Johns Hopkins University Press, 1976).

Descombes, Vincent. 1979. *Le Même et l'autre.* Paris: Minuit. Published in English as *Modern French Philosophy,* trans. L. Scott-Fox and J. M. Harding (Cambridge: Cambridge University Press, 1980).

———. 1996. *Les Institutions du sens.* Paris: Minuit.

Detienne, Marcel. 1977. *Dionysios mis à mort.* Paris: Gallimard, chap. 1.

———. 1980. "Une Mythologie sans illusion." *Le Temps de la réflexion* 1:27–60.

————. 1981. *L'Invention de la mythologie*. Paris. Gallimard. Reprint 1992.

Diamond, Stanley. 1982. "The Myth of Structuralism." In *The Logic of Culture. Advances in Structural Theory and Methods,* ed. Ino Rossi. South Hadley, Mass.: J. F. Bergin, 292–335.

Douglas, Mary. 1967. "The Meaning of Myth, with Special Reference to *La Geste d'Asdiwal.*" In *The Structural Study of Myth and Totemism,* ed. E. R. Leach. London: Tavistock, 49–70.

Dumont, Louis. 1966. "Descent or Intermarriage? A Relational View of Australian Section Systems." *Southwestern Journal of Anthropology* 22, no. 3:231–50.

————. 1971. *Introduction à deux théories d'anthropologie sociale*. The Hague: Mouton.

Eco, Umberto. 1968. *La Struttura assente*. Milano: Bompiani. Published in French as *La Structure absente* (Paris: Mercure de France, 1972), 319–404.

Fleischmann, Eugène. 1966. "L'Esprit humain selon Claude Lévi-Strauss." *Archives européennes de sociologie* 7, no. 1:27–57.

Gardner, Howard. 1972. "Structural Analysis of Protocols and Myths: A Comparison of the Methods of Jean Piaget and Claude Lévi-Strauss." *Semantics* 5, no. 1:31–57.

Geertz, Clifford. 1967. "The Cerebral Savage: On the Works of Claude Lévi-Strauss." *Encounter* 28, no. 4 (April).

————. 1984. "Distinguished Lectures: Anti Anti-relativism." *American Anthropologist* 86, no. 2:263–78.

————. 1988. *Works and Lives: The Anthropologist as Author*. Stanford, Calif.: Stanford University Press.

Genette, Gérard. 1965. "Structuralisme et critique littéraire." *L'Arc* 26:30–54. Reprinted in *Figures* (Paris: Seuil, 1966).

Girard, René. 1972. "Lévi-Strauss, le structuralisme et les règles du mariage." In *La Violence et le sacré*. Paris: Grasset, 305–45. Published in English as "Lévi-Strauss, Structuralism, and Marriage Laws," in *Violence and the Sacred,* trans. Patrick Gregory (Baltimore: Johns Hopkins University Press, 1977), 223–49.

————. 1976. "Differentiation and Undifferentiation in Lévi-Strauss and Current Critical Theory." *Contemporary Literature* 17, no. 3:404–29.

Goddard, D. 1965. "Conceptions of Structures in Lévi-Strauss and British Anthropologists." *Social Research* 32 (winter): 408–27.

Goddard, D. 1970. "Lévi-Strauss and the Anthropologists." *Social Research* 37, no. 3 (fall): 366–78.

Gomez García, P. 1976. "La Estructura mitológica en Lévi-Strauss." *Theorema* 6, no. 1:119–46.

Goodenough, Ward H. 1969. "Frontiers of Cultural Anthropology: Social Organization." *Proceedings of the American Philosophical Society* 113, no. 5:329–35.

Granger, Gilles. 1968. *Essai d'une philosophie du style.* Paris: A. Colin. Republished, Paris: Odile Jacob, 1988, chap. 5.

Guiart, Jean. 1989. "L'analyse structurale des mythes." In Claude Lévi-Strauss, *Des Symboles et leurs doubles.* Paris: Plon, 17–54.

Harris, Marvin. 1968. *The Rise of Anthropological Theory: A History of Theories of Culture.* New York: Thomas Y. Crowell, 482–513.

———. 1976. "Lévi-Strauss et la palourde." *L'Homme* 16, nos. 2–3. (Lévi-Strauss responds to this essay in *Le Regard éloigné* [Paris: Plon, 1983], chap. 8. Published in English as *The View from Afar*, trans. Joachim Neugroschel and Phoebe Hoss [New York: Basic Books, 1985], chap. 8.)

Haskell, R. E. 1985. "Thought-Things: Lévi-Strauss and 'The Modern Mind.'" *Semiotica* 55, nos. 1–2.

Heusch, Luc de. 1963. "Anthropologie structurale et symbolisme." *Cahiers Internationaux du Symbolisme* 2:31–56.

———. 1965a. "Situations et positions de l'anthropologie structurale." *L'Arc* 26.

———. 1965b. "Vers une mytho-logique?" *Critique* 21, nos. 219–20 (August–September). Reprinted in *Pourquoi l'épouser? Et autres essais* (Paris: Gallimard, 1971). Published in English as *Why Marry Her? Society and Symbolic Structures*, trans. Janet Lloyd (Cambridge: Cambridge University Press, 1981).

Hultkrantz, Michel. 1969. "Mythologiques." *American Anthropologist* 71:735–37.

Hymes, Dell H. 1964. *Language in Culture and Society: A Reader in Linguistics and Anthropology.* New York: Harper and Row.

Jakobson, Roman (in collaboration with C. Lévi-Strauss). 1962. " 'Les Chats' de Charles Baudelaire." *L'Homme* 2, no. 1:5–21.

Jameson, Frederic. 1972. *The Prison House of Language: A Critical Account of Structuralism and Russian Formalism.* Princeton, N.J.: Princeton University Press.

Josselin de Jong, J. P. B. de. 1983. "Un Champ d'études ethnologiques en transformation." *L'Ethnographie* 79, no. 7:3–15.

Knight, C. 1983. "Lévi-Strauss and the Dragon: *Mythologiques* Reconsidered in the Light of an Australian Aboriginal Myth." *Man* 18, no. 1:21–50.

Korn, Francis. 1969. "Logic of Some Concepts in Lévi-Strauss." *American Anthropologist* 71 (January).

Kuper, Adam. 1973. "Lévi-Strauss and British Neo-structuralism." In *Anthropologists and Anthropology: The British School, 1922–1972.* New York: Pica Press, 214–26.

Kurzweil, Edith. 1980. *The Age of Structuralism.* New York: Columbia University Press.

Lane, Michael, ed. 1970. *Introduction to Structuralism.* New York: Basic Books.

Leach, Edmund R. 1961. "Lévi-Strauss in the Garden of Eden: An Examination of Some Recent Developments in the Analysis of Myth." *Transactions of the New York Academy of Sciences,* 2d series, 23, no. 4:386–96.

———. 1964. "Telstar et les aborigènes ou *La Pensée sauvage* de Claude Lévi-Strauss." *Annales (Économies–Sociétés–Civilisations)* (November–December).

———, ed. 1967. *The Structural Study of Myth and Totemism.* London: Tavistock.

Lefort, Claude. 1951. "L'Échange et la lutte des hommes." *Les Temps modernes* (February).

Leiris, Michel. "A travers *Tristes tropiques.*" 1956. *Les Cahiers de la république* 2 (July).

Liszka, J. 1982. "Peirce and Lévi-Strauss: The Metaphysics of Semiotics and the Semiosis of Metaphysics." *Idealistic Studies* 12, no. 2:103–34.

Lyotard Jean-François. 1965. "Les Indiens ne cueillent pas les fleurs." *Annales (Économies–Sociétés–Civilisations)* 1 (January–February).

———. 1984. "Le Seuil de l'histoire." *Digraphe* 3:7–56.

Macksey, Richard, and Eugenio Donato, eds. 1970. *The Language of Criticism and the Sciences of Man: The Structuralist Controversy.* Baltimore: Johns Hopkins University Press.

Maranda, Pierre. 1970. "Anthropological Analytics: Lévi-Strauss's Concept of Social Structure." In *The Anthropology of Claude Lévi-Strauss,* ed. H. Nutini and I. Buchler. New York: Appleton-Century-Crofts.

Maybury-Lewis, David. 1969. "Science or Bricolage? *Du miel aux cendres.*" *American Anthropologist* 71, no. 1:114–21.

Mehlmann, Jeffrey. 1974. *A Structural Study of Autobiography: Proust, Leiris, Sartre, Lévi-Strauss.* Ithaca, N.Y.: Cornell University Press.

Merleau-Ponty, Maurice. 1960. "De Mauss à Claude Lévi-Strauss." In *Signes.* Paris: Gallimard.

Needham, Rodney. 1962. *Structure and Sentiment: A Test Case in Social Anthropology.* Chicago: University of Chicago Press.

———, ed. 1971. *Rethinking Kinship and Marriage.* London: Tavistock. (Articles by T. O. Beidelman, A. Forge, J. J. Fox, F. Korn, E. R. Leach, D. McKnight, R. Needham, P. G. Rivière, M. Southwold, and W. D. Wilder.)

Nutini, Hugo G. 1970. "Lévi-Strauss's Conception of Science." In *Echanges et communications: Mélanges offerts à Claude Lévi-Strauss à l'occasion de son 60e anniversaire,* ed. Jean Pouillon and Pierre Maranda. The Hague: Mouton.

———. 1971. "The Ideological Bases of Lévi-Strauss's Structuralism." *American Anthropologist* 73, no. 3:537–44.

Ortigues, Edmond. 1963. "Nature et culture dans l'oeuvre de Lévi-Strauss." *Critique* 189 (February): 142–57.

Pavel, Thomas. 1988. *Le Mirage linguistique.* Paris: Minuit, chap. 2.

Petitot, Jean. 1988. "Approche dynamique de la formule canonique du mythe." *L'Homme* 106–7 (April–September).

Piaget, Jean. 1970. "The Anthropological Structuralism of Claude Lévi-Strauss." In *Structuralism,* trans. Chaninah Maschler. New York: Basic Books, 106–19.

Poirier, Jean. 1983. "Les Catégories de la pensée sauvage: Invariances et spécificétés culturelles." *Bulletin de la Société Française de Philosophie* 67, no. 3:77–114.

Poole, Roger. 1969a. "Introduction to Lévi-Strauss's *Totemism.*" Harmondsworth, England: Penguin.

———. 1969b. "Lévi-Strauss, Myth's Magician: The Language of Anthropology." *New Blackfriars* 50, no. 588 (May): 432–40.

Pouillon, Jean. 1956. "L'Oeuvre de Lévi-Strauss." *Les Temps modernes* 126 (July): 150–72.

———. 1966a. "L'Analyse des mythes." *L'Homme* 6, no. 1:100–105.

———. 1966b. "Présentation: Un essai de définition." *Les Temps modernes* 246 (November): 769–90.

Propp, Vladimir. 1982. "Structure and History in the Study of Folktales (a Reply to Lévi-Strauss)." *Russian Literature* 12, no. 1:58–78.

Remotti, Francesco. 1968. "Modelli e strutture nell'anthropologia di Claude Lévi-Strauss." *Rivista di Filosofia* 59 (October–December): 401–37.

Ricoeur, Paul. 1963a. "Structure et herméneutique." *Esprit* 322 (November).

———. 1963b. "Symbole et temporalité." *Archivio di Filosophia* 1–2.

———. 1967. "La Structure, le mot, l'événement." *Esprit* 360 (35th year, May): 801–21. Republished in P. Ricoeur, *Le Conflit des interprétations* (Paris: Seuil, 1969). Published in English as *The Conflict of Interpretations,* ed. Don Hide (Evanston, Ill.: Northwestern University Press, 1974).

Robey, David, ed. 1973. *Structuralism: An Introduction.* Oxford: Clarendon Press.

Rossi, Ino, ed. 1982. *The Logic of Culture: Advances in Structural Theory and Methods.* South Hadley, Mass.: J. F. Bergin. (Articles by C. Ackerman, P. Bouissac, N. Ross Crumrine, M. Godelier, Fawda El Guindi, W. G. Jilek, L. Jilek-Aall, K. Maddock, P. Maranda, R. Neich, H. Rosenbaum, I. Rossi, and R. T. Zuidema.)

Sahlins, Marshall. 1966. "On the Delphic Writing of Claude Lévi-Strauss." *Scientific American* 215, no. 6:131–36.

———. 1976. *Culture and Practical Reason.* Chicago: University of Chicago Press.

Sartre, Jean-Paul. 1960. *La Critique de la raison dialectique.* Paris: Gallimard, 467–505. Published in English as *Critique of Dialectical Reason,* trans. Alan Sheridan-Smith, ed. Jonathan Rée (London: NLB, 1976).

Scholte, Bob. 1969. "Lévi-Strauss's Peneloppean Effort: The Analysis of Myth." *Semiotica* 1:99–124.

———. 1974. "Lévi-Strauss." In *Handbook of Social and Cultural Anthropology,* ed. John Higman. Chicago: Rand McNally, 676–716.

Schwimmer, Eric. 1978. "Lévi-Strauss and Maori Social Structure." *Anthropologica* 20, nos. 1/2:201–22.

Sebag, Lucien. 1962. "Histoire et structure." *Les Temps modernes* 195 (August).

Sebag, Lucien. 1965. "Le Mythe: Code et message." *Les Temps modernes* (20th year): 1607–23.

Serres, Michel. 1968. *Hermès I ou La Communication.* Paris: Minuit.

Seung, T. 1982. *Structuralism and Hermeneutics.* New York: Columbia University Press.

Smith, Pierre, and Dan Sperber. 1971. "Mythologiques de Georges Dumézil." *Annales (Économies–Sociétés–Civilisations)* 3–4 (26th year; May–August).

Sontag, Susan. 1966. "The Anthropologist as Hero." In *Against Interpretation and Other Essays.* New York: Farrar Strauss, 69–81. Republished in *Claude Lévi-Strauss: The Anthropologist as Hero,* ed. E. and T. Hayes (Cambridge, Mass.: M.I.T. Press, 1970). Originally published as *Symbole, fonction, histoire* (Paris: Hachette, 1979).

Sperber, Dan. 1982. "Claude Lévi-Strauss aujourd'hui." In *Le Savoir des anthropologues.* Paris: Hermann, 87–128. Published in English as "Claude Lévi-Strauss Today," in *On Anthropological Knowledge* (Cambridge: Cambridge University Press, 1985), 64–93.

Todorov, Tzvetan. 1989. *Nous et les autres: La Réflexion française sur la diversité humaine.* Paris: Seuil, 81–109. Published in English as *On Human Diversity: Nationalism, Racism, and Exoticism in French Thought,* trans. Catherine Porter (Cambridge, Mass.: Harvard University Press, 1993).

Vidal-Naquet, Pierre (in collaboration with Jacques Le Goff). 1974. "Lévi-Strauss en Brocéliande: Esquisse pour une analyse du roman courtois." *Critique* 325 (June): 541–71.

Other Works Cited in the Text

Ariès, P. 1954. *Le Temps de l'histoire.* Paris: Plon. [Quotations from this work have been translated by me. *Trans.*]

Augé, M. 1980. *The Anthropological Circle: Symbol, Function, History.* Trans. Martin Thom. Cambridge: Cambridge University Press.

Backès-Clément, C. 1970. *Claude Lévi-Strauss.* Paris: Éditions Seghers. [Quotations from this work have been translated by me. *Trans.*]

Beauvoir, S. de. 1953. *The Second Sex.* Trans. H. M. Parshley. New York: Alfred A. Knopf. Originally published as *Le Deuxième Sexe* (Paris: Gallimard, 1949).

Boas, F. 1911. *Handbook of American Indian Languages.* Part 1. Bulletin no. 40. Washington, D.C.: Bureau of American Ethnology.

Bollème, G. 1990. *Préface à la vie d'écrivain ou Extraits de la correspondance de Gustave Flaubert.* Paris: Seuil. [Quotations from this work have been translated by me. *Trans.*]

Bourbaki, N. 1948. "L'Architecture des mathématiques." In *Les Grands courants de la pensée mathématique.* Ed. Cahiers du Sud. [Quotations of this work cited by Marcel Hénaff were translated by L. Scott-Fox and J. M. Harding in Descombes 1980. *Trans.*]

Braudel, F. 1980. *On History.* Trans. Sarah Matthews. Chicago: University of Chicago Press. Originally published as *Écrits sur l'histoire* (Paris: Flammarion, 1977).

Cahiers pour l'analyse. 1966. No. 4. Paris. [Quotations from this publication have been translated by me. *Trans.*]

Descombes, V. 1980. *Modern French Philosophy.* Trans. L. Scott-Fox and J. M. Harding. Cambridge: Cambridge University Press. Originally published as *Le Même et l'autre* (Paris: Éditions de Minuit, 1979).

Dumézil, G. 1952. *Les Dieux des Indo-Européens.* Paris: Presses Universitaires de France. [Quotations from this work have been translated by me. *Trans.*]

Elkin, A. P. 1931. "The Kopara: The Settlement of Grievances." *Oceania* 2.

Fortes, M. 1969. *Kinship and the Social Order: The Legacy of Lewis Morgan.* Chicago: Adline.

Frazer, J. G. 1910. *Totemism and Exogamy.* London: Macmillan.

———. 1919. *Folklore in the Old Testament.* 3 vols. London: Macmillan.

Granet, M. 1939. *Catégories matrimoniales et relations de proximité dans la Chine ancienne.* Paris: Alcan.

Gurvitch, G., and W. Moore. 1945. *Twentieth Century Sociology.* New York: Philosophical Library.

Héritier, F. 1982. "The Symbolics of Incest and Its Prohibition" In *Between Belief and Transgression,* ed. M. Izard and P. Smith, trans.

John Leavitt. Chicago: University of Chicago Press. Originally published as "Symbolique de l'inceste et de sa prohibition," in *La Fonction symbolique* (Paris: Gallimard, 1979).

Izard, M., and P. Smith, eds. 1982. *Between Belief and Transgression.* Trans. John Leavitt. Chicago: University of Chicago Press. Originally published as *La Fonction symbolique* (Paris: Gallimard, 1979).

Jakobson, R. 1978. *Six Lectures on Sound and Meaning.* Trans. John Mepham. Cambridge, Mass.: MIT Press. Published in French as *Six Leçons sur le son et le sens* (Paris: Éditions de Minuit, 1976).

Kroeber, A. L. 1943. "Structure, Function and Pattern in Biology and Anthropology." *Scientific Monthly* 56.

———. 1948. *Anthropology.* Rev. ed. New York: Harcourt, Brace and World.

Lalande, A. 1983. *Vocabulaire technique et critique de la philosophie.* Paris: Presses Universitaires de France. First published in 1926 (Paris: Alcan). [Quotations from this work have been translated by me. *Trans.*]

Laplanche, J., and J. B. Pontalis. 1967. *Vocabulaire de la psychanalyse.* Paris: Presses Universitaires de France. [Quotations from this work have been translated by me. *Trans.*]

Leach, E. 1966. "The Legitimacy of Solomon." *Archives Européennes de sociologie* 8.

———. 1980. *L'Unité de l'homme.* Paris: Gallimard. [Marcel Hénaff quotes from the preface, which does not seem to have been published in English. I have provided the translation. *Trans.*]

Leenhardt, M. 1930. "Notes d'ethnologie néo-calédonienne." *Travaux et mémoires de l'Institut d'éthnologie* 8. [Quotations from this publication have been translated by me. *Trans.*]

Le Play, F. 1879. *La Méthode sociale.* Tours: Alfred Mame et fils. [Quotations from this work have been translated by me. *Trans.*]

Lévi-Strauss, C. 1945. "The Structural Study of Myths." *Journal of American Folklore* 68.

———. 1948.

———. 1958. "Un Monde des sociétés." *Way Forum* (March). [Quotations from this publication have been translated by me. *Trans.*]

———. 1962. "Sur le caractère distinctif des faits ethnologiques." *Revue des travaux de l'Académie des sciences morales et politiques* 115, 4th series. [Quotations from this publication have been translated by me. *Trans.*]

———. 1965. "The Future of Kinship Studies." Huxley Memorial Lecture for 1965. In *Proceedings of the Royal Anthropological Institute of Great Britain and Ireland*, 13–22.

———. 1966. "Philosophie et anthropologie." *Cahiers de philosophie* 1 (January). [Quotations from this publication have been translated by me. *Trans.*]

Lowie, R. H. 1920. *Primitive Society*. New York: Bonie and Liveright.

Malinowski, B. 1960. *A Scientific Theory of Culture*. New York: Oxford University Press.

Mauss, M. 1972a. "Body Techniques." In *Sociology and Psychology*. Trans. R. Brain. London: Routledge and Kegan Paul. Published as "Les Techniques du corps," in *Sociologie et anthropologie* (Paris: Presses Universitaires de France, 1950). Originally published in *Journal de psychologie* 32, nos. 3–4 (March 13–April 15, 1936).

———. 1972b. "A General Theory of Magic." In *Sociology and Psychology*. Trans. R. Brain. London: Routledge and Kegan Paul. Originally published in *Sociologie et anthropologie* (Paris: Presses Universitaires de France, 1950).

———. 1972c. "Real and Practical Relations between Psychology and Sociology." In *Sociology and Psychology*. Trans. R. Brain. London: Routledge and Kegan Paul. Published as "Rapports réels et pratiques de la psychologie et de la sociologie," in *Sociologie et anthropologie* (Paris: Presses Universitaires de France, 1950). Originally published in *Journal de psychologie normale et pathologique* (1924).

———. 1972d. *Sociology and Psychology*. Trans. R. Brain. London: Routledge and Kegan Paul. Selections from *Sociologie et anthropologie* (Paris: Presses Universitaires de France, 1950).

———. 1990. *The Gift*. Trans. W. D. Halls. London: Routledge. Published in *Sociologie et anthropologie* (Paris: Presses Universitaires de France, 1950). Originally published in *Année sociologique* 1 (1923–24).

Merleau-Ponty, M. 1964. *Signs*. Trans. Richard C. McCleary. Evanston, Ill.: Northwestern University Press. Originally published as *Signes* (Paris: Gallimard, 1960).

Montaigne. 1910. *The Essayes of Michael Lord of Montaigne*. Vol. 1. Trans. John Florio. London: J. M. Dent and Sons. Originally published as *Essais* (1580).

Nadel, S. 1957. *The Theory of Social Structure*. London: Cohen and West.

Nizan, P. 1967. *Aden-Arabie*. Paris: F. Maspero. Originally published in 1932 (Paris: Rieder).

Ortigues, E. 1962. *Le Discours et le symbole*. Paris: Aubier. [Quotations from this work have been translated by me. *Trans.*]

Propp, V. 1968. *Morphology of the Folktale*. Trans. Laurence Scott. Austin: University of Texas Press. Originally published as *Morfologiia Skazki* (Leningrad, 1928).

Radcliffe-Brown, A. R. 1940. "On Social Structure." *Journal of the Royal Anthropological Institute* 70.

———. 1941. "The Study of Kinship Systems." *Journal of the Royal Anthropological Institute* 71.

———. 1952. *Structure and Function in Primitive Society.* New York: The Free Press.

Revel, J.-F. 1957. *Pourquoi des philosophes?* Paris: J. J. Pauvert. [Quotations from this work have been translated by me. *Trans.*]

Ricoeur, P. 1969. *Le Conflit des interprétations.* Paris: Seuil. Published in English as *The Conflict of Interpretations,* ed. Don Hide (Evanston, Ill.: Northwestern University Press, 1974).

Rousseau, J.-J. 1911. *Émile.* Trans. Barbara Foxley. London: Dent. Originally published in French as *Émile* (Paris, 1762).

———. 1964."Discourse on the Origin and Foundations of Inequality among Men." In *The First and Second Discourses.* Ed. R. D. Masters. Trans. R. D. and J. R. Masters. New York: St. Martin's Press. Originally published in 1754 as "Discours sur l'origine et les fondemens de l'inégalité parmi les hommes," in *Oeuvres complètes de Jean-Jacques Rousseau,* vol. 3, Bibliothèque de la Pléiade (Paris: Gallimard, 1964).

Sahlins, M. 1972. *Stone Age Economics.* Chicago: Adline.

Sartre, J.-P. 1956. *Being and Nothingness.* Trans. H. E. Barnes. New York: Philosophical Library. Originally published as *L'Être et le néant* (Paris: Gallimard, 1943).

Segalen, V. 1978. *Essai sur l'exotisme.* Montpellier: Fata Morgana. [Quotations from this work have been translated by me. *Trans.*]

Serres, M. 1995. *The Natural Contract.* Trans. Elizabeth MacArthur and William Paulson. Ann Arbor: University of Michigan Press. Originally published as *Le Contrat naturel* (Paris: Éditions François Bourin, 1990).

Simpson, G. G. 1961. *Principles of Animal Taxonomy.* New York: Columbia University Press.

Southwold, M. 1971. "Meanings of Kinship." In *Rethinking Kinship and Marriage.* Ed. R. Needham. London: Tavistock.

Sperber, D. 1975. *Rethinking Symbolism.* Trans. Alice L. Morton. London: Cambridge University Press. Originally published as *Le Symbolisme en générale* (Paris: Hermann, 1974).

———. 1985a. "Un Esprit psychologue." *Le Magazine littéraire* 223 (October). [Quotations from this publication have been translated by me. *Trans.*]

———. 1985b. *On Anthropological Knowledge.* Cambridge: Cambridge University Press. Originally published as *Le Savoir des anthropologues* (Paris: Hermann, 1982).

Trubetzkoy, N. S. 1933. "La Phonologie actuelle." *Journal de psychologie* 30.

Valéry, P. 1987. *Cahiers I, 1894–1914.* Ed. Nicole Celeyrette-Pietri and Judith Robinson-Valéry. Paris: Gallimard. [Quotations from this work have been translated by me. *Trans.*]

Wiener, N. 1948. *Cybernetics.* New York: Technology Press.

Wittgenstein, L. 1979. *Remarks on Frazer's Golden Bough.* Ed. Rush Rhees. Retford, England: Brynmill Press.

Index

action, 189, 207
addressee, 191, 197
aesthetics, 190, 193, 198
Albus, A., 206
alliance, 36, 38, 44, 48, 49, 56, 57, 61–65, 70, 71, 73–75, 78–80, 82, 87, 89–93, 120, 129, 133, 135, 170, 225, 228–31; exogamous, 6, 16, 42, 115; matrimonial, 36, 39, 45, 48, 49, 64, 98; rules of, 58, 120, 211
Alquié, F., 246
Althusser, L., 4
American Anthropologist, 255
analogical reasoning. *See* thought: analogical
analogy, 163, 175, 187; external, 155; objective, 154
anisogamy, 81
Annales school, 235
anthropocentrism, 242
appellation, 83, 135, 156, 232
Aristotle, 207
Aron, R., 255
art, 120, 132, 190, 203, 211, 224, 240, 258; abstract, 206, 210, 211; academic, 201–3, 208; and aesthetic emotion, 194, 211, 212; Caduveo, 198, 200, 206; classical, 197; contemporary (modern), 191, 197, 200, 201, 204–6; double apprehension of, 192; function of, 191; history of, 201, 209, 190; imitative, 190; nonrepresentational, 191, 195, 207; possessive, 206; primitive, 190, 191, 195, 202, 207, 209; representational, 190, 191, 195–97, 206–8; representative function of, 194; signifying function of, 202; and society, 197, 199–201; structure in, 191, 192, 194; as symbolic appropriation, 197; Western, 196, 201, 207, 208; work of, 142, 143, 177, 190–94, 196, 198, 201, 203, 204, 206, 211–13
Ascoli, M., 250
asymmetry, 199, 200
atemporality, 107
atom of kinship, 86, 89, 90
attitude, 16, 58, 65, 73, 82–84, 87, 89, 96, 132, 232
Augé, M., 5, 101, 102
axiom of amity, 37, 66

Backès-Clément, C., 4, 32
Bataille, G., 253, 255; *L'Érotisme*, 253
Bataillon, M., 253
Bayet, A., 253
Beauvoir, S. de, 246, 252, 253; *The Second Sex*, 253
beliefs, 167, 222, 242
Benedict, R., 251
Benvéniste, E., 4, 7, 18, 253, 255
Berger, G., 252
Blanchot, M., 255
Boas, F., 96, 97, 103, 125, 126, 251
Bouglé, C., 246, 247
Boulez, P., 210
Bourbaki, N., 13, 14
Braque, G., 203
Braudel, F., 23, 229, 235, 247, 255
Bréhier, L., 246
Breton, A., 250, 251
bricolage, 59, 139, 145, 156, 149, 192, 212, 219, 223; intellectual, 144, 157
bricoleur/engineer opposition, 145
Brunschvicg, L., 246

Cahiers pour l'analyse, 2
Caillois, R., 254, 257
Calder, A., 251
Camus, A., 252
Carrington, L., 251
caste, 61, 200
Castro Fara, L. de, 248
categories, 120, 143, 173; logical, 117, 118, 120; of the mind, 181, 202; transcendental, 112; unconscious, 94–96, 102, 103
causality, 229, 231, 232, 235; chronological, 189; historical, 209
Charbonnier, G., 34, 195, 207, 255; *Conversations with Claude Lévi-Strauss*, 34, 207, 255
Chomsky, N., 74, 107, 110
circulation of women, 73, 74
clan, 58, 59, 77, 223
class, matrimonial, 58–60, 68. *See also* system: class
classification, 109, 135, 147, 148, 151, 152, 155–58, 185; formal, 158; of natural species, 26; savage, 142, 146, 148, 157, 225; system of, 220, 225, 241; totemic, 108, 116, 145, 151, 177

Marcel Hénaff, a philosopher and anthropologist, is a professor at the University of California, San Diego, and a program director at the Collège International de Philosophie, Paris. Among his many publications are *Sade, l'invention du corps libertin* (forthcoming in English translation from the University of Minnesota Press) and *Le Prix de la vérite: Le don, l'argent, la philosophie* (forthcoming in Paris). He is completing a book on the modern city and the crisis of public space.

Mary Baker is a freelance translator who lives in Montreal.